Every Decker book is accompanied by a CD-ROM.

The disc appears in the front of each copy, in its own sealed jacket. Affixed to the front of the book will be a distinctive BĉD sticker **"Book *cum* disc."**

The disc contains the complete text and illustrations of the book, in fully searchable PDF files. The book and disc are sold *only* as a package; neither is available independently, and no prices are available for the items individually.

BC Decker Inc is committed to providing high-quality electronic publications that complement traditional information and learning methods.

We trust you will find the book/CD package invaluable and invite your comments and suggestions.

Brian C. Decker
CEO and Publisher

Herb-Drug Interactions in Oncology

Barrie R. Cassileth, PhD
Chief, Integrative Medicine Service
Memorial Sloan-Kettering Cancer Center
New York, New York

Member, Board of Directors
American Cancer Society
Atlanta, Georgia

Charles D. Lucarelli, MS, RPh
Director, Division of Pharmacy Services
Memorial Sloan-Kettering Cancer Center
New York, New York

2003
BC Decker Inc
Hamilton · London

BC Decker Inc
P.O. Box 620, L.C.D. 1
Hamilton, Ontario L8N 3K7
Tel: 905-522-7017; 800-568-7281
Fax: 905-522-7839; 888-311-4987
E-mail: customercare@bcdecker.com
www.bcdecker.com

03 04 05 06/PC/9 8 7 6 5 4 3 2 1
Printed in Canada

ISBN 1-55009-245-6

Sales and Distribution

United States
BC Decker Inc
P.O. Box 785
Lewiston, NY 14092-0785
Tel: 905-522-7017; 800-568-7281
Fax: 905-522-7839; 888-311-4987
E-mail: info@bcdecker.com
www.bcdecker.com

Canada
BC Decker Inc
20 Hughson Street South
P.O. Box 620, LCD 1
Hamilton, Ontario L8N 3K7
Tel: 905-522-7017; 800-568-7281
Fax: 905-522-7839; 888-311-4987
E-mail: info@bcdecker.com
www.bcdecker.com

Foreign Rights
John Scott & Company
International Publishers' Agency
P.O. Box 878
Kimberton, PA 19442
Tel: 610-827-1640
Fax: 610-827-1671
E-mail: jsco@voicenet.com

Japan
Igaku-Shoin Ltd.
Foreign Publications Department
3-24-17 Hongo
Bunkyo-ku, Tokyo, Japan 113-8719
Tel: 3 3817 5680
Fax: 3 3815 6776
E-mail: fd@igaku-shoin.co.jp

U.K., Europe, Scandinavia, Middle East
Elsevier Science
Customer Service Department
Foots Cray High Street
Sidcup, Kent
DA14 5HP, UK
Tel: 44 (0) 208 308 5760
Fax: 44 (0) 181 308 5702
E-mail: cservice@harcourt.com

Singapore, Malaysia,Thailand, Philippines, Indonesia, Vietnam, Pacific Rim, Korea
Elsevier Science Asia
583 Orchard Road
#09/01, Forum
Singapore 238884
Tel: 65-737-3593
Fax: 65-753-2145

Australia, New Zealand
Elsevier Science Australia
Customer Service Department
STM Division
Locked Bag 16
St. Peters, New South Wales, 2044
Australia
Tel: 61 02 9517-8999
Fax: 61 02 9517-2249
E-mail: stmp@harcourt.com.au
www.harcourt.com.au

Mexico and Central America
ETM SA de CV
Calle de Tula 59
Colonia Condesa
06140 Mexico DF, Mexico
Tel: 52-5-5553-6657
Fax: 52-5-5211-8468
E-mail:
editoresdetextosmex@prodigy.net.
mx

Argentina
CLM (Cuspide Libros Medicos)
Av. Córdoba 2067 - (1120)
Buenos Aires, Argentina
Tel: (5411) 4961-0042/(5411) 4964-0848
Fax: (5411) 4963-7988
E-mail: clm@cuspide.com

Brazil
Tecmedd
Av. Maurílio Biagi, 2850
City Ribeirão Preto – SP – CEP: 14021-000
Tel: 0800 992236
Fax: (16) 3993-9000
E-mail: tecmedd@tecmedd.com.br

Contents

Preface

The use of herbs, botanicals, vitamin combinations, and other over-the-counter agents is increasingly common in North America. Shelves of health food stores are lined with hundreds of remedies. The US Institute of Medicine estimates the US food supplement industry at $16 billion annually. Herbs and other agents are equally popular around the world.

Despite long-term use of such products, high-quality research has been sparse, resulting in a major information gap for health professionals and the general public. Problems of poor manufacturing practices, product contamination, absence of standardization, highly varied amounts of assumed active ingredients even from the same manufacturer, incorrect or absent understanding of active ingredients, and serious herb-drug interactions continue to create major problems, including deaths.

In addition to over-the-counter agents, many bogus alternative therapies are falsely promoted as viable cancer treatment options for use in lieu of surgery, chemotherapy, radiation therapy, and other mainstream approaches to oncologic care. These products and regimens tend to be in vogue for varying periods of time. Often they are reinvented, as was Laetrile, decades after hard data revealed their uselessness and caused them to fade from favor. The vogue-like character of botanicals as well as alternative regimens provides yet another layer of complexity for professionals and patients.

In 1999, an Integrative Medicine Service was created at Memorial Sloan-Kettering Cancer Center. We developed this department to provide helpful complementary therapies, conduct research, provide education programs, and develop Web-based information about herbs and other products and regimens. We began serious research efforts to determine the antitumor potential of herbs and botanical compounds. At the same time, we developed a universally available Web site called Aboutherbs. It is designed to be used by both the physician and the patient. To access it, anyone can go to the Internet, insert <MSKCC.com/aboutherbs> and find timely, useful, scientifically accurate information about herbal remedies. The Web site will tell the reader if an herb may interact with other medications and whether it is known to affect heart rate, cause excessive bleeding during surgery, or produce any other problem. It assesses each remedy's medicinal value, based on reliable scientific information. The Web site is updated regularly, and more data on additional herbs and other remedies are entered as scientific investigations continue.

This manual is based on information provided on our Web site. It includes all of the information our researchers, pharmacists, and experts in botanicals had assembled on herbal and other "natural" remedies at the time of publication.

It is essential that everyone know the benefits and the dangers of ANY medication prior to use. This book will help physicians, pharmacists, and the public determine whether a supplement or remedy is dangerous or useful.

Barrie R. Cassileth, PhD
May 2003

Acknowledgments

The editors wish to acknowledge the important contributions of the following individuals:

James Dougherty, MD
Angela Donato
Jason Epstein
Donald Garrity, RD
Jenny Stillwaggon
Glenn Schulman, PharmD
Simon Yeung, MBA, MS, RPh, LAc

714X

COMMON NAME
714X

SCIENTIFIC NAME
Trimethylaminohydroxybicyclo-
heptane chloride

KEY WORDS
Gaston Naessens 714X, 714-X,
Naessens 714X

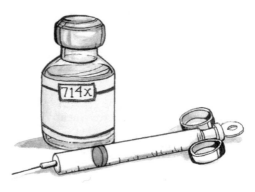

A.DONATO

CLINICAL SUMMARY
Proprietary product developed and manufactured by Cerbe Inc., Canada. Patients use this product to prevent and treat cancer or human immunodeficiency virus/acquired immune deficiency syndrome (HIV/AIDS), lupus, fibromyalgia, and chronic fatigue syndrome. 714X is promoted as a sterile, isotonic formulation that contains nitrates (~5%), ammonium (~1.4%), and camphor (< 0.01%). 714X is not legal in the United States and is available only in Canada under the Compassionate Use Program. 714X is injected intralymphatically in the groin area daily for 21 days followed by 3 days off treatment. This cycle is repeated a minimum of three times. Inhalation therapy is used concomitantly for patients with head and neck or lung cancer. Injection site reactions, including redness and soreness, may occur. There are no published data evaluating 714X for any of the proposed claims.

CONSTITUENTS
Water (94%), camphor (~< 0.01%), nitrate (~5%), ammonium (~1.4%), sodium chloride (~1%), ethanol (~1%), trace elements (insignificant amounts).[1]

WARNINGS
714X is not legal in the United States.

MECHANISM OF ACTION
Developed by Gaston Naessens, 714X is said to produce disease regression, revitalize the immune system, and support host defense mechanisms. The promoters claim that the camphor has selective affinity for cancer cells, whereas the nitrate component fulfills the nitrogen requirement of cancer cells, thereby protecting immune cells. The nitrogen-enriched camphor supposedly antagonizes the secretion of cocancerogenic K factor by cancer cells. There are no data in the literature to support the proposed mechanisms of action or benefits claimed by the manufacturer.[1-3]

USAGE
Cancer prevention, cancer treatment, chronic fatigue syndrome, human immunodeficiency virus (HIV) and acquired immune deficiency syndrome (AIDS), muscle pain, rheumatoid arthritis, systemic lupus erythematosus.

ADVERSE REACTIONS
Common: Injection site reactions, such as redness, inflammation, and soreness.[2]

DRUG INTERACTIONS
Cerbe, Inc. states that decreased efficacy of 714X may occur if administered concurrently with vitamin B_{12}, vitamin E, and shark or bovine cartilage.[2]

DOSAGE
Intralymphatic Injection: Perinodular injection in right inguinal area. First cycle: 0.1 mL day 1, 0.2 mL day 2, increasing to a target dose of 0.5 mL on days 5 to 21. No titration is used for subsequent cycles. Cycles are 21 days followed by a 2- to 3-day rest period. *Inhalation:* Nebulizer treatments are suggested for head/neck and lung cancers. Therapy with 0.6 mL of 714X in 1.9 mL normal saline initiated during the second cycle of intralymphatic injections. Nebulizer treatments are given 12 hours prior to or following daily injections.[2,3]

LITERATURE SUMMARY AND CRITIQUE
No published clinical trials, case reports, or in vitro data support the use of 714X for any proposed claims. Anecdotal reports of animal studies suggest that 714X produces few side effects and is generally well tolerated, but no efficacy data have been reported.

REFERENCES

1   Kurtzweil P. Investigators' report: promoter of 714X cure-all faces prison for selling unapproved drug. FDA Consumer Magazine [online]. http://www. fda.gov/fdac/departs/996_irs.html (accessed Jan 25, 2002).

2. 714X: technical data. Cerbe Inc. Available at: http://www.cerbe.com/index.html (accessed Jan 30, 2002).

3. Kaegi E. Unconventional therapies for cancer: 6. 714-X. Task Force on Alternative Therapeutic of the Canadian Breast Cancer Research Initiative. Can Med Assoc J 1998;158:1621–4.

Aloe Vera

A.DONATO

COMMON NAMES
Aloe gel, aloe leaf

SCIENTIFIC NAMES
Aloe barbadensis, Aloe capensis

CLINICAL SUMMARY

Derived from the leaves of the plant. Topical administration of aloe vera gel is generally safe. It may help reduce radiation-induced skin changes, but clinical trial results are inconsistent. Aloe vera gel should not be confused with aloe juice or aloe latex, both of which contain anthraquinone, a cathartic laxative. Oral and parenteral administration of aloe vera should be avoided owing to potential toxicities and lack of clinical efficacy demonstrated in humans. The US Food and Drug Administration (FDA) rules that aloe is not safe as a stimulant laxative. Cancer therapy using injections of acemannan, a mucopolysaccharide derived from aloe vera, resulted in the deaths of several patients.

CONSTITUENTS

Mono- and polysaccharides, tannins, sterols, organic acids, enzymes, saponins, vitamins, minerals, glucomannan and acemannan, lipids: cholesterol, gamolenic acid.

WARNINGS

Aloe vera gel should not be confused with aloe juice or aloe latex, both of which contain anthraquinone, a cathartic laxative. Aloe vera taken for internal use should be discouraged owing to possible adverse effects and inconclusive clinical data. Aloe vera injections for cancer patients have resulted in several deaths. The FDA rules that aloe is not safe as a stimulant laxative.[1,2]

MECHANISM OF ACTION

It is presently believed that some of the beneficial effects of aloe result from inhibition of bradykinin by a contained carboxypeptidase. Aloe is also believed to hinder the formation of thromboxane, the activity of which is detrimental to burn wound healing. Antiprostaglandin activity has also been reported. Aloe has antibacterial and antifungal properties. The laxative effect of aloe juice and aloe latex is caused by anthraquinone glycosides aloin A and B. Anthraquinone and anthrones are thought to increase colonic peristalsis and increase intestinal water content via modulation of chloride-ion channels.[3]

USAGE

Burns, cold sores, dry skin, inflammation, pain, pruritus.

ADVERSE REACTIONS

Reported (Oral): Gastrointestinal upset, nausea and vomiting, occasional rash (dermatitis).
Toxicity: Seizures, potassium loss, and electrolyte abnormalities.[4]

DRUG INTERACTIONS
Oral

Glyburide: Aloe may increase hypoglycemic effects.
Diuretics: Aloe may have an additive hypokalemic effect owing to diarrhea if used for a prolonged period.
Digoxin: Aloe may have an additive hypokalemic effect owing to diarrhea if used for a prolonged period.

Topical

Hydrocortisone: Aloe may increase anti-inflammatory effects.[5]

DOSAGE

Oral: Not recommended.
Parenteral: Not recommended.
Topical: Apply gel three to five times a day. Gel is available in several different purity strengths.

LITERATURE SUMMARY AND CRITIQUE

Owing to the many different aloe vera formulations and compounds used in clinical studies, it is difficult to interpret the studies fairly. There are few controlled studies using aloe vera gel. The evidence does support topical use for minor burns, frostbite, wound healing, and anti-inflammatory purposes, especially combined with hydrocortisone. Conflicting data exist regarding use of aloe vera to prevent skin erythema and pruritus following radiation therapy.

Williams MS, et al. Phase III double-blind evaluation of an aloe vera gel as a prophylactic agent for radiation-induced skin toxicity. Int J Radiat Oncol Biol Phys 1996;36:345–9.
A randomized, prospective, double-blind evaluation of 98% pure aloe vera gel versus placebo in 194 breast cancer patients receiving chest wall irradiation. Skin care with either aloe vera or placebo gel was started within 3 days of initial radiation treatment and applied twice daily. Data analysis revealed no statistical difference between the treatment arms with respect to radiation-induced dermatitis. A second phase of the trial randomized 107 breast cancer patients to either 98% pure aloe vera gel or observation only; no advantage was seen for patients receiving aloe vera. The author concludes that aloe vera gel does not protect against radiation-induced dermatitis.

Olsen DL, et al. The effect of aloe vera/mild soap versus mild soap in preventing skin reactions in patients undergoing radiation therapy. Oncol Nurs Forum 2001;28:543–7.
A randomized, blinded, prospective study of patients undergoing radiation therapy. Seventy patients were randomized to receive skin care with either aloe vera and mild soap or mild soap alone. Time to skin change (texture, erythema, tanning, pruritus) was the primary measured outcome. Aloe vera product contained pure aloe vera gel in addition to d-α-tocopherol, triethanolamine, and methylparaben. There was no statistically significant difference between the treatment arms. Patients who received aloe/soap and received a cumulative radiation dose greater than 2,700 cGy exhibited increased time to skin changes versus soap.

REFERENCES
1. License revoked for aloe vera use. Nat Med Law 1998;1:1–2.
2. Gearan A. Doctor injected desperate cancer patients with aloe vera. Associated Press [online]. http://www.athensnewspapers.com/1997/100997/1009.a3aloevera.html (accessed November 16, 2001).
3. Tyler V. Herbs of choice, the therapeutical use of phytomedicinals. Binghamton (NY): Pharmaceutical Press; 1994.
4. Bisset NG. Herbal drugs and phytopharmaceuticals. Boca Raton (FL): CRC Press; 1994.
5. Brinker F. Herb contraindications and drug interactions. 3rd ed. Sandy (OR): Eclectic Med; 2001.

Alpha-Lipoic Acid

COMMON NAMES

Thioctic acid, lipoate, lipoic acid,
1,2-dithilpolane-3-valeric acid,
6,8-thioctic acid, ALA, thioctan

SCIENTIFIC NAME

1,2-Dithiolane-3-pentanoic acid

A DONATO

CLINICAL SUMMARY

Endogenous cofactor found in all eukaryotic and prokaryotic cells and obtained in the diet. Patients take this supplement to treat and prevent cancer and to treat diabetic neu ropathies, human immunodeficiency virus/acquired immune deficiency syndrome (HIV/AIDS), and liver disease. Alpha-lipoic acid (ALA) is an essential cofactor in the production of energy and acts as a potent antioxidant. Oral supplementation results in variable bioavailability, and the elimination half-life ranges from 10 to 30 minutes. No significant adverse effects are reported, with repeated dosing up to 1,200 mg/d. No drug interactions are reported, but it is debated whether the antioxidant activity of ALA may antagonize the effects of chemotherapy and radiation therapy. Clinical data suggest that ALA is ineffective for reversing neuropathies or liver disease. Additional research is required to evaluate its role in cancer prevention, diabetic-related complications, and drug-induced toxicity to the auditory nerve.

MECHANISM OF ACTION

ALA acts as a lipophilic free radical scavenger. Dihydrolipoic acid (DHLA), a product of the reduction of lipoic acid, has more pronounced antioxidant effects than does lipoic acid. Both DHLA and lipoic acid have metal chelating and free radical scavenging capacities, whereas only DHLA is able to repair oxidative damage and regenerate endogenous antioxidants such as vitamin C, vitamin E, and glutathione. As a lipoamide, ALA functions as a cofactor in various multienzyme systems involved in the decarboxylation of α-keto acids such as pyruvate.[1-3]

USAGE
Cancer prevention, cancer treatment, diabetes, HIV and AIDS, liver disease.

PHARMACOKINETICS
Absorption: Endogenous synthesis of lipoic acid takes place in humans and animals. Lipoic acid is bound to proteins in food, specifically lysine. It appears that digestive enzymes do not effectively cleave the peptide bond between lipoic acid and lysine. Oral bioavailability for a 200 mg dose of ALA is estimated to be 30%. De novo synthesis from fatty acids and cysteine also yields lipoic acid.

Distribution: Small amounts of lipoic acid enter the circulation from food or endogenous biosynthesis. After oral administration of supplements, high levels of free lipoic acid can be detected in the serum, and this form is thought to be most important therapeutically. Free lipoic acid distributes widely throughout the body and can be detected in body tissues. The mean plasma half-life is approximately 30 minutes. An absolute bioavailability value has been calculated to be approximately 20 to 38% depending on the isomer and the formula administered.

Metabolism/Excretion: Enzymatic reduction of lipoic acid takes place in the mitochondria and cytosol. Mitochondrial β-oxidation also occurs. In general, a variety of reductive enzymes in body tissues contribute to the high clearance of lipoic acid. Urine appears to be the major excretory pathway, with some fecal loss. The metabolism of lipoic acid in humans has not been studied extensively.[1-6]

ADVERSE REACTIONS
Reported: Hypoglycemia.[1-7]

DRUG INTERACTIONS
None known.

DOSAGE
Oral: No Recommended Dietary Allowances have been set for lipoic acid. Clinical studies have used intravenous and oral doses ranging from 100 to 1,200 mg in split doses three times a day.

LITERATURE SUMMARY AND CRITIQUE

Ziegler D, et al. Effects of treatment with the antioxidant alpha-lipoic acid on cardiac autonomic neuropathy in NIDDM patients: a 4-month randomized controlled multicenter trial (DEKAN Study). Diabetes Care 1997;20:369–73.

A small, prospective, randomized, double-blind evaluation of 800 mg of ALA or placebo on non–insulin-dependent diabetes mellitus (NIDDM) patients with cardiac autonomic neuropathy. Subjects took one tablet four times daily of either 200 mg ALA ($n = 29$) or placebo ($n = 35$) for 4 months. The primary outcome measured was improvement in heart rate variability (HRV) evaluated at baseline and 2 and 4 months. Change in hemoglobin A_{1c}, creatine, and electrolytes was also evaluated. Following 4 months of supplementation, a decrease in HRV was seen in the ALA arm, whereas a slight increase occurred in the placebo group, -6.9% and $+3.6\%$, respectively. The difference was not statistically significant, and clinical significance appears to be minimal. The rate of adverse events was similar between the treatment arms. The trial had stringent exclusion criteria; therefore, the results are not applicable to all NIDDM patients. ALA does not appear to be effective in altering cardiac autonomic neuropathy, but additional studies should be performed.

Marshall AW, et al. Treatment of alcohol-related liver disease with thioctic acid: a six month randomized double-blind trial. Gut 1982;23:1088–93.

A prospective, randomized, double-blind evaluation of thioctic acid, also known as ALA, on patients with alcohol-related liver disease. Patients had a history of 80 g/d alcohol consumption and a precirrhotic liver based on biopsy. Patients received either 100 mg of thioctic acid ($n = 20$) or placebo ($n = 20$) three times a day for 6 months. Primary outcomes were change in serum gamma-glutamyl transpeptidase, total bilirubin, mean corpuscular volume, and liver fibrosis and inflammation. Alcohol intake was assessed at regular intervals and consisted of subject self-reporting. Following 24 weeks of supplementation, no indication was found that thioctic acid improved laboratory indices or liver histology. No significant adverse effects were reported. The authors suggest that thioctic acid, although safe, does not affect alcohol-related liver disease.

REFERENCES

1. Biewenga GP, Haenen GR, Bast A. The pharmacology of the antioxidant lipoic acid. Gen Pharmacol 1997;29:315–31.
2. Packer L. Alpha-lipoic acid: a metabolic antioxidant which regulates NF-κB signal transduction and protects against oxidative injury. Drug Metab Rev 1998;30:245–75.
3. Schupke H, et al. New metabolic pathways of α-lipoic acid. Drug Metab Disp 2001;29:855–62.
4. Sen CK, Packer L. Thiol homeostasis and supplements in physical exercise. Am J Clin Nutr 2000;72 Suppl:653S–69S.
5. Teichert J, et al. Investigations on the pharmacokinetics of alpha-lipoic acid in healthy volunteers. Int J Clin Pharmacol Ther 1998;36:625–8.
6. Breithaupt-Grogler K, et al. Dose-proportionality of oral thioctic acid—coincidence of assessments via pooled plasma and individual data. Eur J Pharm Sci 1999;8:57–65.
7. Jacob S, et al. Oral administration of RAC-alpha-lipoic acid modulates insulin sensitivity in patients with type-2 diabetes mellitus: a placebo-controlled pilot trial. Free Radic Biol Med 1999;27:309–14.

Amygdalin

A.DONATO

COMMON NAMES
Apricot pits, vitamin B_{17}, mandelonitrile-β-glucuronide (semisynthetic), mandelonitrile β-D-gentiobioside (natural product), levorotatory and mandelonitrile, prunasin

SCIENTIFIC NAME
D-Mandelonitrile-β-D-glucosido-6-β-D-glucoside

KEY WORDS
Laetrile, vitamin B_{17}

CLINICAL SUMMARY
A naturally occurring cyanogenic glycoside derived from nuts, plants, and the pits of certain fruits, primarily apricots. Although patients use amygdalin, commonly called Laetrile, research has demonstrated only the absence of beneficial effect. Amygdalin is metabolized by β-glucosidase to cyanide, benzaldehyde, and prunasin. Oral administration has resulted in cyanide toxicity and death. Amygdalin is illegal in the United States but remains available in Tijuana clinics and via the Internet. Pharmaceutical evaluation of the parenteral formulation showed contamination with both pyrogens and microbes, and both oral and parenteral formulations did not contain labeled amounts of amygdalin. Patients should not use this supplement.

CONSTITUENTS
D-Mandelonitrile-β-D-glucosido-6-β-D-glucoside.

WARNINGS
Amygdalin is not approved for use in the United States. Pharmaceutical evaluation of the injectable formulation showed pyrogen and microbial contamination, and both injectable and oral dosage forms did not contain labeled amount of amygdalin.[1]

MECHANISM OF ACTION

The mechanism of action is unknown. Claims for amygdalin's activity rely on the theory, now proven false, that cancer cells contain elevated amounts of β-glucosidase and reduced levels of rhodanese compared with normal cells. Based on this incorrect assumption, cancer cells were claimed to metabolize amygdalin into cyanide and die, whereas healthy cells would convert cyanide to benign thiocyanate via rhodanese. Limited in vitro data support the idea that cyanide, benzaldehyde, and prunasin are cytotoxic. It has also been postulated that cancer develops owing to deficiencies in vitamin B_{17}, but no data substantiate this idea.[2,3]

USAGE

Cancer prevention, cancer treatment.

PHARMACOKINETICS

Hydrocyanic acid, or cyanide, and benzaldehyde are formed from mandelonitrile when amygdalin is metabolized by β-glucosidase enzymes in the cell. Administration of amygdalin 4.5 g/m^2 intravenously to cancer patients displays two-compartment open-model kinetics. Elimination half-life is approximately 2 hours, with a mean clearance of 99 mL/min. No changes in whole blood levels of cyanide or thiocyanate were noted with parenteral administration. Repeated oral administration of amygdalin 500 mg tablets in cancer patients resulted in increased whole blood cyanide levels averaging approximately 1 μg/mL (range 0–3 μg/mL).[3–5]

ADVERSE REACTIONS

Reported: Dermatitis and cyanide toxicity consisting of nausea, vomiting, headache, dizziness, mental obtundation, cyanosis, hypotension, ptosis, neuropathies, coma, and death.[4,6,7]

DRUG INTERACTIONS

Ascorbic Acid: Ascorbic acid may increase the toxicity of amygdalin.
Food: β-Glucosidase is found in certain foods (eg, almonds, celery, peaches, carrots) and may increase the toxicity of amygdalin.

LABORATORY INTERACTIONS

Increased temperature, reduced oxygen saturation.

DOSAGE

Not recommended. Amygdalin is illegal in the United States.
Intravenous: Anecdotal reports and Tijuana clinics typically give 4.5 g/m^2 intravenously for 21 days for one cycle.

Oral: Anecdotal reports and Tijuana clinics initiate 500 mg tablets three times a day indefinitely after the initial intravenous cycle.[4]

LITERATURE SUMMARY AND CRITIQUE
Moertel CG, et al. A clinical trial of amygdalin (Laetrile) in the treatment of human cancer. N Engl J Med 1982;306:201–6.
A prospective, open-label evaluation of amygdalin plus "metabolic therapy" on 178 patients with various cancers. All patients were in generally good health, and a third had not received any prior treatment. Patients received 21 days of intravenous amygdalin 4.5 g/m^2 followed by 500 mg amygdalin tablets three times a day. In addition, patients were placed on a metabolic therapy consisting of vitamins (A, C, E, B complex), minerals, and pancreatic enzyme supplementation. A diet restricting eggs, dairy, meats, and caffeinated and alcoholic beverages was also encouraged. Primary outcomes measured were tumor response and survival. Of the 175 evaluable patients, there was one partial response, and 79% had progression of disease after 2 months and 91% by 3 months. Median survival based on all patients was 4.8 months from initiation of therapy. Many adverse effects noted were related to cyanide toxicity, including headache, nausea, vomiting, dizziness, and mental obtundation. The results suggest that amygdalin is ineffective in the treatment of cancer.

REFERENCES
1. Davignon JP, Trissel LA, Kleinman LM. Pharmaceutical assessment of amygdalin (Laetrile) products. Cancer Treat Rep 1978;62:99–104.
2. Newmark J, et al. Amygdalin (Laetrile) and prunasin β-glucosidases: distribution in germ-free rat and in human tumor tissue. Proc Natl Acad Sci U S A 1981;78:6513–6.
3. Ames MM, et al. Pharmacology of amygdalin (Laetrile) in cancer patients. Cancer Chemother Pharmacol 1981;6:51–7.
4. Moertel CG, et al. A clinical trial of amygdalin (Laetrile) in the treatment of human cancer. N Engl J Med 1982;306:201–6.
5. Moertel CG, et al. A pharmacologic and toxicological study of amygdalin. JAMA 1981;245:561–4.
6. Sadoff L, Fuchs K, Hollander J. Rapid death associated with Laetrile ingestion. JAMA 1978;239:1532.
7. Kalyanaraman UP, et al. Neuromyopathy of cyanide intoxication due to "Laetrile" (amygdalin). Cancer 1983;51:2126–33.

Anvirzel

COMMON NAMES
Rose laurel, adelfa, rosenlorbeer, karavira

SCIENTIFIC NAME
Nerium oleander

KEY WORD
Nerium oleander

A. DONATO

CLINICAL SUMMARY
A hot water extract prepared from the aerial leaves of the *N. oleander* plant. Patients use the proprietary product, Anvirzel, to treat cancer, human immunodeficiency virus/acquired immune deficiency syndrome (HIV/AIDS), hepatitis C, and psoriasis. The plant contains cardiac glycosides, primarily oleandrin, which is similar to digitalis (or digoxin). Raw leaves from the plant are toxic. In vitro studies indicate that Anvirzel causes apoptosis in various cancer cell lines. One in vitro study showed that oleandrin increases the sensitivity of PC-3 human prostate cells to radiotherapy, but no animal or human data are available. Possible adverse effects from Anvirzel include nausea, vomiting, diarrhea, pruritus, pain at the injection site, tachycardia, and arrhythmias. No drug interactions have been reported, although a theoretical additive effect may occur when administered with digoxin. The manufacturer (Ozelle Pharmaceuticals, San Antonio, TX) states that a phase I study is complete and several phase II studies are under development. Anvirzel is considered an investigational new drug in the United States and is not available for compassionate use. Until data regarding efficacy and toxicity are available, this product should not be used outside of clinical trials.

CONSTITUENTS
Cardiac glycosides: oleandrin, odoroside, neritaloside, aglycone oleandrigenin; polysaccharides.[1]

WARNINGS
Unprocessed leaves from the *N. oleander* plant are highly toxic.

MECHANISM OF ACTION
The exact mechanism of action is unknown. The cardiac glycosides are cardioactive and have properties similar to digitalis. In vitro studies suggest that Anvirzel's anticancer activity may be attributable to oleandrin, which suppresses the activity of nuclear factor-κB in various cell lines (U937, CaOV3, human epithelial cells, and T cells). Oleandrin also induces apoptosis in PC-3 cells in vitro. One in vitro study shows that oleandrin increases the sensitivity of PC-3 human prostate cells to radiotherapy. Putative mechanisms of action include activation of caspase cascade, inhibition of sodium-potassium adenosine triphosphatase causing increased intracellular calcium, and improved cellular export of fibroblast growth factor-2. The inventor also claims that Anvirzel has analgesic properties.[2-6]

USAGE
Cancer treatment, congestive heart failure, hepatitis, HIV and AIDS, psoriasis, rheumatoid arthritis.

PHARMACOKINETICS
Oleandrin, the principal glycoside in *N. oleander*, is well absorbed following oral administration. Biologic half-life is not determined, but pharmacodynamic activity lasts for approximately 2.5 days. About half of circulating oleandrin is bound to plasma proteins. Both biliary and renal elimination have been shown.[7]

ADVERSE REACTIONS
Reported (Anvirzel): Nausea, vomiting, diarrhea, pruritus, pain at injection site, tumor pain, mastalgia, leukocytosis, tachycardia, and arrhythmias.
Common (Raw Botanical): Consumption of one *N. oleander* leaf may be fatal. Onset of toxicity occurs several hours following consumption and includes vomiting, abdominal pain, cyanosis, hypotension, hypothermia, vertigo, respiratory paralysis, and death.

DRUG INTERACTIONS
Digoxin: Theoretically, the cardiac glycosides in *N. oleander* may have an additive effect with digoxin, causing toxicity.

CONTRAINDICATIONS
Patients with hypercalcemia, hypokalemia, bradycardia, ventricular tachycardia, or New York Heart Association stage III or IV heart failure should not use this product.[7]

DOSAGE

Route of administration varies with type and location of disease.

Parenteral: 0.3 to 0.7 mL intramuscularly daily or every other day. Therapy continues until remission of disease.

Oral: 0.3 to 0.7 mL three times a day after meals (maximum of 2 mL per dose reported in patent).

Gargle: 5% mouthwash used daily.[4]

LITERATURE SUMMARY AND CRITIQUE

According to the manufacturer's Web site (<http://www.ozelle.com>), a phase I clinical trial commenced on April 10, 2000, at the Cleveland Clinic, Cleveland, Ohio. The maximum intramuscular dose was 2.4 mL given once daily. The results of the study are not yet available, despite the Web site claim that they would be available to the company during the third quarter of 2001.

REFERENCES

1. Wang X, et al. LC/MS/MS analysis of an oleander extract for cancer treatment. Anal Chem 2000;72:3547–52.
2. Smith JA, et al. Inhibition of export of fibroblast growth factor-2 (FGF-2) from the prostate cancer cell lines PC3 and DU145 by Anvirzel and its cardiac glycoside component, oleandrin. Biochem Pharmacol 2001;62:469–72.
3. Manna SK, et al. Oleandrin suppresses activation of nuclear transcription factor-κB, activator protein-1, and c-Jun NH2-terminal kinase. Cancer Res 2000;60:3838–47.
4. Ozel HZ. Extracts of *Nerium* species, methods of preparation, and use therefore. US patent 5,135,745. 1992 Aug 4.
5. Pathak S, et al. Anvirzel™, an extract of *Nerium oleander*, induces cell death in human but not murine cancer cells. Anticancer Drugs 2000;11:455–63.
6. Nasu S, et al. Enhancement of radiotherapy by oleandrin is a caspase-3 dependent process. Cancer Lett 2002;185:145–51.
7. Schulz V, et al. Rational phytotherapy: a physician's guide to herbal medicine. 4th ed. New York: Springer; 2001.

Arnica

COMMON NAMES
Mountain tobacco, leopard's bane, wolf's bane, mountain arnica

SCIENTIFIC NAME
Arnica montana

KEY WORDS
Arnica montana, wolf's bane

CLINICAL SUMMARY

Derived from the flowers and rhizome. No data from clinical trials support the use of homeopathic or herbal preparations of oral arnica for any of the claims proposed for it (postoperative antibacterial, muscle pain following exercise, bruising, pain and bleeding following dental procedure). Side effects following oral administration of the herb (but not the homeopathic preparation) include gastrointestinal distress, hypotension, tachycardia, shortness of breath, coma, and death. Topical administration is relatively benign but can cause contact dermatitis, irritation, and burning.

CONSTITUENTS

Amines: betaine, choline, trimethylamine; carbohydrates: mucilage, polysaccharides including inulin; coumarins: scopoletin, umbelliferone; flavonoids: betuletol, eupafolin, flavonol, glucuronides, kaempferol, luteolin, quercetin, spinacetin, tricin; terpenoids: sesquiterpenes, arnifolin, helenalin; volatile oil: thymol; other constituents: arnicin, caffeic acid, carotenoids, phytosterols, resin, tannin.[1]

WARNINGS

Internal use of arnica is not advised. The effects of arnica on the lungs, heart, and uterus have not been sufficiently tested to justify the risks associated with oral use. A fatal case of poisoning has been reported following ingestion of 70 g of arnica tincture. The US Food and Drug Administration considers oral arnica an unsafe herb. External use appears to pose no risk.[2,3]

MECHANISM OF ACTION

Experimental studies on the effects of arnica preparations have demonstrated anti-microbial, anti-inflammatory, respiratory-stimulant, positive inotropic, and tonus-increasing actions. The anti-inflammatory effects are attributed to helenalin, whose actions include a marked antiedemic effect that has been confirmed in experimental models. The external use of arnica preparations can cause dermatitis in individuals sensitized by sesquiterpenes of the helenalin type.[4]

USAGE

Inflammation, sprains.

ADVERSE REACTIONS

Common (Oral): Gastrointestinal distress, tachycardia, shortness of breath, coma, and death.
Infrequent (Topical): Contact dermatitis, irritation, burning.[5]

DRUG INTERACTIONS

Antihypertensives: Arnica may reduce hypotensive effects.
Anticoagulants/Antiplatelets: Arnica may potentiate the anticoagulant effect owing to the coumarin constituents. This effect has not been documented in humans. Use with caution.

DOSAGE

Oral: The homeopathic preparations seem to be the most popular. Unless otherwise prescribed: *Tea:* 2 g arnica in 100 mL water; *Tincture:* Poultices—tincture diluted in 3 to 10 times amount of water.
Topical: Mouthwash: Tincture diluted 10 times; **DO NOT SWALLOW**.[6]

LITERATURE SUMMARY AND CRITIQUE

No human studies have been performed to validate its use.

REFERENCES

1. Newall CA, et al. Herbal medicines: a guide for health-care professionals. London: Pharmaceutical Press; 1996.
2. Brinker F. Herb contraindications and drug interactions. 3rd ed. Sandy (OR): Eclectic Medical Publications; 2001.
3. Schulz V, et al. Rational phytotherapy, a physician's guide to herbal medicine. 3rd ed. New York: Springer; 1996.
4. US Food and Drug Administration/Center for Food Safety and Applied Nutrition/Office of Plant and Dairy Foods and Beverages. Poisonous plant database—vascular plant list [online] 1999 May 14 [cited 2001 July 12]. http://vm.cfsan.fda.gov/~djw/plantnam.html (accessed July 12, 2001).
5. Blumenthal M, et al. Herbal medicine, expanded Commission E monographs. Austin (TX): American Botanical Council; 2000.
6. Wichtl M. Herbal drugs and phytopharmaceuticals. Boca Raton (FL): CRC Press; 1994.

Astragalus

COMMON NAMES
Huang Chi, Huang Qi, milk vetch, *Radix astragali*

SCIENTIFIC NAME
Astragalus membranaceus

KEY WORDS
Radix astragali, Huang Chi, Huang Qi

CLINICAL SUMMARY
Derived from the root of the plant. This product is primarily used for its immunostimulating properties. In vitro, animal, and anecdotal human data show reduction of immune suppression following chemotherapy. Chinese studies suggest that astragalus, when used with angelica, has renal protective effects. Astragalus increases M-cholinergic receptor density in senile rats. This suggests that astragalus may have a role in combating brain senility. To date, no significant adverse events have been reported. Patients on immunosuppressants (eg, tacrolimus or cyclosporine) should not take this supplement. Herbal astragalus preparations should be administered only by oral route.

CONSTITUENTS
Triterpenoid saponins (cycloastragenol, astragaloside I to VIII, cyclocanthoside), cycloartane triterpene, polysaccharide, isoflavonoids, amino acids.[1]

MECHANISM OF ACTION
Astragalus works by stimulating several factors of the immune system. The polysaccharides potentiate in vitro the immune-mediated antitumor activity of interleukin-2 (IL-2), improve the responses of lymphocytes from normal subjects and cancer patients, and

enhance the natural killer cell (NKC) activity of normal subjects and potentiate activity of monocytes. The saponins potentiate NKC activity and restore steroid-inhibited NKC activity in vitro. They also increase phagocytosis and demonstrate hepatoprotective effects on chemically induced liver injury in vitro and in vivo. Chinese studies suggest that astragalus, when used with angelica, has renal protective effects by mediating gene expression. Astragalus increases M-cholinergic receptor density in senile rats. This suggests that astragalus may have a role in combating brain senility.[2–4]

USAGE

Cardiovascular disease, chemotherapy side effects, common cold, diabetes, human immunodeficiency virus (HIV) and acquired immune deficiency syndrome (AIDS), immunostimulation, microbial infection, strength and stamina.

ADVERSE REACTIONS

No adverse effects have been reported.

DRUG INTERACTIONS

Immunosuppressants: Astragalus may antagonize the effects of immunosuppressants such as tacrolimus and cyclosporine.
Aldesleukin: Concomitant treatment with astragalus has resulted in a 10-fold potentiation of tumoricidal activity with decreased side effects.
Cyclophosphamide: Astragalus may decrease immunosuppression following treatment.[5–7]

DOSAGE

Oral: 250 to 500 mg in capsules/tablets four times a day. Also available as a tea, tincture, dried root, and fluid extract.

LITERATURE SUMMARY AND CRITIQUE

The clinical evidence to justify its use as a chemoprotective agent, immunostimulant, and hepatoprotective agent consists of animal and in vitro studies. No significant human studies have been conducted.

Qun L, et al. Effects of astragalus on IL-2/IL-2R system in patients with maintained hemodialysis [letter]. Clin Nephrol 1999;52:333–4.
Prospective evaluation of 31 patients in end-stage renal disease on hemodialysis. Participants were randomized to receive either intravenous astragalus or placebo. After 2 months of treatment, the astragalus group had significantly higher levels of IL-2 compared with placebo.

REFERENCES

1. Tang W, et al. Chinese drugs of plant origin. Berlin: Springer-Verlag; 1992.
2. Bone K. Clinical applications of Ayurvedic and Chinese herbs. Queensland (Australia): Phytotherapy Press; 1996.
3. Shi R, et al. The regulatory action of *Radix astragali* on M-cholinergic receptor of the brain of senile rats. J Tradit Chin Med 2001;21:232–5.
4. Yu L, et al. Identification of a gene associated with astragalus and angelica's renal protective effects by silver staining mRNA differential display. Chin Med J (Engl) 2002;115:923–7.
5. Upton R. Astragalus root: analytical, quality control and therapeutic monograph. American Herbal Pharmacopoeia Scotts Valley, California 1999;1:1–25.
6. Chu DT, et al. Fractionated extract of astragalus, a Chinese medicinal herb, potentiates LAK cell cytotoxicity generated by a low dose of recombinant interleukin-2. J Clin Lab Immunol 1988;26:183–7.
7. Chu DT, Wong WL, Mavligit GM. Immunotherapy with Chinese medicinal herbs. II. Reversal of cyclophosphamide-induced immune suppression by administration of fractionated *Astragalus membranaceus* in vivo. J Clin Lab Immunol 1988;25:125–9.

Ayurveda

COMMON NAMES
Ayurvedic medicine, traditional
Indian medicine

CLINICAL SUMMARY

From the Sanskrit words "ayur" (life) and "veda" (knowledge), Ayurveda originated in India over 3,000 years ago. Treatment is patient tailored and consists of oral formulations containing herbal, mineral, spice, and animal components; mental balance through yoga or meditation; purgatives; and dietary and lifestyle changes. It is available in at least 10 clinics in North America, but there is no licensure for practicing Ayurveda in the United States. Ayurvedic medicinal compounds, which can contain from a few to hundreds of components, are commonly used to treat chronic diseases such as diabetes, rheumatoid arthritis, Parkinson's disease, acne, obesity, and cancer, as well as acute conditions. Many of the more frequently used herbs have been studied extensively in vitro and in vivo and show antioxidant, antitumor, antimicrobial, immunomodulatory, hypoglycemic, or anti-inflammatory properties. Clinical trials show weak benefit of various formulations in treating acne, rheumatoid arthritis, diabetes, hepatitis, obesity, and constipation. Meditation reduces anxiety, lowers blood pressure, and enhances general well-being in clinical trials. The World Bank is funding research in India to evaluate Ayurvedic medicines for anemia, edema during pregnancy, and postpartum complications. Little is known about the drug interactions between Ayurvedic and modern drugs. As with any unregulated products, the medicinals used in Ayurveda may be substandard or contaminated; numerous cases of lead poisoning from Ayurvedic preparations have been reported.

WARNINGS
Like many imported traditional medicines, some Ayurvedic preparations have been found to be contaminated with pathogens, heavy metals, undeclared prescription drugs (eg, corticosteroids), and other products.

MECHANISM OF ACTION
Ayurveda emphasizes both health maintenance *(Svasthavritha)* and diagnosis and treatment *(Athuravritha)*. Patients are classified by their prominent *dosha*, or physical, emotional, and metabolic type *(Kapha, Pitta, or Vata)*, each located in specific organs and associated with two of the five elements (earth, fire, water, air, and ether) and five senses. The *dosha* represents properties shared by the organs, body, environment, and cosmos. When a patient's unique state of *dosha* is out of balance, illness occurs. Therapy is personalized to the individual's problems and metabolic characteristics to restore individual *dosha* balance through diet and lifestyle modifications, medicinals (herbs, spices, metals, and/or animal products), breathing exercises, and meditation. Detoxification *(panchakarma)* occurs before medicines begin, including bloodletting, induced vomiting, and bowel purging. The therapeutic approach seeks to cure the disease by reversing the steps that led to it, balancing the *dosha* (eg, administering cooling medicines if *Pitta*, the hot *dosha*, is predominant).

Many of the more frequently used herbs, such as ashwagandha *(Withania somnifera)*, guggul *(Commiphora mukul)*, boswellia *(Boswellia serrata)*, gotu kola *(Centella asiatica)*, curcumin *(Curcuma longa)*, ginger *(Zingiber officinale)*, aloe *(Aloe barbadensis)*, and garlic *(Allium sativum)*, have been studied extensively in vitro and in vivo and show antioxidant, antitumor, antimicrobial, immunomodulatory, or anti-inflammatory properties. (See chapters on those herbs for more information.) *Rasayana* herbs (said to promote positive health) such as ashwagandha, *Asparagus racemosus, Emblica officinalis, Piper longum*, and *Terminalia chebula* show immunostimulant and adaptogenic activities in an animal study. *Mucuna pruriens*, used in preparations for Parkinson's disease, contains L-dopa. Ayurvedic gold preparations (eg, Swarna Bhasma) have antioxidant and restorative effects in animal models of ischemia. The herbs most often used to treat diabetes, *Gymnema sylvestre, Momordica charantia*, fenugreek, *Coccinia indica*, and *Pterocarpus marsupium*, show hypoglycemic activity in vitro and in vivo. The herbal mixtures Maharishi Amrit Kalash-4 and -5 have antioxidant properties, inhibit low-density lipoprotein (LDL) oxidation in vitro, inhibit platelet aggregation, and cause a reduction in aortic arch atheroma in hyperlipidemic rabbits. Maharasnadi Quathar is used to treat rheumatoid arthritis, increases antioxidant enzyme activity, decreases thiobarbituric acids reactive substances (TBARS) generation, and improves symptoms in human subjects.[1-14]

USAGE
Acne, atherosclerosis, cancer prevention, cancer treatment, cardiovascular disease, depression, diabetes, health maintenance, hepatitis, high cholesterol, hypertension, indigestion, infections, memory loss, Parkinson's disease, rheumatoid arthritis, weight loss.

ADVERSE REACTIONS

Reported (General): Headache, gastrointestinal complaints. Several herbs in Ayurvedic preparations can cause photosensitivity, whereas some contain arsenic or mercury that can produce skin lesions.

Common (Mineral Tonics): Ayurvedic preparations can contain varying amounts of lead (0.9–72,990 µg Pb/g) and have caused severe gastrointestinal symptoms and anemia owing to lead poisoning.

Common (**Adhatoda vasica**)*:* This herb, often used for respiratory tract ailments, is reported to have oxytocic and abortifacient effects.[5–13]

DRUG INTERACTIONS

Phenytoin: The Ayurvedic syrup shankhapushpi causes decreased blood concentrations of phenytoin.[10,15]

DOSAGE

Varies by preparation.

LITERATURE SUMMARY AND CRITIQUE

Almost all clinical trials reported in the literature are conducted in India. Only a few are published in English. No research dealing with cancer was uncovered.

Nagashayana N, et al. Association of L-DOPA with recovery following Ayurveda medication in Parkinson's disease. J Neurol Sci 2000;176:124–7.
A prospective study of an Ayurveda remedy containing cow's milk, *M. pruriens, Hyoscyamus reticulatus, Withania somnifera,* and *Sida cordifolia* with or without *panchakarma* (cleansing therapy) in 18 patients with Parkinson's disease. Thirteen patients underwent 28 days of cleansing, consisting of oleation, purgation, and enemas, prior to 56 days of the medicinal herb, and 5 patients received the medicinal herb alone for 84 days. A significantly greater proportion of patients receiving medicinal compounds plus *panchakarma* experienced improvements in activities of daily living, motor function, and symptoms, which the authors attributed to cleansing of the intestine to allow increased absorption. Patient demographic data and detailed protocol were not provided.

Paranjpe P, Kulkarni PH. Comparative efficacy of four Ayurvedic formulations in the treatment of acne vulgaris: a double-blind randomized placebo-controlled evaluation. J Ethnopharmacol 1995;49:127–32.
A randomized, double-blind evaluation of four oral herbal/mineral formulations in 82 patients ages 18 to 28 with moderate acne. Split into five groups, subjects received two tablets three times daily of Sookshma Triphala (*n* = 16), Thiostanin (*n* = 17), Shankhabhasma Vati (*n* = 14), Sunder Vati (*n* = 20), or placebo (*n* = 15). Only the Sunder Vati arm experienced significant decreases in number of inflammatory and noninflammatory

lesions by 6 weeks. Sunder Vati contains *Phyllanthus emblica* (Amalaki), *Embelia ribes* (Vidanga), *Holarrhena antidysenterica* (Kutaj bark), and *Z. officinale* (Sunth or ginger).

Ramesh PR, et al. Managing morphine-induced constipation: a controlled comparison of an Ayurvedic formulation and senna. J Pain Symptom Manage 1998;16:240–4.
A small, open, controlled trial evaluating prophylactic Misrakasneham, a liquid purgative containing 21 herbs, castor oil, ghee, and milk, versus senna laxative tablet (Sofsena) in patients receiving oral morphine for advanced cancer. Patients received 2.5 mL of Misrakasneham mixed with warm milk ($n = 20$) or 120 mg senna tablet ($n = 16$) before initiation of morphine therapy; doses were escalated if a prior dose was ineffective after 2 days. Daily "satisfactory" bowel movements were measured. The difference in efficacy between treatment arms was not significant: 85% of the Misrakasneham group and 69% of the senna group had satisfactory bowel movements.

Chopra A, et al. Randomized double blind trial of an Ayurvedic plant derived formulation for treatment of rheumatoid arthritis. J Rheumatol 2000;27:1365–71.
A randomized, double-blind trial evaluating RA-1, a standardized formulation of *W. somnifera* (ashwagandha), *B. serrata* (gugulla), *Z. officinale* (ginger), and *C. longa* (circumin) in patients with active rheumatoid arthritis. Patients received 444 mg RA-1 extract in split doses ($n = 89$) or placebo ($n = 93$) for 16 weeks and were required to discontinue nonsteroidal anti-inflammatory drug therapy 3 to 5 days prior to entry, but stable prednisolone use not exceeding 7.5 mg was permitted. A significantly greater proportion of patients in the RA-1 group showed > 50% reduction in joint swelling. Both the RA-1 group and the placebo group showed significant improvement from baseline in functional criteria, including joint count pain, joint count swelling, pain VAS, Stanford Health Assessment Questionnaire, and patient and physician global assessment; RA-1 showed numerically, but not statistically, greater improvement than placebo. Adverse events, consisting of headache and nausea, were similar between groups. Subjects were enrolled from free community arthritic camps, which may have led to selection bias toward women and lower socioeconomic classes.

Paranjpe P, Patki P, Patwardhan B. Ayurvedic treatment of obesity: a randomized double-blind, placebo-controlled clinical trial. J Ethnopharmacol 1990;29:1–11.
A randomized, double-blind trial of four Ayurvedic medicinal compounds versus placebo in 70 otherwise healthy patients at least 20% in excess of ideal body weight. Patients were randomized to receive 250 mg three times daily of Triphala guggul and 250 mg three times daily of Gokshuradi guggul (group I), 250 mg three times daily of Triphala guggul and 100 mg three times daily of Sinhanad guggul (group II), 250 mg three times daily of Triphala guggul and 250 mg three times daily of Chandraprabhavati (group III), or 250 mg three times daily of placebo (group IV). Dietary intake was not controlled. Body weight, skinfold thickness, body measurements, and serum cholesterol and triglycerides were significantly lower after 3 months in groups I, II, and III compared with the placebo group. Results did not differ significantly between active groups. Treatment did not result in changes in blood pressure, pulse rate, or body temperature. Diar-

rhea and nausea were reported side effects. The four medicinal compounds contain a variety of Ayurvedic herbs but have in common guggul *(Commiphora mukul)*, hirda *(T. chebula)*, beheda *(T. belerica)*, and amalaki *(Emblica officinalis)*.

REFERENCES

1. Cassileth BR. The alternative medicine handbook. New York: WW Norton & Co; 1998.
2. Chopra A, Doiphode VV. Ayurvedic medicine: core concept, therapeutic principles, and current relevance. Med Clin North Am 2002;86:75–89.
3. Nagashayana N, et al. Association of L-DOPA with recovery following Ayurveda medication in Parkinson's disease. J Neurol Sci 2000;176:124–7.
4. Sundaram V, et al. Inhibition of low-density lipoprotein oxidation by oral herbal mixtures Maharishi Amrit Kalash-4 and Maharishi Amrit Kalash-5 in hyperlipidemic patients. Am J Med Sci 1997;314:303–9.
5. Ayurvedic interventions for diabetes mellitus: a systematic review. Evid Rep Technol Assess 2001;41.
6. Rege NN, Thatte UM, Dahanukar SA. Adaptogenic properties of six Rasayana herbs used in Ayurvedic medicine. Phytother Res 1999;13:275–91.
7. Shah ZA, Vohora SB. Antioxidant/restorative effects of calcined gold preparations used in Indian systems of medicine against global and focal models of ischemia. Pharmacol Toxicol 2002;90:254–9.
8. Thabrew MI, et al. Antioxidant potential of two polyherbal preparations used in Ayurveda for the treatment of rheumatoid arthritis. J Ethnopharmacol 2001;76:285–91.
9. Ernst E. Adverse effects of herbal drugs in dermatology. Br J Dermatol 2000;143:923–9.
10. Prpic-Majic D, et al. Lead poisoning associated with the use of Ayurvedic metal-mineral tonics. J Toxicol Clin Toxicol 1996;34:417–23.
11. Claeson UP, et al. Adhatoda vasica: a critical review of ethnopharmacological and toxicological data. J Ethnopharmacol 2000;72:1–20.
12. van Vonderen MG, et al. Severe gastrointestinal symptoms due to lead poisoning from Indian traditional medicine. Am J Gastroenterol 2000;95:1591–2.
13. Spriewald BM, et al. Lead induced anaemia due to traditional Indian medicine: a case report. Occup Environ Med 1999;56:282–3.
14. Chopra A. Ayurvedic medicine and arthritis. Rheum Dis Clin North Am 2000;26:133–43.
15. Fugh-Berman A. Herb-drug interactions. Lancet 2000;355:134–8.

Bee Pollen

COMMON NAMES
Buckwheat pollen, pine pollen, pu huang

CLINICAL SUMMARY
Produced by bees from a combination of flower pollen and nectar. The use of bee pollen is relatively benign. Aside from its nutritional value, no clinical data show any benefit from its use. Patients who are allergic to bee venom (ie, bee stings) or to honey, ragweed, or chrysanthemum should not take this product. Adverse effects consist of possible hypersensitivity reactions.

CONSTITUENTS
Polysaccharides, protein, amino acids, minerals, carbohydrates, lipids, essential fatty acids (α-linolenic and linolenic).[1]

MECHANISM OF ACTION
Unknown.

USAGE
Alcoholism, allergies, appetite, asthma, benign prostatic hypertrophy, cancer prevention, diabetes, gastrointestinal disorders, health maintenance, strength and stamina.

ADVERSE REACTIONS

Reported: Hypersensitivity reaction causing pruritus, headache, swelling, sneezing, ana-phylaxis, hypereosinophilia, and eosinophilic gastroenteritis consisting of nausea, abdominal pain, and diarrhea.[2]

DRUG INTERACTIONS

None known at this time.

LABORATORY INTERACTIONS

None known at this time.

CONTRAINDICATIONS

Patients with an allergy to bee stings (bee venom), intolerance to honey, or allergy to rag-weed/chrysanthemums should avoid bee pollen products.

DOSAGE

Oral: 500 to 1,000 mg two to three times a day. Available in tablets, capsules, and granules.

LITERATURE SUMMARY AND CRITIQUE

No significant studies to report. Most studies on bee pollen are small, uncontrolled human studies or animal studies. No significant clinical efficacy is reported other than that of its nutritive value.

Steben RE, Boudreaux P. The effects of pollen and protein extracts on selected blood factors and performance of athletes. J Sports Med 1978;18:221–6.
Small randomized study evaluating the effect of bee pollen supplement on 18 male high school students. Three treatment arms were established to compare bee pollen to protein extract to placebo. Following 12 weeks of training and supplementation, no effect of the bee pollen, protein extract, or placebo was seen on performance, hemoglobin, or serum electrolytes. This small study was probably incapable of detecting a statistically signifi-cant difference between treatment groups. No adverse events were reported with supple-mentation.

REFERENCES

1. Mirkin G. Can bee pollen benefit health? JAMA 1989;262:1854.
2. Leung AY, et al. Encyclopedia of natural ingredients. New York: Wiley and Sons; 1996.

Beta-carotene

COMMON NAMES

Provitamin A carotenoid, beta
carotene, betacarotene

CLINICAL SUMMARY

A natural pigment synthesized by plants. Beta-carotene supplements are used as an antioxidant and an immunostimulant and to prevent or treat cancer, human immunodeficiency virus (HIV), heart disease, and leukoplakia. Beta-carotene, along with α-carotene and β-cryptoxanthin, can be converted to retinol and is classified as a provitamin A carotenoid. Supplementation with beta-carotene does not increase overall vitamin A levels or lead to vitamin A toxicity. Data on chemoprevention for cancer are inconsistent. Several large epidemiologic studies produced conflicting results, including possible increased risk of lung cancer in male smokers over age 40. Available data also conflict on beta-carotene supplementation in HIV-positive patients and concerning effects on CD4 counts. One large-scale cohort study in the Netherlands suggests that alcohol consumption has a negative effect on the chemopreventive property of beta-carotene. No significant adverse reactions are reported. There is no recommended dose or daily intake amount of beta-carotene.

MECHANISM OF ACTION

Beta-carotene is a provitamin A carotenoid and therefore converts into retinol. Supplementation with beta-carotene does not increase overall vitamin A levels or lead to vitamin A toxicity. Proposed mechanisms of action for beta-carotene for cancer prevention include inhibition of cancer growth, induction of differentiation by modulation of cell-cycle regulatory proteins, alterations in insulin-like growth factor-1, prevention of oxidative DNA damage, and possible enhancement of carcinogen metabolizing enzymes. Beta-carotene may enhance macrophage function and natural killer cell cytotoxicity and increase T helper lymphocytes. Carotenoids are also associated with various health effects, including decreased risk for macular degeneration and cataracts, cancers, and cardiovascular events.[1-3]

USAGE

Cancer prevention, cardiovascular disease, cataracts, HIV and acquired immune deficiency syndrome (AIDS), immunostimulation, macular degeneration, oral leukoplakia.

PHARMACOKINETICS

Absorption: Intestinal absorption of carotenoids, including beta-carotene, is facilitated by the formation of bile acid micelles. The presence of fat in the small intestine stimulates the secretion of bile acids from the gallbladder and improves the absorption of carotenoids by increasing the size and stability of the micelles, thus allowing more carotenoids to be solubilized. Beta-carotene may be absorbed intact or cleaved to form vitamin A. Source, dose, and presence of other carotenoids affect its bioavailability.

Distribution: The concentration of beta-carotene in human serum and tissues is highly variable and depends on food sources, efficiency of absorption, and amount of fat in the diet. Beta-carotene is transported in the blood primarily by low-density lipoproteins. The serum concentration of carotenoids after a single dose peaks at 24 to 48 hours postdose. The earliest postprandial serum appearance of carotenoids is in the chylomicron fraction. Beta-carotene is primarily stored in adipose tissue and liver.

Metabolism/Excretion: Beta-carotene may be cleaved to form vitamin A while being absorbed from the stomach. Cleavage is accomplished either by the intestinal mucosal enzyme beta-carotene 15-15'-dioxygenase or by noncentral cleavage mechanisms. The extent of conversion of a highly bioavailable source of dietary beta-carotene to vitamin A in humans has been shown to be between 60 and 75%, with an additional 15% of the beta-carotene absorbed intact. Noncentral cleavage of carotenoids yields a wide variety of metabolic products, including aldehydes, acid, alcohol, and epoxide derivatives. It is assumed that beta-carotene is eliminated in bile and urine.[1,4,5]

ADVERSE REACTIONS

No common adverse effects have been reported.

Toxicity: Carotenodermia is a harmless but clearly documented effect of high carotenoid intake. A yellowish discoloration of the skin has resulted following chronic intake of food and supplements containing large amounts of carotenoids.[1,4,6]

DRUG INTERACTIONS

Ethanol: May block the conversion of beta-carotene to vitamin A. The hepatotoxic effects of ethanol may be potentiated by high doses of beta-carotene. One large-scale cohort study in the Netherlands suggests that alcohol consumption has a negative effect on the chemopreventive property of beta-carotene.[2,7]

DOSAGE

No standard dosing exists. Supplementation for the general population is not recommended. *Tolerable upper intake level:* None set.[1]

LITERATURE SUMMARY AND CRITIQUE

Hennekens CH, et al. Lack of effect of long-term supplementation with beta carotene on the incident of malignant neoplasms and cardiovascular disease. N Engl J Med 1996;334:1145–9.

A prospective, double-blind evaluation of male physicians, ages 40 to 84, randomized to receive 325 mg of aspirin plus 50 mg of beta-carotene every other day, one active and one placebo, or two placebos. A total of 11,036 patients received beta-carotene only and 11,035 patients received placebo over a 12-year treatment period. Statistical analysis suggests that beta-carotene supplementation offers no increased or decreased risk for development of any cancer. Beta-carotene supplements do not appear to influence the risk of cardiovascular events. A subset analysis of subjects who smoked suggested no increase or decrease in cancer risk.

Alpha-Tocopherol, Beta Carotene Cancer Prevention Study Group. The effect of vitamin E and beta carotene on the incidence of lung cancer and other cancers in male smokers. N Engl J Med 1994;330:1029–35.

A prospective, randomized evaluation of male smokers, ages 50 to 69, from Finland. Subjects received supplementation with 20 mg of beta-carotene alone ($n = 7,282$), 50 mg of α-tocopherol alone ($n = 7,286$), combination ($n = 7,278$), or placebo ($n = 7,287$). Patients were followed for 5 to 8 years or until death. The primary end point was incidence of lung cancer. Data analysis revealed an increased number of deaths from lung cancer, ischemic heart disease, and hemorrhagic stroke for subjects receiving beta-carotene, with an 8% higher mortality rate over those not receiving beta-carotene. The authors suggest that although beta-carotene has previously been shown to reduce the incidence of certain cancer, male smokers may be at an increased risk of lung cancer when administered beta-carotene supplements.

Coodley GO, et al. Beta-carotene in HIV infection: an extended evaluation. Cancer 1996;10:967–73.

A prospective, intent-to-treat evaluation of HIV-positive patients randomized to receive 3 months of either 60 mg of beta-carotene three times daily ($n = 36$) or placebo ($n = 36$). The primary outcomes were changes in CD4 cells, CD4/CD8 ration, Karnofsky Performance Scale score, natural killer cells, and total white blood cell count. No significant advantage was demonstrated in patients supplemented with beta-carotene for any of the end points. Although previous pilot studies suggested improvements in CD4 cell counts following beta-carotene supplementation, no benefit could be demonstrated in this study.

REFERENCES

1. Dietary Reference Intakes for vitamin C, vitamin E, selenium, and carotenoids. Washington (DC): National Academy Press; 2000.
2. Leo MA, Lieber CS. Alcohol, vitamin A, and β-carotene: adverse interactions, including hepatotoxicity and carcinogenicity. Am J Clin Nutr 1999;69:1071–85.
3. Zhang LX, et al. Carotenoids enhance gap junctional communication and inhibit lipid peroxidation in C3H/10T1/2 cells: relationship to their cancer chemopreventive action. Carcinogenesis 1991;12:2109–14.
4. Brody T. Nutritional biochemistry. San Diego (CA): Academic Press; 1999.
5. Nierenberg DW, et al. Determinants of increase in plasma concentration of β-carotene after chronic oral supplementation. The Skin Cancer Prevention Study Group. Am J Clin Nutr 1991;53:443–9.
6. Pronsky ZM. Power's and Moore's food-medication interactions. 11th ed. Pottstown (PA): Food Medication Interactions; 2000.
7. Schuurman A, et al. A prospective cohort study on intake of retinol, vitamins C and E, and carotenoids and prostate cancer risk (Netherlands). Cancer Causes Control 2002;13:573–82.
8. Holick CN, et al. Dietary carotenoids, serum beta-carotene, and retinol and risk of lung cancer in the α-tocopherol, beta-carotene cohort study. Am J Epidemiol 2002;156:536–47.
9. Olmedilla B, et al. A European multicentre, placebo-controlled supplementation study with α-tocopherol, carotene-rich palm oil, lutein or lycopene; analysis of serum responses. Clin Sci (Lond) 2002;102:447–56.

Bilberry Fruit

COMMON NAMES
Dwarf bilberry, bog bilberry,
European blueberry, huckleberry,
whortleberry

SCIENTIFIC NAME
Vaccinium myrtillus

KEY WORD
Vaccinium myrtillus

CLINICAL SUMMARY
Derived from the fruit of the tree. Numerous human studies suggest that bilberry anthocyanosides prevent diabetic retinopathy and improve visual acuity and retinal function. Products should be standardized to 25% anthocyanosides. Coumarins present in bilberry may interact with platelets and have an additive effect with blood thinners. No adverse reactions have been reported. Bilberry fruit should not be confused with bilberry leaf, which may cause hypoglycemia.

CONSTITUENTS
Tannins: 5 to 10% catechin tannins; carbohydrates: 30% invert sugar and pectins; flavonols: flavonol glycosides including astragalin, hyperoside, isoquercitrin, quercetin; phenolic acids; anthocyanosides.[1]

MECHANISM OF ACTION
Bilberry has shown vasoprotective, antiedematous, antioxidant, anti-inflammatory, and astringent actions. It has demonstrated free radical scavenging and inhibition of cyclic adenosine monophosphate phosphodiesterase actions. In vitro and in vivo clinical studies show inhibition of platelet aggregation and stimulation of vascular prostacyclin.

Preliminary human trials indicate vasoprotective properties. Bilberry anthocyanins regenerate rhodopsin and are indicated in treatment of poor night vision, mascular degeneration, glaucoma, and cataracts.[2,3]

USAGE

Cancer prevention, cataracts, circulatory disorders, diabetic retinopathy, diarrhea, glaucoma, hemorrhoids, macular degeneration, mucositis, varicose veins, visual acuity.

PHARMACOKINETICS

Intravenous and oral studies were performed in male rats with bilberry anthocyanosides. Oral administration showed moderate gastrointestinal absorption, with bioavailability less than 2%. Peak levels were achieved within 15 minutes with a three-compartment distribution and elimination shown. Elimination was primarily through urine and bile. There are no reports regarding the pharmacokinetics of whole bilberry extract.[4]

ADVERSE REACTIONS

None reported.

DRUG INTERACTIONS

Anticoagulants/Antiplatelets: Bilberry may potentiate the risk of bleeding if used concurrently owing to platelet aggregation inhibition and prostaglandin modulation.

LABORATORY INTERACTIONS

Coumarin content in bilberry may increase prothrombin time/partial thromboplastin time and inhibit platelet activity.

DOSAGE

Dosage varies considerably. Standardized dosage of 25% anthocyanoside content recommended. *Night vision*: 60 to 120 mg of extract by mouth daily. *Visual and circulatory problems*: 240 to 480 mg two or three times a day.

LITERATURE SUMMARY AND CRITIQUE

Several clinical trials have found no short- or long-term improvements in night vision attributable to bilberry. Numerous human studies have shown that bilberry in a standardized extract form of 25% anthocyanosides is effective in preventing diabetic retinopathy and improving visual acuity and retinal function.[5-7]

Muth ER, Laurent JM, Jasper P. The effect of bilberry nutritional supplementation on night visual acuity and contrast sensitivity. Altern Med Rev 2000;5:164–73.
A prospective, randomized, placebo-controlled crossover evaluation of bilberry supplementation in 15 healthy male air force personnel. All subjects had visual acuity of 20/20 or better at baseline. Two 3-week treatment periods with a 1-month washout period between evaluated the effects of bilberry or placebo on night visual acuity and night contrast sensitivity. No change was detected in either outcome. Bilberry did not augment night visual acuity or contrast sensitivity in subjects with no prior deficiencies.

REFERENCES

1. Bisset NG, et al. Herbal drugs and phytopharmaceuticals. 2nd ed. Boca Raton (FL): Medpharm CRC Press; 1994.
2. Blumenthal M, et al. Herbal medicine, expanded Commission E monographs. 1st ed. Austin (TX): American Botanical Council; 2000.
3. Bruneton J. Pharmacognosy, phytochemistry, medicinal plants. Paris: Lavoisier Publishing; 1995.
4. Morazzoni P, et al. *Vaccinium myrtillus* anthocyanosides pharmacokinetics in rats. *Arzneimittelforschung* 1991;41:128–31.
5. Muth ER, et al. The effect of bilberry nutritional supplementation on night visual acuity and contrast sensitivity. Altern Med Rev 2000;5:164–73.
6. Zadok D, et al. The effect of anthocyanosides on night vision tests. Invest Ophthalmol Vis Sci 1997;38 Suppl:633.
7. Perossini M, et al. Diabetic and hypertensive retinopathy therapy with anthocyanosides double blind placebo-controlled clinical trial. Ann Ottal Clin Ocul 1987;113:1173–90.

Bioresonance Therapy

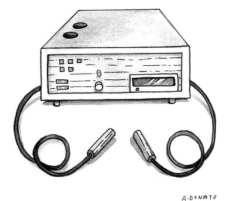

A·D·NATO

COMMON NAMES
Electrodermal testing, biophysical information therapy (BIT), bio-energetic therapy, energy medicine, vibrational medicine

KEY WORDS
Electrodermal testing, energy medicine

CLINICAL SUMMARY

Bioresonance therapy is available in clinics in Europe, Mexico, Florida, and elsewhere in the United States. It is used to diagnose and treat cancer, allergies, arthritis, and various chronic degenerative diseases. A variation known as electrodermal testing was developed as an aid in prescribing homeopathic remedies and is used widely in Europe for the diagnosis of allergies. Bioresonance is based on the claim that electromagnetic oscillations emitted by diseased organs and cancer cells vary from those emitted by healthy cells owing to their differences in cell metabolism and deoxyribonucleic acid (DNA) damage. An electrical galvanic device supposedly detects these differences by measuring the electrical resistance at the skin along acupuncture points or meridians and thus determines which organs are affected. Some practitioners claim that the measurements relate to the energy circulation (Qi) throughout the organs and meridians of the body. Patients can be treated with a "radiofrequency electrical signal," said to normalize electrical conductance at specific points, strengthen the body's natural oscillations, cancel pathologic oscillations via destructive wave interference, and normalize cell metabolism. No evidence supports these claims. Treatment may also involve removal and replacement of dental alloys or amalgams, which are said to carry currents that "alter the body's electromagnetic circulatory system." The US Food and Drug Administration has prosecuted numerous purveyors of electrical devices for making unsubstantiated health benefit claims. A randomized, double-blind trial of bioresonance in treatment of atopic dermatitis in children failed to show efficacy. Clinical trials evaluating electrodermal testing show no reliability in diagnosing allergies. No clinical trials evaluate bioresonance therapy for use in cancer, likely owing to its spurious scientific basis. The American Cancer Society advises patients not to seek treatment with unproved electronic devices.

WARNINGS

The American Cancer Society urges cancer patients not to seek treatment with bioresonance or other electronic devices.[1]

MECHANISM OF ACTION

Bioresonance is based on the unproved premise that the electromagnetic oscillations emitted by damaged organs and cancer cells vary from those emitted by healthy cells owing to their differences in cell metabolism and DNA damage. An electrical device supposedly detects these differences with probes that measure the electrical resistance along acupuncture points or held in the patient's hands and can thus determine which organs are affected. Low resistance is said to indicate pathology or allergy. Electrodermal testing developed as an aid in prescribing homeopathic remedies; medicines are tested "to determine how well they resonate with the individual or how similar they are to the body frequencies needing enhancement to overcome an illness." Practitioners claim that the wave emission from homeopathic medicines or allergens is measured through the device and is modulated through the patient's autonomic nervous system, influencing skin resistance. In bioresonance therapy, patients are treated through the probe with a "radiofrequency electrical signal," which purportedly normalizes electrical conductance at specific points, strengthens the body's natural oscillations, and cancels pathologic oscillations via destructive wave interference, thereby normalizing cell metabolism and allowing self-healing. No evidence supports these claims. Some proponents claim that the device naturally kills tumor cells by releasing "suppressed" tumor suppressor genes or attenuating overactive oncogenes. This hypothesis is untenable because of the irreversibility of most cancer-causing genetic mutations. In actuality, galvanic devices make medically irrelevant measurements of electrical resistance of a patient's skin, which varies with skin moisture and with pressure of the probe. An evaluation of one device found that a galvanic skin response of low resistance was not a reliable indicator of vertebral pathology and that the device produced a low-resistance reading after 5 seconds of application to any point on the body. Proponents of bioresonance often confuse electric current with electromagnetic waves, which have different physiologic effects.[1–8]

USAGE

Allergies, asthma, atopic dermatitis, cancer treatment, rheumatoid arthritis.

ADVERSE REACTIONS
None known.

DRUG INTERACTIONS
None known.

DOSAGE
A clinical trial administered bioresonance therapy twice a week for at least 4 weeks. Sessions consist of a combination of "elementary therapy," "gut-regulating therapy," "geopathic therapy," "extinction therapy," and "elimination" of allergies.

LITERATURE SUMMARY AND CRITIQUE
Lewith GT, et al. Is electrodermal testing as effective as skin prick tests for diagnosing allergies? A double blind, randomized block design study. BMJ 2001;322:131–4.
A randomized, double-blind evaluation of electrodermal testing in reproducing allergy diagnosis made 2 to 16 weeks prior by skin prick test in 15 atopic and 15 healthy controls. Subjects underwent nine sessions of electrodermal testing with the Vegatest protocol by three different experienced operators, six allergens per session (two house dust mite, two cat dander, two distilled water). Subjects were classified as "allergic" or "not allergic" to each allergen by the operator, who was prohibited from asking questions about the subject's health history. Vegatest "allergic" diagnoses did not differ significantly between atopic and control groups: 24% versus 22% for cat dander, 28% versus 29% for dust mites, and 26% versus 23% for distilled water, respectively. No operator was more reliable than any other, and no subjects were consistently correctly diagnosed.

Krop J, et al. A double-blind comparison of electrodermal testing with serial dilution end-point titration and skin prick tests for allergy to house dust mite. Am J Acupuncture 1998;26:53–62.
An evaluation of the reliability of electrodermal testing (EDT) compared to the skin prick test and serial dilution end-point titration (SDEPT) in predicting allergy to dust mites in 57 patients with undiagnosed multisystem allergic disorders. Subjects were tested first with a Vegatest II, followed by a skin prick test and an SDEPT test. Whereas SDEPT and EDT positive diagnoses concurred in 91% of cases, skin prick test and EDT positive diagnoses agreed in only 41% of cases. The study did not control for patient characteristics, diet, or seasonal variation in allergies, and presenting conditions ranged from migraine to irritable bowel syndrome to diabetes. Although the authors question the reliability of skin prick tests in favor of EDT, it seems more likely that EDT and SDEPT both have high false-positive rates.

Schoni MH, Nikolaizik WH, Schoni-Affolter F. Efficacy trial of bioresonance in children with atopic dermatitis. Int Arch Allergy Immunol 1997;112:238–46.
A double-blind, parallel-group study in 32 children, ages 1.5 to 16.8 years, hospitalized with persistent atopic dermatitis in Switzerland. Patients were randomized by sex, age, and severity of disease to receive conventional therapy and either active or placebo bioresonance (BIT) therapy twice a week for at least 4 weeks. Each session consisted of so-called "elementary therapy" and "gut-regulating therapy." "Geopathic therapy" and "extinction therapy" for heavy metals were also performed in the first few sessions. Follow-up sessions allegedly involved "elimination" of allergies. Outcomes measured were skin symptom scores, sleep and itch scores, blood cell activation markers of allergy, and a 1-year follow-up questionnaire. Both treatment arms experienced immediate and sustained amelioration of disease; BIT did not appear to have a significant additive effect on any outcome. Schoni and colleagues concluded that, in light of its high costs, BIT has no place in the treatment of children with atopic dermatitis.

REFERENCES

1. American Cancer Society. Questionable methods of cancer management: electronic devices. CA Cancer J Clin 1994;44:115–27.
2. New Hope Clinic. Available at: http://newhopeclinic.com (accessed Apr 9, 2002).
3. Barrett S. 'Electrodiagnostic' devices. BioResonance Tumor Therapy. Quackwatch. Available at: http://www. quackwatch.com (accessed Apr 9, 2002).
4. Schoni MH, Nikolaizik WH, Schoni-Affolter F. Efficacy trial of bioresonance in children with atopic dermatitis. Int Arch Allergy Immunol 1997;112:238–46.
5. Nansel DD, Jansen RD. Concordance between galvanic skin response and spinal palpation findings in pain-free males. J Manipulative Physiol Ther 1988;11:267–72.
6. Royal FF, Royal DF. Homeopathy and EDT: upheld by modern science—with case histories. Am J Acupuncture 1992;20:55–66.
7. Lewith GT, et al. Is electrodermal testing as effective as skin prick tests for diagnosing allergies? A double blind, randomized block design study. BMJ 2001;322:131–4.
8. Krop J, et al. A double-blind comparison of electrodermal testing with serial dilution endpoint titration and skin prick tests for allergy to house dust mite. Am J Acupuncture 1998;26:53–62.

Bitter Melon

A. DONATO

COMMON NAMES
Bitter gourd, bitter apple, wild cucumber, bitter cucumber, balsam apple, balsam pear, margose, la-kwa, leprosy gourd, karela

SCIENTIFIC NAME
Momordica charantia

KEY WORDS
Momordica charantia, karela

CLINICAL SUMMARY
Derived from the fruit and seed of the tree. Bitter melon has been used to treat diabetes, cancer, viral infections, and immune disorders. Data suggest that a significant hypoglycemic effect occurs in both healthy and diabetic patients. However, bitter melon should not be used in place of mainstream therapies. In vitro and animal studies indicate antiviral activity against human immunodeficiency virus (HIV) and herpes, a cytotoxic effect against leukemic cells, and a cytostatic effect in breast cancer, but related human studies have not been conducted. Children and pregnant women should not use bitter melon because of its potential toxicity. Reported adverse effects include hypoglycemia and hepatotoxicity. There is a potential for additive effect when bitter melon is combined with insulin or oral hypoglycemic agents.

CONSTITUENTS (FRUIT)
Glycosides: momordin, charantin; alkaloids: momordicin; others: polypeptide P; oils (seed only): stearic, linoleic, oleic acids; glycoproteins: α-momorcharin, β-momorcharin, lectins; others: vicine (pyrimidine nucleoside), protein MAP30.[1]

WARNINGS

Red arils (covering on seed) are reportedly toxic in children, causing vomiting, diarrhea, and death.[1]

MECHANISM OF ACTION

Vicine, charantin, and polypeptide P in both animals and humans increase glucose uptake and glycogen synthesis in the liver, muscle, and adipose tissue and improve glucose tolerance. Studies with hepatic enzymes in mice revealed reduction in glucose-6-phosphatase and fructose-1,6-bisphosphatase activity and increased glucose oxidation by the glucose-6-phosphate dehydrogenase pathway. Bitter melon displays cytotoxic activity against leukemic cells in vitro (guanylate cyclase inhibitor). The MAP30 extract has a cytostatic effect on MDA-MB-231 human breast cancer cells xenografted into mice. MAP30 also demonstrates dose-dependent inhibition of HIV-1 integrase leading to poor viral deoxyribonucleic acid (DNA) integration, thus inhibiting T lymphocytes and monocytes.[1-3]

USAGE

Cancer prevention, diabetes, fever, HIV and AIDS, infections, menstrual disorder.

ADVERSE REACTIONS

Reported: Hypoglycemia, hepatotoxicity (animal studies).
Toxicity: Ingestion of vicine (seed) may cause favism characterized by headache, fever, abdominal pain, and coma.

DRUG INTERACTIONS

Insulin: Bitter melon may have an additive effect when used concomitantly.
Hypoglycemics: Bitter melon may have an additive effect when used concomitantly.[4,5]

CONTRAINDICATIONS

Pregnant women should not use; may induce bleeding, contractions, and abortion.

DOSAGE

Oral: No standard dosage has been used. Wide variations in potency are related to method of preparation and dosage form. *Dried fruit:* Doses ranging from 50 mg/kg to 5,000 mg up to three times a day have been used. *Liquid extract:* Dose depends on preparation.

LITERATURE SUMMARY AND CRITIQUE

Only small, uncontrolled human trials have evaluated the hypoglycemic properties of bitter melon.

Welihinda J, et al. Effect of *Momordica charantia* on the glucose tolerance in maturity onset diabetes. J Ethnopharmacol 1986;17:277–82.
A prospective evaluation of 18 newly diagnosed adult diabetics comparing blood glucose level with and without bitter melon administration 30 minutes prior to an oral glucose tolerance test. Patients had not started any hypoglycemic therapy (eg, insulin or sulfonylureas). A statistically significant reduction in blood sugar after administration of bitter melon, approximately 20 to 30%, was demonstrated. Larger randomized trials are necessary to establish long-term effects.

REFERENCES

1. DerMarderosian A, editor. The review of natural products. St. Louis: Facts and Comparisons; 1999.
2. Huang KC. The pharmacology of Chinese herbs. 2nd ed. New York: CRC Press; 1999.
3. Lee-Huang S, et al. Inhibition of MDA-MD-231 human breast tumor xenografts and HER2 expression by anti-tumor agents GAP31 and MAP30. Anticancer Res 2000;20:653–9.
4. Brinker F. Herb contraindications and drug interactions. 3rd ed. Sandy (OR): Eclectic Medical Publications; 2001.
5. Srivastava Y, et al. Antidiabetic and adaptogenic properties of *Momordica charantia* extract: an experimental and clinical evaluation. Phytother Res 1993;7:285–9.

Black Cohosh

COMMON NAMES
Black snakeroot, rattlesnake root, squawroot

SCIENTIFIC NAME
Cimicifuga racemosa

KEY WORDS
Cimicifuga racemosa, Remifemin

A. DONATO

CLINICAL SUMMARY
Obtained from the root of the plant. Black cohosh is used to palliate the symptoms of menopause and dysmenorrhea. The mechanism of action is not known. Whether black cohosh has estrogenic activity is under debate; caution should be used in patients with hormone-sensitive disease. Clinical studies demonstrate efficacy in reducing menopausal symptoms, but several of these trials were open label or were not placebo controlled. Studies evaluating black cohosh to treat hot flashes in women after breast cancer treatment showed efficacy in reducing sweating but not other symptoms. It should be noted that all studies reported were conducted with the brand-name product Remifemin, which is standardized to contain 1 mg of 27-deoxyacteine. No significant adverse events have been reported for this product.

CONSTITUENTS
Triterpene glycosides (actein, 12-acetylactein, and cimigoside); tannins; isoflavone: small amounts of formononetin (may not be present in commercially available formulations); other constituents such as acetic acid, butyric acid, formic acid, isoferulic acid, palmitic acid, salicylic acid, racemosin, phytosterols, and cimicifugin 15 to 20%.[1]

WARNINGS
Black cohosh should not be confused with blue cohosh.

PRECAUTION
It is still quite controversial whether black cohosh possesses estrogenic activity. This product should be used under the supervision of a physician.

MECHANISM OF ACTION
Unknown. Black cohosh was believed to have estrogenic properties and to decrease luteinizing hormone (LH) levels. However, recent studies have shown no estrogenic effects and no effect on LH, follicle-stimulating hormone (FSH), prolactin (PRL), or estradiol (E_2). It is unknown whether it has a cardiovascular effect or an effect on osteoporosis.[2-4]

USAGE
Cough, dysmenorrhea, menopausal symptoms, premenstrual syndrome, rheumatoid arthritis, sedation.

ADVERSE REACTIONS
Reported: Gastrointestinal upset.

DRUG INTERACTIONS
Tamoxifen: Black cohosh may have an additive antiproliferative effect.

DOSAGE
Oral: Dose varies according to product. It is available as a tincture, capsules/tablets, and tea. Remifemin, the most studied product, is standardized on the basis of triterpene glycosides; each tablet contains 1 mg of 27-deoxyacteine. *Remifemin*: One to two tablets by mouth twice a day.[3]

LITERATURE SUMMARY AND CRITIQUE
All studies on black cohosh were done in Europe using the German product Remifemin.

Liske E, et al. Physiological investigation of a unique extract of black cohosh (*Cimicifugae racemosae rhizoma*): a 6-month clinical study demonstrates no systemic estrogenic effect. J Womens Health Gend Based Med 2002;11:163–74.
A randomized, double-blind, parallel-group study conducted at four clinics in Poland. One hundred forty-nine peri- and postmenopausal women with moderate to severe symptoms received either Remifemin 39 mg/d ($n = 74$) or 127.3 mg/d ($n = 75$) for 12 to

24 weeks. The high-dose group tended to have more perimenopausal women, but all other characteristics were comparable. The Kupperman Menopause Index and Self-Rating Depression Scale improved significantly in both groups; both doses were tolerable. Both doses caused a slight but insignificant increase in vaginal cell proliferation, karyopyknotic index, and eosinophilic index, from which the authors inferred a lack of estrogenic effect of Remifemin. No changes in levels of E_2, LH, FSH, PRL, or sex hormone–binding globulin (SHBG) were found in postmenopausal women. Studies of longer duration may be helpful.

Jacobson JS, et al. Randomized trial of black cohosh for the treatment of hot flashes among women with a history of breast cancer. J Clin Oncol 2001;19:2739–45.
A prospective, randomized, double-blind evaluation of black cohosh extract on hot flashes in women who had completed primary breast cancer treatment. Patients were stratified based on concurrent tamoxifen treatment and instructed to take one tablet of black cohosh ($n = 42$) or placebo ($n = 43$) twice daily for 2 months. The primary outcome measured was change in frequency and intensity of hot flashes. Serum levels of FSH and LH were also measured. Patients receiving black cohosh did have a statistically significant decrease in sweating, but all other symptom improvements were similar between treatment groups. No significant increases in FSH or LH were noted. Of the adverse events reported, none were attributed to black cohosh. Additional studies are required to assess the safety of black cohosh in patients with breast cancer.

Liske E, et al. Therapy of climacteric complaints with *C. racemosa*: herbal medicine with clinically proven evidence. Menopause 1998;5:250.
An open, controlled study of 60 patients was divided into three groups. Group 1 received black cohosh (Remifemin) 40 drops twice a day, group 2 received 2 mg of diazepam daily, and group 3 received conjugated estrogens 0.625 mg/d. Symptom reduction in the three groups was similar. After 3 months, the black cohosh group did show a statistically significant decrease of menopausal symptoms.

Liske E, et al. Therapeutic efficacy and safety of *Cimicifuga racemosa* for gynecologic disorders. Adv Ther 1998;15:45–53.
This study showed good therapeutic efficacy and tolerability profiles for *C. racemosa*. In addition, clinical and experimental investigations indicate that *C. racemosa* does not show hormone-like activity, as was originally postulated.

Schaper and Brümmers. Remifemin: a plant based gyn agent [scientific brochure]. Germany; 1997.
A randomized, double-blind study of 152 patients with moderate degree of menopausal symptoms. One group received black cohosh (Remifemin) two tablets twice a day and the other group received one tablet twice a day. In both groups, menopausal symptoms improved significantly by the same amount. However, no changes were seen in vaginal cytology or levels of LH, FSH, PRL, E_2, or SHBG.

Duker EM, et al. **Effects of extracts of** *Cimicifuga racemosa* **(Remifemin) on gonadotropin release in menopausal women and ovariectomized rats. Planta Med 1991;57:420.**
An open-label, controlled, comparative trial of 110 female patients was conducted to evaluate the estrogenic activity of *C. racemosa*. In group 1 ($n = 55$), patients received 8 mg of extract daily for 8 weeks, whereas group 2 ($n = 55$) received placebo for 8 weeks. The results showed a significant LH reduction in the placebo group. No significant change in FSH concentrations was noted in either group. The authors concluded that *Cimicifuga* (Remifemin) possesses estrogenic activity but, unlike estrogens, does not affect the release of PRL and FSH. Researchers then fractionated the extract into three distinct types of active compounds based on the ability to reduce LH secretion in ovariectomized rats and to compete in vitro with E_2-17α for estrogen receptor binding sites. They concluded that the LH suppressive effect of *Cimicifuga* is caused by at least three different synergistically acting compounds.

Stoll W, et al. **Phytopharmacon influences atrophic vaginal epithelium. Double-blind study:** *Cimicifuga* **vs. estrogenic substances. Therapeuticum 1987;1:23.**
A study of 80 patients randomized into three groups. Group 1 received two tablets of a black cohosh extract (Remifemin) twice a day. Group 2 received 0.625 mg of conjugated estrogens. Group 3 received placebo. After 12 weeks, the black cohosh group produced a notable increase in vaginal epithelium and significant improvements in somatic measures and neurovegetative and psychological symptoms compared with estrogen and placebo. The number of hot flashes dropped from an average of five daily to less than one in the black cohosh group, whereas in the estrogen group, hot flashes dropped from 5 to 3.5 average daily occurrences.

REFERENCES

1. Newall C, et al. Herbal medicines, a guide for health care professionals. London: Pharmaceutical Press; 1996.
2. Liske E, et al. Therapeutic efficacy and safety of *Cimicifuga racemosa* for gynecologic disorders. Adv Ther 1998;15:45–53.
3. Remifemin: a plant-based gynecological agent [scientific brochure]. Germany: Schaper & Brümmer; 1997.
4. Zierau O, et al. Antiestrogenic activities of *Cimicifuga racemosa* extracts. J Steroid Biochem Mol Biol 2002;80:125–30.

Blue-Green Algae

COMMON NAMES
Pond scum, *Spirulina platensis,*
Spirulina fusiformis, AFA-algae,
Arthrospira platensis, tecuitlatl,
BGA

SCIENTIFIC NAMES
Spirulina sp, Aphanizomenon
flos-aquae

KEY WORDS
Spirulina, Aphanizomenon
flos-aquae

CLINICAL SUMMARY

Blue-green algae are primitive autotrophic prokaryotes (also known as *Cyanobacteria*). *Spirulina* species are cultured in alkaline fresh water, whereas *Aphanizomenon flos aquae* (AFA) is naturally grown and harvested from Upper Klamath Lake, Oregon. Blue-green algae products frequently contain one or both of these strains of algae. Patients take blue-green algae supplements to prevent and treat cancer and viral infections and for weight loss. Blue-green algae are used as a source of food in parts of the world. Although no human clinical data support its use for any of the proposed claims, studies suggest that *Spirulina* has chemoprotective and radioprotective effects in animals. Blue-green algae may be contaminated by strains of algae (eg, microcystin species) that are toxic. Adverse effects are uncommon except when products are contaminated; contaminant toxins can cause hepatotoxicity, renal failure, and neurotoxicity. To date, there are no known drug interactions. Supplementation with blue-green algae provides protein and small amounts of vitamins and minerals, but no research supports their value.

CONSTITUENTS
Proteins (50–70%): all essential amino acids; carbohydrates: rhamnose, ribose, mannose, fructose, polysaccharides; vitamins: A, E, cyanocobalamin, niacin, choline, folic acid, thiamine; other: chlorophyll, copper, magnesium, zinc, potassium.[1,2]

WARNINGS
Microcystin contamination can cause hepatotoxicity, renal failure, and neurotoxicity. Products should be certified free from contamination.

MECHANISM OF ACTION
The mechanism of action is unknown. The protein and vitamin content may contribute to any alleviation of fatigue. Calcium spirulan, a polysaccharide extract from *S. platensis*, demonstrates inhibition of human immunodeficiency virus (HIV)-1 viral replication via possible binding and disruption of CD4-glycoprotein p120 interaction in vitro, although the clinical significance of this is unknown. In vitro, calcium spirulan also inhibits replication of herpes simplex 1, cytomegalovirus, and influenza. Studies performed in healthy humans suggest that AFA-algae increases the level of circulating natural killer cells. In vitro studies also suggest that AFA-algae has antiviral and antimutagenic activity. Other studies suggest that spirulina has chemoprotective and radioprotective effects in animals through the stimulation of the hemopoietic system. Although uncommon, several toxins from *Microcystis* species of algae may contaminate AFA-algae and *Spirulina* algae blooms. Anatoxin can cause paralysis of respiratory muscles owing to irreversible binding and sustained action of the nicotinic acetylcholine receptor. Saxitoxin contamination is thought to block nerve cell neuronal transmission owing to binding to voltage-gated sodium channels. Microcystins are cyclic heptapeptides that induce hepatotoxicity.[1–8]

USAGE
Appetite suppression, attention-deficit/hyperactivity disorder, cancer prevention, cancer treatment, fatigue, HIV and acquired immune deficiency syndrome (AIDS), immunostimulation, oral leukoplakia, viral infections, weight loss.

ADVERSE REACTIONS
Infrequent: Nausea, vomiting, anxiety, insomnia.
Rare: Cyanotoxin (eg, anatoxin, saxitoxin, microcystins) contamination of AFA-algae and possibly *Spirulina* may cause hepatotoxicity, renal failure, neurotoxicity, seizures, respiratory arrest, acute pancreatitis, and cardiomyopathy.[2,6]

DRUG INTERACTIONS
No known interactions at this time.

DOSAGE

Oral: Consumption of 1 to 12 g dried blue-green algae per meal has been reported.

LITERATURE SUMMARY AND CRITIQUE

Mathew B, et al. Evaluation of chemoprevention of oral cancer with *Spirulina fusiformis.* **Nutr Cancer 1995;24:197–202.**

A prospective, randomized, double-blind evaluation of blue-green algae supplementation in patients with homogeneous and nonhomogeneous oral leukoplakia. Patients were pan tobacco chewers recruited from Kerala, India. Following 12 months of supplementation with 1 g/d of *S. fusiformis* (n = 45) or placebo (n = 43), conversion of oral leukoplakia lesions was increased for the active group. However, conversion of nonhomogeneous lesions was similar between the active and placebo groups, one and two cases, respectively. Although the results suggest that blue-green algae supplementation may be efficacious as chemoprevention for oral cancer, the long-term efficacy is unknown, and extrapolations to other populations may not be appropriate.

REFERENCES

1. Foster S, Tyler VE. Tyler's honest herbal: a sensible guide to the use of herbs and related remedies. 4th ed. New York: Haworth Herbal Press; 1999.
2. Ziegler R. *Aphanizomenon flos-aquae* (AFA-algae). A food supplement with dubious health claims. Meeting of the Swiss Study Group for Complementary and Alternative Methods in Cancer, Weiskirchen, Switzerland; 2001 Nov 9.
3. Ayehunie S, et al. Inhibition of HIV-1 replication by an aqueous extract of *Spirulina platensis* (*Arthrospira platensis*). J Acquir Immune Defic Syndr Hum Retrovirol 1998;18:7–12.
4. Hayashi T, et al. Calcium spirulan, an inhibitor of enveloped virus replication, from a blue-green algae *Spirulina platensis*. J Nat Prod 1996;59:83–7.
5. Draisci R, et al. Identification of anatoxins in blue-green algae food supplements using liquid chromatography-tandem mass spectrometry. Food Addit Contam 2001;18:525–31.
6. Patocka J. The toxins of *Cyanobacteria*. Acta Med 2001;44:69–75.
7. Zhang H, et al. Chemo- and radio-protective effects of polysaccharide of *Spirulina platensis* on hemopoietic system of mice and dogs. Acta Pharmacol Sin 2001;22:1121–4.
8. Premkumar K, et al. Effect of *Spirulina fusiformis* on cyclophosphamide and mitomycin-C induced genotoxicity and oxidative stress in mice. Fitoterapia 2001;72:906–11.

Borage

COMMON NAMES
Bee plant, bee bread, borage seed oil, ox's tongue, starflower oil

SCIENTIFIC NAME
Borago officinalis

A.DONATO

CLINICAL SUMMARY
Oil derived from the plant. Used as a source of gamma-linoleic acid (GLA) and to treat rheumatoid arthritis; routinely consumed as an alternative to evening primrose oil. Limited clinical data support claims made for borage oil. One study showed that borage oil has no overall efficacy in atopic eczema. Borage oil contains a pyrrolizidine alkaloid, amabiline, which is hepatotoxic. The risk of hepatic damage increases with length of exposure and cumulative dose consumed. Patients should use borage oil certified free of unsaturated pyrrolizidine alkaloids (UPAs). Borage oil may be unsafe during pregnancy.

CONSTITUENTS
Alkaloids: contains small amounts of many pyrrolizidine types, especially amabiline (hepatotoxin); fatty acids: linoleic acid, GLA, oleic and saturated fatty acids; mucilages: glucose, galactose, arabinose; acids: acetic, lactic, malic, silicic; tannins; saponins.[1]

WARNINGS
Borage contains small amounts of the alkaloid amabiline, which is hepatotoxic. Consumption of 1 to 2 g of borage seed oil daily can result in an intake of toxic UPAs approaching 10 μg. The German Federal Health Agency now specifies that consumption

of such products should be limited to no more than 1 μg of UPA daily. Borage oil products should be certified free of UPAs (meet the criterion of no more than 0.5–1 μg/g).[2]

MECHANISM OF ACTION
Borage's seed oils seem to be responsible for its action. The GLA from the seeds may have anti-inflammatory properties. GLA can be converted to the prostaglandin precursor dihomo-GLA, which has anti-inflammatory activity. The mucilage constituent has an expectorant-like action, and malic acid has a mild diuretic effect. The tannin constituent may have mild astringent and constipating actions.[3,4]

USAGE
Arthritis, chest congestion, cough, depression, infantile seborrheic dermatitis, menopausal symptoms.

ADVERSE REACTIONS
Common: Constipation may occur after administration.
Rare: Hepatotoxicity has been reported following chronic administration.

DRUG INTERACTIONS
Phenothiazines: Theoretically, borage oil may lower the seizure threshold owing to its GLA content. Seizures have been documented with evening primrose oil but not borage oil.
Tricyclic Antidepressants: Theoretically, may lower seizure threshold owing to GLA content. Seizures have been documented with evening primrose oil but not borage oil.
Nonsteroidal Anti-inflammatory Drugs (NSAIDs): Theoretically, concomitant use with borage oil would decrease the effects of borage oil as NSAIDs interfere with the synthesis of prostaglandin E.[5,6]

CONTRAINDICATIONS
Pregnancy: Preliminary studies suggest that borage oil has a teratogenic effect and that its prostaglandin E agonist action may cause premature labor.[6]

DOSAGE
Oral: No specific dosage is recommended. Clinical studies have used doses ranging from 1,000 to 4,000 mg/d standardized to 10 to 25% GLA.[7,8]

LITERATURE SUMMARY AND CRITIQUE
Henz BM, et al. Double-blind, multicentre analysis of the efficacy of borage oil in patients with atopic eczema. Br J Dermatol 1999;140:685–8.

A double-blind, multicenter study of borage oil (23% GLA) in 167 adults with stable atopic eczema of moderate severity. Patients were randomized to take daily either 500 mg of borage oil–containing capsules or the bland lipid miglyol as a placebo over a 24-week period. The primary end point was the amount of rescue medication (topical diflucortolone-21 valerate cream) used until response; the secondary end point was clinical improvement. Patients taking borage oil experienced small but insignificant clinical improvements compared with placebo; a subgroup excluding noncompliant patients and those who failed to show increased erythrocyte dihomo-GLA levels showed a significant benefit.

Leventhal LJ, et al. Treatment of rheumatoid arthritis with gamma-linoleic acid. Ann Intern Med 1993;119:867–73.
A randomized, double-blind, placebo-controlled, 24-week trial of 37 patients with rheumatoid arthritis and active synovitis. The treatment group receiving GLA 1.4 g experienced a 36% reduction in the number of tender joints and a 28% reduction in swollen joints. The placebo group did not show significant improvement in any measure. No significant adverse effects were reported.

Pullman-Mooar S, et al. Alteration of the cellular fatty acid profile and the production of eicosanoids in human monocytes by gamma-linolenic acid. Arthritis Rheum 1990;22:1526–33.
In an uncontrolled trial, borage seed oil 1.1 g was given to seven healthy patients and seven patients with rheumatoid arthritis for 12 weeks. Eighty-five percent of the arthritic group experienced relief, possibly owing to the GLA in the borage oil.[9–11]

REFERENCES
1. Newell CA, et al. Herbal medicine: a guide for healthcare professionals. London: Pharmaceutical Press; 1996.
2. Tyler V. Herbs of choice, the therapeutical use of phytomedicinals. Binghamton (NY): Pharmaceutical Press; 1994.
3. Pierce A. The American Pharmaceutical Association practical guide to natural medicines. New York: The Stonesong Press Inc; 1999.
4. Belch JJ, Hill A. Evening primrose oil and borage oil in rheumatologic conditions. Am J Clin Nutr 2000;71 Suppl:352S–6S.
5. Brinker F. Herb contraindications and drug interactions. 3rd ed. Sandy (OR): Eclectic Medical Publications; 2001.
6. Kast RE. Borage oil reduction of rheumatoid arthritis activity may be medicated by increased cAMP that suppresses tumor necrosis factor-alpha. Int Immunopharmacol 2001;2197–99.
7. Leventhal LJ, et al. Treatment of rheumatoid arthritis with gamma-linoleic acid. Ann Intern Med 1993;119:867–73.
8. Pullman-Mooar S, et al. Alteration of the cellular fatty acid profile and the production of eicosanoids in human monocytes by gamma-linolenic acid. Arthritis Rheum 1990;22:1526–33.
9. Hoffman D. The herb users guide: the basic skills of medical herbalism. Wellingborough (UK): Thorsons; 1987.
10. Tollesson A, Frithz A. Borage oil, an effective new treatment for infantile seborrhoeic dermatitis. Br J Dermatol 1993;129:95.
11. Henz BM, et al. Double-blind, multicentre analysis of the efficacy of borage oil in patients with atopic eczema. Br J Dermatol 1999;140:685–8.

Bovine Cartilage

COMMON NAME
Bovine tracheal cartilage

KEY WORDS
Catrix, Psoriacin

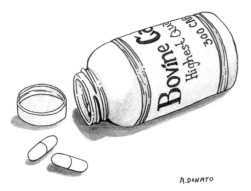

A.DONATO

CLINICAL SUMMARY
Derived from the cartilage, usually the trachea, of cows. This product should not be confused with shark cartilage. Bovine cartilage is used to prevent and treat cancer and to treat human immunodeficiency virus/acquired immune deficiency syndrome (HIV/AIDS); it may be administered by both oral and parenteral routes. Few published clinical trials demonstrate its efficacy. Nausea and vomiting are commonly reported adverse events. Other events reported include changes in taste perception, fatigue, dizziness, and dyspepsia. Inflammation and irritation at injection sites are common following parenteral administration. No drug interactions are known.

CONSTITUENTS
Acidic mucopolysaccharide complex: glycosaminoglycans, primarily chondroitin sulfate, polysaccharides.[1]

WARNINGS
Bovine cartilage should not be confused with shark cartilage.

MECHANISM OF ACTION

Immunoregulatory effects are believed to enhance antibody responses to T-independent and T-dependent antigens, indicating that its activity is attributable in part to a direct effect on B cells or an indirect effect mediated by macrophages. It is believed to support the resynthesis of cartilage in osteoarthritis.[2]

USAGE

Cancer prevention, cancer treatment, HIV and AIDS.

ADVERSE REACTIONS

Common: Nausea and vomiting are the primary adverse effects.
Reported: Altered sense of taste, fatigue, dyspepsia, fever, dizziness, and edema of the scrotum following treatment with Catrix bovine cartilage product.
Common (Parenteral Only): Inflammation and redness at the injection site.[3–5]

DRUG INTERACTIONS

None reported.

DOSAGE

Parenteral (for Cancer): Loading dose administered subcutaneously in 25 to 50 mL increments for a total dose of 100 mL in the thighs, flanks, or back. This was repeated daily to weekly until a cumulative subcutaneous dose of 2,000 mg was reached.
Oral (for Cancer): 9 g daily, divided into at least two doses.[4] *Osteoarthritis:* Both intravenous and oral dosages vary.

LITERATURE SUMMARY AND CRITIQUE

Bovine cartilage data are inconclusive and mostly testimonial. Further research is needed in cancer.

Durie BG, et al. Antitumor activity of bovine cartilage extract (Catrix®) in the human tumor stem cell assay. J Biol Response Mod 1985;4:590–5.
The human tumor assay system used three human tumor cell lines and fresh biopsy specimens from 22 patients with malignant tumors. In vitro efficacy was demonstrated with high-dose, continuous exposure to Catrix, particularly against the 8226 human myeloma cell line, as well as ovarian, pancreatic, colon, testicular, and sarcoma biopsy specimens. The level of sensitivity was less than or equal to 30% survival of colon growth in vitro. Because the in vitro concentrations may be achievable in vivo, the results justify more detailed in vitro evaluation as well as potential clinical trials.

Prudden JF. The treatment of human cancer with agents prepared from bovine cartilage. J Biol Response Mod 1985;4:551–84.
Case report series presented on oral and subcutaneous administration of specific preparations of Catrix. Responses were observed following full-dose therapy over prolonged courses of therapy, up to 11 years. Nineteen cases of complete response, 10 cases of partial response, and 1 case of stable disease were documented. Eighteen patients received conventional therapy within 1 year of bovine cartilage treatment. Nine patients received concurrent conventional therapy in addition to study medication. An additional seven patients received conventional therapy both prior to and during the treatment period. It is difficult to interpret efficacy from this series owing to variations in treatment, dose, route of administration, and reporting of data.

Romano CF, et al. A phase II study of Catrix-S in solid tumors. J Biol Response Mod 1985;4:585–9.
Catrix-S was administered by weekly subcutaneous injection (5–7.5 g/wk) to nine patients with progressive metastatic malignancy. One complete response was seen in a patient with metastatic renal cell carcinoma to the lung. Eight patients experienced disease progression. No undue toxicity was noted.

REFERENCES

1. Cancer Net: National Cancer Institute. Cartilage (bovine and shark) [online]. http://www.cancer.gov/cancer_information/doc.aspx?viewid=4AABA6FA-8A2E-4BF7-941F-7DC416B41233 (accessed Aug 30, 2001).
2. Rosen J. Immunoregulatory effects of Catrix. J Biol Response Mod 1988;7:498–512.
3. Prudden JF, Balassa LL. The biological activity of bovine cartilage preparations. Clinical demonstration of their potent anti-inflammatory capacity with supplementary notes on certain relevant fundamental supportive studies. Semin Arthritis Rheum 1974;3:287–321.
4. Prudden JF. The treatment of human cancer with agents prepared from bovine cartilage. J Biol Response Mod 1985;4:551–84.
5. Romano CF, et al. A phase II study of Catrix-S in solid tumors. J Biol Response Mod 1985;4:585–9.

Bromelain

SCIENTIFIC NAMES
Sulfydryl proteolytic enzyme, cysteine proteinase

CLINICAL SUMMARY
Enzyme obtained from the stem of the pineapple. Bromelain belongs to a group of plant-derived proteolytic enzymes that also includes papain and has a wide range of applications. In vitro and some in vivo studies demonstrate its ability to prevent edema formation and reduce existing edema. Bromelain can reduce blood levels of fibrinogen and support fibrinolysis. It activates plasmin and prolongs prothrombin and partial thromboplastin times.

MECHANISM OF ACTION
Studies show that bromelain prevents platelet aggregation and the adhesion of platelets to blood vessel endothelial cells. It can act as an anti-inflammatory agent via its ability to reduce levels of prostaglandin E_2 and thromboxane A_2. Bromelain promotes the absorption of antibiotic drugs and, topically, supports the skin débridement of burns. The mechanism of action of bromelain is thought to be attributable to its proteolytic activity. Oral enzymes such as bromelain have been proposed as additive agents for cancer therapy. Proposed anticancer mechanisms include down-regulation of the immunosuppressive cytokine transforming growth factor-β, direct inhibition of tumor cell growth, modulation of immune cell function, modulation of cell adhesion molecules, and the effects on platelet aggregation and thrombosis mentioned above.[1–4]

USAGE
Arthritis, bruises, burns, cancer prevention, cancer treatment, circulatory disorders, edema, indigestion.

PHARMACOKINETICS
Absorption: Orally administered bromelain is absorbed intact from the intestine. Because of its proteolytic activity, about 50% of bromelain is rapidly complexed with an antiproteinase, namely α_2-macroglobulin. Proteolytic activity is maintained within this protective molecule but reduced. In a recent human study, plasma half-life was determined

to be 6 to 9 hours. Orally administered bromelain is absorbed at a rate of 40% in animal studies.

Distribution: Bromelain is distributed in the blood and plasma.

Metabolism/Excretion: The pathways of metabolism and excretion are not fully known.

ADVERSE REACTIONS

Reported: Diarrhea, gastrointestinal disturbance, allergic reactions.[1,5]

DRUG INTERACTIONS

Antibiotics/Tetracyclines: Bromelain may increase blood and urine levels. *Anticoagulants:* Bromelain may increase bleeding risk owing to its antithrombotic effects.

Chemotherapy: Bromelain may increase the efficacy of drugs such as 5-fluorouracil and vincristine.[5]

DOSAGE

No standard dosing exists.

LITERATURE SUMMARY AND CRITIQUE

Desser L, et al. Oral therapy with proteolytic enzymes decreases excessive TGF-β levels in human blood. Cancer Chemother Pharmacol 2001;47 Suppl:S10–5.

The effect of a combination of oral proteolytic enzymes containing papain, bromelain, trypsin, and chymotrypsin on the levels of cytokine-transforming growth factor-β (TGF-β) was studied. Overproduction of TGF-β is involved in chronic inflammation and delayed wound healing and is associated with adverse effects from chemo- and radiation therapy. Fifty-two patients with rheumatoid arthritis, osteomyelofibrosis, or herpes zoster were recruited. Seventy-eight healthy volunteers served as controls. Oral proteolytic enzymes were shown to reduce TGF-β-1 only in patients with elevated TGF-β-1 concentration (> 50 ng/mL serum). This study was well designed and has a relatively high level of statistical significance. However, it included other oral proteolytic enzymes in addition to bromelain, leaving the possibility that the outcome was attributable to a synergy of all of the oral proteolytic enzymes. The effect of bromelain alone was not identified.[6,7]

REFERENCES

1. Maurer HR. Bromelain: biochemistry, pharmacology and medical use. Cell Mol Life Sci 2001;58:1234–45.
2. Klasen HJ. A review on the non-operative removal of necrotic tissue from burn wounds. Burns 2000;26:207–22.
3. Desser L, et al. Oral enzymes as additive cancer therapy. Int J Immunother 2001;17:153–61.
4. Desser L, et al. Oral therapy with proteolytic enzyes decreases excessive TGF-β levels in human blood. Cancer Chemother Pharmacol 2001;47:S10–5.

5. Herr SM. Herb-drug interaction handbook. 2nd ed. Nassau (NY): Church Street Books; 2002.
6. Petry JJ. Surgically significant nutritional supplements. Plast Reconstr Surg 1996;97:233–40.
7. Castell JV, et al. Intestinal absorption of undegraded proteins in men: presence of bromelain in plasma after oral intake. Am J Physiol 1997;273:G139–46.

Bupleurum

COMMON NAMES
Chai-Hu, hare's ear root, thoroughwax root, saiko

SCIENTIFIC NAMES
Bupleurum chinense, Bupleurum scorzoneraefolium

KEY WORDS
Chai-Hu, saiko

CLINICAL SUMMARY
Derived from the root of the plant. Bupleurum is a common herb used in traditional Chinese and Japanese medicine. It is frequently prescribed in combination with other herbs to treat cold, fever, malaria, gastrointestinal disorders, and chronic liver diseases. In vitro studies show that bupleurum has anti-inflammatory and antiviral activities. Classic herbal formulas, such as Xiao Chai Hu Tang (Sho-saiko-to), using bupleurum as the major ingredient have been found to be effective in treating hepatitis and liver cancers. The major components, saikosaponins, are believed to contribute to bupleurum's medicinal properties. Large doses of bupleurum may cause nausea and vomiting.

CONSTITUENTS
Saikosaponins (a, b1, b2, c, d), bupleurumol, essential oils, fat.[1]

WARNINGS
Bupleurum is the major ingredient in a herbal formula, Sho-saiko-to, that has been associated with interstitial pneumonitis.

MECHANISM OF ACTION

The saikosaponins in bupleurum are mainly responsible for the plant's medicinal activities. In vitro studies indicate that saikosaponins have anti-inflammatory effects by inhibiting arachidonic acid metabolism. Saikosaponin d has immunoregulatory action by promoting interleukin-2 production and receptor expression as well as modulating the T-lymphocyte function. Its apoptotic effect is thought to be partly mediated by increases in c-myc and p53 messenger ribonucleic acid (mRNA) levels accompanied by a decrease in bcl-2 mRNA level. Bupleurum may also have antibiotic and antiviral properties.[2-7]

USAGE

Cancer treatment, cirrhosis, common cold, fever, hepatitis, infections, inflammation, liver disease, malaria.

ADVERSE REACTIONS

Large doses of bupleurum can cause nausea and vomiting, facial and extremity edema, gastrointestinal distention, and constipation.[1,2]

DOSAGE

Three to 12 g orally per day. Usually brewed in decoction or prepared as a powder extract in combination with other herbs.[2]

LITERATURE SUMMARY AND CRITIQUE

Most of the clinical studies published involving bupleurum have been performed in Japan using formulas such as Sho-saiko-to.

REFERENCES

1. Huang KC. The pharmacology of Chinese herbs. 2nd ed. New York: CRC Press; 1999.
2. Bensky D, Gamble A. Chinese herbal medicine: materia medica. Rev. ed. Seattle: Eastland Press; 1993.
3. Kato M, et al. Characterization of the immunoregulatory action of saikosaponin-d. Cell Immunol 1994;159:15–25.
4. Bermejo Benito P, et al. In vivo and in vitro antiinflammatory activity of saikosaponins. Life Sci 1998;63:1147–56.
5. Wu W, Hsu H. Involvement of p-15(INK4b) and p-16(INK4a) gene expression in saikosaponin a and TPA-induced growth inhibition of HepG2 cells. Biochem Biophys Res Commun 2001;285:183–7.
6. Hsu M, et al. Effect of saikosaponin, a triterpene saponin, on apoptosis in lymphocytes: association with c-myc, p53, and bcl-2 mRNA. Br J Pharmacol 2000;131:1285–93.
7. Ushio Y, Abe H. Inactivation of measles virus and herpes simplex virus by saikosaponin d. Planta Med 1992;58:171–3.

Burdock

COMMON NAMES
Lappa, edible burdock, gobo, wild gobo, happy major

SCIENTIFIC NAME
Arctium majus

KEY WORD
Arctium majus

A.DONATO

CLINICAL SUMMARY
Derived from the root or seeds of the plant. Historically, burdock has been used as a diuretic and to lower blood sugar. It is used to treat anorexia, gout, cancer, and human immunodeficiency virus (HIV), although no published clinical studies have evaluated these claims. Animal studies indicate a possible hypoglycemic effect; patients should be warned against combining with insulin and hypoglycemics. Pregnant or nursing women should not consume burdock. Several cases of burdock tea contaminated with belladonna alkaloids have been reported in Europe and the United States. The product should be certified against contamination and labeled accordingly.

CONSTITUENTS
Acids: acetic, butyric, caffeic, chlorogenic, trans-2-hexanoic, isovaleric, lauric, linoleic, propionic, stearic acid; aldehydes: acetaldehyde, benzaldehyde, butyraldehyde, isovaleraldehyde, valeraldehyde; carbohydrates: inulin, mucilage, pectin; flavonols: kaempferol, quercetin; polyacetylenes; other constituents: volatile oils, sesquiterpene lactone (arctiopicrin), bitters (lappatin), phytosterols (sitosterol and stigmasterol), tannins.[1]

WARNINGS

Burdock tea has been contaminated with belladonna alkaloids (atropine). Products should be certified against contamination.

MECHANISM OF ACTION

The exact mechanism of action is unknown. In vitro studies have shown the polyacetylene component to have antibacterial and fungistatic properties. Animal studies have shown the root extract to induce hypoglycemia and increase carbohydrate tolerance, stimulate uterine smooth muscle, and have antimutagenic activity. The lignan and sesquiterpene extracts have been shown to inhibit platelet activating factor in vitro. In mice, the tannin extract has induced a macrophage response.[2,3]

USAGE

Anorexia, arthritis, cancer treatment, detoxification, diabetes, eczema, health maintenance, HIV and acquired immune deficiency syndrome (AIDS), microbial infection, promotion of urination, psoriasis.

ADVERSE REACTIONS

Reported: Hypoglycemia (animal models).

DRUG INTERACTIONS

Hypoglycemics: Theoretically, large doses of burdock may have an additive effect.

CONTRAINDICATIONS

Patients allergic to chrysanthemums may exhibit cross-sensitivity to burdock. Burdock may cause uterine stimulation and should be avoided by pregnant women.[4]

DOSAGE

Oral: 2 mL liquid extract three times a day.[1]

REFERENCES

1. Newall CA, et al. Herbal medicines: a guide for health-care professionals. London: Pharmaceutical Press; 1996.
2. Foster S, et al. Tyler's honest herbal: a sensible guide to the use of herbs and related remedies. New York: Hawthorn Herbal Press; 1999.
3. Tamayo C, et al. The chemistry and biological acitivity of herbs used in Flor-essence herbal tonic and Essiac. Phytother Res 2000;14:1–14.
4. Bryson PD. Burdock root tea poisoning. Case report involving a commercial preparation. JAMA 1978;239:2157.

Butcher's Broom

A.DONATO

COMMON NAMES
Box holly, sweet broom, knee holly, pettigree, jew's myrtle, thorny fragon

SCIENTIFIC NAME
Ruscus aculeatus

KEY WORDS
Ruscus aculeatus

CLINICAL SUMMARY

Derived from the root of the plant. Taken orally or applied topically, this herb has been used for varicose veins, hemorrhoids, and lymph edema. Clinical studies in lymph edema and varicose veins have revealed efficacy without achieving statistical significance compared with control groups. Minimal side effects have been reported, but the Cyclo 3 product has more frequent reports of diarrhea and abdominal discomfort. May interact with monoamine oxidase inhibitors (MAOIs; phenelzine [Nardil], tranylcypromine [Parnate]) and possibly anticoagulants.

CONSTITUENTS

Steroidal saponins (neoruscogenin ruscogenin); flavonoids; tetracosanoic acid; chrysophanic acid; sitosterol, campesterol, stigmasterol; coumarins; sparteine; tyramine; glycolic acid.[1]

MECHANISM OF ACTION

Butcher's broom steroidal saponins may be responsible for stimulating the postjunctional α-adrenergic receptors of the smooth muscle cells of the vascular wall and may produce vasoconstriction. It may also have anti-inflammatory effects and increase lymphatic flow.[2]

USAGE

Circulatory disorders, constipation, hemorrhoids, inflammation, leg cramps, lymphedema, promotion of urination, varicose veins.

ADVERSE REACTIONS

Common: Diarrhea has been frequently reported with the product Cyclo 3 but is less common with use of other formulations of butcher's broom.

DRUG INTERACTIONS

MAOI: Owing to the tyramine constituent in butcher's broom, avoid concurrent use with MAOIs such as phenelzine and tranylcypromine.

Anticoagulants/Antiplatelets: Butcher's broom contains coumarins that may inhibit platelet activity and potentiate response to anticoagulants.

DOSAGE

Oral: Capsules standardized to 7 to 11 mg ruscogenins; daily dosage is 72 to 75 mg of dry extract from butcher's broom rhizome daily in two divided doses.

Topical: Apply small amount once or twice daily.[3,4]

LITERATURE SUMMARY AND CRITIQUE

Cluzan RV, et al. Treatment of secondary lymphedema of the upper limb with butcher's broom and hesperidin methyl chalcone (Cyclo 3 Fort). Lymphology 1996;29:29–35.

Fifty-seven patients with secondary lymphedema of the upper limb after previous treatment for breast cancer were treated for 3 months with an extract of *Ruscus* and hesperidin methyl chalcone (Cyclo 3 Fort) or placebo according to a double-blind protocol. All patients also underwent manual lymphatic drainage twice a week for at least 1 month. With Cyclo 3 Fort, the reduction in volume of arm edema, the main assessment criterion, was 12.9% after 3 months of treatment compared with a placebo ($p = .009$). Decreased edema appeared to be more marked in the forearm compared with the upper arm, where excess fat deposition seemed to dominate over excess fluid accumulation. Minimal adverse reactions were noted.

Cappelli R, et al. Use of extract of *Ruscus aculeatus* in venous disease in the lower limbs. Drugs Exp Clin Res 1988;14:277–83.

The effectiveness and tolerability of a venotropic drug (RAES) composed of an extract of *R. aculeatus* (16.5 mg), hesperidin (75 mg), and ascorbic acid (50 mg) was evaluated in

40 patients suffering from chronic phlebopathy of the lower limbs. The crossover, double-blind trial involved two periods of treatment of 2 months with the drug (two capsules three times a day) or placebo and an interim period of 15 days for washout. An overall tendency for improvement occurred that was more distinct during the periods of treatment with the drug. In fact, symptoms and plethysmographic parameters immediately changed significantly in correspondence with the administration of RAES. The biologic and clinical tolerability were excellent.

Vanscheidt W, et al. Efficacy and safety of a butcher's broom preparation (*Ruscus aculeatus* L. extract) compared to placebo in patients suffering from chronic venous insufficiency. Arzneimittelforschung 2002;52:243–50.

This was a multicenter, double-blind, randomized, placebo-controlled trial studying 148 women with chronic venous insufficiency. They were divided into treatment and placebo groups. The treatment group received capsules containing 36.0 to 37.5 mg of dry butcher's broom extract twice daily for 12 weeks. Changes in leg volume, circumference of the lower leg and ankle, subjective symptoms, and quality of life were monitored. At 8 and 12 weeks, there were significant improvements on all of the parameters on the treatment group compared with the placebo group. Few adverse effects were reported. In general, the herb was well tolerated. This study was well designed. The number of subjects studied was large enough to provide statistically significant results. However, it only involved female patients and lasted only 12 weeks. Future studies should include men; long-term effects should also be monitored.

REFERENCES

1. Blumenthal M, et al. The complete German Commission E monographs: therapeutic guide to herbal medicines. Austin (TX): American Botanical Council; 1998.
2. Foster S, et al. Tyler's honest herbal: a sensible guide to the use of herbs and related remedies. 3rd ed. New York: Haworth Herbal Press; 1993.
3. Blumenthal M, et al. Herbal medicine expanded Commission E monographs. 1st ed. Austin (TX): American Botanical Council; 2000.
4. Vanscheidt W, et al. Efficacy and safety of a butcher's broom preparation (*Ruscus aculeatus* L. extract) compared to placebo in patients suffering from chronic venous insufficiency. Arzneimittelforschung 2002;52:243–50.

Calcium Glucarate

COMMON NAMES
Glucarate, calcium-D-glucarate, calcium saccharate, calcium-D-saccharate

SCIENTIFIC NAME
D-Glucaric acid salt

KEY WORD
D-Glucaric acid salt

A.DONATO

CLINICAL SUMMARY
Calcium glucarate occurs naturally in a variety of foods and is also synthetically manufactured. Clinically used to stabilize the parenteral formulation of calcium gluconate, it has been used to prevent and treat cancer. Patients with breast cancer often self-medicate with supplements of calcium glucarate following surgery or adjunctive treatments. The glucarate component, not the calcium, is thought to account for its activity. Following administration, glucarate is converted to D-glucaro-1,4-lactone, which inhibits β-glucuronidase. Anecdotal in vitro and animal data suggest that inhibition of β-glucuronidase may prevent carcinogenesis, as well as inhibit the initiation and promotion of cancer cells. Increased elimination of carcinogens and hormones, including estrogen, also has been shown. No human trials evaluating the safety or efficacy of calcium glucarate are published. The potential for interactions with drugs metabolized by glucuronidation is unknown.

MECHANISM OF ACTION
The glucarate component, not the calcium, accounts for the activity of this supplement. Calcium glucarate is absorbed from the gut as D-glucaric acid. D-Glucaric acid is further converted to D-glucaro-1,4-lactone, which is thought to inhibit the activity of β-glucuronidase. β-Glucuronidase has been shown to decrease the rate of elimination of

estrogen and carcinogens (eg, polycyclic aromatic hydrocarbons and nitrosamines) by deconjugation. Inhibition of β-glucuronidase activity with calcium glucarate is thought to improve excretion of metabolized estrogen and carcinogens. D-Glucarate can also be metabolized by gut bacteria, inhibit bacterial β-glucuronidase, and potentially alter the enterohepatic cycle. D-Glucarate may also interact with signal transduction pathways, altering promotion and initiation of cancer cells.[1-4]

USAGE

Cancer prevention, cancer treatment, detoxification.

PHARMACOKINETICS

Animal Studies: D-Glucarate salts are absorbed in the stomach as D-glucaric acid or metabolized by gut bacteria. D-Glucaric acid is converted to D-glucaro-1,4-lactone and D-glucaro-6,3-lactone. D-Glucaro-1,4-lactone is extensively distributed throughout the body, present in all tissues and body fluids. Excretion is primarily in the urine with minimal amounts present in feces and bile.[2,3,5]

ADVERSE REACTIONS

No adverse reactions have been reported.

DRUG INTERACTIONS

Oral Birth Control/Hormone Replacement: Theoretically, glucarate may reduce serum levels of estradiol and other hormones metabolized by the glucuronidation pathway.
Entacapone: Theoretically, glucarate may alter the metabolism and excretion of entacapone.[3]

DOSAGE

Oral: Optimal dose has not been defined. Doses ranging from 200 to 1,200 mg daily in divided doses have been used.

LITERATURE SUMMARY AND CRITIQUE

Several animal studies indicate low toxicity and possible effectiveness, but human clinical trials are necessary and as yet unavailable.

REFERENCES

  1. Heerdt AS, et al. Calcium glucarate as a chemopreventive agent in breast cancer. Isr J Med Sci 1995;31:101–5.
  2. Abou-issa H, et al. Relative efficacy of glucarate on the initiation and promotion phases of rat mammary carcinogenesis. Anticancer Res 1995;15:805–10.

3. Walaszek Z, et al. Metabolism, uptake, and excretion of a D-glucaric acid salt and its potential use in cancer prevention. Cancer Detect Prevent 1997;21:178–90.
4. Yoshimi N, et al. Inhibition of azoxymethane-induced rat colon carcinogenesis by potassium hydrogen D-glucarate. Int J Oncol 2000;16:43–8.
5. Dwivedi C, et al. Effect of calcium glucarate on α-glucuronidase activity and glucarate content of certain vegetables and fruits. Biochem Med Metab Biol 1990;43:83–92.

CanCell

A.DONATO

COMMON NAMES
Entelev, Sheridan's formula, JS-114, JS-101, 126-F, Jim's Juice, Quantrol

KEY WORDS
Entelev, Cantron

CLINICAL SUMMARY

Unproven alternative treatment containing a variety of ingredients depending on the manufacturer (eg, catechol, nitric acid, sodium sulfite, potassium hydroxide, sulfuric acid, crocinic acid, and various minerals and vitamins). Patients use this product to prevent and treat cancer, human immunodeficiency virus/acquired immune deficiency syndrome (HIV/AIDS), epilepsy, Alzheimer's disease, and other immunologic and degenerative diseases. Created by James Sheridan in the 1930s, this product purportedly balances the vibrational frequency of cancer cells and returns them to their healthy state. No studies have been published evaluating the use of CanCell for any proposed claims. Fatigue is the only reported adverse event. Manufacturers of CanCell discourage the combination of CanCell with conventional oncology treatments. Patients should be warned against using this product.

CONSTITUENTS

Nitric acid, sodium sulfite, potassium hydroxide, sulfuric acid, catechol, crocinic acid, inositol, minerals, vitamins.[1]

MECHANISM OF ACTION

The manufacturers of CanCell and Cantron offer different theories, both unfounded, explaining their product's anticancer activity. CanCell's use is based on the assumption that cancer cells function at a "critical point" of cellular respiration, above which normal cells function aerobically and below which abnormal anaerobic cells are destroyed as foreign matter. The catechol component is claimed to inhibit cellular respiration in cancer cells so that they might fall from the "critical point" to a primitive state and self-destruct. In addition, CanCell supposedly balances the vibrational frequency of cancer cells, returning them to a normal state. The manufacturers of Cantron claim that imbalance in cellular respiration results in cellular damage. Cantron allegedly helps maintain balance through the electrolyte and antioxidant properties of its hydroxyquinone and catechol components. Neither set of claims is substantiated by scientific data or consistent with any scientific construct.[1,2]

USAGE

Alzheimer's disease, cancer treatment, cystic fibrosis, diabetes, emphysema, epilepsy, hemophilia, herpes, HIV and AIDS, hypertension, hypotension, multiple sclerosis, scleroderma, systemic lupus erythematosus, viral infections.

PHARMACOKINETICS

No formal pharmacokinetic studies exist. The manufacturer states that the product is absorbed orally, sublingually, topically, and rectally.[1]

ADVERSE REACTIONS

Reported: Fatigue. Cancer patients may have progression of disease if they follow the manufacturer's recommendation not to combine CanCell and mainstream cancer treatment.[1]

DRUG INTERACTIONS

The manufacturer suggests that CanCell not be combined with vitamins or smoking and discourages concomitant use of conventional cancer treatments.[1]

DOSAGE

No dose-ranging studies have been performed.
Oral: Anecdotal use of one-quarter teaspoon held under the tongue for 4 minutes and then swallowed, repeated every 6 hours around the clock.
Rectal: Anecdotal use of one-quarter teaspoon injected into the rectum every 6 hours around the clock.

Topical: Topical application has been used in combination with oral or rectal administration. The wrist or ball of the foot is first cleaned with soap and water, several drops of dimethylsulfoxide are applied, and cotton gauze soaked with CanCell is applied to the skin and left for several hours.[1]

LITERATURE SUMMARY AND CRITIQUE

No published human, animal, or in vitro studies evaluate CanCell for any proposed claim. Although the manufacturers of CanCell maintain that extensive studies in mice and humans document its efficacy, no results have been published in peer-reviewed journals. In 1978 and 1980, the National Cancer Institute (NCI) conducted animal studies with CanCell and found that the product lacked significant antitumor activity. The NCI's In Vitro Anticancer Drug Discovery Program evaluated CanCell in 1990–1991, also with negative results. Neither study was published. It was determined that no further research on CanCell/Entelev was warranted. (See <http://cis.nci.nih.gov/fact/9_13.htm>.)

REFERENCES

1. American Cancer Society. Questionable methods of cancer management: Cancell/Entelev. CA Cancer J Clin 1993;43:57–62.
2. Grossgebauer K. The 'Cancell' theory of carcinogenesis: re-evolution of an ancient, holistic neoplastic unicellular concept of cancer. Med Hypotheses 1995;45:545–55.

Capsaicin

COMMON NAMES
Cayenne, chili pepper, capsaicin, African chilies, green bell pepper, red pepper, tabasco pepper

SCIENTIFIC NAME
Capsicum sp

KEY WORDS
Cayenne, chili pepper, Zostrix

CLINICAL SUMMARY
Derived from the fruit. Topically applied preparations are thought to decrease substance P and improve neuropathic and arthritic conditions. Onset of pain relief requires at least 4 weeks of treatment. Use of gloves is recommended when applying topically. After application, common adverse events include skin redness and burning, which subside in a subset of patients following repeated administration. There is no literature regarding oral administration of capsicum. Although it has been used safely as a spice, toxicities following overdoses include gastroenteritis and renal damage. Topical and oral supplementation of capsicum may interact with sedatives, theophylline, and antihypertensives. Patients receiving capsicum with an angiotensin-converting enzyme (ACE) inhibitor may be at an increased risk of developing cough.

CONSTITUENTS
Capsaicinoids: capsaicin, dihydrocapsaicin, nordihydrocapsaicin; volatile oils: trace amounts; proteins; carotenoid pigments.[1]

WARNINGS
Capsicum can be extremely irritating to the mucous membranes and to the eyes. Avoid contact with eyes and irritated or broken skin. Use gloves when applying topically, except when treating the hands.

MECHANISM OF ACTION

Topically, capsaicin may block pain fibers by destroying substance P, which normally would mediate pain signals to the brain. Depletion of substance P does not occur immediately. Effective use of the cream requires topical application four or five times daily for a period of at least 4 weeks.[2]

USAGE

Circulatory disorders, colic, diabetic neuropathy, diarrhea, headaches, herpes zoster neuropathy, high cholesterol, motion sickness, muscle pain, osteoarthritis, rheumatoid arthritis, spasms, stomach and intestinal gas, toothache.

ADVERSE REACTIONS

Common (Oral): Gastrointestinal irritation, sweating, flushing, lacrimation, rhinorrhea.
Toxicity (Oral): Gastroenteritis, renal damage.
Common (Topical): Burning, urticaria, contact dermatitis.[3]

DRUG INTERACTIONS

ACE Inhibitors: Capsaicin, orally or topically, can increase the incidence of cough that is associated with ACE inhibitors.
Sedatives: Capsaicin may increase sedation.
Theophylline: Concurrent administration with capsaicin may increase absorption.
Monoamine Oxidase Inhibitors: Capsaicin may increase catecholamine secretion.
Antihypertensives: Capsaicin may increase catecholamine secretion and antagonize hypotensive effects.[4]

DOSAGE

Oral: 30 to 120 mg three times a day.
Topical: 0.025 to 0.075% capsaicin creams may be applied three to four times a day and have a duration of action of about 4 to 6 hours. If applied with fingers, wash hands afterwards with a diluted vinegar solution.

LITERATURE SUMMARY AND CRITIQUE

Paice JA, et al. Topical capsaicin in the management of HIV-associated peripheral neuropathy. J Pain Symptom Manage 2000;19:45–52.
A multicenter, controlled, randomized trial studied the efficacy of capsaicin in patients with HIV-associated distal symmetric peripheral neuropathy (DSPN) and compared measures of pain intensity, pain relief, quality of life, etc. The results suggest that capsaicin was ineffective in relieving pain associated with HIV-associated DSPN.

Ellison N, et al. Phase III placebo-controlled trial of capsaicin cream in the management of surgical neuropathic pain in cancer patients. J Clin Oncol 1997;15:2974–80.
Ninety-nine cancer patients with postsurgery neuropathic pain were given capsaicin cream 0.075% or placebo applied four times a day for 8 weeks. At the end of the 8 weeks, there was a 53% reduction in pain in the capsaicin group compared with 17% in the placebo group. There was significant burning and redness in the capsaicin group.

Dasgupta P, et al. Chilies: from antiquity to urology. Br J Urol 1997;80:845–52.
In a study of six patients, an intravesical capsaicin injection was shown to reduce urinary urgency, bladder capacity, and the micturition threshold pressure. The authors suggest that capsaicin induces diuresis through stimulation of the vesicorenal reflex.

McCarthy GM, et al. Effect of topical capsaicin in the therapy of painful osteoarthritis of the hands. J Rheumatol 1992;19:604–7.
In a study of 21 patients, capsaicin cream improved tenderness and pain in joints with osteoarthritis but had no effect in patients with rheumatoid arthritis.

Deal CL, et al. Treatment of arthritis with topical capsaicin: a double-blind trial. Clin Ther 1991;13:383–95.
A study in which 70 patients with osteoarthritis and 31 patients with rheumatoid arthritis were treated with capsaicin 0.025% cream or placebo four times a day for 4 weeks. The results show that the placebo response was high, up to 48% in 1 week. Burning occurred in 44% of patients. Both the osteoarthritis and rheumatoid arthritis groups experienced a reduction in knee pain during treatment with capsaicin cream.

Bernstein JE, et al. Effects of topically applied capsaicin on moderate and severe psoriasis vulgaris. J Am Acad Dermatol 1986;15:504–7.
In a double-blind study, 44 patients with moderate to severe psoriasis were treated with capsaicin 0.01%, capsaicin 0.025%, or placebo. At 6 weeks, overall clinical improvement was observed in the capsaicin group. Burning, stinging, and redness occurred in approximately 50% of the patients. The 0.01% cream was as effective as the 0.025%, with less burning.

REFERENCES

1. Blumenthal M, et al. Herbal medicine: expanded Commission E monographs. Austin (TX): American Botanical Council; 2000.
2. Tyler V. Herbs of choice, the therapeutic use of phytomedicinals. Binghamton (NY): Pharmaceutical Products Press; 1994.
3. Newall CA, et al. Herbal medicines: a guide for health care professionals. London: Pharmaceutical Press; 1996.
4. Brinker F. Herb contraindications and drug interactions. 2nd ed. Sandy (OR): Eclectic Medical Publications; 1998.

Carnitine

COMMON NAMES
Levocarnitine, vitamin B_T, vitamin B_7, propionyl-L-carnitine

SCIENTIFIC NAME
β-Hydroxy-gamma-trimethylaminobutyric acid

CLINICAL SUMMARY
Endogenous cofactor in intermediary metabolism. Patients use this supplement to enhance physical performance and to treat fatigue and cachexia associated with carnitine deficiency caused by end-stage renal disease, cardiovascular disease, cancer, diabetes, chronic fatigue syndrome, and human immunodeficiency virus/acquired immune deficiency syndrome (HIV/AIDS). Endogenous treatment is thought to enhance mitochondrial integrity and function. Studies of oral carnitine for enhanced exercise performance in healthy individuals are poorly designed and show no consistent benefit. Preliminary data suggest efficacy in ameliorating chemotherapy-related fatigue and improving physical performance in patients undergoing dialysis for end-stage renal disease, but larger trials must be conducted. L-Carnitine inhibits cisplatin-induced injury of the kidney and small intestine in animal models. The role of adjunctive carnitine therapy in ischemic heart disease is still speculative. One study suggests that L-carnitine could be used to prevent skeletal muscle myopathy in heart failure and to block apoptosis. Several trials have shown enhanced physical performance, mitochondrial metabolism, or survival. Beneficial performance effects of both carnitine and propionyl-L-carnitine are seen in trials of peripheral arterial disease. Over-the-counter preparations may have poor dissolution properties and low oral bioavailability. Reported adverse effects include flu-like syndrome, injection site reaction, pain, pharyngitis, headache, diarrhea, and hypertension, whereas high doses may result in an unpleasant body odor.

MECHANISM OF ACTION
Carnitine facilitates the transport of long-chain fatty acyl coenzyme A (CoA) esters across the inner mitochondrial membrane, facilitating β-oxidation of fatty acids and acting as an intracellular energy reservoir of acetyl groups. In conditions of ischemia and carnitine deficiency, these acyl esters accumulate and cause deleterious effects, including inhibition of adenine nucleotide translocase, causing inhibition of adenosine triphosphate

production. Carnitine modulates the ratio of CoA to CoA-SH, is involved in trapping acyl residues from peroxisomes and mitochondria, and stabilizes cellular membranes. Carnitine is a free radical scavenger and may take part in nuclear transcription.

High serum carnitine levels generally correlate with better functional capacity in clinical trials. Exogenous carnitine enhances mitochondrial function in several studies, thought to be attributable to an increase in fatty acid oxidation and conservation of glycogen or a decrease in levels of acetyl CoA, which inhibits pyruvate dehydrogenase. In ischemic animal models, carnitine reduces loss of high-energy phosphates, enhances glucose oxidation, preserves myocardial carnitine stores, reduces accumulation of fatty acid esters, and enhances lactate extraction. Numerous studies report that carnitine supplementation improves cardiac performance in animal models of cardiomyopathy or ischemic insult, including improved myocardial metabolic patterns, reduced necrosis, diminished enzymatic infarct size, and preserved left ventricular function. L-Carnitine has been shown to inhibit cisplatin-induced injury of the kidney and small intestine in animal models. One study suggested that L-carnitine inhibits caspases and decreases levels of tumor necrosis factor-α. Long-term carnitine supplementation in humans is correlated with improved myocardial mechanical performance, reduction in ventricular arrhythmias, and increased exercise tolerance. Carnitine administration to rats ameliorates tumor-induced increase in plasma triglycerides. Carnitine is a peripheral antagonist of thyroid hormone action.[1-11]

USAGE

Alzheimer's disease, angina, cancer-related cachexia, cardiovascular disease, chemotherapy side effects, chronic fatigue syndrome, chronic obstructive pulmonary disorders, circulatory disorders, diabetes, high cholesterol, HIV- and AIDS-associated wasting, infertility, strength and stamina.

PHARMACOKINETICS

Absorption: Endogenous synthesis of carnitine takes place primarily in the liver and, to a lesser extent, the kidneys and brain. The dietary precursors for this synthesis are lysine and methionine. Intestinal absorption of dietary carnitine is saturable and can increase in response to carnitine deficiency. Intravenous L-carnitine shows linear kinetics and a long time to steady state. Following administration of 2 g of L-carnitine for 4 days, C_{max} is about 80 ìmol/L and occurs at 3.3 hours. Oral bioavailability is approximately 15%. Mucosal absorption of carnitine is saturated by 2 g doses, and oral fractionated treatment is required for higher doses.

Distribution: Total-body carnitine stores have been estimated to be between 20 and 25 g. The concentration of free muscle carnitine is approximately 4 mmol/kg. The quantity stored is influenced by muscle mass, nutritional status, and age. The adrenal glands exhibit the highest tissue concentrations of carnitine. Skeletal muscle (98%), liver (1.5%), heart, and other tissues with fatty acid metabolism also contain high levels of carnitine but are incapable of synthesizing it.

Metabolism/Excretion: More than 95% of dietary carnitine is excreted in the urine. Mean apparent terminal elimination half-life of an intravenous carnitine formulation is 17.4 hours.[12,13]

ADVERSE REACTIONS

Rare: Dyspepsia, heartburn, blurred vision, transient hair loss, skin rash, and seizures. Mild myasthenia has been reported in uremic patients receiving D,L- carnitine.
Reported: Flu syndrome, injection-site reaction, pain, pharyngitis, headache, diarrhea, and hypertension.
Toxicity: No notable clinical toxicities have been reported, but high oral doses of L-carnitine may cause an unpleasant body odor.[5,6,9,12]

DRUG INTERACTIONS
None known.

CONTRAINDICATIONS

A patient with riboflavin-responsive mild multiple acyl CoA dehydrogenation deficiency of the ethylmalonic-adipic aciduria type experienced repeated hypoglycemic episodes while taking L-carnitine supplements. Patients with defective oxidation of medium- or short-chain fatty acyl CoA esters should use carnitine supplementation with caution.[14]

DOSAGE

No Recommended Dietary Allowances have been set for carnitine. Daily intake needed to maintain the body's stores ranges from 8 to 11 mg/d.
Oral: Oral doses range between 500 mg/d and 4 g/d, but doses up to 15 g are well tolerated. Carnitine may be absorbed better if taken on an empty stomach. *Infertility caused by prostatovesiculoepididymitis*: 1 g carnitine and 500 mg acetyl carnitine every 12 hours for 3 months.
Intravenous: 10 to 20 mg/kg after each dialysis session for hemodialysis patients.[3,10]

LITERATURE SUMMARY AND CRITIQUE

Graziano F, et al. **Potential role of levocarnitine supplementation for the treatment of chemotherapy-induced fatigue in non-anaemic cancer patients. Br J Cancer 2002;86:1854–7.**
A prospective evaluation of 4 g daily oral carnitine supplementation in 50 nonanemic patients with solid tumors and good performance status who experienced fatigue during chemotherapy. Chemotherapy was cisplatin based in 44 patients and ifosfamide based in 6 patients. All patients had low baseline plasma levels of free carnitine (< 30 μM). Carnitine was administered in 2 g doses every 12 hours for the 7 days of chemotherapy. Patients were evaluated weekly with physical examinations, blood chemistries, and Func-

tional Assessment of Cancer Therapy-Fatigue (FACT-F) questionnaires until the next chemotherapy cycle. After 1 week, all patients had plasma free carnitine levels > 30 µM and 45 patients reported ameliorated fatigue. Mean FACT-F scores improved significantly from baseline (19.7) to the first week (34.9) ($p < .001$). Chemotherapy efficacy was not affected. Randomized, placebo-controlled trials are necessary to verify the efficacy of carnitine in reducing cancer fatigue.

Brass EP, et al. Intravenous L-carnitine increases plasma carnitine, reduces fatigue, and may preserve exercise capacity in hemodialysis patients. Am J Kidney Dis 2001;37:1018–28.
Two randomized, controlled, multicenter studies of the effect of intravenous L-carnitine on blood carnitine levels, exercise capacity, and quality of life in patients with end-stage renal disease, on maintenance hemodialysis therapy, and receiving erythropoietin (EPO). After each dialysis session, patients received either 20 mg/kg intravenous L-carnitine ($n = 28$) or placebo ($n = 28$) for 24 weeks (study A) or 10 ($n = 32$), 20 ($n = 30$), or 40 mg/kg ($n = 32$) L-carnitine or placebo ($n = 33$) for 24 weeks (study B). Blood parameters were measured at baseline and every 4 weeks, and maximal exercise testing, Kidney Disease Questionnaire, and VO_{2max} were assessed at baseline and 12 and 24 weeks. When corrected for body weight, carnitine (any dose) resulted in a significantly smaller decrease in VO_{2max} (-0.05 ± 0.19 mL/kg/min) over 24 weeks than placebo (-0.88 ± 0.26 mL/kg/min, $p = .009$); the clinical significance of this VO_{2max} maintenance is uncertain, however. Patients receiving all doses of carnitine reported a significantly improved sense of fatigue and experienced dose-dependent increases in serum carnitine. Side effects reported for both treatment arms included flu syndrome, injection-site reaction, pain, pharyngitis, headache, and hypertension.

Hurot JM, et al. Effects of L-carnitine supplementation in maintenance hemodialysis patients: a systematic review. J Am Soc Nephrol 2002;13:708–14.
An exploratory meta-analysis of 482 patients in 18 randomized, controlled trials from 1978 to 1999 evaluating the effects of L-carnitine supplementation on blood chemistry, EPO dose, and symptoms in patients undergoing maintenance hemodialysis. In nine trials evaluating serum lipid profile, effects on serum triglycerides were heterogeneous, and no effect was seen on serum total cholesterol. Carnitine supplementation increased hemoglobin levels in three pre-EPO trials by a clinically significant amount. A significant reduction in EPO dose with constant hemoglobin or hematocrit was seen in carnitine-treated groups in four of six trials. The effect of carnitine on exercise capacity, cardiovascular instability, or quality of life was not assessed because of the heterogeneity in recording methods between trials. Most trials included in this review were small and not double-blind, and the meta-analysis did not take into account route of administration.

Ellaway CJ, et al. Medium-term open label trial of L-carnitine in Rett syndrome. Brain Dev 2001;23:S85–S89.
A small open-label study of the effects of L-carnitine supplementation on symptomatology, sleep, hand apraxia, physical activity, and parental quality of life in 21 females with Rett syn-

drome versus 62 untreated female controls. Subjects received 100 mg/kg/d L-carnitine in two divided doses for a 6-month period. Outcomes were assessed at baseline and after 6 months. All treatment patients, 10 of whom had low serum carnitine at baseline, experienced increases in serum carnitine to normal or high levels. Compared with controls, patients receiving carnitine showed statistically significant and clinically meaningful improvements in sleep efficiency, energy level, and communication skills ($p < .05$). Further studies are necessary to understand the empiric treatment of Rett syndrome with L-carnitine.

Loignon M, Toma E. L-Carnitine for the treatment of highly active antiretroviral therapy-related hypertriglyceridemia in HIV-infected adults. AIDS 2001;15:1194–5.
A small pilot study evaluating the effect of 3 g/d oral L-carnitine supplementation on hypertriglyceridemia in 15 men and 1 woman infected with HIV on highly active antiretroviral therapy (HAART). Treatment lasted 8.9 ± 5 months. Biochemical and metabolic parameters were measured at months 1 and 2, at the first change of HAART, and at the end of therapy. Serum triglyceride levels decreased by 39% at month 1, 28% at month 2, 23% when HAART was first changed, and 34.7% at the last measurement. Near-normal triglyceride levels (≤ 3 mmol/L) were obtained in 54% of patients by 2 months and in 69% of patients at the last measurement. Larger, controlled, randomized trials are necessary to support the promising results of this pilot study.

Benvenga S, et al. Usefulness of L-carnitine, a naturally occurring peripheral antagonist of thyroid hormone action, in iatrogenic hyperthyroidism: a randomized, double-blind, placebo-controlled clinical trial. J Clin Endocrinol Metab 2001;86:3579–94.
A randomized, double-blind, placebo-controlled, crossover design trial evaluating 4 months of 2 or 4 g daily carnitine supplementation versus 2 months placebo in 50 otherwise healthy women with hyperthyroidism. All patients received a thyroid-stimulating hormone–suppressive dose of L-thyroxine. Patients were evaluated clinically and biochemically at baseline and every month thereafter. Bone mineral density was measured at baseline and at the study's end. Carnitine (any dose) was associated with slight decreases in serum aspartate transaminase, alanine transaminase, gamma-glutamyltransferase, sex hormone–binding globulin, and ferritin and increases in urinary excretion of OH-proline and serum osteocalcin, which are all up-regulated by thyroid hormone. In all carnitine groups, symptomatology (asthenia, palpitations, nervousness, insomnia, and heart rate) decreased during active treatment and worsened during placebo. Transient nausea and gastralgia were the only adverse events reported.

Plioplys AV, Plioplys S. Amantadine and L-carnitine treatment of chronic fatigue syndrome. Neuropsychobiology 1997;35:16–23.
A crossover trial evaluating 2 months of L-carnitine and 2 months of amantadine with a 2-week washout period in 28 patients with chronic fatigue syndrome (CFS). Fourteen patients received 3 g/d L-carnitine first, whereas the other 14 received 100 to 200 mg/d amantadine first. Outcomes measured were the Fatigue Severity Scale, Beck Depression Inventory, Symptom Checklist 90-R, CFS Impairment Index, and CFS Severity Index. Nonsteroidal anti-inflammatory drugs could be taken when needed, but use was not

recorded. All 28 patients were able to tolerate L-carnitine, whereas 13 patients discontinued amantadine before 8 weeks owing to side effects. In 12 of the 18 psychometric tests and subtests, a statistically significant improvement was recorded at 8 weeks in the L-carnitine group; no tests or subtests deteriorated. No difference in response was seen between those treated with L-carnitine first or second. Degree of improvement was correlated with the severity of CFS at the beginning of the study.

Cacciatore L, et al. The therapeutic effect of L-carnitine in patients with exercise-induced stable angina: a controlled study. Drugs Exp Clin Res 1991;17:225–35.
A multicenter, controlled trial examining the effects of carnitine in 200 patients aged 40 to 65 with exercise-induced stable angina New York Heart Association functional class I or II. One hundred patients received 2 g oral L-carnitine for 6 months in addition to conventional therapy; the other 100 received only conventional therapy. Blood glucose, triglyceride, total cholesterol, and high-density lipoprotein levels were measured; an electrocardiogram was performed; and cardioactive drug intake was evaluated at baseline and at months 1, 2, 3, and 6. Exercise testing was performed at baseline and 6 months. The carnitine-treated group showed a significant reduction in the number of premature ventricular contractions and exercise-induced electrocardiographic signs of ischemia and increased exercise tolerance. Significant reductions in drug consumption and total cholesterol and triglyceride levels were observed in the carnitine-treated group alone. This study is flawed, lacking blinding, randomization, and use of placebo. More recent studies use a derivative of carnitine, propionyl-L-carnitine, in ischemic conditions and cardiovascular disease with positive results.

REFERENCES

1. Arsenian MA. Carnitine and its derivatives in cardiovascular disease. Prog Cardiovasc Dis 1997;40:265–86.
2. Brody T. Nutritional biochemistry. San Diego (CA): Academic Press; 1999.
3. Benvenga S, et al. Usefulness of L-carnitine, a naturally occuring peripheral antagonist of thyroid hormone action, in iatrogenic hyperthyroidism: a randomized, double-blind, placebo-controlled clinical trial. J Clin Endocrinol Metab 2001;86:3579–94.
4. Breitkreutz R, et al. Effect of carnitine on muscular glutamate uptake and intramuscular glutathione in malignant diseases. Br J Cancer 2000;82:399–403.
5. Lango R, et al. Influence of L-carnitine and its derivatives on myocardial metabolism and function in ischemic heart disease and during cardiopulmonary bypass. Cardiovasc Res 2001;51:21–9.
6. Plioplys AV, Plioplys S. Amantadine and L-carnitine treatment of chronic fatigue syndrome. Neuropsychobiology 1997;35:16–23.
7. Rizos I. Three-year survival of patients with heart failure caused by dilated cardiomyopathy and L-carnitine administration. Am Heart J 2000;139: S120–3.
8. Atar D, et al. Carnitine—from cellular mechanisms to potential clinical applications in heart disease. Eur J Clin Invest 1997;27:973–6.
9. Brass EP, et al. Intravenous L-carnitine increases plasma carnitine, reduces fatigue, and may preserve exercise capacity in hemodialysis patients. Am J Kidney Dis 2001;37:1018–28.
10. Chang B, et al. L-Carnitine inhibits cisplatin-induced injury of the kidney and small intestine. Arch Biochem Biophys 2002;405:55.

11. Vescovo G, et al. L-Carnitine: a potential treatment for blocking apoptosis and preventing skeletal muscle myopathy in heart failure. Am J Physiol Cell Physiol 2002;283:C802–10.
12. US Food and Drug Administration. Carnitor® (levocarnitine). New drug application # 18-948/S-022, 19-257/S-010 & 20-182/S-008. Available at: http://www.fda.gov/cder/approval/index.htm (accessed Jun 10, 2002).
13. Green A, et al. Possible deleterious effect of L-carnitine supplementation in a patient with mild multiple acyl-CoA dehydrogenation deficiency (ethylmalonic-adipic aciduria). J Inherit Metab Dis 1991;14:691–7.
14. Vicari E, Calogero AE. Effects of treatment with carnitines in infertile patients with prostato-vesiculo-epididymitis. Hum Reprod 2001;16:2338–42.

Cascara

COMMON NAME
Cascara sagrada

SCIENTIFIC NAME
Rhamnus purshiana

CLINICAL SUMMARY

Derived from the bark of the plant. Cascara is mainly used to relieve constipation. The major constituents are cascarosides that stimulate the large intestine and produce a laxative effect. Cascara is one of the herbs incorporated in the Hoxsey herbal therapy. In vitro studies suggest that an active ingredient, aloe-emodin, may have antiproliferative activities. No controlled human trials are available to confirm these effects. Cascara is not indicated for long-term use. Prolonged use or overdose may cause diarrhea and electrolyte imbalance. The US Food and Drug Administration (FDA) rules that cascara is not as safe as a stimulant laxative.

CONSTITUENTS

Anthracene glycosides: cascarosides, aloins, chrysaloins, aloe-emodin, chrysophanol, emodin, physcion; others: linoleic acid, myristic acid, syringic acid, lipids, resin, tannin.[1]

WARNINGS

Chronic use may cause electrolyte imbalance, especially hypokalemia. The FDA rules that cascara is not safe as a stimulant laxative.[2,3]

MECHANISM OF ACTION

The major constituents, cascarosides, stimulate the large intestine and produce a well-documented laxative effect. Cascarosides increase intestinal motility and lead to propulsive contractions. This results in an increased water and electrolyte content in the lumen, which further facilitates bowel passage. Cascara's anticancer activities may arise from its emodin and aloe-emodin content. In vitro studies show that aloe-emodin induces p53 and p21 expression, resulting in cell-cycle arrest in the G_1 phase. However, more studies are needed to confirm this effect. Studies on the carcinogenic effects of cascara have produced conflicting results.[1,3–6]

USAGE

Cancer treatment, constipation.

PHARMACOKINETICS

After ingestion, cascara glycosides pass through the small intestine unchanged. On reaching the large intestine, glycosides are hydrolyzed and activated by local bacteria. Studies show that the dimeric aglycones are well absorbed through the intestinal wall and strongly bind to plasma proteins. Aglycones are excreted through the bile.[7]

ADVERSE REACTIONS

Reported: Fresh cascara contains anthrones, which may cause vomiting and intestinal cramps.
Toxicity: Excessive use can cause diarrhea and weakness.
Rare: Cascara has been associated with cholestatic hepatitis.[2,3,8]

DRUG INTERACTIONS

Diuretics: Cascara can cause excessive loss of potassium.
Digoxin: Cascara may potentiate cardiac effects.

LABORATORY INTERACTIONS

Decreased serum potassium. Anthraquinones in cascara may discolor the urine and interfere with diagnostic tests.[3]

CONTRAINDICATIONS

Cascara should not be used by patients with intestinal obstruction or undiagnosed abdominal symptoms. Patients with inflammatory bowel disease should use caution with this supplement. Anthraquinone-containing laxatives such as cascara should not be used by pregnant or nursing mothers.

DOSAGE

Infusion: 2 g dried bark in 150 mL boiling water daily.

Extract: 2 to 5 mL daily.

Other Preparations: Equivalent to 20 to 30 mg of hydroxanthracene derivatives, calculated as cascaroside A, daily.[1]

LITERATURE SUMMARY AND CRITIQUE

No clinical studies document the anticancer effect of cascara. In vitro studies of aloe-emodin, an active ingredient, suggest antiproliferative activities.

REFERENCES

1. Barnes J, et al. Herbal medicines. 2nd ed. London: Pharmaceutical Press; 2002.
2. DerMarderosian A, editor. The review of natural products. St. Louis: Facts and Comparisons; 1999.
3. Gruenwald J, et al. PDR for herbal medicines. Montvale (NJ): Medical Economics Company; 1998.
4. Mereto E, et al. Evaluation of the potential carcinogenic activity of senna and cascara glycosides for the rat colon. Cancer Lett 1996;101:79–83.
5. Kuo P, et al. The antiproliferative activity of aloe-emodin is through p53-dependent and p21-dependent apoptotic pathway in human hepatoma cell lines. Life Sci 2002;71:1879–92.
6. Koyama J, et al. Chemopreventive effects of emodin and cassiamin B in mouse skin carcinogenesis. Cancer Lett 2002;182:135–9.
7. DeWitte P, et al. Bicascarosides in fluid extracts of cascara. Planta Med 1991;57:440–3.
8. Nadir A, et al. Cascara sagrada-induced intrahepatic cholestasis causing portal hypertension: case report and review of herbal hepatotoxicity. Am J Gastroenterol 2000;95:3634–7.

Cat's Claw

COMMON NAMES
Una de gato, life-giving vine of Peru, hawk's claw

SCIENTIFIC NAME
Uncaria tomentosa

KEY WORD
Uncaria tomentosa

CLINICAL SUMMARY

Derived from the bark of the tree. In vitro studies show that its pentacyclic oxindole alkaloids enhance phagocytosis, display immunomodulatory properties specifically against nuclear factor κB and tumor necrosis factor (TNF)-α, and alleviate inflammation. However, no human studies have been conducted to evaluate efficacy. Reported adverse reactions include hypotension and diarrhea. An additive effect with anticoagulants or hypotensives is possible; therefore, caution should be exercised. Cat's claw should be avoided in patients with autoimmune disorders (eg, systemic lupus erythematosus).

CONSTITUENTS

Oxindole alkaloids: isopteropodine, pteropodine, rhynchophylline, mytraphylline, speciphylline; indole alkaloidal glucosides: cadambine, 3-dihydrocadambine, and 3-isodihydrocadambine; hirsutine; quinovic acid glycosides; tannins; polyphenols; catechins; β-sitosterol.[1,2]

MECHANISM OF ACTION

The oxindole alkaloids are claimed to have immunostimulating properties in vitro to increase phagocytotic activity and synthesis of white blood cells and enhance T helper cell function. The major alkaloid rhynchophylline is claimed to be antihypertensive, relax the blood vessels of endothelial cells, dilate peripheral blood vessels, inhibit sympathetic nervous system activities, lower the heart rate, and lower blood cholesterol. The alkaloid mytraphylline has diuretic properties, and hirsutine inhibits urinary bladder contractions and possesses local anesthetic properties. The anti-inflammatory activity may be caused by the inhibition of TNF-α production. *Uncaria tomentosa* water extracts have been shown to enhance deoxyribonucleic acid (DNA) repair after chemotherapy-induced damage.[3-11]

USAGE
Birth control, cancer treatment, gastrointestinal disorders, human immunodeficiency virus (HIV) and acquired immune deficiency syndrome (AIDS), inflammation.

ADVERSE REACTIONS
Common: May cause diarrhea and lower blood pressure.
Case Report: Acute renal failure in a patient with systemic lupus erythematosus.[12]

DRUG INTERACTIONS
Antihypertensives: Cat's claw may cause an additive or a synergistic hypotensive effect.
Anticoagulants/Antiplatelets: Cat's claw may have an additive anticoagulant effect.
CYP3A4: In vitro, cat's claw inhibits CYP3A4, indicating that it, theoretically, may increase the serum levels of drugs such as protease inhibitors, non-nucleoside reverse-transcriptase inhibitors, cyclosporine, some benzodiazepines, and many others.[13]

DOSAGE
Oral: 250 to 1,000 mg daily available in many strengths and formulations. Also available as a tea.

LITERATURE SUMMARY AND CRITIQUE
Animal and in vitro data exist in cancer, immunostimulant, inflammation, and antiviral studies. Human studies are lacking, and further research is needed.

REFERENCES
1. Wirth C, et al. Pharmacologically active procyanidines from the bark of *Uncaria tomentosa*. Phytomedicine 1997;4:265–6.
2. Hemingway SR, Phillipson JD. Proceedings: alkaloids from South American species of *Uncaria* (Rubiaceae). J Pharm Pharmacol 1974;26 Suppl:113.
3. Rizzi R, et al. Mutagenic and antimutagenic activities of *Uncaria tomentosa* and its extracts. J Ethnopharmacol 1993;38:63–77.

4. Paulsen SM. Use of herbal products and dietary supplements by oncology patients—informed decisions? Highlights Oncol Pract 1998;15:94–106.
5. Aquino R, et al. Plant metabolites: new compounds and anti-inflammatory activity of *Uncaria tomentosa*. J Nat Prod 1991;54:453–9.
6. Sheng Y, Bryngelsson C, Pero R. Enhanced DNA repair, immune function and reduced toxicity of C-MED-100, a novel aqueous extract from *Uncaria tomentosa*. J Ethnopharmacol 2000;69:115–26.
7. Charbonnet R, et al. Cat's claw inhibits TNFalpha production and scavenges free radicals: role in cytoprotection. Free Radic Biol Med 2000;29:71–8.
8. Riva L, et al. The antiproliferative effects of *Uncaria tomentosa* extracts and fractions on the growth of breast cancer cell line. Anticancer Res 2001;21:2457–61.
9. Sandoval M, et al. Anti-inflammatory and antioxidant activities of cat's claw (*Uncaria tomentosa* and *Uncaria guianensis*) are independent of their alkaloid content. Phytomedicine 2002;9:325–37.
10. Mur E, et al. Randomized double blind trial of an extract for the pentacyclic alkaloid-chemotype of *Uncaria tomentosa* for the treatment of rheumatoid arthritis. J Rheumatol 2002;29:678–81.
11. Sheng Y, et al. DNA repair of aqueous extracts of *Uncaria tomentosa* in a human volunteer study. Phytomedicine 2001;8:275–82.
12. Hilepo JN, et al. Acute renal failure caused by 'cat's claw' herbal remedy in a patient with systemic lupus erythematosus. Nephron 1997;77:361.
13. Scott GN, Elmer GW. Update on natural product-drug interactions. Am J Health Syst Pharm 2002;59:339–47.

Chamomile (German)

COMMON NAMES
Hungarian chamomile, wild chamomile, *Chamomilla recutita*

SCIENTIFIC NAME
Matricaria recutita L.

KEY WORD
Matricaria recutita

A. DONATO

CLINICAL SUMMARY
Derived from the flower. Chamomile is widely used in teas for its relaxing effect. Topical and oral administrations are safe except in patients with allergies to ragweed or chrysanthemums. Studies of chamomile mouthwash produced conflicting results regarding its benefit in reducing 5-fluorouracil (FU)-induced mucositis. Potential drug interactions include platelet inhibition leading to additive anticoagulant effect and potentially increased sedation from sedatives or hypnotics. The usual oral dose is 3 g (approximately 1 tablespoon) of flower heads for one cup of tea up to four times a day. Oral rinse is 10 to 15 drops of chamomile extract in 100 mL of water administered three times a day.

CONSTITUENTS (FLOWER HEAD)
Coumarins; flavonoids (up to 8%): quercetin, rutin, apigenin, luteolin, apigetrin, apiin; volatile oils: α-bisabolol (up to 50%), azulene, chamazulene; other constituents: amino acids, choline polysaccharide, plant and fatty acids, tannin, triterpene hydrocarbons.[1]

MECHANISM OF ACTION
In animal studies, a wide range of pharmacologic activities has been documented, including antibacterial, anti-inflammatory, antispasmodic, antiulcer, antiviral, and hypouremic activ-

ities. Apigenin, a flavone, interacts with γ-aminobutyric acid $(GABA)_A$-benzodiazepine receptors in vitro and inhibits locomoter behavior in rats. The azulene components of the volatile oil are thought to contribute by inhibiting histamine release and have been reported to prevent allergic seizures in animals. Matricin, the precursor to chamazulene, is reported to be a more effective anti-inflammatory agent than chamazulene. Anti-inflammatory and antiulcerogenic activity has also been documented for the α-bisabolol compound. Antibacterial activity has been documented for the coumarin constituents. Antispasmodic activity has been documented for the flavonoid and bisabolol constituents.[2,3,6]

USAGE
Colic, gastrointestinal disorders, hemorrhoids, infections, inflammation, mastitis, mucositis, sedation, skin ulcers, spasms, stomach and intestinal gas.

ADVERSE REACTIONS
Reported: Hypersensitivity reactions in people allergic to ragweed or members of the Compositae family, ranging from contact dermatitis to anaphylaxis.[2,4]

DRUG INTERACTIONS
Anticoagulants/Antiplatelets: Chamomile may increase anticoagulant effects and inhibit platelets owing to coumarin content.
Sedatives: Chamomile may cause additive drowsiness.[5]

LABORATORY INTERACTIONS
May increase prothrombin time, activated partial thromboplastin time, and international normalized ratio (INR).

CONTRAINDICATIONS
People allergic to ragweed or members of the Compositae family, such as chrysanthemums, should avoid this product.

DOSAGE
Oral: Tea: 3 g (1 tablespoonful) of flower heads, taken up to four times a day. *Oral rinse:* 10 to 15 drops of chamomile liquid extract in 100 mL of warm water three times a day.

LITERATURE SUMMARY AND CRITIQUE
Fidler P, et al. Prospective evaluation of a chamomile mouthwash for prevention of 5-FU-induced oral mucositis. Cancer 1996;77:522–5.
A phase III, double-blind, placebo-controlled clinical trial with 164 patients equally randomized to both treatment groups. Patients received 30 minutes of oral cryotherapy

prior to bolus of 5-FU-based chemotherapy. Chamomile or placebo mouthwash was used three times a day for 14 days beginning on the first day of chemotherapy. Graded stomatitis scores were not significantly different between the two treatment groups. Chamomile mouthwash did not appear to be beneficial in the prevention of 5-FU-induced stomatitis.

Carl W, et al. Management of oral mucositis during local radiation and systemic chemotherapy: a study of 98 patients. J Prosthet Dent 1991;30:395–6.

Twenty patients treated with radiation and 46 patients receiving systemic chemotherapy participated in prophylactic oral care with a chamomile oral rinse. Thirty-two patients were treated therapeutically after mucositis had developed. Prophylactic use of the rinse prevented the occurrence of mucositis in 78% of the patients receiving chemotherapy and delayed the onset and reduced the intensity of radiation-induced mucositis.

REFERENCES

1. Blumenthal M, et al. Herbal medicine, expanded Commission E monographs. 1st ed. Austin (TX): American Botanical Council; 2000.
2. Newall C, et al. Herbal medicines: a guide for health-care professionals. London: Pharmaceutical Press; 1996.
3. Avallone R, et al. Pharmacological profile of apigenin, a flavonoid isolated from *Matricaria chamomilla*. Biochem Pharmacol 2000;59:1387–94.
4. Tyler V. Herbs of choice, the therapeutic use of phytomedicinals. Binghamton (NY): Pharmaceutical Press; 1994.
5. Brinker F. Herb contraindications and drug interactions. 3rd ed. Sandy (OR): Eclectic Medical Publications; 2001.
6. Kyokong O, et al. Efficacy of chamomile-extract spray for prevention of post-operative sore throat. J Med Assoc Thai 2002;85 Suppl:S180–5.
7. Budzinski JW, et al. An in vitro evaluation of human cytochrome P450 3A4 inhibition by selected commercial herbal extracts and tinctures. Phytomedicine 2000;7:273–82.

Chaparral

COMMON NAMES
Creosate bush, greasewood, hediondilla

SCIENTIFIC NAMES
Larrea tridentate, Larrea divaricata

KEY WORDS
Larrea tridentate, creosate

CLINICAL SUMMARY

Derived from the leaves and flowers of the plant. Several clinical trials have been conducted, but none support the promotional claims. Numerous reports indicate hepatotoxicity following the use of chaparral. Although a small-scale study indicated that relatively small intake of *Larrea tincture* (< 10%) appears to have no adverse effect, correlation between length of exposure and risk is not yet determined. Owing to case reports involving both reversible and irreversible liver damage, the US Food and Drug Administration (FDA) issued a health warning urging withdrawal of these products in 1992.

CONSTITUENTS

Amino acids: arginine, aspartine, cystine, glutamic acid, glycine, isoleucine, leucine, phenylalanine, tryptophan, tyrosine, valine; flavonoids: more than 20 different reported, including isorhamnetin, kaempferol, and quercetin and their glycosidic and ether derivatives; gossypetin, herbacetin, and their acetate derivatives; lignans: nordihydroguaiaretic acid (NDGA), norisoguaiacin, dihydroguaiaretic acid; resins: a number of flavone and flavonol glycosides; volatile oils: terpene components include calamene, eudesmol, limonene; others: two pentacyclic triterpenes and saponins. A cytotoxic naphthoquinone derivative, larreantin, has been isolated from the roots.[1]

WARNINGS

Chaparral has been associated with severe hepatotoxicity, with some cases requiring liver transplantation.

MECHANISM OF ACTION

NDGA, a lipoxygenase inhibitor, may be responsible for the biologic activity of chaparral. It is believed that NDGA may have anticancer activity by blocking cellular respiration in vitro. However, later studies found no effect in vivo.[2,3]

USAGE

Arthritis, bronchitis, cancer prevention, cancer treatment, common cold, inflammation, menstrual cramps, promotion of urination, spasms.

ADVERSE REACTIONS

Reported: Fatigue, contact dermatitis, gastrointestinal upset, jaundice, hepatotoxicity, cirrhosis, acute hepatitis, kidney failure, and renal cell carcinoma[1,4–6]

DRUG INTERACTIONS

Monoamine Oxidase Inhibitors (MAOIs): Excessive doses of chaparral may interfere with MAOI therapy owing to the documented amino acid constituents.[1]

LABORATORY INTERACTIONS

Elevated liver function tests.

DOSAGE

Not recommended in any dosage form.

LITERATURE SUMMARY AND CRITIQUE

Sheikh NM, et al. Chaparral-associated hepatotoxicity. Arch Intern Med 1997; 157:913–9.

Eighteen case reports of adverse events associated with the ingestion of chaparral reported to the FDA between 1992 and 1994 were reviewed. The results showed evidence of hepatotoxicity in 13 cases. Jaundice occurred 3 to 52 weeks after ingestion of chaparral, and the predominant pattern of liver injury was characterized as toxic or drug-induced cholestatic hepatitis. In four patients, progression to cirrhosis occurred, and two patients required liver transplants.

Batchelor WB, et al. Chaparral-induced hepatic injury. Am J Gastroenterol 1995;90:831–3.

Two case studies of hepatitis after daily ingestion of chaparral were presented. Both patients remained well after abstinence from chaparral.

Gordon DW, et al. Chaparral ingestion. The broadening spectrum of liver injury caused by herbal medications. JAMA 1995;273:489–90.

Case study of a patient who developed severe hepatitis after consuming chaparral for 10 months and subsequently required a liver transplant.

Heron S, Yarnell E. The safety of low-dose *Larrea tridentate* (DC) Coville (creosote bush or chaparral): a retrospective clinical study. J Altern Complement Med 2001;7:175–85.

This study was a retrospective review of 35 patients who used *Larrea* or a combination of *Larrea* and other herbs either internally or externally over a 22-month period. No patient showed signs of organ damage. Four patients before and after blood chemistry showed no indication of liver damage. Although the results suggested that *Larrea* in low doses appears to be safe, the study was based solely on retrospective observation. Of 35 patients, only 4 patients' outcome could be verified through blood chemistry. More studies have to be done to before a clinically safe dose level can be established.

REFERENCES

1. Newall CA, et al. Herbal medicines: a guide for health-care professionals. London: Pharmaceutical Press; 1996.
2. Cunningham DC, et al. Proliferative responses of normal human mammary and MCF-7 breast cancer cells to linoleic, CLA and eicosanoid synthesis inhibitors in culture. Anticancer Res 1997;17:197–203.
3. Pavani M, et al. Inhibition of tumoral cell respiration and growth by nordihydroguaiaretic acid. Biochem Pharmacol 1994;48:1935–42.
4. Sheikh NM, et al. Chaparral-associated hepatotoxicity. Arch Intern Med 1997;157:913–9.
5. Tyler V, et al. The honest herbal. New York: Pharmaceutical Press; 1993.
6. Heron S, Yarnell E. The safety of low-dose *Larrea tridentata* (DC) Coville (creosote bush or chaparral): a retrospective clinical study. J Altern Complement Med 2001;7:175–85.

Chasteberry

COMMON NAMES
Chaste tree fruit, monk's pepper

SCIENTIFIC NAME
Vitex agnus castus

KEY WORDS
Vitex, Agnus castus

A. DONATO

CLINICAL SUMMARY
Derived from the fruit of the tree. This herb contains steroidal precursors and active moieties, including progesterone, testosterone, and androstenedione. Several clinical studies in women suggest efficacy in reducing symptoms associated with premenstrual syndrome (PMS). Chasteberry may interact with oral contraceptives, other hormonal therapy, and dopamine antagonists (such as haloperidol and prochlorperazine). Adverse effects reported include nausea, rash, headache, and agitation.

CONSTITUENTS
Flavonoids: casticin, penduletin, chrysophanol D; iridoid alkaloids: viticin, angnoside, aucubin; progestins: progesterone, hydroxyprogesterone, testosterone, epitestosterone, androstenedione; volatile oils.[1]

MECHANISM OF ACTION
In animal studies, chasteberry has been reported to diminish release of follicle-stimulating hormone from the anterior pituitary while increasing the release of luteinizing hormone (LH) and prolactin. It also contains constituents that bind to dopamine (D_1 and D_2) receptors and seem to inhibit prolactin release. In human studies, it has been found to

restore progesterone concentrations, prolong the hyperthermic phase in the basal temperature curve, and restore the LH–releasing hormone test to normal. It is thought to act on the pituitary-hypothalamic axis rather than directly on the ovaries.[2-5]

USAGE
Dysmenorrhea, mastalgia, menopausal symptoms, uterine bleeding.

ADVERSE REACTIONS
Reported: Gastrointestinal upset, nausea, rash, urticaria, headaches, and agitation.[6,7]

DRUG INTERACTIONS
Oral Contraceptives: Chasteberry may interfere with efficacy owing to its hormone-regulating activity.
Dopamine D$_2$ Antagonists: Chasteberry may interfere with the action of drugs that antagonize dopamine receptors (eg, chlorpromazine, haloperidol, prochlorperazine).[1,8]

DOSAGE
Oral: Typical dose is 20 to 40 mg once a day. *Extract:* 40 drops each morning on an empty stomach.

LITERATURE SUMMARY AND CRITIQUE
Schellenberg R. Treatment for the premenstrual syndrome with agnus castus fruit extract: prospective, randomized, placebo controlled study over three menstrual cycles. BMJ 2001;322:134–7.
A double-blind, placebo-controlled study of 178 women found that treatment with chasteberry over three menstrual cycles significantly reduced PMS symptoms. Responder rates were 52% and 24% for the active and placebo groups, respectively. The dose used was one tablet of chasteberry dry extract three times a day. Women in the treatment group experienced significant improvements in symptoms, including depression, headache, irritability, and breast tenderness.

Loch EG, Selle H, Boblitz N. Treatment of premenstrual syndrome with a phytopharmaceutical formulation containing *Vitex agnus castus*. J Womens Health Gend Based Med 2000;9:315–20.
A noninterventional review of 1,634 female German patients suffering from PMS who were treated with a *Vitex* preparation. Questionnaires, completed by the physician at baseline and after three menstrual cycles, evaluated the symptoms of PMS and efficacy of herbal supplement. The results indicate that a reduction in PMS symptoms, including depression, anxiety, bloating, and headache, occurred. Reported adverse events included

13 cases of skin symptoms (pruritus, rash, eczema, hair loss) and 6 reports of mild gastrointestinal complaints (nausea, vomiting, diarrhea, stomach pain).

REFERENCES

1. Schulz V, et al. Rational phytotherapy, a physician's guide to herbal medicine. 3rd ed. New York: Springer; 1996.
2. Newall C, et al. Herbal medicines: a guide for health-care professionals. London: Pharmaceutical Press; 1996.
3. Berger D, et al. Efficacy of *Vitex agnus castus* L. extract Ze 440 in patients with pre-menstrual syndrome (PMS). Arch Gyncecol Obstet 2000;264:150–3.
4. Meier B, et al. Pharmacological activities of *Vitex agnus-castus* extracts in vitro. Phytomedicine 2000;7:373–81.
5. Schellenberg R. Treatment for the premenstrual syndrome with *agnus castus* fruit extract: prospective, randomised, placebo controlled study. BMJ 2001;322:134–7.
6. Foster S. Herbs for your health. Loveland (CO): Interweave Press; 1996.
7. Mills S, et al. Principles and practice of phytotherapy. London: Churchill Livingstone; 2000.
8. Brinker F. Herb contraindications & drug interactions. 2nd ed. Sandy (OR): Eclectic Medical Publications; 1998.

Chinese Asparagus

COMMON NAMES
Tian Dong, Tian Men Dong, *Asparagi radix*, tenmondo, asparagus root

SCIENTIFIC NAME
Asparagus cochinchinensis

KEY WORD
Tian Men Dong

CLINICAL SUMMARY
Derived from the root of the plant. Chinese asparagus is used in traditional Chinese medicine to treat a variety of conditions, including breast cancer and liver disease, and as a tonic. Asparamide and β-sitosterol are thought to be responsible for its antineoplastic activity in vitro. No adverse events or drug interactions are known for this supplement. Additional research must be conducted to assess its safety and efficacy.

CONSTITUENTS
Saponins: officinalisnin I and II, asparasaponin I and II, asparagosides A to I; asparamide; β-sitosterol.[1,2]

MECHANISM OF ACTION
In vitro studies suggest that the β-sitosterol constituent has activity against mouse S-180 leukemia and lung cancer. An aqueous extract of asparagus root inhibits tumor necrosis factor-α secretion in mouse astrocytes. Asparagus root also reduces alcohol-induced hepatotoxicity in Hep G2 cell lines.[3,4]

USAGE
Cancer treatment, constipation, cough, health maintenance, hepatitis.

ADVERSE REACTIONS
None reported.

DRUG INTERACTIONS
None known.

DOSAGE
Oral: In traditional Chinese medicine, 6 to 15 g of the raw herb are used in a decoction with other herbs, but no standard dose is recognized.

LITERATURE SUMMARY AND CRITIQUE
No clinical trials have been performed evaluating Chinese asparagus for any proposed claim.

REFERENCES
1. Huang KC. The pharmacology of Chinese herbs. 2nd ed. New York: CRC Press; 1999.
2. Konishi T, Shoji J. Studies on the constituents of *Asparagi radix*. I. On the structures of furostanol oligosides of *Asparagus cochinchinensis* (loureio) merrill. Chem Pharm Bull 1979;27:3086–94.
3. Koo HN, et al. Inhibition of tumor necrosis factor-α-induced apoptosis by *Asparagus cochinchinensis* in Hep G2 cells. J Ethnopharmacol 2000;73:137–43.
4. Kim H, et al. Inhibitory effect of *Asparagus cochinchinensis* on tumor necrosis factor-α secretion from astrocytes. Int J Immunopharmacol 1998;20:153–62.

Chitosan

COMMON NAMES
Chitosan, kitosan, chitin

SCIENTIFIC NAME
Deacetylated chitin bipolymer

KEY WORDS
Kitosan, Fat Trapper

A. DONATO

CLINICAL SUMMARY

Chitin is extracted from the exoskeleton of crustaceans, including shrimp, lobster, and clams. A derivative of chitin, chitosan is used as an excipient in pharmaceutical formulations for weight loss, hyperlipidemia, and wound healing. Although it is said to bind fat in the gut, several clinical trials found no increase in fecal excretion of fat or weight loss compared with placebo. Chitosan may lower low-density lipoprotein (LDL) cholesterol, although an optimal dose and long-term efficacy are not yet established. Limited clinical data are available regarding efficacy for anemia of chronic renal failure, although chitosan did show benefit in a small randomized study. Reported adverse events include constipation and gastrointestinal distress. Patients allergic to shellfish should not use this supplement. Pregnant women should not consume owing to binding of fat-soluble vitamins (A, D, E, and K) and calcium.

CONSTITUENTS

Polymers: cationic polysaccharides, similar to cellulose, consisting of glucosamine and N-acetylated glucosamine linked by glycosidic bonds.[1]

WARNINGS

In April 2000, the Federal Trade Commission (FTC) issued a court order against Enforma Natural Products, Inc., manufacturers of Fat Trapper and Fat Trapper Plus, for making unsubstantiated and deceptive claims about the health benefits of these products. The order prohibits Enforma from using the name "Fat Trapper" and requires them to disclose in advertising that dieting and/or exercise are required to lose weight. The FTC report is available at <http://www.ftc.gov/opa/2002/07/enforma.htm>.

MECHANISM OF ACTION

The exact mechanism of action is not known. Following oral administration, chitosan forms a positively charged gel matrix in stomach acid able to bind bile acids, nitrogen metabolites, phospholipids, unesterified cholesterol, fat-soluble vitamins, and calcium. Increased elimination of fat has not been demonstrated. Topical application enhances wound healing by stimulation of granulation tissue. Possible mechanisms of action include formation of a gel-like fibronectin matrix that facilitates inward epithelial cell migration and the formation of heparin-chitosan complexes that ultimately activate growth factors that bind to stabilized heparin.[2–4]

USAGE

High cholesterol, weight loss, wound healing.

PHARMACOKINETICS

Not absorbed systemically.

ADVERSE REACTIONS

Reported: Constipation, flatulence, and gastrointestinal distress symptoms.[5]

DRUG INTERACTIONS

Vitamins A, D, E, and K: Chitosan may bind fat-soluble vitamins and decrease absorption.[1]

LABORATORY INTERACTIONS

Total cholesterol, LDL.

CONTRAINDICATIONS

Patients with shellfish allergy should not use chitosan. Pregnant women should not consume chitosan owing to a possible reduction in calcium and vitamin D absorption.

DOSAGE

Products vary in percentage of chitosan content.
Oral: 2 to 6 g chitosan administered in divided doses daily.

LITERATURE SUMMARY AND CRITIQUE

Pittler MH, et al. Randomized, double-blind trial of chitosan for body weight reduction. Eur J Clin Nutr 1999;53:379–81.
Placebo-controlled, randomized, intent-to-treat analysis of 30 overweight individuals who maintained their current diet with the addition of either 1,000 mg chitosan or placebo twice daily. Prospective evaluation on days 14 and 28 revealed no significant reduction in weight, body mass index, total cholesterol, triglycerides, or quality of life when compared with placebo. The authors state that the dosage may have been inadequate owing to variations between the manufacturer's labeled content of chitosan versus independent testing for chitosan content, 71% versus 42%, respectively. No serious adverse events were reported.

Jing SB, et al. Effect of chitosan on renal function in patients with chronic renal failure. J Pharm Pharmacol 1997;49:721–3.
Prospective trial of patients receiving thrice-weekly hemodialysis for longer than 13 months, randomized to receive placebo or 1,400 mg chitosan three times a day for 12 weeks. No significant adverse events were reported. A significant increase in hemoglobin was noted for the treatment arm pre- and post-treatment, 5.8 g/dL and 6.8 g/dL, respectively, compared with placebo pre- and post-treatment, 5.9 g/dL to 5.8 g/dL. A significant reduction in total cholesterol was also noted for chitosan pre- and post-treatment, 10.14 mM to 5.82 mM. The researchers also noted a reduction in uremic pruritus but no change in electrolytes. Although the authors conclude that chitosan is effective for improving anemia associated with hemodialysis and renal failure, it is not stated whether erythropoietin or blood transfusions were administered.

Stone CA, et al. Healing at skin graft donor sites dressed with chitosan. Br J Plast Surg 2000;53:601–6.
Prospective evaluation of 20 patients receiving skin grafts from either the thigh or the forearm. Patients served as their own control. Half of the donor site was dressed with conventional material and the other half with chitosan. Time to healing was the primary end point. No donor site infections or adverse reactions were noted. Chitosan had a similar healing time to Kaltostat control dressing, but a significantly shorter healing time compared with Mepitel control dressing. Observational data suggest that chitosan improved re-epithelialization, nerve, and capillary regeneration, but further research is needed.

Tai TS, et al. Effect of chitosan on plasma lipoprotein concentrations in type-two diabetic subjects with hypercholesterolemia. Diabetes Care 2000;23:1703–4.
Prospective evaluation of 33 patients with type 2 diabetes randomized to a placebo-controlled crossover evaluation of chitosan 450 mg three times daily. Chitosan groups

experienced a statistically significant reduction in total cholesterol and LDL concentrations. No significant changes in triglycerides, high-density lipoprotein, hemoglobin A_{1c}, or fasting glucose were noted.

Guerciolini R, et al. Comparative evaluation of fecal fat excretion induced by orlistat and chitosan. Obes Res 2001;9:364–7.

A prospective, randomized, open-label, crossover study comparing fecal fat excretion induced by either orlistat (Xenical) or chitosan (Fat Trapper). Patients received thrice-daily supplementation of 120 mg orlistat or 890 mg chitosan for 7 days. A total of 12 healthy patients were enrolled. Feces were collected for days 4 to 7 and analyzed for fat content. Baseline excretion of fat was 1.36 ± 0.45 g/d. Supplementation with chitosan did not significantly increase fat excretion (0.27 ± 1.02 g/d) compared with baseline. Orlistat significantly increased excretion compared with baseline (16.13 ± 7.27 g/d). The claim that chitosan binds fat and helps to eliminate it from the body was not substantiated in this trial.

REFERENCES

1. Koide SS. Chitin—chitosan: properties, benefits, and risks. Nutr Res 1998;18:1091–101.
2. Maezaki Y, et al. Hypocholesterolemic effect of chitosan in adult males. Biosci Biotech Biochem 1993;57:1439–44.
3. Stone CA, et al. Healing at skin graft donor sites dressed with chitosan. Br J Plast Surg 2000;53:601–6.
4. Guerciolini R, et al. Comparative evaluation of fecal fat excretion induced by orlistat and chitosan. Obes Res 2001;9:364–7.
5. Pittler MH, et al. Randomized, double-blind trial of chitosan for body weight reduction. Eur J Clin Nutr 1999;53:379–81.

Chromium

COMMON NAMES
Chromium III, chromium
picolinate, niacin-bound
chromium, chromium chloride

SCIENTIFIC NAME
Trivalent chromium

KEY WORD
Niacin-bound chromium

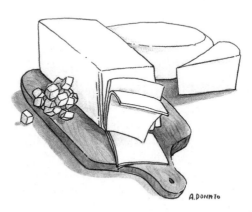

A.DONATO

CLINICAL SUMMARY

Chromium, a naturally occurring element obtained from food, is considered an essential trace element. Patients take this supplement for diabetes and weight loss and to improve muscle mass. Chromium is poorly absorbed following oral administration, although the salt forms (eg, chromium picolinate, niacin-bound chromium, and chromium chloride) appear to have better bioavailability. Chromium is believed necessary for glucose and lipid metabolism. It is involved with the activity of insulin. The role of chromium in weight loss or muscle mass improvement is unclear. Most clinical trials have inadequate sample size or other major design flaws. Chromium supplementation appears to be effective in lowering glucose and insulin levels in type 2 diabetic patients, although additional studies are required. Reported adverse effects for chromium include sporadic case reports of renal failure, rhabdomyolysis, liver damage, and dermatitis. Chromium requires transferrin to be absorbed and is renally eliminated; therefore, patients with renal and hepatic dysfunction should not be routinely supplemented. To date, there are no known drug interactions. Optimal dosage remains undetermined.

CONSTITUENTS

Trivalent chromium; salt formed with picolinic acid, niacin, amino acids, or chloride.

MECHANISM OF ACTION

Chromium is an essential trace element involved with glucose and lipid metabolism, circulating insulin levels, and the peripheral activity of insulin. In vitro and in vivo studies suggest that chromium potentiates the activity of insulin. This is thought to occur via enhanced intracellular tyrosine kinase activity that results from an interaction between chromium, low-molecular-weight chromium-binding substance, and activated cell surface insulin receptors.[1–3]

USAGE

Diabetes, strength and stamina, weight gain, weight loss.

PHARMACOKINETICS

Absorption: The bioavailability of trivalent chromium is relatively low, ranging from 0.4 to 2.5% of the orally administered dose. Chromium picolinate, trivalent chromium bound to picolinic acid, has a bioavailability of approximately 3%.

Distribution: Trivalent chromium binds to transferrin and albumin. It distributes throughout the body but appears to concentrate in the kidney, liver, soft tissue, and spleen. Chromium fits a three-compartment pharmacokinetic model.

Excretion: The biologic half-life for urinary excretion of chromium ranges from 0.97 to 1.51 days. Analysis of third-compartment excretion shows a terminal half-life ranging from 231 to 346 days. Unabsorbed chromium is excreted in the feces, whereas absorbed chromium is primarily eliminated renally.[4,5]

ADVERSE REACTIONS

Rare: Hepatic toxicity.

Case Reports: Two cases of renal failure; one case of acute generalized exanthematous pustulosis, characterized by erythematous lesions, fever, edema, leukocytosis, and eosinophilia; one report of rhabdomyolysis in a patient taking chromium picolinate in addition to other dietary supplements.[5–9]

DRUG INTERACTIONS

Sulfonylureas/Insulin: Theoretically, chromium may have additive hypoglycemic effects.

LABORATORY INTERACTIONS

Lower hemoglobin A_{1c}, blood glucose, serum insulin, total cholesterol. Small increase in high-density lipoprotein.

CONTRAINDICATIONS

Patients with liver or renal insufficiency may have increased susceptibility to adverse effects.[4]

DOSAGE

Oral: Supplements: 100 to 1,000 µg/d have been used.
Recommended Dietary Allowances:
Men
   19–50 years: 35 µg/d
   > 50 years: 25 µg/d
Women
   19–50 years: 25 µg/d
   > 50 years: 20 µg/d[4]

LITERATURE SUMMARY AND CRITIQUE

Several clinical trials have evaluated the efficacy of chromium supplementation for weight loss and muscle mass. Most trials had small sample sizes, and conclusive data are lacking. To date, no study supports the use of chromium supplements for weight loss or improvements in muscle mass.

Anderson RA, et al. Elevated intakes of supplemental chromium improve glucose and insulin variable in individuals with type 2 diabetes. Diabetes 1997;46:1786–91.
A prospective, double-blind, randomized evaluation of chromium supplementation in type 2 diabetic patients ages 35 to 65 years. A total of 180 patients were randomized to 4 months of placebo, 100 µg of chromium twice daily, or 500 µg of chromium twice daily. Primary outcomes measured were change in fasting glucose, hemoglobin A_{1c}, fasting insulin, and 2-hour postprandial glucose levels. The authors report that patients receiving 500 µg of chromium twice daily had statistically significant lower fasting glucose and 2-hour postprandial glucose levels at 2 and 4 months. Both treatment groups had significantly lower fasting and 2-hour postprandial insulin levels at 2 and 4 months, and hemoglobin A_{1c} levels at 4 months decreased by 1 to 2 g/dL in each treatment group. The authors did not publish actual baseline values, and the statistical methods used are questionable. No adverse events were reported. The long-term effect and withdrawal of chromium supplementation are not addressed.

REFERENCES

1. Porter DJ, Raymond LW, Anastasio GD. Chromium: friend or foe? Arch Fam Med 1999;8: 386–90.
2. Vincent JB. The biochemistry of chromium. J Nutr 2000;130:715–8.
3. Cefalu WT, et al. Oral chromium picolinate improves carbohydrate and lipid metabolism and enhances skeletal muscle Glut-4 translocation in obese, hyperinsulinemic (JCR-LA corpulent) rats. J Nutr 2002;132:1107–14.
4. Dietary Reference Intakes for vitamin A, vitamin K, arsenic, boron, chromium, copper, iodine, iron, manganese, molybdenum, nickel, silicon, vanadium, and zinc. Washington (DC): National Academy Press; 2001.
5. Jeejeebhoy KN. The role of chromium in nutrition and therapeutics and as a potential toxin. Nutr Rev 1999;57:329–35.

6. Young PC, et al. Acute generalized exanthematous pustulosis induced by chromium picolinate. J Am Acad Dermatol 1999; 41:820–3.
7. Wasser WG, Feldman NS, D'Agati VD. Chronic renal failure after ingestion of over-the-counter chromium picolinate. Ann Intern Med 1997;126:410.
8. Martin WR, Fuller RE. Suspected chromium picolinate-induced rhabdomyolysis. Pharmacotherapy 1998;18:860–2.
9. Cerulli J, et al. Chromium picolinate toxicity. Ann Pharmacother 1998;32:428–31.

Chrysanthemum

COMMON NAMES
Chrysanthemum sinense,
Chrysanthemum japonense,
mum, ju hua, chu hua

SCIENTIFIC NAME
Chrysanthemum morifolium

KEY WORDS
Mum, ju hua

A.DONATO

CLINICAL SUMMARY

Derived from the flower and aerial parts of the plant. Chrysanthemum is used frequently in traditional Chinese medicine. Historically applied to treat hypertension, angina, and fevers. No clinical studies evaluating efficacy in humans have been performed. Animal data suggest possible anti-inflammatory and antipyretic activity. Hypersensitivity and photosensitivity reactions are documented. Patients allergic to ragweed should avoid this herb. Chrysanthemum is one of the eight components of PC-SPES.

CONSTITUENTS

Essential oils: bornol; alkaloids: stachydrine; sesquiterpenes: alantolactone; glycosides: acacetin-7-rhamnoglucose, cosmosin, acacetin-7-glucose, diosmetin-7-glucose; other compounds: adenine, choline, camphor.[1]

WARNINGS

May cause photosensitivity.

MECHANISM OF ACTION

The flower increases coronary vasodilatation and coronary blood flow but has little effect on cardiac contractility or oxygen consumption. It reduces the capillary permeability induced by histamine and operates as an antibacterial and antipyretic agent. Some studies indicate that chrysanthemum may have cytotoxic acitivities.[1-3]

USAGE

Angina, common cold, fever, hypertension.

ADVERSE REACTIONS

Reported: Contact dermatitis, hypersensitivity reaction, photosensitivity.[4,5]

DRUG INTERACTIONS

Antihypertensives: Theoretically, chrysanthemum may have an additive hypotensive effect.

LABORATORY INTERACTIONS

Blood pressure.

CONTRAINDICATIONS

Patients with allergy to ragweed should avoid this herb.

DOSAGE

Oral: No standardized dose.
Dried flower tops are a part of traditional Chinese medicine. *Water extract:* 25 mL three times a day.

LITERATURE SUMMARY AND CRITIQUE

No clinical studies have been performed with chrysanthemum on humans.

REFERENCES

1. Huang KC. The pharmacology of Chinese herbs. 2nd ed. New York: CRC Press; 1999.
2. Lee JR, et al. A new guaianolide as apoptosis inhibitor from *Chrysanthemum boreale*. Planta Med 2001;67:585–7.
3. Sharma SC, Tanwar RC, Kaur S. Contact dermatitis from chrysanthemums in India. Contact Dermatitis 1989;21:69–71.
4. Kuno Y, Kawabe Y, Sakakibara S. Allergic contact dermatitis associated with photosensitivity, from alantolactone in a chrysanthemum farmer. Contact Dermatitis 1999;40:224–5.
5. Ukiya M, et al. Constitutents of Compositae plants III. Anti-tumor promoting effects and cytotoxic activity against human cancer cell lines of triterpene diols and triols from edible chrysanthemum flowers. Cancer Lett 2002;177:7–12.

Coenzyme Q_{10}

COMMON NAMES
Ubiquinone, ubidecarenone, ubiquinol, CoQ, CoQ_{10}

SCIENTIFIC NAME
2,3-Dimethoxy-5-methyl-6-decaprenyl benzoquinone

KEY WORDS
CoQ_{10}, ubiquinone

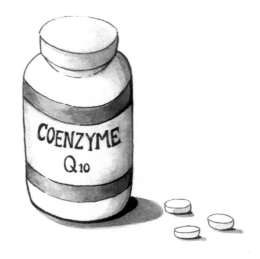

CLINICAL SUMMARY
Synthesized endogenously by mammals. Patients use this supplement to treat cancer, congestive heart failure, arrhythmias, Parkinson's disease, and hypertension and to prevent anthracycline cardiomyopathy. Coenzyme Q_{10} (CoQ_{10}) is essential for the production of adenosine triphosphate (ATP). It also has antioxidant membrane-stabilizing properties, prevents mitochondrial deformity, and maintains myocardial calcium ion channels during ischemic insults. CoQ_{10} has low bioavailability following oral administration and distributes widely throughout the body. Metabolites are excreted via the biliary tree. Data on effects on congestive heart failure do not concur. Case reports describing efficacy for breast cancer exist in the literature, but there are no controlled clinical trials. Use of CoQ_{10} to prevent anthracycline-induced cardiomyopathy requires additional research. A recent study also shows that CoQ_{10} may be effective in early Parkinson's disease. No significant adverse effects are reported. CoQ_{10} is structurally similar to vitamin K and therefore may antagonize the effects of warfarin. It may antagonize the effects of chemotherapy via antioxidant activity. Ubiquinone may reduce the effect of radiation therapy. UbiQgel, a CoQ_{10} formulation, is a US Food and Drug Administration (FDA)-approved orphan drug under study in mitochondrial diseases (eg, MELAS [mitochondrial encephalopathy, lactic acidosis, and stroke-like episodes] syndrome, Kearns-Sayre syndrome). Additional research is required to establish the role of CoQ_{10} supplementation.

MECHANISM OF ACTION

CoQ_{10}, known to have antioxidant and membrane-stabilizing properties, is the only endogenously produced lipid with a redox function in mammals. All cells are capable of synthesizing CoQ_{10}, and no redistribution between organs occurs through the blood. CoQ_{10} is necessary for ATP production. Its role as a mobile electron carrier in the mitochondrial electron transfer process of respiration and coupled phosphorylation is well established. It has a direct regulatory role on succinyl and reduced nicotinamide adenine dinucleotide dehydrogenases. Like vitamin E, CoQ_{10} is a lipid-soluble antioxidant. Like vitamin C, reduced CoQ_{10} effectively regenerates α-tocopherol from the α-tocopheroxyl radical. CoQ_{10} has been demonstrated to scavenge free radicals produced by lipid peroxidation and prevent mitochondrial deformity during episodes of ischemia, and it may have some ability to maintain the integrity of myocardial calcium ion channels during ischemic insults. Its major mechanism of action is protection of ischemic tissue from reperfusion damage. CoQ_{10} appears to be capable of stabilizing cellular membranes and preventing depletion of metabolites required for ATP resynthesis.[1,2,6]

USAGE

Angina, cancer prevention, cardiovascular disease, chemotherapy side effects, congestive heart failure, human immunodeficiency virus (HIV) and acquired immune deficiency syndrome (AIDS), hypertension, infertility, migraine prophylaxis, Parkinson's disease, periodontal disease, strength and stamina.

PHARMACOKINETICS

Absorption: Uptake of dietary CoQ_{10} in the liver does not affect the synthesis of endogenous CoQ_{10}, which supports the notion that CoQ_{10} does not exert any feedback inhibition on its own biosynthesis. Animal studies demonstrate a bioavailability of 2 to 3%. With high doses of dietary CoQ_{10}, the blood concentration in both rats and humans can be increased about two- to fourfold. Following ingestion of 100 mg of CoQ_{10}, peak plasma levels occur between 5 and 10 hours. T_{max} is approximately 6.5 hours, which indicates slow absorption from the gastrointestinal tract, possibly owing to the high molecular weight and low water solubility of CoQ_{10}.

Distribution: The mean plasma levels after a single 100 mg oral dose of CoQ_{10} in human subjects is 1.004 ± 0.37 mg/mL. In humans, CoQ_{10} is found in relatively high concentrations in the heart, liver, kidney, and pancreas. The plasma half-life of CoQ_{10} in different tissues varies between 49 and 125 hours. Following absorption from the gastrointestinal tract, CoQ_{10} is taken up by chylomicrons. The major portion of an exogenous dose of CoQ_{10} is deposited in the liver and packaged into very-low-density lipoprotein.

Metabolism/Excretion: It is assumed that metabolism and excretion of exogenous CoQ_{10} are analogous to endogenously produced CoQ_{10}. The excretion of CoQ_{10} is predominantly via the biliary tract.[1,2]

ADVERSE REACTIONS
Infrequent: Nausea, diarrhea, and appetite suppression.[3]

DRUG INTERACTIONS
3-Hydroxy-3-methylglutaryl (HMG)-CoA Reductase Inhibitors: Endogenous levels of CoQ$_{10}$ may be reduced by lovastatin, atorvastatin, and simvastatin. The HMG-CoA reductase enzyme is responsible for catalyzing the conversion of acetyl CoA to cholesterol and synthesis of CoQ$_{10}$.
Warfarin: CoQ$_{10}$ may antagonize the effects of warfarin. CoQ$_{10}$ is structurally similar to vitamin K.
Chemotherapy: Theoretically, CoQ$_{10}$ may decrease the efficacy of chemotherapy owing to antioxidant activity.[4,5]

CONTRAINDICATIONS
Ubiquinone intake may reduce the effect of radiation therapy.[6]

DOSAGE
Oral: Dosages used in clinical trials: *Chronic heart failure:* 100 to 200 mg/d; *Hypertension:* 100 to 200 mg/d; *HIV/AIDS:* 100 mg/d; *Breast cancer:* 90 to 390 mg/d; *Periodontal disease:* 50 mg/d; *Early Parkinson's disease:* 1,200 mg/d.[7]

LITERATURE SUMMARY AND CRITIQUE
Shults CW, et al. Effects of coenzyme Q$_{10}$ in early Parkinson disease. Arch Neurol 2002;59:1541–50.
A multicenter, randomized, placebo-controlled, double-blind, dose-ranging trial in 80 otherwise healthy patients with early Parkinson's disease. Patients received placebo or CoQ$_{10}$ at dosages of 300, 600, or 1,200 mg daily, split into four doses. Recent or concurrent use of antioxidants was not permitted. Patients were followed for up to 16 months or until treatment with levodopa was required. The primary outcome measured was the Unified Parkinson Disease Rating Scale (UPDRS); the study was projected to have 73% power to detect a difference of 6 points in the total UPDRS score. Mean total change was +11.99 in the placebo group and +6.69 in the 1,200 mg/d group ($p = .4$). Time until treatment with levodopa was not affected by treatment. The side-effect profile for all doses of CoQ$_{10}$ was mild and similar to that for placebo. These results must be confirmed with larger studies, but this study does suggest that dosages of < 200 mg/d in previous trials may have been inadequate.

Khatta M. The effect of coenzyme Q$_{10}$ in patients with congestive heart failure. Ann Intern Med 2000;132:636–40.
A prospective, randomized, double-blind, placebo-controlled trial evaluating CoQ$_{10}$ supplementation in patients with New York Heart Association Class III or IV heart failure.

Patients were randomized to receive 200 mg/d of CoQ_{10} ($n = 23$) or placebo ($n = 23$) for 6 months. The study was designed to detect a 2.8 mL/kg/min difference in peak oxygen consumption. Other outcomes measured were changes in left ventricular ejection fraction and exercise duration. No adverse events were reported. No significant improvement was noted in patients supplemented with 200 mg/d of CoQ_{10}.

Watson PS, et al. Lack of effect of coenzyme Q on left ventricular function in patients with congestive heart failure. J Am Coll Cardiol 1999;33:1549–52.
A prospective, randomized, double-blind, crossover design study evaluating 99 mg/d CoQ_{10} on 30 patients with chronic heart failure and left ventricular dysfunction. Patients received either placebo or 33 mg CoQ_{10} thrice daily for 3 weeks followed by a 1-week washout period. Treatment groups crossed over to alternate treatment for 12 weeks. Transthoracic echocardiogram, Swan-Ganz catheterization, and quality of life assessments were conducted prior to and following each treatment period. No adverse events were reported during the study. No significant improvements were documented following 12 weeks of supplementation with CoQ_{10}. However, as Shults and colleagues (2002) suggest, doses < 200 mg/d may be inadequate.

Lockwood K, et al. Partial and complete regression of breast cancer in patients in relation to dosage of coenzyme Q_{10}. Biochem Biophys Res Commun 1994;199:1504–8.
A case report series, originally presented at the Eighth International Symposium on the Biomedical and Clinical Aspects of Coenzyme Q, November 1993, in Stockholm. Lockwood supplemented 32 breast cancer patients with 90 mg of CoQ_{10}, linolenic acid, fatty acids, beta-carotene, vitamin C, vitamin E, and selenium. A trial is reported in which 32 breast cancer patients were supplemented with 90 mg/d CoQ_{10}, resulting in 6 complete remissions. However, the results were not statistically significant because CoQ_{10} levels were similar to a comparison group. The authors present two case reports of patients with intraductal carcinoma, both status postsurgical resection, with recurrent local disease who went into remission with CoQ_{10} doses up to 390 mg/d. No additional data from the trial are provided. The authors suggest CoQ_{10} as a viable treatment alternative for breast cancer, although clinical trials are lacking.

Lockwood K, et al. Progress on therapy of breast cancer with vitamin Q_{10} and the regression of metastasis. Biochem Biophys Res Commun 1995;212:172–7.
Additional case report series describing complete remission of three patients with metastatic intraductal carcinoma treated with 390 mg/d of CoQ_{10}.

REFERENCES

1. Greenberg S, Frishman WH. Coenzyme Q_{10}: a new drug for cardiovascular disease. J Clin Pharmacol 1990;30:596–608.
2. Dallner G, Sindelar PJ. Regulation of ubiquinone metabolism. Free Radic Biol Med 2000;29:285–94.
3. Fuke C, Krikorian SA, Couris RR. Coenzyme Q_{10}: a review of essential functions and clinical trials. US Pharmacist 2000;25:28–41.

4. Folkers K, et al. Lovastatin decreases coenzyme Q levels in humans. Proc Natl Acad Sci U S A 1990;87:8931–4.
5. Pronsky ZM. Power's and Moore's food-medication interactions. 11th ed. Pottstown (PA): Food Medication Interactions; 2000.
6. Lund E, el al. Effect of radiation therapy on small-cell lung cancer is reduced by ubiquinone intake. Folia Microbiol 1998;4:505–6.
7. Shults CW, et al. Effects of coenzyme Q$_{10}$ in early Parkinson disease. Arch Neurol 2002;59: 1541–50.
8. Rozen TD, et al. Open label trial of coenzyme Q$_{10}$ as a migraine preventive. Cephalalgia 2002;22:137–41.
9. Lister RE. An open, pilot study to evaulate the potential benefits of coenzyme Q$_{10}$ combined with ginkgo biloba extract in fibromyalgia syndrome. J Int Med Res 2002;30:195–9.

Comfrey

COMMON NAMES
Slippery root, knitbone, blackwort, bruisewort

SCIENTIFIC NAME
Symphytum officinale

KEY WORD
Symphytum officinale

CLINICAL SUMMARY
Derived from the root, leaves, and branches. In June 2001, the US Food and Drug Administration (FDA) asked all manufacturers to remove products containing comfrey from the market. No clinical studies support the use of oral comfrey, and there is an extensive literature concerning hepatotoxicity. The risk of systemic absorption following the use of topical comfrey preparations is unknown.

CONSTITUENTS
Alkaloids (pyrrolizidine type): symphytine, symlandine, echimidine, intermidine, lycopsamine, myoscorpine, acetyllycopsamine, acetylintermidine, lasiocarpine, heliosupine, viridiflorine, echiumine; carbohydrates: gums (arabinose, glucuronic acid, mannose, rhamnose, xylose), glucose, fructose; tannins (pyrocatechol type): 2.4%; triterpenes: sitosterol and stigmasterol (phytosterols), steroidal saponins, isobauerenol; other constituents: allantoin, caffeic acid, carotene, chlorogenic acid, choline, lithospermic acid, rosmarinic acid, silicic acid.[1]

WARNINGS

On July 6, 2001, the FDA, along with the Center for Food Safety and Applied Nutrition, advised all dietary supplement manufacturers to remove products containing comfrey from the market. (Full text is available at <http://www.cfsan.fda.gov/~dms/dspltr06.html>.) Comfrey contains unsaturated pyrrolizidine alkaloids, which are hepatotoxic and hepatocarcinogenic.[2–4]

MECHANISM OF ACTION

Whatever therapeutic value comfrey may possess is attributed to its content of allantoin, a cell proliferant, and rosmarinic acid, an anti-inflammatory agent and inhibitor of microvascular pulmonary injury.[5]

USAGE

Bronchitis, cancer treatment, inflammation, peptic ulcers, rheumatoid arthritis, wound healing.

ADVERSE REACTIONS

Reported: Hepatotoxicity.

DOSAGE

Oral: Not recommended owing to hepatotoxicity.
Topical: 5 to 20% ointments applied daily. Not to be used for more than 10 days.[6]

LITERATURE SUMMARY AND CRITIQUE

There are no clinical studies that document any positive effects of comfrey, but many studies have shown hepatotoxicity.[7–12]

REFERENCES

1. Newall C, et al. Herbal medicines: a guide for health-care professionals. London: Pharmaceutical Press; 1996.
2. Schulz V, et al. Rational phytotherapy: a physician's guide to the use of herbs and related remedies. 3rd ed. Berlin: Springer; 1998.
3. Awang DVC. Comfrey. Can Pharm J 1987;120:101–4.
4. FDA advises dietary supplement manufacturers to remove products containing comfrey from the market [talk paper online] 2001 Jul 6. http://www.cfsan.fda.gov/~dms/ dspltr06.html (accessed November 2, 2001).
5. Tyler V. Herbs of choice: the therapeutic use of phytomedicinals. Binghamton (NY): Pharmaceutical Products Press; 1994.
6. Foster S, et al. Tyler's honest herbal: a sensible guide to the use of herbs and related remedies. 3rd ed. Binghamton: Haworth Herbal Press; 1993.
7. Ridker PN, McDermott WV. Hepatotoxicity due to comfrey herb tea. Am J Med 1989;87:701.

8. Ridker PN, McDermott WV. Comfrey herb tea and hepatic veno-occlusive disease. Lancet 1989;i:657–8.

9. Ridker PM, et al. Hepatic veno-occlusive disease associated with the consumption of pyrrolizidine-containing dietary supplements. Gastroenterology 1985;88:1050–4.

10. Yeong ML, et al. Hepatic veno-occlusive disease associated with comfrey ingestion. J Gastroenterol Hepatol 1990;5:211–4.

11. Weston CFM, et al. Veno-occlusive disease of the liver secondary to ingestion of comfrey. BMJ 1987;295:183.

12. Roitman JN. Comfrey and liver damage [letter]. Lancet 1981;i:944.

Cordyceps

COMMON NAMES
Vegetable caterpillar, Chinese caterpillar fungus, dong chong xia cao, semitake, hsia ts'ao tung ch'ung, yarsha gumba

SCIENTIFIC NAMES
Cordyceps sinensis, Sphaeria sinensis

KEY WORDS
Sphaeria sinensis, dong chong xia cao

A.DONATO

CLINICAL SUMMARY
Cordyceps includes fungus that grows on caterpillar larvae, *Hepialus armoricanus oberthuer*. Both are contained in the product and both are consumed. Cordyceps is used for a wide range of conditions including fatigue, sexual dysfunction, and coughs and as an adaptogen or immune stimulant. In addition to anecdotal data regarding efficacy, small clinical trials have been performed, but only review articles are available in English. No adverse effects have been reported. Although no known drug interactions exist, blood glucose should be monitored in diabetics using cordyceps owing to possible hypoglycemic effect. In addition, animal studies show proliferation of progenitor red blood cells; therefore, cordyceps should not be used by those with myelogenous-type cancers.

CONSTITUENTS
Protein: amino acids; sterol: ergosterol; polyamines: spermine, spermidine, putrescine, 1,3-diaminopropane; fatty acids: oleic, linoleic, palmitic, stearic; nucleosides: 3-deoxyadenosine (cordycepin); saccharides: D-mannitol, galactomannin.[1]

MECHANISM OF ACTION

Cordyceps stimulates the number of T helper cells, prolongs the survival of lymphocytes, increases tumor necrosis factor-α (TNF-α) and interleukin-1, and increases the activity of natural killer cells in cultured rat Kupffer's cells. Enhanced proliferation of erythroid progenitor cell in the bone marrow of mice has also been shown. One study suggested that cordyceps can stimulate progesterone production in animal cells. Another study shows that cordyceps may be effective against tumor cells by down-regulating major histocompatibility complex (MHC) class II antigen expression. In addition, anecdotal information suggests reduction of cyclosporine and aminoglycoside-induced renal toxicity, although the mechanism of action is not known.[2–7]

USAGE

Bronchitis, chronic obstructive pulmonary disorders, cough, fatigue, hepatitis, high cholesterol, immunostimulation, sexual dysfunction, strength and stamina.

ADVERSE REACTIONS

None reported.

DRUG INTERACTIONS

Hypoglycemics/Insulin: Cordyceps may have an additive hypoglycemic effect. Monitor blood glucose.[1]

DOSAGE

Oral: 3 to 5 g/d.

LITERATURE SUMMARY AND CRITIQUE

Zhu JS, Halpern GM, Jones K. The scientific rediscovery of a precious ancient Chinese herbal regime: *Cordyceps sinensis*. Parts I and II. J Altern Complement Med 1998;4: 289–303 and 1998;4:429–57.

A series of studies, which were not always controlled, claimed to show the following:

*   Elderly patients with asthenia had significant improvements in fatigue, dizziness, and intolerance to cold, tinnitus, frequent nocturia, hyposexuality, and amnesia at a dose of 3 g.
*   Improved quality of life in a study of 64 chronic heart failure patients at a dose of 3 to 4 g of cordyceps.
*   Patients with chronic obstructive pulmonary disease had improvements in their pulmonary symptoms, appetite, and energy.
*   Several studies showed significant improvements in all respiratory symptoms at a dose range of 3 to 4.5 g of cordyceps. Improvements were in shortness of breath, cough and expectoration, and sleep.

- Improved renal function in 30 patients with chronic renal failure. Improvements were seen in creatinine clearance, blood urea nitrogen, serum creatinine, and reduction in urinary protein.
- In patients with lung cancer, cordyceps administered at 2 to 3 g resulted in more patients completing radiation and chemotherapy compared with the control group.

Xu F, et al. Amelioration of cyclosporin nephrotoxicity by *Cordyceps sinensis* in kidney-transplant recipients. Nephrol Dial Transplant 1995;10:142–3.
A brief letter summarizing results of a randomized, placebo-controlled study that found that 3 g of cordyceps daily has a protective effect against cyclosporine-induced nephrotoxicity. Sixty-nine kidney transplant patients with at least 3 months of stable renal function following transplant were given cyclosporine 5 mg/kg/d and received either 3 g of cordyceps or placebo for 15 days. It is not mentioned why cyclosporine was initiated in these patients as it appears that they were not previously taking the medication. Serum creatinine and blood urea nitrogen were statistically lower for patients receiving cordyceps compared with the placebo group. It must be noted that the cyclosporine levels appeared to be lower in the cordyceps group, but this was not statistically significant. Cordyceps appears to reduce cyclosporine-induced renal toxicity, but larger trials are needed.

REFERENCES

1. Huang KC. The pharmacology of Chinese herbs. 2nd ed. Boca Raton (FL): CRC Press; 1999.
2. Zhu JS, Halpern GM, Jones K. The scientific rediscovery of a precious ancient Chinese herbal regime: *Cordyceps sinensis,* part I. J Altern Complement Med 1998;4:289–303.
3. Zhu JS, Halpern GM, Jones K. The scientific rediscovery of a precious ancient Chinese herbal regime: *Cordyceps sinensis,* part II. J Altern Complement Med 1998;4:429–57.
4. Xu F, et al. Amelioration of cyclosporin nephrotoxicity by *Cordyceps sinensis* in kidney-transplant recipients. Nephrol Dial Transplant 1995;10:142–3.
5. Huang B, et al. *Cordyceps sinensis* and its fractions stimulate MA-10 mouse Leydig tumor cell steroidogenesis. J Androl 2001;22:831–7.
6. Nakamura K, et al. Inhibitory effect of *Cordyceps sinensis* on spontaneous liver metastasis of Lewis lung carcinoma and B16 melanoma cells in syngeneic mice. Jpn J Pharmacol 1999;79:335–41.
7. Hiu JH, et al. *Cordyceps sinensis* increases the expression of major histocompatibility complex class II antigens in human hepatoma cell line HA22T/VGH cells. Am J Chin Med 1998; 26:59–70.

Coriolus versicolor

COMMON NAMES
PSK, PSP, *Trametes versicolor*

SCIENTIFIC NAMES
Coriolus versicolor, Trametes versicolor, Polyporus versicolor

KEY WORDS
PSK, *Trametes versicolor*, yun zhi

CLINICAL SUMMARY
Water extract of the fruiting body and mycelium of the mushroom. Patients use *Coriolus versicolor* or its constituents polysaccharide K (PSK) and polysaccharide P (PSP) to stimulate the immune system, reduce chemotherapy toxicity, and increase the effectiveness of chemotherapy or radiotherapy for cancer. The β-glucans PSK and PSP show antiproliferative activity in animal models and immunostimulant activity in both animal and human studies. PSK extracts are available for clinical use in Japan. Toxicity is low; only darkening of the fingernails is reported. When used in conjunction with chemotherapy, PSK appears to improve survival rates in gastric and colorectal cancer patients after surgery. Outcomes in breast cancer, hepatocellular carcinoma (HCC), and leukemia are less impressive. No clinical trials evaluating PSP are published in the peer-reviewed literature.

CONSTITUENTS
Proteoglycans: PSK, a β-1,4-glucan (isolated from the CM-101 strain), PSP (isolated from the COV-1 strain).

MECHANISM OF ACTION
Coriolus versicolor is thought to be a biologic response modifier. The proteoglycan constituents (PSK and PSP, discussed below) are thought to be responsible for its immunostimulant and anticancer activities.

PSK is thought to enhance both humoral and cellular immunity. It inhibits tumor growth in vitro and in several allogeneic and syngeneic tumor models in mice and rats.

Animal models show additive effects and prevention of side effects when PSK is given with chemotherapeutic agents, including 5-fluorouracil (5-FU), doxorubicin, cyclophosphamide, tegafur, cisplatin, and mitomycin C (MMC). Recovery of depressed humoral immunity is observed when PSK is combined with radiotherapy in mice. Animal studies support the contention that PSK induces T killer cell activity and restores depressed immune parameters while inhibiting immunosuppressive substances. In vitro, PSK induces cytokine expression in human peripheral blood mononuclear cells. Tumor necrosis factor-α and interleukin-8 gene expression are significantly induced after PSK administration in healthy volunteers and gastric cancer patients, although individual response varies. In a number of animal models, oral PSK increases survival and/or suppresses the formation and metastasis of carcinogen- or radiation-induced tumors. PSK also inhibits postsurgical growth of recurrent or metastatic tumor cells in animal models, possibly through inhibition of tumor cell migration, intravasation, attachment to endothelial cells, and growth. Several animal studies report synergism between PSK and biologic therapies, including a concanavalin A–bound L1210 vaccine and the immunoglobulin G2a monoclonal antibody against human colon cancer cells.

PSP induces cytokine production and T-cell proliferation and prevents cyclophosphamide immune depression in animal models. Peritoneal macrophages isolated from mice fed PSP show increased production of reactive nitrogen intermediates, superoxide anions, and tumor necrosis factor. No in vitro cytotoxicity is seen, but PSP inhibits proliferation of several tumor cell lines and enhances the effects of radiation against rat glioma cells in vitro and in vivo. In animal studies, oral administration inhibits growth of lung adenocarcinoma; intraperitoneal administration inhibits Lewis Lung carcinoma (LLC) and sarcoma 180 growth. A small trial of breast cancer patients treated with PSP shows maintenance of peripheral white blood counts and platelet counts after three cycles of chemotherapy. In vitro, PSP inhibits the interaction between human immunodeficiency virus (HIV)-1 glycoprotein p120 and CD4 receptor, HIV-1 transcriptase activity, and glycohydrolase enzyme activity associated with viral glycosylation, but no clinical trials support its use as an antiviral agent in vivo. PSP also shows analgesic activity in mouse models.[1–5]

USAGE

Cancer prevention, cancer treatment, chemotherapy side effects, hepatitis, herpes, immunostimulation, infections, radiation therapy side effects, strength and stamina.

PHARMACOKINETICS

Absorption: Animal studies with radiolabeled PSK show that it is partially decomposed to small molecular products in the digestive tract. The full molecular spectrum of labeled PSK is absorbed within 24 hours following oral administration in mice. Peak plasma levels of low-molecular-weight substances occur at 0.5 to 1 hour in rats and 1 to 2 hours in rabbits, whereas molecules the size of PSK appear in serum after 4, 10, and 24 hours.

Distribution: Radiolabeled PSK or its metabolites are detected in the digestive tract, bone marrow, salivary glands, thymus, adrenal gland, brain, liver, spleen, pancreas, and tumor tissue in sarcoma-bearing mice. Activity remains high longest in the liver and bone marrow.

Excretion: Approximately 70% of radiolabeled PSK is excreted in expired air, 20% in feces, 10% in urine, and 0.8% in bile. Approximately 86% is excreted within 24 hours.

ADVERSE REACTIONS

Infrequent: Darkening of the fingernails, coughing during administration of powder drug.

DRUG INTERACTIONS

Acetaminophen: Theoretically, *Coriolus versicolor* may protect against acetaminophen-induced liver injury.

LABORATORY INTERACTIONS

None known.

DOSAGE

Oral: Up to 15 g/d has been taken long term without noticeable adverse effects.

LITERATURE SUMMARY AND CRITIQUE

Niimoto M, et al. Postoperative adjuvant immunochemotherapy with mitomycin C, futraful, and PSK for gastric cancer. An analysis of data on 579 patients followed for five years. Jpn J Surg 1988;18:681–6.
A randomized, controlled trial of adjuvant chemotherapy with or without PSK in 579 patients after curative gastrectomy. MMC 20 mg was administered on the day of surgery, plus an additional 10 mg the following day for special cases. One to 2 weeks postsurgery, group A received 3 g PSK, group B 600 to 800 mg futraful (FT), and group C both PSK and FT for 1 year. Patient characteristics were comparable between groups but were not noted. Five-year survival rates were 64.1% for group A, 58.5% for group B, and 71.7% in group C. The difference between groups B and C was significant ($p < .01$) but not between A and C. This suggests that PSK enhances the effects of adjuvant chemotherapy after gastrectomy.

Nakazato H, et al. Efficacy of immunochemotherapy as adjuvant treatment after curative resection of gastric cancer. Lancet 1994;343:1122–6.
A randomized, controlled, multicenter evaluation of chemotherapy with or without PSK in 262 patients after curative gastrectomy. Chemotherapy consisted of intravenous MMC on postoperative days 1 and 7 plus 150 mg/d of oral 5-FU. The PSK group received 3 g/d

of oral PSK for 4 weeks alternating with 4 weeks of 5-FU, whereas control patients received only 5-FU alternated with 4 weeks without treatment. Ten courses were given to both groups. PSK patients experienced a greater 5-year disease-free rate (70.7% versus 59.4%) and 5-year survival rate (73% versus 60%) than the control group. Because eligibility criteria included a positive purified protein derivative test, this trial represents only the benefits of PSK in patients with a preserved immune response.

Mitomi T, et al. Randomized, controlled study on adjuvant immunochemotherapy with PSK in curatively resected colorectal cancer. The Cooperative Study Group of Surgical Adjuvant Immunochemotherapy for Cancer of Colon and Rectum (Kanagawa). Dis Colon Rectum 1992;35:123–30.
A multicenter trial of MMC and 5-FU with or without PSK in 448 patients with curatively resected colon cancer. Patients received 6 mg/m^2 MMC on the day of and day after surgery and 200 mg/d of oral 5-FU for 6 months either with ($n = 221$) or without ($n = 227$) 3 g/d of oral PSK for over 3 years. Demographics and clinical characteristics were similar between groups, except that PSK patients had significantly larger rectal tumors than controls. Patients were followed up for 3 to 5 years. Both disease-free and overall survival curves were significantly better for patients receiving PSK ($p = .013$). The 3-year survival estimate for PSK patients was 85.8% compared with 79.2% for controls.

Torisu M, et al. Significant prolongation of disease-free period gained by oral polysaccharide K (PSK) administration after curative surgical operation of colorectal cancer. Cancer Immunol Immunother 1990;31:261–8.
A randomized, double-blind evaluation of PSK ($n = 56$) versus placebo ($n = 55$) in patients after curative surgery of colorectal cancer. Starting 10 to 15 days after surgery, patients received 3 g/d PSK or placebo for 2 months and then 2 g/d until 24 months and 1 g/d thereafter. Clinical characteristics were similar between groups, although tumor size was not addressed. Overall and disease-free survival were significantly higher in the PSK group compared with the placebo group ($p < .05$, both). Polymorphonuclear monocytes from patients receiving PSK showed increased phagocytic and locomotive activity. Other measured immune parameters, such as skin reactivity, lymphocyte counts, and immunoglobulin levels, did not differ significantly between groups. Survival and disease-free survival rates were generally worse than in other trials combining PSK and chemotherapeutic agents, indicating that PSK alone is not as effective after curative surgery of colorectal cancer.

Iino Y, et al. Immunochemotherapies versus chemotherapy as adjuvant treatment after curative resection of operable breast cancer. Anticancer Res 1995;15:2907–11.
A randomized evaluation of combination chemotherapy (5-FU, cyclophosphamide, MMC, and predonisolone [FEMP]) with 3 g/d of PSK or 150 mg/d of levamisole (LMS) in 227 patients with operable breast cancer with vascular invasion in the tumor and/or in the metastatic lymph node. Each treatment, FEMP, FEMP + LMS, or FEMP + PSK, lasted 28 days and was carried out at 6-month intervals for 5 years. Patients receiving FEMP + PSK had a slightly better survival curve than the FEMP group ($p = .0706$),

although differences in overall survival and disease-free survival were not significant between the three groups. Ten-year disease-free survival rates were 64.6% in the FEMP, 70.7% in the FEMP + LMS, and 74.1% in the FEMP + PSK groups.

Ohno R, et al. A randomized trial of chemoimmunotherapy of acute nonlymphocytic leukemia in adults using a protein-bound polysaccharide preparation. Cancer Immunol Immunother 1984;18:149–54.
A randomized, controlled trial of maintenance chemotherapy with ($n = 36$) or without ($n = 31$) PSK in 17 patients with acute nonlymphocytic leukemia who had achieved complete remission and had received consolidation therapy. Maintenance chemotherapy was given alternately every fifth week for 2 years. Three grams of PSK were given every day indefinitely except during maintenance chemotherapy. Remission duration and survival length analyzed 6 months after the last entry showed a borderline beneficial effect of PSK ($p = .089$), but analysis at 24 months showed no significant difference.

Suto T, et al. Clinical study of biological response modifiers as maintenance therapy for hepatocellular carcinoma. Cancer Chemother Pharmacol 1994;33:145–8.
A randomized, controlled trial comparing 100 to 150 mg of 5-FU with or without PSK, lentinan, or OK-432 as a maintenance therapy for HCC after treatment with percutaneous ethanol injection (PEI), transcatheter arterial embolization, or arterial infusion of antitumor agents. All patients received 100 to 150 mg/d of 5-FU. Group I ($n = 15$) was given 3 g/d of oral PSK for 7 days every 2 weeks, group II ($n = 15$) received an intravenous injection of 2 mg of lentinan once a week; group III ($n = 12$) received OK-432 once a week, and group IV ($n = 16$) received 5-FU only. Patient characteristics were comparable except that group I patients tended to have worse reserve liver function, and PEI was performed more often in group IV. Mean survival time did not differ significantly between groups.

REFERENCES

1. Kim HS, Kacew S, Lee BM. In vitro chemopreventive effects of plant polysaccharides (*Aloe barbadensis Miller, Lentinus edodes, Ganoderma lucidum* and *Coriolus versicolor*). Carcinogenesis 1999;23:1637–40.
2. Kato M, Hirose K, Hakozaki M, et al. Induction of gene expression for immunomodulating cytokines in peripheral blood mononuclear cells in response to orally administered PSK , an immunomodulating protein-bound polysaccharide. Cancer Immunol Immunother 1995;40:152–6.
3. Kobayashi H, Matsunaga K, Fujii M. PSK as a chemopreventive agent. Cancer Epidemiol Biomarkers Prev 1993;2:271–6.
4. Tsukagoshi S, et al. Krestin (PSK). Cancer Treat Rev 1984;11:131–55.
5. Kobayashi H, Matsunaga K, Oguchi Y. Antimetastatic effects of PSK (Krestin), a protein-bound polysaccharide obtained from basidiomycetes: an overview. Cancer Epidemiol Biomarkers Prev 1995;4:275–81.
6. Nakazato H, et al. Efficacy of immunochemotherapy as adjuvant treatment after curative resection of gastric cancer. Lancet 1994;343:1122–6.

7. Kanoh T, Saito K, Matsunaga K, et al. Enhancement of the antitumor effect by the concurrent use of a monoclonal antibody and the protein-bound polysaccharide PSK in mice bearing a human cancer cell line. In Vivo 1994;8:241–5.
8. Ng TB. A review of research on the protein-bound polysaccharide (polysaccharopeptide, PSP) from the mushroom *Coriolus versicolor* (Basidomycetes: polyporacae). Gen Pharmacol 1998;30:1–4.
9. Liu WK, et al. Activation of peritoneal macrophages by polysaccharopeptide from the mushroom, *Coriolus versicolor*. Immunopharmacology 1993;26:139–46.
10. Mao XW. Evaluation of polysaccharopeptide effects against C6 glioma in combination with radiation. Oncology 2001;61:243–53.
11. Dong Y, et al. Antitumor effects of a refined polysaccharide peptide fraction isolated from *Coriolus versicolor*: in vitro and in vivo studies. Res Commun Mol Pathol Pharmacol 1996; 92:140–8.
12. Shiu WCT, Leung TWT, Tao M. A clinical study of PSP on peripheral blood counts during chemotherapy. Phytother Res 1992;6:217–8.
13. Ng TB, Chan WY. Polysaccharopeptide from the mushroom *Coriolus versicolor* possesses analgesic acitivity but does not produce adverse effects on female reproductive or embryonic development in mice. Gen Pharmacol 1997;29:269–73.
14. Kidd PM. The use of mushroom glucans and proteoglycans in cancer treatment. Altern Med Rev 2000;5:4–27.
15. Ikuzawa M, et al. Fate and distribution of an antitumor protein-bound polysaccharide PSK (Krestin). Int J Immunopharmacol 1988;10:415–23.

Devil's Claw

COMMON NAMES
Grapple plant, wood spider

SCIENTIFIC NAME
Harpagophytum procumbens

KEY WORD
Harpagophytum procumbens

CLINICAL SUMMARY

Derived from the root or tuber. Clinical studies reveal conflicting data about the efficacy of devil's claw as an anti-inflammatory or analgesic. It has been thought that the iridoid glucosides may be responsible for activity, but they are not active when administered separately from whole root extract. The basis for chemical standardization is unknown. Analysis of commercial products reveals wide variance in chemical components. Limited side effects have been reported; diarrhea and bradycardia also occur. Devil's claw increases gastric acid secretions and may interfere with the activity of antacids and histamine-2 (H_2) blockers (eg, ranitidine and famotidine). Other possible drug interactions include increased activity of anticoagulants and cardiac and antiarrhythmic drugs.

CONSTITUENTS

Iridoid glucosides: harpagoside, harpagide, and procumbide; phytosterols: β-sitosterol, oleanolic acid; flavonoids: kaempferol and luteolin; phenolic acids; glycosidic phenyl-propanoic esters: verbascoside and isoacteoside.[1]

MECHANISM OF ACTION

In animal studies, an aqueous extract containing chiefly harpagoside showed significant dose-dependent anti-inflammatory and analgesic effects. Harpagoside is not implicated in the anti-inflammatory action, but, along with other constituents, it does appear to be involved in the peripheral analgesic properties. Devil's claw also has antioxidant effects by scavenging both superoxide and peroxyl in a dose-dependent manner. The bitter iridoids are responsible for the use of the herb as a stomachic. In vitro and in vivo animal studies have shown some evidence that devil's claw might be cardioactive. Lower doses seem to cause bradycardia and increase the strength of contraction, and high doses seem to weaken heart contractions and coronary blood flow.[2,3]

USAGE

Anorexia, gastrointestinal disorders, inflammation, muscle pain, osteoarthritis, pain.

ADVERSE REACTIONS

Reported: Diarrhea, possible bradycardia.

DRUG INTERACTIONS

Antacids/H₂ Antagonists: Devil's claw may reduce efficacy owing to increased production of stomach acid.
Beta-Blockers/Digoxin: Devil's claw may cause bradycardia and weaken heart contractions and coronary blood flow.
Anticoagulants: Devil's claw may have additive anticoagulant activity.

DOSAGE

Anorexia: 1.5 g of crude herb.
Arthritis: 4.5 g of crude herb.[4,5]

LITERATURE SUMMARY AND CRITIQUE

Conflicting reports have been documented in the scarce clinical studies on the anti-inflammatory activity of devil's claw. Owing to the inconclusive data, it may have very little activity as a single agent. Futher research is needed with standardized iridoid glycosides to test efficacy.

REFERENCES

1. Newall CA, et al. Herbal medicine: a guide for health-care professionals. London: Pharmaceutical Press; 1996.
2. Wichtl MW. Herbal drugs and phytopharmaceuticals. Boca Raton (FL): CRC Press; 1994.

3. Langmead L, et al. Antioxidant effects of herbal therapies used by patients with inflammatory bowel disease: an in vitro study. Aliment Pharmacol Ther 2002;16:197–205.
4. Fiebich BL, et al. Inhibition of TNF-α synthesis in LPS-stimulated primary human monocytes by *Harpagophytum* extract SteiHap 69. Phytomedicine 2001;8:28–30.
5. Schulz V, et al. Rational phytotherapy: a physician's guide to the use of herbs and related remedies. 3rd ed. Berlin: Springer; 1998.

Di Bella Multitherapy

COMMON NAMES
Di Bella's tetralogy, DBM, Di Bella regimen

CLINICAL SUMMARY
Alternative therapy composed of somatostatin, melatonin, bromocriptine, a solution of retinoids, and low doses of cyclophosphamide or hydroxyurea. Physiologist Luigi Di Bella developed the regimen and promotes it as an effective treatment for cancer, retinitis pigmentosa, multiple sclerosis, amyotrophic lateral sclerosis, and Alzheimer's disease. Treatment is tailored to the individual patient and purportedly stimulates the body's self-healing without the toxicity of conventional chemotherapy. Di Bella multitherapy (DBM) is based on the theory that growth hormone (GH) and prolactin are involved in neoplastic growth. Somatostatin and its analog octreotide inhibit GH and insulin-like growth factor (IGF)-1 secretion in humans, whereas bromocriptine is a prolactin inhibitor. This treatment was very popular in Italy in the late 1990s as Di Bella claimed that he cured thousands on an outpatient basis, and physicians in other countries, such as Canada, also prescribed it. DBM was highly publicized and politicized in Italy, raising the issue of "freedom of treatment" for patients who could not afford the expensive regimen. In response, local judges ordered that somatostatin be added to the list of effective reimbursable medications, and the Italian National Institute of Health supported 11 separate open-label uncontrolled phase II studies of eight different cancers, organized by Di Bella and the National Cancer Advisory Committee. These trials, which have been criticized for design flaws, found no complete responses, 0.8% partial response rate, and considerable toxicity. However, a small phase II study of late-stage non-Hodgkin's lymphoma patients revealed a 70% response rate. Adverse effects include increased pain at tumor site, nausea, vomiting, anorexia, diarrhea, and somnolence. Somatostatin may reduce or eliminate the efficacy of painkillers (eg, methadone, morphine). This therapy cannot be recommended.

CONSTITUENTS
Somatostatin; solution of retinoic acid, vitamin A, beta-carotene, vitamin E; melatonin; bromocriptine; variable: adrenocorticotropic hormone (ACTH) and low oral doses of cyclophosphamide and hydroxyurea.

MECHANISM OF ACTION

The DBM is based on the theory that GH and prolactin are involved in neoplastic growth, particularly in lymphomas and leukemias.

Somatostatin is a hypothalamic neurohormone that inhibits GH secretion. Its synthetic analog, octreotide, shows antineoplastic activity in vitro and in vivo and is used clinically for the treatment of acromegaly and neuroendocrine tumors. Their biologic effects are mediated via high-affinity plasma membrane receptors (SSTR-1 through SSTR-5) that are coupled to various signal transduction pathways and are found throughout the body and on many human tumors. Clinical studies show a reduction in serum IGF-1 and IGF-1 gene expression after treatment with octreotide. Somatostatin and analogs also enhance secretion and expression of IGF binding protein-1, which negatively regulates plasma IGF-1 while inhibiting mitogens and secretion of gastrointestinal hormones implicated in tumor growth. Somatostatin analogs also show immune-modulating activity in vitro and inhibit angiogenesis and directly induce cell growth arrest and apoptosis in vivo and in vitro.

Melatonin is a free radical scavenger and displays antiproliferative effects on various cancer cell lines in vitro, but no human studies show evidence of antitumor activity. Melatonin shows antimyelodysplastic activity and reduces bone marrow toxicity of chemotherapeutic agents in animal models.

Bromocriptine is a dopamine agonist and prolactin inhibitor. Prolactin stimulates growth of lymphomas in vivo and in vitro, and prolactin receptors are present on normal and neoplastic lymphoid cells. Retinoids act as antioxidants and immunostimulants, cause cell growth arrest in B-cell lymphomas in vitro, and have shown benefit in trials of promyelocytic leukemia and cutaneous T-cell lymphoma. ACTH receptors can be found on T and B lymphocytes, and ACTH has been seen to depress lymphocyte blastogenesis and modulate natural killer cell activity in vitro.[1–7]

USAGE

Alzheimer's disease, cancer treatment, Lou Gehrig's disease, multiple sclerosis, retinitis pigmentosa.

PHARMACOKINETICS

No formal pharmacokinetic studies have been performed on the DBM.

Somatostatin peptides have a short half-life of approximately 1 minute, whereas its synthetic analog octreotide exhibits a half-life of 80 to 100 minutes. Octreotide plasma levels are proportional to the dose administered intravenously or subcutaneously. Peak plasma levels occur after 30 minutes, and octreotide displays linear pharmacokinetics. Octreotide is found mainly in the plasma, bound to lipoprotein and albumin. Continuous infusion of somatostatin is necessary to maintain desired plasma concentrations.

Melatonin is absorbed following oral administration but undergoes extensive first-pass metabolism. Melatonin is metabolized rapidly in the liver to hydroxy metabolites, possibly by cytochrome P-450 isoenzymes 1A2 and 2C19. Oral bioavailability is estimated to be 15% for the parent compound. Elimination half-life is approximately 45 minutes, with a total-body clearance of 10 hours for a 3 mg dose.

Approximately 28% of oral bromocriptine is absorbed through the gastrointestinal tract, and only 6% reaches systemic circulation after extensive first-pass metabolism. Peak plasma levels are attained in 1 to 1.5 hours, where 90 to 96% of bromocriptine is bound to serum albumin. Bromocriptine does not distribute appreciably into erythrocytes. Metabolism takes place in the liver by cytochrome P-450IIIA isoenzymes and excretion occurs principally in the feces via biliary elimination, with a small amount in the urine. Elimination time is 4 to 4.5 hours for the initial phase and 45 to 50 hours for the terminal phase.[7–10]

ADVERSE REACTIONS

Reported (DBM): Increased pain at the tumor site in advanced cancer patients; somnolence, diarrhea, nausea, vomiting, anorexia, grade I hyperglycemia, ankle-feet edema; and anemia and thrombocytopenia were noted in trials using cyclophosphamide.

Case Report (DBM): A breast cancer patient with lung and liver metastases developed acute myeloid leukemia, which her physicians associated with chronic cyclophosphamide use, after treatment with DBM. Her leukemia led rapidly to death owing to cerebral hemorrhage.

Common (Somatostatin): Gastrointestinal complaints (diarrhea, vomiting, and nausea), cholelithiasis, and effects on glucose metabolism.

Toxicity (Somatostatin): Pain at injection site, allergic reactions, hair loss, a few cases of reversible hepatic dysfunction.

Reported (Bromocriptine): Hypotension, peripheral vasoconstriction, dyskinesias, fatigue, nausea, vomiting, postpartum myocardial infarction, headache, dizziness, psychosis.

Reported (Melatonin): Drowsiness, alterations in sleep patterns, altered mental status, disorientation, tachycardia, flushing, pruritus, abdominal cramps, headache, hypothermia.[6–8,11–15]

DRUG INTERACTIONS

Opiates: Somatostatin has opioid antagonist properties and has been observed to decrease or eliminate the analgesic effects of methadone and morphine in advanced cancer patients requiring pain relief.

Immunosuppressants (eg, Cyclosporine, Tacrolimus): Bromocriptine is thought to inhibit the cytochrome P-450IIIA isoenzyme family and reduce the metabolism of drugs such as cyclosporine and tacrolimus, increasing the risk of toxicity from these medications.

Macrolides: Potentiate adverse effects of bromocriptine.

Efavirenz: Increases the effect of bromocriptine.

Protease Inhibitors: Bromocriptine may potentiate their effect.

Antihypertension Drugs: Bromocriptine may have an added hypotensive effect. Bromocriptine is inhibited by drugs that increase prolactin concentration (eg, amitriptyline, butyrophenones, imipramine, methyldopa, phenothiazines, and reserpine).
Nifedipine: Concomitant administration of melatonin and nifedipine has resulted in elevations in blood pressure and heart rate.
Fluvoxamine: Fluvoxamine may increase circulating plasma levels of melatonin, resulting in sedation.
Succinylcholine: Cyclophosphamide potentiates the effect of succinylcholine.
Digoxin: Cyclophosphamide decreases the effect of digoxin.
St. John's Wort: May decrease the effect of cyclophosphamide.[9,11,16,17]

DOSAGE
The drug regimen is tailored to the patient. The following dosages were used in the 1998 prospective Italian study of the DBM:
Oral: Melatonin 20 mg/d, bromocriptine 2.5 mg/d, and solution of retinoids 7 g/d. Hydroxyurea 1 mg/d or cyclophosphamide 50 mg/d.
Parenteral: Somatostatin 3 mg/d over 8 hours or octreotide 1 mg/d.[12]

LITERATURE SUMMARY AND CRITIQUE
Italian Study Group for the Di Bella Multitherapy Trials. Evaluation of an unconventional cancer treatment (the Di Bella multitherapy): results of phase II trials in Italy. BMJ 1999;318:224–8.
A set of 11 independent, uncontrolled, open-label phase II studies of 395 patients with eight types of cancer at 26 Italian hospitals. The main end point was objective tumor response. Patients were refractory to or ineligible for standard treatment and had aggressive non-Hodgkin's lymphoma (NHL); chronic lymphoid leukemia; stage IV breast cancer; metastatic non–small cell lung cancer (NSCLC); advanced colorectal cancer; metastatic or recurrent squamous cell head, neck, or esophagus cancer; recurrent glioblastoma; or advanced solid neoplasms in terminally ill patients. Patients with advanced pancreatic cancer or NSCLC who had not undergone conventional therapy were also included. The number of patients in each cancer group ranged from 20 to 65. Patients received daily melatonin 20 mg, bromocriptine 2.5 mg, somatostatin 3 mg (slow subcutaneous injection) or octreotide 1 mg (subcutaneous injection), and a solution of retinoids, 7 g. Hydroxyurea 1 mg/d was administered to the glioblastoma patients, and all others (except those with solid tumors and stage IV breast cancer) received 50 mg/d cyclophosphamide. Ascorbic acid 1 to 2 g and dihydrotachysterol 0.4 to 0.9 mg were added to the treatment in April to May of 1998 at Di Bella's request. The average treatment time was 2 months. Tumor size was assessed after 1, 2, or 3 months. No patient had a complete response; partial response was seen in one patient with NHL, one patient with breast cancer, and one patient with pancreatic cancer. These patients had disease progression after 350 days, 182 days, and 255 days, respectively. At the second examination,

12% (47) of patients had stable disease, 52% (199) progressed, and 25% (97) died. At the end of the trial, 4 to 8 months after the start of therapy, 219 (57%) patients had died. Adverse effects, including diarrhea, vomiting, nausea, and somnolence, were reported in 40% of patients. Anemia and thrombocytopenia were noted in trials using cyclophosphamide. The study group concluded that a phase III trial of the DBM is not warranted as only a 0.8% response rate and considerable toxicity were found with its use. Di Bella and his followers later criticized the study for its biased selection of terminally ill patients, and its protocol's variance from that which Di Bella had adopted. Experts have criticized the trial's hasty, flawed design and lack of randomization.[18,19]

Buiatti E, et al. Results from a historical survey of the survival of cancer patients given Di Bella Multitherapy. Cancer 1999;86:2143–9.
A retrospective evaluation of survival in cancer patients treated with the DBM between 1971 and 1997. Cases were searched in cancer registries for diagnostic confirmation, date of diagnosis, and follow-up and were matched individually (by site, gender, age, period of diagnosis) to cases from Italian cancer registries to compare survival. DBM patients received varying drug regimens, depending on case and period of treatment (1971–1984, 1985–1997), for variable lengths of time. Only 4 of 248 evaluable patients used DBM as their only cancer therapy; of these, one survived 4 years and another is still alive 2 years past diagnosis. Five-year survival rates for children with leukemia and adult cancer patients were both 29.4%. Five-year survival was significantly lower than control cases in patients with childhood leukemia, breast carcinoma, and adult leukemia and for all patients combined. Twenty-seven patients survived 10 or more years from diagnosis and 20 from first DBM treatment; all were previously treated with conventional cancer therapies. A primary flaw of this study is its lack of data concerning stage of disease; as patients could not be matched to controls with the same stage, the Di Bella cohort may have selected for more advanced, desperate cases. The small site-specific groups, variability of treatment between patients, and small percentage of Di Bella's patients studied (248 of 1,523 with documented cancer) cast further doubt on the significance of the results.

Todisco M, Casaccia P, Rossi N. Cyclophosphamide plus somatostatin, bromocriptine, retinoids, melatonin and ACTH in the treatment of low-grade non-Hodgkin's lymphomas at advanced stage: results of a phase II trial. Cancer Biother Radiopharm 2001;16:171–7.
A prospective phase II evaluation of a multidrug therapy similar to the Di Bella regimen in 20 patients with low-grade stage III or IV NHL. Patients had performance status between 0 and 3 and a bidimensionally measurable lesion and had undergone from zero to three previous conventional cancer treatments. Patients received 75 mg/d of oral cyclophosphamide in split doses; 1.5 mg/d of subcutaneous somatostatin over 8 hours or 0.5 mg/d of octreotide in a single injection; 2.5 mg/d of bromocriptine in split doses; 5 mg of all-*trans* retinoic acid, 5,000 IU of vitamin A palmitate, and 20 mg/d of beta-carotene; 20 mg/d of melatonin in split doses; and 1 mg/wk of ACTH intramuscularly. Patients were treated for 1 month, at which time those with a partial response or stable

disease were treated for an additional 2 months or more. Primary outcome was change in lesion size or onset of new lesions. After the first month, 14 (70%) had a partial response ($\geq$ 50% reduction in size for at least 4 weeks), 4 (20%) had stable disease, and 2 (10%) progressed on therapy. After an average of 21 months follow-up time (range = 7 to 25), none of the 14 partial response patients experienced progression of disease and 7 had a complete response. Of the 4 patients with stable disease after 1 month, 1 had a partial response and 3 progressed within an average of 14.3 months. Response to therapy was found to be dependent on the type of previous therapy and time from last treatment; only those patients with a time from last treatment $\geq$ 1.5 months refractory to single-agent or combination chemotherapy did not show a response. The most common side effects were diarrhea (25%), nausea or vomiting (20%), anorexia (25%), drowsiness (20%), grade I hyperglycemia (25%), and ankle and/or face edema (20%), which were treated with dose adjustments. Larger trials in low-grade NHL are warranted.

REFERENCES

1. Bousquet C, at al. Antiproliferative effects of somatostatin and analogs. Chemotherapy 2001;47 Suppl 2:30–9.
2. Xi SC, et al. Inhibition of androgen-sensitive LNCaP prostate cancer growth in vivo by melatonin: association of antiproliferative action of the pineal hormone with mt1 receptor protein expression. Prostate 2001;46:52–61.
3. Cos S, Garcia-Bolado A, Sanchez-Barcelo EJ. Direct antiproliferative effects of melatonin on two metastatic cell sublines of mouse melanoma (B18BL6 and PG19). Melanoma Res 2001;11:197–201.
4. Blask E, Wilson ST, Zalatan F. Physiological melatonin inhibition of human breast cancer cell growth in vitro: evidence for a glutathione-mediated pathway. Cancer Res 1997;57:1909–14.
5. Karbownik M, Reiter RJ. Antioxidative effects of melatonin in protection against cellular damage caused by ionizing radiation. Proc Soc Exp Biol Med 2000;225:9–22.
6. Todisco M, Casaccia P, Rossi N. Cyclophosphamide plus somatostatin, bromocriptine, retinoids, melatonin and ACTH in the treatment of low-grade non-Hodgkin's lymphomas at advanced stage: results of a phase II trial. Cancer Biother Radiopharm 2001;16:171–7.
7. Scarpignato C, Pelosini I. Somatostatin analogs for cancer treatment and diagnosis: an overview. Chemotherapy 2001;47 Suppl 2:1–29.
8. Sack RL, Lewy AJ, Hughes RJ. Use of melatonin for sleep and circadian rhythm disorders. Ann Med 1998;30:115–21.
9. Hartter S, et al. Increased bioavailability of oral melatonin after fluvoxamine coadministration. Clin Pharmacol Ther 2000;67:1–6.
10. DeMuro RL, et al. The absolute bioavailability of oral melatonin. J Clin Pharmacol 2000;40:781–4.
11. Ripamonti C, et al. Can somatostatin be administered in association with morphine in advanced cancer patients with pain? Ann Oncol 1998;9:921–4.
12. Italian Study Group for the Di Bella Multitherapy Trials. Evaluation of an unconventional cancer treatment (the Di Bella multitherapy): results of phase II trials in Italy. BMJ 1999;318:224–8.
13. Sacco C, Patriarca F. Acute myeloid leukemia following chronic low-dose cyclophosphamide for metastatic breast cancer. Tumori 2001;87:101–3.
14. Avery D, Lenz M, Landis C. Guidelines for prescribing melatonin. Ann Med 1998;30:122–30.
15. Brzezinski A. Melatonin in humans. N Engl J Med 1997;336:186–95.

16. Lusordi P, Piazza E, Fogari R. Cardiovascular effects of melatonin in hypertensive patients well controlled by nifedipine: a 24-hour study. Br J Clin Pharmacol 2000;49:423.

17. Von Bahr C, et al. Fluvoxamine but not citalopram increases serum melatonin in healthy subjects—an indication that cytochrome P450 CYP1A2 and CYP2C19 hydroxylate melatonin. Eur J Clin Pharmacol 2000;56:123–7.

18. Mullner M. Di Bella's therapy: the last word? The evidence would be stronger if the researchers had randomised their studies. BMJ 1999;318:208–9.

19. Remuzzi G, Schieppati A. Lessons from the Di Bella affair. Lancet 1999;353:1289–90.

Dong Quai

COMMON NAMES
Chinese angelica, dang gui, tang kuei, tan kue

SCIENTIFIC NAME
Angelica sinensis

KEY WORD
Angelica sinensis

CLINICAL SUMMARY

Derived from the root of the plant. Traditionally used for menstrual symptoms and as a female "tonic." Primary active ingredients include psoralens and safrole, both of which are thought to be carcinogenic. To date, clinical data regarding the use of dong quai for its proposed claims are inconclusive. Reported adverse events include diarrhea, photosensitivity, and gynecomastia. Owing to the coumarin content, the activity of anticoagulants may be potentiated.

CONSTITUENTS

Volatile oils: safrole, isosafrole, n-butylphthalide; coumarin derivatives: psoralens, bergapten, osthol, imperatorin, oxypeucedanin; ferulic acid.[1]

WARNINGS

Psoralens are photocarcinogenic and mutagenic, and safrole is carcinogenic. Pregnant and breast-feeding patients must not ingest dong quai.[2,3]

MECHANISM OF ACTION

The coumarins exert vasodilatory, antispasmodic effects, and central nervous system stimulation.[4,7]

USAGE

Dysmenorrhea, health maintenance, menopausal symptoms, premenstrual syndrome, spasms.

PHARMACOKINETICS

Unknown.

ADVERSE REACTIONS

Reported: Photosensitivity, photodermatitis (may potentiate response to radiation therapy owing to psoralens content), gynecomastia, bleeding, diarrhea, and fever.[5]

DRUG INTERACTIONS

Anticoagulants: Dong quai may have an additive anticoagulant effect.[6]

LABORATORY INTERACTIONS

Elevated prothrombin time/international normalized ratio.[6]

DOSAGE

Oral: Varies widely owing to variety of formulations. Studies have used extracts, capsules, or roots.

LITERATURE SUMMARY AND CRITIQUE

Hirata JD, et al. Does dong quai have estrogenic effects in postmenopausal women? A double-blind, placebo-controlled trial. Fertil Steril 1997;68:981–6.

A double-blind, randomized, placebo-controlled trial of 71 women. The results suggest that dong quai is no more efficacious than placebo in relieving menopausal symptoms and does not alter endometrial thickness, vaginal maturation, or estrogen levels.

REFERENCES

1. Bone K. Clinical applications of Ayurvedic and Chinese Herbs. Queensland (Australia): Phytotherapy Press; 1997.
2. Tyler V. The honest herbal: a sensible guide to herbs and related remedies. Philadelphia (PA): George Stickley Company; 1982.

 3. DerMarderosian A, editor. The review of natural products. St. Louis: Facts and Comparisons; 1999.
 4. Huang KC. The pharmacology of Chinese herbs. 2nd ed. Boca Raton (FL): CRC Press; 1999.
 5. Goh SY, Koh KC. Gynaecomastia and the herbal tonic "dong quai." Singapore Med J 2001; 42:115–6.
 6. Page RL, Lawrence JD. Potentiation of warfarin by dong quai. Pharmacotherapy 1999; 19:870–6.
 7. Foster S, et al. Tyler's honest herbal: a sensible guide to the use of herbs and related remedies. 3rd ed. New York: Haworth Herbal Press; 1993.
 8. Tyler VE. Rejuvex for postmenopausal symptoms. JAMA 1994;271:1210.
 9. Hirata JD, et al. Does dong quai have estrogenic effects in postmenopausal women? A double-blind, placebo-controlled trial. Fertil Steril 1997;68:981–6.
10. Amato P, Christophe S, Mellon PL. Estrogenic activity of herbs commonly used as remedies for menopausal symptoms. Menopause 2002;9:145–50.

Echinacea

COMMON NAMES
Coneflower, purple coneflower, black Sampson, Sampson root, sonnenhut, igelkopfwurzel

SCIENTIFIC NAMES
Echinacea purpura, Echinacea angustifolia, Echinacea pallida

KEY WORD
Coneflower

A. DONATO

CLINICAL SUMMARY
Derived from the root and aerial parts of the plant. Patients primarily use echinacea to prevent and treat the common cold. The alkylamide, alkaloid, and polyacetylene fractions are thought to be responsible for stimulating leukocytes and increasing the release of tumor necrosis factor (TNF) and interleukin (IL)-1. Although several randomized, placebo-controlled trials have been conducted on the prophylaxis of infections, the results conflict, and more research is required. Double-blind, randomized studies for the treatment of the common cold suggest that, if initiated within 24 hours of onset, echinacea may shorten the duration of colds but not reduce the severity of symptoms. Echinacea may reduce the efficacy of immunosuppressants (eg, tacrolimus, cyclosporine). Reported adverse effects include headache, dizziness, gastrointestinal complaints, and rare allergic reactions. Because several species of echinacea are incorporated into a variety of formulations (eg, liquid extract, capsules, tea), there is no standardization between products or doses used.

CONSTITUENTS
Alkaloids: isotussilagine, tussilagine; amides: echnacein, isobutylamides; carbohydrates: echinacin, polysaccharides, inulin, fructose, glucose, pentose; glycosides: echinacoside;

139

terpenoid: germacrane (sesquiterpene lactone ester); others: cichoric acid, betaine, methylparahydroxycinnamate, vanillin, phytosterol, volatile oils.[1]

MECHANISM OF ACTION

Several components in echinacea appear to be responsible for its activity. In vitro and in vivo studies suggest that echinacea stimulates phagocytosis, enhances mobility of leuko-cytes, stimulates TNF and IL-1 secretion from macrophages and lymphocytes, and improves respiratory activity. Nonspecific T-cell activation is thought to occur via bind-ing of the polyacetylene fraction of echinacea to cell-surface carbohydrate receptors, resulting in antiviral and immunostimulant activity. Some components of echinacea appear to have anti-inflammatory, local anesthetic, and antibacterial activity.[1–5]

USAGE

Common cold, immunostimulation, infections, viral infections, wound healing.

ADVERSE REACTIONS

Common: Headache, dizziness, nausea, constipation, and mild epigastric pain.
Rare: Dermatitis, anaphylaxis.[1,6,7]

DRUG INTERACTIONS

Immunosuppressants: Theoretically, echinacea may antagonize the effects of immuno-suppressants.
CYP3A4: Echinacea inhibits CYP3A4 in vitro, indicating that it could, theoretically, increase serum levels and adverse effects of drugs such as alprazolam, calcium-channel blockers, and protease inhibitors.[8,9]

CONTRAINDICATIONS

Theoretically, because of potential aggravation of an underlying disease state, patients with autoimmune disorders (eg, systemic lupus erythematosus and rheumatoid arthri-tis), multiple sclerosis, other progressive collagenous disorders, tuberculosis, human immunodeficiency virus (HIV), and acquired immune deficiency syndrome (AIDS) should not consume echinacea.[8]

DOSAGE

Oral: Owing to variations in echinacea species and methods of preparation, product labeling must be reviewed to determine suggested dosing. It is suggested that echinacea not be used for more than 8 weeks at a time. *Juice from pressed aerial parts:* 2 to 3 mL three times a day. *Liquid extract:* 1:1 in 45% alcohol 0.25 to 1 mL three times a day; 1:5 in 45% alcohol 1 to 2 mL three times a day. *Dried root:* 500 to 1,000 mg three times a day has been used. *Capsules:* Available in strengths ranging from 200 to 1,000 mg administered up to three times a day.[1,2,10]

LITERATURE SUMMARY AND CRITIQUE

Melchart D, et al. Echinacea for preventing and treating the common cold. Cochrane Database Syst Rev 2001;4:1–15.

A complete search of the literature was performed and trials conducted in a randomized fashion were included. Sixteen trials were found in the literature: eight studying efficacy as prophylaxis and eight for the treatment of the common cold and viral infections. Echinacea did not exhibit any pooled effect for the prophylaxis of infections when compared with placebo. Trials studying echinacea for the treatment of infections were poorly designed, and pooled effects could not be determined. The authors state that the variety of products used and lack of consistent evidence indicate that further research is necessary. The reported adverse event rate was similar to placebo.

Schulten B, et al. Efficacy of *Echinacea purpurea* in patients with a common cold. A placebo-controlled, randomized, double-blind clinical trial. Arzneimittelforschung 2001;51:563–8.

A prospective, adequately randomized, placebo-controlled evaluation of echinacea extract given to patients at the first signs of a cold. A total of 80 patients were included in the intent-to-treat analysis. Patients were randomized to receive 5 mL of freshly pressed juice from the aerial parts of *E. purpura* stabilized in alcohol or placebo twice daily. Primary outcomes measured were severity of symptoms (using the Jackson score) and number of sick days. Seven patients were excluded from the study owing to compliance and three patients withdrew, one because of side effects from echinacea. The duration of illness was significantly shorter in the active treatment group: 6 days versus 9 days for placebo ($p = .0112$). Adverse events were similar between treatment groups and consisted primarily of gastrointestinal complaints. The study suggests that echinacea reduces the duration of the common cold but not necessarily the symptoms associated with it.

REFERENCES

1. Newall C, et al. Herbal medicines: a guide for health-care professionals. 1st ed. London: Pharmaceutical Press; 1996.
2. Schulz V, et al. Rational phytotherapy: a physician's guide to herbal medicine. 4th ed. New York: Springer; 2001.
3. Foster S, et al. Tyler's honest herbal: a sensible guide to the use of herbs and related remedies. New York: Haworth Herbal Press; 1999.
4. Melchart D, et al. Polysaccharides isolated from *Echinacea purpurea* herbal cell cultures to counteract undesired effects of chemotherapy—a pilot study. Phytother Res 2002;16:138–42.
5. Kim LS, et al. Immunological activity of larch arabinogalactan and echinacea: a preliminary, randomized, double-blind, placebo-controlled trial. Altern Med Rev 2002;7:138–49.
6. Giles JT, et al. Evaluation of echinacea for treatment of the common cold. Pharmacotherapy 2000;20:690–7.

 7. Grimm W, Muller H. A randomized controlled trial of the effect of fluid extract of *Echinacea purpurea* on the incidence and severity of colds and respiratory infections. Am J Med 1999;106:138–43.
 8. Brinker F. Herb contraindications and drug interactions. 3rd ed. Sandy (OR): Eclectic Medical Publications; 2001.
 9. Scott GN, Elmer GW. Update on natural product-drug interactions. Am J Health Syst Pharm 2002;59:339–47.
10. Blumenthal M, et al. The complete German Commission E monographs: therapeutic guide to herbal medicines. Austin (TX): American Botanical Council; 1998.
11. Gallo M, Koren G. Can herbal products be used safely during pregnancy? Focus on echinacea. Can Fam Physician 2001;47:1727–8.
12. Budzinski JW, et al. An in vitro evaluation of human cytochrome P450 3A4 inhibition by selected commercial herbal extracts and tinctures. Phytomedicine 2000;7:273–82.

Ephedra

COMMON NAMES
Ma Huang, herbal ecstasy

SCIENTIFIC NAMES
Ephedra sinica, Ephedra equisetina

KEY WORD
Ma Huang

CLINICAL SUMMARY
Derived from the dried rhizome and root of the plant, ephedra has been used as a medicinal herb for thousands of

years in India and China. It is commonly consumed in low doses and in combination with other herbs to promote urination and to treat asthma, bronchitis, and coughs. Ephedrine and pseudoephedrine, the major constituents, are nonselective sympathomimetic agents with both alpha and beta activities and have direct and indirect central nervous system (CNS) stimulation effects. These effects account for the medicinal properties of the herb. Ephedra also has antibacterial and anti-inflammatory activities. Recently, ephedra has been widely promoted as a natural stimulant and appetite suppressant. Although limited clinical data support this use, an evaluation of adverse events related to ephedra reported several cases of stroke, myocardial infarction, and death in patients with no prior history of vascular disease. Misuse and overdose of ephedra have resulted in heart attack, stroke, seizure, psychosis, and death. Drug-herb interactions are major concerns. The US Food and Drug Administration (FDA) has issued warnings against the consumption of dietary supplements that contain ephedra.

CONSTITUENTS
Alkaloids: L-Ephedrine, D-pseudoephedrine, methylephedrine, D-*N*-methylpseudoephedrine, and L-norephedrine.[1,2]

WARNINGS

The FDA warns consumers not to purchase or consume ephedrine-containing dietary supplements marketed as "Ecstasy." These products have made unsubstantiated claims and may pose significant health risks. Possible adverse effects include hypertension, palpitations, heart attack, stroke, seizures, psychosis, and death.[3,4]

MECHANISM OF ACTION

The major alkaloids in ephedra, ephedrine and pseudoephedrine, are CNS stimulants. They are nonselective sympathomimetic agents with both alpha and beta activities. These alkaloids can be use as decongestants because they constrict peripheral blood vessels, but, in high doses, they also raise blood pressure. The CNS stimulation property contributes to ephedra's appetite suppressant effects and its reputation as a weight loss agent. This effect, however, may lead to other cardiovascular adverse reactions, such as stroke and heart attack. Ephedra's antiasthmatic effect arises from its ability to relax bronchial smooth muscle. Studies indicate that ephedra also has antibacterial, anti-inflammatory, and uterine stimulatory activities.[5-10]

USAGE

Asthma, bronchitis, common cold, cough, infections, promotion of urination, strength and stamina, weight loss.

PHARMACOKINETICS

Ephedra alkaloids are absorbed in the intestine. A small amount is metabolized in the liver, but most is excreted in the urine unchanged. Excretion rate is adversely affected by the urine pH value. Serum half-life is 3 to 6 hours for ephedrine and 5 to 8 hours for pseudoephedrine.[5,10]

ADVERSE REACTIONS

Reported: Hypertension, palpitations, heart attack, stroke, seizures, insomnia, psychosis, and death.[3,4]

DRUG INTERACTIONS

Aspirin: May increase risk of cerebral hemorrhage.
Benzodiazepines and Other Sedatives: Effects may be antagonized by ephedra.
β-Adrenergic Agonists: Ephedra may potentiate effects of β-adrenergic agonists.
CNS Stimulants: May increase stimulatory effects.
Monoamine Oxidase Inhibitors: Concomitant use can cause hypertensive crisis.
Theophylline: May increase stimulatory effects.
Digoxin: Concomitant use can cause arrhythmia.[1,5,11]

LABORATORY INTERACTIONS

Consumption of ephedra alkaloids may interfere with a urine amphetamine test, resulting in false-positive readings. Ephedra may increase blood glucose levels.[11]

CONTRAINDICATIONS

Anxiety, hypertension, heart disease, glaucoma, prostate enlargement, and hyperthyroidism. The safety of ephedra for use during pregnancy has not been established. Because ephedra can stimulate uterine contraction, women who are pregnant should not consume this product.[9,10]

DOSAGE

Oral: 15 to 30 mg of total alkaloid per dose, up to 300 mg/d. *Tea:* 1 to 4 g of raw herb three times daily. *Tincture (1:4):* 6 to 8 mL three times daily.[1]

LITERATURE SUMMARY AND CRITIQUE

Boozer C, et al. An herbal supplement containing ma huang-guarana for weight loss: a randomized, double-blind trial. Int J Obes Relat Metab Disord 2001;25:316–24.

Sixty-seven subjects participated in a randomized, double-blind, placebo-controlled study. They were given supplements containing 72 mg of ephedra and 240 mg of caffeine per day. After 8 weeks, subjects from the active treatment group lost an average of 4.0 kg compared with 0.4 kg in the placebo group. Serum triglyceride and hip circumference were also reduced in the active treatment group. The study concluded that this mixture effectively promoted short-term weight and fat loss. However, adverse symptoms such as dry mouth, insomnia, and headache were reported. More studies are needed to explore the long-term effects.

Samenuk D, et al. Adverse cardiovascular events temporally associated with ma huang, an herbal source of ephedrine. Mayo Clin Proc 2002;77:12–6.

Based on the data obtained from the comprehensive database Adverse Reaction Monitoring System of the FDA, the authors found 926 cases of possible ephedra toxicity reported between 1995 and 1997. Analysis of 37 cases indicated that ephedra and related products can cause stroke, myocardial infarction, and sudden death. These adverse effects are not dose related and can happen to patients with no prior history of vascular disease.

REFERENCES

1. Gruenwald J, et al. PDR for herbal medicines. 2nd ed. Montvale (NJ): Medical Economics Company; 1998.
2. Huang KC. The pharmacology of Chinese herbs. 2nd ed. New York: CRC Press; 1999.
3. FDA statement on street drugs containing botanical ephedrine. HHS News. U.S. Department of Health and Human Services; 1996 Apr 10.
4. Haller C, Benowitz N. Adverse cardiovascular and central nervous system events associated with dietary supplements containing *Ephedra* alkaloids. N Engl J Med 2000;343:1833–8.

5. Barnes J, et al. Herbal medicines. 2nd ed. London: Pharmaceutical Press; 2002.
6. Bensky D, Gamble A. Chinese herbal medicine: materia medica. Rev. ed. Seattle: Eastland Press; 1993.
7. Foster S, et al. Tyler's honest herbal: a sensible guide to the use of herbs and related remedies. New York: Haworth Herbal Press; 1999.
8. Boozer C, et al. An herbal supplement containing ma huang-guarana for weight loss: a randomized, double-blind trial. Int J Obes Relat Metab Disord 2001;25:316–24.
9. Samenuk D, et al. Adverse cardiovascular events temporally associated with ma huang, an herbal source of ephedrine. Mayo Clin Proc 2002;77:12–6.
10. Haller C, et al. Pharmacology of *Ephedra* alkaloids and caffeine after single-dose dietary supplement use. Clin Pharmacol Ther 2002;71:421–32.
11. Jellin J, editor. Natural medicines comprehensive database. Therapeutic Reseach Faculty; 2002.

Essiac

SCIENTIFIC NAMES

Burdock root *(Arctium lappa)*, sheep sorrel *(Rumex acetosella)*, slippery elm bark *(Ulmus fulva)*, turkish rhubarb root *(Rheum palmatum)*

KEY WORD

Vitaltea

CLINICAL SUMMARY

This product is composed of four botanicals: cut or dried burdock root, powdered sheep sorrel root, powdered slippery elm bark, and powdered rhubarb root. The formula is consumed as a tea. Promoters claim that this product boosts the immune system, acts as a tonic, and treats cancer and human immunodeficiency virus (HIV). To date, however, no data or published clinical trials show efficacy for any claims made. Possible adverse effects include nausea, vomiting, diarrhea, constipation, hypoglycemia, and renal and hepatic toxicity with chronic consumption. Case reports indicate that burdock root contaminated with belladonna have caused atropine-like toxicity. No drug interactions are documented except for a single case report of decreased clearance of chemotherapy possibly owing to inhibition of hepatic metabolism. Additional research is required to establish whether essiac is safe and effective for any of its proposed claims.

CONSTITUENTS

Sheep Sorrel (**R. acetosella**): Derived from the aerial parts of the plant. Sheep sorrel historically has been used to treat inflammation, scurvy, cancer, and diarrhea. The major constituents of sheep sorrel include anthraquinones, oxalates, and various vitamins, including A, B complex, C, D, E, and K. Consumption of large doses may result in diarrhea from the anthraquinone content and renal and liver damage from the oxalate content. There are no published trials evaluating the efficacy of sheep sorrel for any of the proposed claims.

Slippery Elm (**U. fulva**): Derived from the inner bark of the tree. Slippery elm has been used historically for gastrointestinal disorders, skin ulcers or abscesses, cancers, cough, fevers, and inflammation. The primary constituent, mucilage, is thought to account for the demulcent effects. To date, no human or animal studies have been performed to evaluate the efficacy of any of the proposed claims. Toxicity of slippery elm is low, based on chemical components. No adverse reactions or drug interactions are reported in the literature. Slippery elm appears to be safe for coughs and minor gastrointestinal complaints. However, it should not be used to treat severe conditions such as cancer or bronchitis.

Burdock (**A. lappa**): Derived from the root or seeds of the plant. Historically, burdock has been used as a diuretic and to reduce blood sugar levels. It is claimed to treat anorexia, gout, cancer, and HIV, although no clinical studies are reported in the literature. Animal studies indicate possible hypoglycemic effect; therefore, a theoretical interaction exists with insulin and hypoglycemics. Several cases of burdock tea contaminated with belladonna alkaloids have been reported in Europe and the United States. Product should be certified against contamination and labeled accordingly.

Rhubarb (**R. palmatum**): Derived from the root of the plant. Rhubarb has been used for a variety of conditions including cancer, immunosuppression, constipation, diarrhea, gastrointestinal ulcers, and chronic renal failure. The anthraquinone and tannins are thought to be responsible for the laxative and constipating effects, respectively. There are limited human clinical data for any of the claims made. Animal data show antitumor effects in mice, but this has not been studied in humans. Adverse effects are primarily gastrointestinal. Chronic consumption can cause hypokalemia owing to diarrhea, possible renal and hepatic damage from oxalates, and theoretical hypokalemia when combined with diuretics and altered response to digoxin.

MECHANISM OF ACTION

The mechanism of action is not established. Rhubarb and sheep sorrel contain anthraquinones that stimulate secretion of mucosa and water, as well as stimulate peristalsis. Additional activities of anthraquinones isolated from rhubarb show stimulation of interleukin (IL)-1, IL-6, and tumor necrosis factor in vitro and tumor necrosis against sarcoma 37, breast cancer, and Ehrlich cell lines in mice. Burdock root can induce hypoglycemia in animal models. Tannin extract may induce a macrophage response, and the lignan and sesquiterpene extracts were shown to inhibit platelet activating factor in vitro.[1,2]

USAGE

Cancer treatment, health maintenance, HIV and acquired immune deficiency syndrome (AIDS), immunostimulation.

ADVERSE REACTIONS

Reported: Nausea, vomiting, diarrhea, hypokalemia owing to chronic diarrhea, contact dermatitis, anaphylaxis.[3]

CONTRAINDICATIONS

Theoretically, patients with renal or hepatic insufficiency should not consume this product.

DOSAGE

Oral: Products vary in the amount by weight of each botanical. *Tea:* 1 to 13 times a day on an empty stomach. No standard dose has been established.

LITERATURE SUMMARY AND CRITIQUE

No clinical studies have been published evaluating the claims made for essiac.

REFERENCES

1. Tamayo C, et al. The chemistry and biological activity of herbs used in Flor-essence herbal tonic and Essiac. Phytother Res 2000;14:1–14.
2. Locock RA. Essiac. Can Pharm J 1997;130:18–19, 51.
3. Kaegi E. Unconventional therapies for cancer: 1. Essiac. The Task Force on Alternative Therapies of the Canadian Breast Cancer Research Initiative. Can Med Assoc J 1998;158:897–902.

Evening Primrose Oil

A. DONATO

COMMON NAMES
EPO, night willow herb, fever plant, king's cure-all

SCIENTIFIC NAME
Oenothera biennis

KEY WORD
Oenothera biennis

CLINICAL SUMMARY

Oil derived from the plant. Evening primrose oil (EPO) is used for rheumatoid arthritis, premenstrual syndrome (PMS), mastalgia, eczema, fatigue, and diabetic neuropathy. EPO contains gamma-linolenic acid (GLA), a primary fixed oil that is converted to dihomo-gamma-linolenic acid, a prostaglandin precursor. Clinical efficacy data are inconsistent. Adverse reactions include headache and gastrointestinal disturbances. EPO should not be taken during pregnancy. One study reports a reduced seizure threshold when EPO was combined with phenothiazine antipsychotics. Although EPO does not have intrinsic estrogenic properties, several manufacturers do combine EPO with phytoestrogens, and product labels should be carefully reviewed.

CONSTITUENTS

Fixed oils: *cis*-linoleic acid, *cis*-GLA, oleic acid, palmitic acid, stearic acid.[1]

MECHANISM OF ACTION

Theoretically, GLA can be converted directly to the prostaglandin precursor dihomo-GLA. The administration of the oil might be beneficial to individuals unable to metabolize *cis-*

linolenic acid to GLA and to produce subsequent intermediates of considerable metabolic significance, including prostaglandins.[2,3]

USAGE

Cancer treatment, diabetic neuropathy, eczema, gastrointestinal disorders, high cholesterol, mastalgia, menopausal symptoms, PMS, rheumatoid arthritis.

PHARMACOKINETICS

Repeated oral administration of EPO (480 mg/d GLA/d) to health volunteers resulted in a mean C_{max} of approximately 20.7 to 22.6 µg/mL. GLA levels were approximately 4.5 times greater from baseline in all patients, but serum levels of other fatty acids did not change significantly from baseline. Gastric absorption and T_{max} for morning doses was longer than T_{max} for identical doses given in the evening.[4]

ADVERSE REACTIONS

Reported: Headache, gastrointestinal upset, nausea, and increased risk of pregnancy complications.

DRUG INTERACTIONS

Phenothiazines (eg, fluphenazine): EPO may lower the seizure threshold and precipitate seizures in patients taking phenothiazines.[5]

CONTRAINDICATIONS

Pregnant women should not take EPO owing to increased risk of pregnancy complications.

DOSAGE

Oral: Dose varies depending on formulation. *Mastalgia:* 3,000 to 4,000 mg daily. *PMS:* 2,000 to 4,000 mg daily. *Rheumatoid arthritis:* 540 to 2,800 mg daily.

LITERATURE SUMMARY AND CRITIQUE

Zurier RB, et al. Gamma-linolenic acid treatment of rheumatoid arthritis. A randomized, placebo-controlled trial. Arthritis Rheum 1996;39:1808–17.
Fifty-six patients enrolled in this double-blind GLA study that showed both statistically and clinically meaningful improvements in the active treatment group. Both groups were given GLA for an additional 6 months, and an added benefit was demonstrated. Overall, 16 of 21 patients given GLA for a full year showed significant relief of symptoms.

Budeiri D, et al. Is evening primrose oil of value in the treatment of premenstrual syndrome? Control Clin Trials 1996;17:60–8.
A systematic literature search of clinical trials of EPO for the treatment of PMS was carried out with a view to performing a meta-analysis. Seven placebo-controlled trials were found, but in only five trials was randomization clearly indicated. The two well-controlled studies failed to show any beneficial effects for EPO, although modest effects cannot be excluded given that the trials were relatively small. Nonetheless, on current evidence, EPO is of little value in the management of PMS.

Keen H, et al. Treatment of diabetic neuropathy with gamma-linolenic acid. Diabetes Care 1993;16:8–15.
A double-blind, randomized, multicenter, placebo-controlled study of 111 patients who were administered 6 g/d GLA and followed for 12 months. The treated group showed statistically significant improvements in well-controlled diabetes. However, no effects on serum glucose levels were observed.

Pye JK, et al. Clinical experience of drug treatment for mastalgia. Lancet 1985;ii:373–7.
In open studies in the United Kingdom, EPO has been found to produce positive effects in 44% of women with cyclical mastalgia. This was about the same benefit as seen from bromocriptine, but danazol was more effective (70% response rate).

REFERENCES

1. Newall C. Herbal medicines, a guide for health care professionals. London: Pharmaceutical Press; 1997.
2. Tyler V. Herbs of choice, the therapeutic use of phytomedicinals. Binghamton (NY): Pharmaceutical Press; 1994.
3. Belch JJ, Hill A. Evening primrose oil and borage oil in rheumatologic conditions. Am J Clin Nutr 2000;71:352S–6S.
4. Martens-Lobenhoffer J, Meyer FP. Pharmacokinetic data of gamma-linoleic acid in healthy volunteers after the administration of evening primrose oil (Epogam). Int J Clin Pharmacol Ther 1998;36:363–6.
5. Holman CP, et al. A trial of evening primrose oil in the treatment of chronic schizophrenia. J Orthomol Psychiatry 1983;12:302–4.
6. Theander E, et al. Gammalinolenic acid treatment of fatigue associated with primary Sjögren's syndrome. Scand J Rheumatol 2002;31:72–9.
7. Ziboh VA, et al. Gamma-linolenic acid-containing diet attenuates bleomycin-induced lung fibrosis in hamsters. Lipids 1997;32:759–67.
8. Rahbeeni F, et al. The effect of evening primrose oil on the radiation response and blood flow of mouse normal and tumour tissue. Int J Radiat Biol 2000;76:871–7.

Fenugreek

COMMON NAMES
Bird's foot, Greek hayseed, *Trigonella*, bockshornsame, Methi, hu lu ba

SCIENTIFIC NAME
Trigonella foenum-graecum

KEY WORD
Trigonella

CLINICAL SUMMARY
Derived from the dried seeds of the plant, fenugreek is used traditionally as a demulcent, laxative, and lactation stimulant and to treat various conditions, including diabetes, high cholesterol, wounds, inflammation, and gastrointestinal complaints. It is a common constituent of Ayurvedic medicinals. Fenugreek exhibits hypocholesterolemic, hypolipidemic, and hypoglycemic activity in healthy and diabetic animals and humans. The defatted seed material may reduce gastrointestinal glucose and cholesterol absorption and increase bile acid secretion. Diabetic patients taking fenugreek should monitor their blood glucose closely and may require dose adjustments of antidiabetic agents. This herb may potentiate the activity of anticoagulants and has theoretical interactions with monoamine oxidase inhibitors (MAOIs) and hormonal agents. Pregnant women should not use this herb owing to its uterine stimulant activity. Insufficient evidence is available to evaluate its use as a lactation stimulant. Bleeding, bruising, gastrointestinal disturbances, and hypoglycemia are reported side effects. The US Food and Drug Administration lists fenugreek as "generally regarded as safe."

CONSTITUENTS
Alkaloids: trigonelline (yields nicotinic acid with roasting), gentianine, carpaine, choline; proteins and amino acids: 4-hydroxyisoleucine, histidine, lysine, arginine; flavonoids: apigenin, luteolin, orientin, vitexin, quercetin; saponins: graecunins, fenugrin B, fenugreekine, trigofoenosides A to G; steroidal sapinogens: yamogenin, diosgenin, smilagenin, sarsasapogenin, tigogenin, neotigogenin, gitogenin, neogitogenin, yuccagenin; fiber: gum, neutral detergent fiber; other: coumarin, lipids, vitamins, minerals.[1-3]

WARNINGS

Ingestion of fenugreek seeds or tea by infants or late-term pregnant women can lead to false diagnosis of maple syrup urine disease in the infant owing to the presence of sotolone in the urine.[4,5]

MECHANISM OF ACTION

Most traditional uses of fenugreek are likely attributable to its high fiber content. Fenugreek exhibits hypocholesterolemic, hypolipidemic, and hypoglycemic activity in healthy and diabetic animals and humans. The mechanism is uncertain, but its activity is associated with the defatted seed material, whose galactomannan fiber and saponin components may reduce gastrointestinal glucose and cholesterol absorption and increase bile acid excretion. Hypoglycemic activity is also attributed to the trigonelline, nicotinic acid, and coumarin fractions. 4-Hydroxyisoleucine, an amino acid constituent of fenugreek, potentiates insulin secretion in rats with non–insulin-dependent diabetes mellitus when administered intraperitoneally. Fenugreek intake in humans is associated with an increase in molar insulin binding sites of erythrocytes, which may enhance glucose use. In addition to lower fasting and postprandial glucose levels, fenugreek-treated diabetic rats have higher hemoglobin, reduced glutathione (GSH), and plasma antioxidant levels and lower glycosylated hemoglobin, plasma lipids, and thiobarbituric acid reactive substances (TBARS) levels than diabetic controls. Dietary fenugreek normalizes the activities of glucose and lipid-metabolizing enzymes in diabetic rats. In healthy mice and rats, dietary fenugreek is associated with increased serum thyroxine (T_4), liver GSH, glyoxalase I activity and glutathione S-transferase (GST) activity, and decreased triiodothyronine (T_3) levels and T_3-to-T_4 ratio. Extracts of fenugreek show antimicrobial and nematocidal activity in vitro. In vitro uterine stimulation is documented.[1,6–16,18]

USAGE

Alopecia, arthritis, cancer treatment, diabetes, gastrointestinal disorders, high cholesterol, inducement of childbirth, infections, inflammation, lactation stimulation, lymphadenitis, muscle pain, promotion of urination, skin ulcers, wound healing.

PHARMACOKINETICS

The hypoglycemic action of fenugreek in animal models is still significant 24 hours after administration. Mouse studies conclude that the LD50 of fenugreek alcohol extract in the rat is 5 g/kg intraperitoneally.[1]

ADVERSE REACTIONS

Common: Doses of 100 g/d of fenugreek cause flatulence, diarrhea, and other gastrointestinal symptoms.

Reported: Bleeding, bruising, hypoglycemia. Repeated topical use can cause skin sensitization. Inhalation of the powder can cause asthma and allergic symptoms.[17]

DRUG INTERACTIONS

Anticoagulants: Fenugreek may potentiate effects owing to coumarin content.
Antidiabetic Agents: Possible enhanced glucose-lowering effects. May require dosage adjustments.
Insulin: Insulin dosage may have to be adjusted with regular use of fenugreek.
Other Oral Medications: Absorption of other oral medications administered concomitantly may be impaired owing to high mucilaginous fiber content of fenugreek seeds.
MAOIs: Fenugreek may potentiate their effect owing to amine content.[17]

LABORATORY INTERACTIONS

Increased prothrombin time, international normalized ratio. Decreased blood glucose.
Urine odor: False diagnosis of maple syrup urine disease in the infant owing to presence of sotolone in the urine.[4,5]

CONTRAINDICATIONS

Pregnant women should not use fenugreek because of the risk of oxytocic action. People with a known allergy to fenugreek should not consume it.[17]

DOSAGE

Oral: Seeds: 1 to 6 g three times daily. Doses up to 100 g/d have been used in clinical trials. *Tea:* 500 mg seed in 150 mL cold water for 3 hours; strain.
Topical: Powdered drug: 50 g in one-quarter liter of water applied topically.[17]

LITERATURE SUMMARY AND CRITIQUE

Sharma RD, et al. Hypolipidaemic effect of fenugreek seeds: a chronic study in non-insulin dependent diabetic patients. Phytother Res 1996;10:332–4.
A prospective, one-arm study of dietary fenugreek in 60 patients with non–insulin-dependent diabetes of differing severity levels. Forty patients were taking oral hypoglycemic drugs. Each subject underwent 7 days of control diet followed by 24 weeks of consuming 25 g/d fenugreek seed powder prepared in a soup. Diets in each period were similar in calorie and nutrient composition, except for higher fiber content in the fenugreek diet. Mean serum cholesterol decreased from baseline (approximately 241 mg/dL) to 24 weeks (approximately 199 mg/dL), as did low-density lipoprotein (LDL) cholesterol (approximately 143 to 114 mg/dL), LDL + very-low-density lipoprotein (VLDL) cholesterol (approximately 179 to 148 mg/dL), and triglycerides (approximately 187 to 159 mg/dL). Diarrhea and flatulence were reported in a few patients.

Raghuram TC, Sharma RD, Sivakumar B. Effect of fenugreek seeds on intravenous glucose disposition in non-insulin dependent diabetic patients. Phytother Res 1994;8:83–6.
A randomized, controlled, crossover evaluation of dietary fenugreek in 10 non–insulin-dependent diabetic patients taking glibenclamide, 2.5 to 7.5 mg/d, with a stabilized diet and drug dose. The study consisted of two 15-day periods: 5 patients received bread containing 25 g fenugreek powder daily for the first 15 days, whereas the other 5 received it in the second 15-day period. Control bread contained the same nutrient content without fenugreek. Food intake and body weight were similar between treatment arms. An intravenous glucose tolerance test at the end of each period showed significantly lower mean plasma glucose levels at 40, 50, and 60 minutes and an 11% reduction in the area under the curve in the fenugreek group. Erythrocyte insulin receptors were significantly higher in number in the fenugreek group. A washout period should have been instituted between test periods.

Sharma RD, Raghuram TC, Rao NS. Effect of fenugreek seeds on blood glucose and serum lipids in type I diabetes. Eur J Clin Nutr 1990;44:301–6.
A prospective, controlled crossover evaluation of high-dose dietary fenugreek in 10 insulin-dependent diabetic patients. In two 10-day periods, patients consumed isocaloric diets with or without 100 g defatted fenugreek seed powder in divided doses. Five patients received the fenugreek diet in the first period, and the rest received it in the second period. Patients were maintained on suboptimal insulin doses so that the effects of fenugreek could be seen. Oral glucose tolerance tests (administered with insulin) at the end of each study period showed significantly reduced blood glucose levels ($p < .01$) but unchanged serum insulin levels. Urinary sugar excretion ($p < .01$), serum total cholesterol ($p < .001$), VLDL and LDL cholesterol ($p < .01$), and triglyceride levels ($p < .01$) were also reduced in the fenugreek group.

REFERENCES

1. Newall C, et al. Herbal medicines: a guide for health-care professionals. 2nd ed. London: Pharmaceutical Press; 1998.
2. DerMarderosian A, editor. The review of natural products. St. Louis: Facts and Comparisons; 1999.
3. Barnes J, Anderson LA, Phillipson JD. Herbal medicines: a guide for healthcare professionals. 2nd ed. London: Pharmaceutical Press; 2002.
4. Korman SH, Cohen E, Preminger A. Pseudo-maple syrup urine disease due to maternal prenatal ingestion of fenugreek. J Paediatr Child Health 2001;37:403–4.
5. Sewell AC, Mosandl A, Bohles H. False diagnosis of maple syrup urine disease owing to ingestion of herbal tea. N Engl J Med 1999;341:769.
6. Bordia A, Verma SK, Srivastava KC. Effect of ginger (*Zingiber officinale* Rosc.) and fenugreek (*Trigonella foenumgraecum* L.) on blood lipids, blood sugar, and platelet aggregation in patients with coronary artery disease. Prostaglandins Leukot Essent Fatty Acids 1997;56: 379–84.
7. Raghuram TC, Sharma RD, Sivakumar B. Effect of fenugreek seeds on intravenous glucose disposition in non-insulin dependent diabetic patients. Phytother Res 1994;8:83–6.

8. Ravikumar P, Anuradha CV. Effect of fenugreek seeds on blood lipid peroxidation and antioxidants in diabetic rats. Phytother Res 1999;13:197–201.

9. Choudhary D, et al. Modulation of glyoxalase, glutathione S-transferase and antioxidant enzymes in the liver, spleen and erythrocytes of mice by dietary administration of fenugreek seeds. Food Chem Toxicol 2001;39:989–97.

10. Raju J, et al. *Trigonella foenum graecum* (fenugreek) seed powder improves glucose homeostasis in alloxan diabetic rat tissues by reversing the altered glycolytic, gluconeogenic and lipogenic enzymes. Mol Cell Biochem 2001;224:45–51.

11. Broca C, et al. 4-Hydroxyisoleucine: experimental evidence of its insulinotropic and antidiabetic properties. Am J Physiol 1999;277:E617–23.

12. Sur P, et al. *Trigonella foenum graecum* (fenugreek) seed extract as an antineoplastic agent. Phytother Res 2001;15:257–9.

13. Panda S, Tahiliani P, Kar A. Inhibition of triiodothyronine production by fenugreek seed extract in mice and rats. Pharmacol Res 1999;40:405–9.

14. Zia T, Siddiqui IA, Hasnain N. Nematicidal activity of *Trigonella foenum-graecum* L. Phytother Res 2001;15:538–40.

15. Sharma RD, et al. Hypolipidaemic effect of fenugreek seeds: a chronic study in non-insulin dependent diabetic patients. Phytother Res 1996;10:332–4.

16. Sharma RD, et al. Effect of fenugreek seeds on blood glucose and serum lipids in type I diabetes. Eur J Clin Nutr 1990;44:301–6.

17. Fetrow CW, et al. Professional's handbook of complementary and alternative medicines. Philadelphia: Springhouse; 1999.

18. Langmead L, et al. Antioxidant effects of herbal therapies used by patients with inflammatory bowel disease: an in vitro study. Aliment Pharmacol Ther 2002;16:197–205.

Feverfew

COMMON NAMES
Bachelor's button, featherfew, Santa Maria, wild chamomile, wild quinine

SCIENTIFIC NAME
Tanacetum parthenium

KEY WORD
Tanacetum parthenium

CLINICAL SUMMARY
Derived from the leaves of the plant. This herb is used primarily to treat migraine headaches, although clinical data regarding efficacy are contradictory. Feverfew leaves should be administered via capsules or tablets. Oral ulceration has occurred among those who chew the raw leaves or consume them as a tea. Products should be standardized to a 0.2% parthenolide concentration. In vitro studies indicate that this product may interfere with the function of platelets. Feverfew should not be used concomitantly with anticoagulants.

CONSTITUENTS
Terpenoids: chrysantemonin, chrysanthemolide, magnoliolide, parthenolide, santamarine, reynosin; volatile oils: camphor, borneol, farnesene and their esters; pyrethrin; flavonols; tannins.[1]

MECHANISM OF ACTION
It is suggested that the sesquiterpene lactones, particularly parthenolide, are the active ingredient and are responsible for feverfew's anti-inflammatory mechanism of action. A recent study found that parthenolide attenuates activation of the nuclear factor-κB complex to block transcription of inflammatory proteins. It is believed that all of the feverfew constituents have a synergistic effect in preventing migraines. Some researchers believe that the flavonol content has anti-inflammatory action.[2–5]

USAGE

Arthritis, dysmenorrhea, migraine prophylaxis, psoriasis.

ADVERSE REACTIONS

Common: Minor gastrointestinal distress. Mouth ulcerations may result from chewing fresh feverfew leaves.
Withdrawal: Muscle stiffness, anxiety, and moderate pain usually occur following cessation of long-term feverfew use (postfeverfew syndrome).[6]

DRUG INTERACTIONS

Anticoagulants/Antiplatelets: Theoretically, feverfew may have an additive effect.

LABORATORY INTERACTIONS

Theoretically may increase prothrombin time, partial thromboplastin time, and international normalized ratio.

CONTRAINDICATIONS

Patients allergic to ragweed, chrysanthemums, marigolds, or other members of the Compositae family may have cross-sensitivity to feverfew.

DOSAGE

Oral: Migraine prophylaxis: 100 to 250 mg standardized to contain 0.2% parthenolide.
Anti-inflammatory and arthritis: 250 mg three times a day standardized to contain 0.2% parthenolide.

LITERATURE SUMMARY AND CRITIQUE

Clinical studies do not support the use of feverfew in the management of rheumatoid arthritis. Many studies conflict regarding the utility of feverfew as prophylaxis against migraine headaches. The following trials did demonstrate efficacy.

Murphy JJ, et al. Randomized, double-blind, placebo-controlled trial of feverfew in migraine prevention. Lancet 1988;23:189–92.
A prospective, randomized, double-blind, placebo-controlled trial of feverfew conducted in 72 patients who reported at least 2 years of a minimum of one migraine per month. Fifty-nine patients finished the study with a 24% reduction in the number of attacks in the feverfew group compared with the placebo group. A significant reduction in associated nausea and vomiting was noted in the feverfew group. An assessment of blinding revealed that 59% of the patients taking feverfew stated efficacy compared with 24% receiving placebo. The authors' conclusions suggest that feverfew is safe and effective in the prophylaxis of migraine headaches.

Johnson ES, et al. Efficacy of feverfew as prophylactic treatment of migraine. BMJ 1985;291:569–73.

A study of 17 patients previously taking feverfew, randomized to either placebo or feverfew 50 mg daily for six periods of 4 weeks. The authors reported that the placebo group experienced a significant increase in the frequency and severity of headache. Those given the feverfew had no change. It was later suggested that the placebo group suffered from postfeverfew withdrawal symptoms.

REFERENCES

1. European Scientific Cooperative on Phytotherapy. ESCOP monographs on the medicinal uses of plant drugs. Exeter, London: 1996.
2. Tyler V. Herbs of choice, the therapeutical use of phytomedicinals. Binghamton (NY): Pharmaceutical Press; 1994.
3. de Weerdt GJ, et al. Herbal medicines in migraine prevention: randomized double-blind placebo-controlled crossover trial of a feverfew preparation. Phytomedicine 1996;3:225–30.
4. Williams CA, et al. A biologically active lipophilic flavonol from *Tanacetum parthenium*. Phytochemistry 1995;38:267–70.
5. Reuter U, et al. Nuclear factor-kappaB as a molecular target for migraine therapy. Ann Neurol 2002;51:507–16.
6. Johnson ES, et al. Efficacy of feverfew as prophylactic treatment of migraine. BMJ 1985;291:569–73.

Forskolin

COMMON NAME
Makandi

SCIENTIFIC NAME
Coleus forskohlii

KEY WORD
Coleus forskohlii

CLINICAL SUMMARY
Derived from the root of the plant. Diterpenes are thought to be the active components of this herb. Animal studies show that forskolin promotes the activation of adenylate cyclase and increases intracellular concentrations of cyclic adenosine monophosphate. This supplement is used for a variety of conditions, including cancer, obesity, glaucoma, asthma, and heart failure. Sparse anecdotal reports describe use in asthma, glaucoma, and heart failure. Controlled clinical trials are lacking. Forskolin should not be combined with anticoagulants owing to platelet inhibition activity and may cause additive hypotension when combined with antihypertensives. Reported adverse events include hypotension and tachycardia. Only the oral formulation is available in the United States.

CONSTITUENTS
Diterpenes: forskolin, essential oils.

MECHANISM OF ACTION
Forskolin achieves activation of adenylate cyclase through direct stimulation of the catalytic subunit. This characteristic of forskolin led to its extensive use as a biochemical tool. Forskolin inhibits membrane transport and channel proteins. It stimulates lipolysis in adipocytes and also inhibits glucose uptake by adipocytes owing to the binding of forskolin to glucose transport proteins. Forskolin's activity leads to inhibition of platelet aggregation, bronchodilation, potentiation of the secretagogue effects of glucose, and stimulation of the release of somatostatin and glucagon. Forskolin has a positive inotropic effect on the heart without increasing myocardial oxygen.[1–3]

161

USAGE

Allergies, asthma, cancer treatment, congestive heart failure, glaucoma, hypertension, weight loss.

ADVERSE REACTIONS

Reported: Hypotension, tachycardia.[1]

DRUG INTERACTIONS

Antihypertensives: Forskolin may have additive hypotensive effect with beta-blockers, vasodilators, calcium channel blockers, etc.
Anticoagulants: Forskolin may cause bleeding owing to additive platelet inhibition.[1]

DOSAGE

Ophthalmic: No sterile eye drop formulation is available. Formulations not made for ophthalmic use should **NOT BE PLACED DIRECTLY IN THE EYE.**
Parenteral: Not available in the United States.
Oral: Doses of 50 to 100 mg (standardized to 10 to 20% forskolin) administered two to three times a day have been used. *Fluid extract:* 6 to 12 mL daily, but forskolin concentrations vary. *Dried root:* 6 to 12 g daily.[1]

LITERATURE SUMMARY AND CRITIQUE

Very limited data are available concerning the efficacy of forskolin. Most studies performed with forskolin have been human trials; those performed on patients with heart failure and glaucoma are inconclusive.

REFERENCES

1. Bone K. Clinical applications of Ayurvedic and Chinese herbs. Queensland (Australia): Phytotherapy Press; 1996.
2. Baumann G, et al. Cardiovascular effects of forskolin (HL 362) in patients with idiopathic congestive cardiomyopathy. A comparative study with dobutamine and sodium nitroprusside. J Cardiovasc Pharmacol 1990;16:93–100.
3. Meyer BH, et al. The effects of forskolin eye drops on intraocular pressure. S Afr Med J 1987;71:570.

Garlic

COMMON NAMES
Nectar of the gods, camphor of the poor, da-suan, la-suan, stinking rose

SCIENTIFIC NAME
Allium sativum

KEY WORDS
Allium sativum, Kwai, Kyolic

A. DONATO

CLINICAL SUMMARY
Derived from the bulb or clove of the plant. Garlic is used as a spice and to treat hyperlipidemia, hypertension, atherosclerosis, cancer, and infections. Processing can have a substantial effect on the chemical content in garlic; the volatile oil components are sensitive to heat, and certain enzymes are acid labile. Several oral garlic formulations are available, and clinical studies have addressed a variety of the proposed claims. Placebo-controlled trials repeatedly show a reduction in total cholesterol, low-density lipoprotein cholesterol, and triglycerides at 4 to 12 weeks with aged or dried garlic preparations. However, a sustained response has not been found. Studies evaluating the antithrombotic effects repeatedly have shown modest reduction in platelet aggregation but varying levels of fibrinolytic activity. Research shows mixed effects with regard to reductions in blood glucose, blood pressure, or risk of cardiovascular disease. Frequently reported adverse events include bad breath, headache, fatigue, gastrointestinal upset, diarrhea, sweating, and possible hypoglycemia. Because garlic is known to decrease platelet aggregation and potentially elevate the international normalized ratio (INR), it should not be used with anticoagulants or in patients with platelet dysfunction. Garlic appears to induce cytochrome P-450 3A4 and may enhance the metabolism of many medications (eg, cyclosporine and saquinavir).

CONSTITUENTS

Aged Garlic Extract: Water-soluble compounds: S-allyl cysteine, S-allyl mercaptocysteine, saponins; volatile oils: small amount of oil-soluble sulfur compounds including alliin, small amount of allicin, ajoene, diallyl trisulphide; terpenes such as citral, geraniol, linalool; other constituents: S-methyl-l-cysteine sulfoxide, protein, minerals, vitamins, lipids, amino acids, prostaglandins (A_2 and $F_{1\alpha}$); enzymes: alliinase, peroxidases, myrosinase.

Crushed Raw Garlic: Volatile oils: contains most allicin (approximately 3.7 mg/g), alliin, ajoene, diallyl trisulphide; terpenes such as citral, geraniol, linalool; water-soluble compounds: S-allyl cysteine (SAC), S-allyl mercaptocysteine, saponins; other constituents: S-methyl-l-cysteine sulfoxide, protein, minerals, vitamins, lipids, amino acids, prostaglandins (A_2 and $F_{1\alpha}$); enzymes: alliinase, peroxidases, myrosinase.

Garlic Powder: Volatile oils: does not contain allicin; contains alliin (approximately 1%), small amount of oil-soluble sulfur compounds; other constituents: S-methyl-l-cysteine sulfoxide, protein, minerals, vitamins, lipids, amino acids, prostaglandins (A_2 and $F_{1\alpha}$); enzymes: alliinase, peroxidases, myrosinase.

Garlic Essential Oil: No allicin or water-soluble components; not well standardized; volatile oils: contains 1% or less oil-soluble sulfur compounds.[1,2]

WARNINGS

Discontinue use of garlic at least 7 days prior to surgery.[3]

MECHANISM OF ACTION

The intact cells of garlic contain an odorless, sulfur-containing amino acid derivative known as alliin. When the cells are crushed, alliin comes into contact with the enzyme alliinase located in neighboring cells and is converted to allicin. Allicin is a potent antibiotic, but it is highly odoriferous and unstable. The ajoenes are apparently responsible for the antithrombotic properties of garlic. Allicin is described as possessing antiplatelet, antibiotic, and antihyperlipidemic activity. Most authorities agree that the best measure of the total activity of garlic is its ability to produce allicin, which, in turn, results in the formation of other active principles. In hyperlipidemic patients, garlic might lower cholesterol levels by acting as a 3-hydroxy-3-methylglutaryl-coenzyme A (CoA) reductase inhibitor. For atherosclerosis, garlic is believed to reduce oxidative stress and low-density lipoprotein oxidation and have antithrombotic effects. For hypertension, it is thought to reduce blood pressure by causing smooth muscle relaxation and vasodilation by activating the production of endothelium-derived relaxation factor. Garlic might stimulate both humoral and cellular immunity, causing T-cell proliferation, restoring suppressed antibody responses, and stimulating macrophage cytotoxicity on tumor cells. Garlic might increase selenium absorption with possible protection against tumorigenesis.[4-10]

USAGE

Atherosclerosis, cancer prevention, cancer treatment, cardiovascular disease, circulatory disorders, high cholesterol, hypertension, microbial infection, skin infections.

PHARMACOKINETICS

Preparation of garlic, such as heating, microwaving, or drying, can substantially reduce the allyl sulfur compounds (allicin and alliin). Crushed raw garlic is highest in these components. SAC is well absorbed after oral administration and can be detected in the plasma, liver, and kidney. It is metabolized to *N*-acetyl-SAC and excreted in the urine. Allicin has not been detected in the bloodstream and is thought to undergo extensive first-pass hepatic metabolism. Allinase, required to convert alliin to allicin, is acid labile.[11]

ADVERSE REACTIONS

Reported (Oral): Headache, fatigue, altered platelet function with potential for bleeding, offensive odor, gastrointestinal upset, diarrhea, sweating, changes in the intestinal flora, hypoglycemia.
Case Report (Oral): Prolonged bleeding time with spinal epidural hematoma and platelet dysfunction has occurred following excessive usage of garlic.
Reported (Topical): Contact dermatitis.[12,13]

DRUG INTERACTIONS

Insulin: Dose of insulin may require adjustment owing to the hypoglycemic effects of garlic.
Warfarin: Anticoagulant activity may be enhanced owing to increased fibrinolytic activity and diminished human platelet aggregation.
Cytochrome P-450 3A4: Garlic may cause induction of the 3A4 isoenzyme, resulting in enhanced metabolism of certain drugs. *Cyclosporine:* Effectiveness might be decreased by garlic's ability to induce metabolism and decrease levels of drugs such as cyclosporine, which are substrates of cytochrome P-450 3A4. It can potentially cause transplant rejection. *Saquinavir (Fortovase, Invirase):* Consuming garlic can significantly decrease serum concentration levels. Garlic can decrease peak levels by 54% and mean trough levels by 49%. These reductions in levels can cause therapeutic failure and increase development. It is suspected that garlic induces the cytochrome P-450 metabolism of saquinavir. Patients taking other protease inhibitors may be affected; however, only saquinavir interaction has been reported.[14,15]

LABORATORY INTERACTIONS

Insulin; increased prothrombin time and INR; decreased cholesterol; change in blood pressure.

DOSAGE

Oral: Many different formulations and dosages have been used in studies. Products should be standardized to allicin content. Garlic enteric-coated tablets protect the active constituents from stomach acids. *Raw garlic cloves:* 4 g/d.[12]

LITERATURE SUMMARY AND CRITIQUE

Kannar D, et al. Hypocholesterolemic effect of an enteric coated garlic supplement. J Am Coll Nutr 2001;20:225–31.
This study demonstrates that enteric-coated garlic powder supplements with 9.6 mg allicin-releasing potential may have value in mild to moderate hypercholesterolemic patients when combined with a low-fat diet. The results suggest that garlic supplementation has a cholesterol-lowering effect, which may be mediated by direct action of a biologically active compound or compounds and, in part, through the effect on food and nutrient intake.

Ackermann RT, et al. Garlic shows promise for improving some cardiovascular risk factors. Arch Intern Med 2001;161:813–24.
Compared with placebo, garlic preparations may lead to small reductions in the total cholesterol level at 1 month and 3 months but not 6 months. Changes in low-density lipoprotein levels and triglyceride levels paralleled total cholesterol level results; no statistically significant changes in high-density lipoprotein levels were observed. Trials also reported significant reductions in platelet aggregation and mixed effects on blood pressure outcomes.

Stevinson C, et al. Garlic for treating hypercholesterolemia: a meta-analysis of randomized clinical trials. Ann Intern Med 2000;133:420–9.
The available data suggest that garlic is superior to placebo in reducing total cholesterol levels. However, the size of the effect is modest, and the robustness of the effect is debatable. The use of garlic for hypercholesterolemia is therefore of questionable value.

Fleischauer AT, et al. Garlic consumption and cancer prevention: meta-analyses of colorectal and stomach cancers. Am J Clin Nutr 2000;72:1047–52.
In this meta-analysis of colorectal and stomach cancer, the reference categories ranged from no consumption to consumption of 3.5 g/wk, whereas the highest categories ranged from any consumption to more than 28.8 g. The results show that high intake of raw and cooked garlic may be associated with a protective effect against stomach and colorectal cancers. Heterogeneity of effect estimates, differences in dose estimation, publication bias, and possible hypotheses preclude sole reliance on summary effect estimates.

Ankri S, et al. Antimicrobial properties of allicin from garlic. Microbes Infect 1999;1:125–9.
Allicin in its pure form was found to exhibit (1) antibacterial activity against a wide range of gram-negative and gram-positive bacteria, including multidrug-resistant enterotoxicogenic strains of *Escherichia coli*, and (2) antifungal activity and antiviral activity. The

main antimicrobial effect of allicin is attributable to its chemical reaction with thiol groups of various enzymes, which can affect essential metabolism of cysteine proteinase activity involved in the virulence of *Entamoeba histolytica*.

Isaacsohn JL, et al. Garlic powder and plasma lipids and lipoproteins: a multicenter, randomized, placebo-controlled trial. Arch Intern Med 1998;158:1189–94.
A randomized, double-blind, placebo-controlled, 12-week, parallel-treatment study carried out in two outpatient lipid clinics. The active treatment arm received tablets containing 300 mg of garlic powder (Kwai) three times a day, given with meals. This is equivalent to 2.7 g or one clove of fresh garlic per day. The results showed that there were no significant lipid or lipoprotein changes in either the placebo or garlic group. Therefore, garlic was ineffective in lowering cholesterol levels in patients with hypercholesterolemia.

Berthold HK, et al. Effect of a garlic oil preparation on serum lipoproteins and cholesterol metabolism: a randomized controlled trial. JAMA 1998;279:1900–2.
The results of this study show that the commercial garlic oil preparation has no influence on serum lipoproteins, cholesterol absorption, or cholesterol synthesis. Garlic therapy for treatment of hypercholesterolemia cannot be recommended on the basis of this study.

Silagy CA, et al. A meta-analysis of the effect of garlic on blood pressure. J Hypertens 1994;12:463–8.
Only randomized, controlled trials of garlic preparations that were at least 4 weeks in duration were deemed eligible for inclusion in the review. The results suggest that this garlic powder (Kwai) may be of some clinical use in patients with mild hypertension. However, there is still insufficient evidence to recommend it as a routine clinical therapy for the treatment of hypertensive patients.

Jain AK, et al. Can garlic reduce levels of serum lipids? A controlled clinical study. Am J Med 1993;94:632–5.
Forty-two healthy adults with a serum total cholesterol level of greater than or equal to 220 mg/dL received, in a randomized, double-blind fashion, 300 mg three times a day of standardized garlic powder in tablet form or placebo. The results showed that a baseline serum total cholesterol level of 262 mg/dL was reduced to 247 mg/dL after 12 weeks of standard garlic treatment. Corresponding values for placebo were 276 mg/dL before and 274 mg/dL after. There were no significant changes in high-density lipoprotein cholesterol, triglycerides, serum glucose, blood pressure, and other monitored parameters.

REFERENCES

1. Newall CA, et al. Herbal medicines: a guide for health care professionals. London: Pharmaceutical Press; 1996.
2. Amagase H, et al. Intake of garlic and its bioactive components. J Nutr 2001;131:955S–62S.
3. Ang-lee M, et al. Herbal medicines and perioperative care [review]. JAMA 2001;286:208–16.
4. Tyler V. Herbs of choice, the therapeutical use of phytomedicinals. Binghamton (NY): Pharmaceutical Press; 1994.
5. Qureshi AA, et al. Suppression of avian hepatic lipid metabolism by solvent extracts of garlic: impact on serum lipids. J Nutr 1983;113:1746–55.

6. Pedraza-Chaverri J, et al. Garlic prevents hypertension induced by chronic inhibition of nitric oxide synthesis. Life Sci 1998;62:71–7.

7. Dirsch VM, et al. Effect of allicin and ajoene, two compounds of garlic, on inducible nitric oxide synthase. Atherosclerosis 1998;139:333–9.

8. Sato T, Miyata G. The nutraceutical benefit, part IV: garlic. Nutrition 2000;16:787–8.

9. Hodge G, et al. *Allium sativum* (garlic) suppresses leukocyte inflammatory cytokine production in vitro: potential therapeutic use in the treatment of inflammatory bowel disease. Cytometry 2002;48:209–15.

10. Hirsch K, et al. Effect of purified allicin, the major ingredient in freshly crushed garlic, on cancer cell proliferation. Nutr Cancer 2000;38:245–54.

11. Song K, Milner JA. The influence of heating on the anticancer properties of garlic. J Nutr 2001;131:1054S–7S.

12. Blumenthal M. Herbal medicine, expanded Commission E monographs. 1st ed. Austin (TX): American Botanical Council; 2000.

13. Rose KD, et al. Spontaneous spina epidural hematoma with associated platelet dysfunction from excessive garlic ingestion: a case report. Neurosurgery 1990;26:880–2.

14. Brinker F. Herb contraindications and drug interactions. 2nd ed. Sandy (OR): Eclectic Medical Publications; 1998.

15. Piscitelli SC, et al. The effect of garlic supplements on the pharmacokinetics of saquinavir. Clin Infect Dis 2002;34:234–8.

Germanium

COMMON NAMES

Inorganic germanium, germanium dioxide (GeO_2), spirogermanium, carboxyethylgermanium sesquioxide (Ge-132), germanium sesquioxide, germanium-lactate-citrate (Ge-lac-cit), organogermanium, germanium elixir

CLINICAL SUMMARY

Germanium is a naturally occurring element. It is promoted for treating cancer, human immunodeficiency virus (HIV), and acquired immune deficiency syndrome (AIDS). Supplementation with germanium has resulted in renal, hepatic, myelogenous, and neurologic toxicities. To date, nine deaths have been reported in the literature from as little as a 15 g cumulative dose. Limited clinical research has been conducted in humans. The toxicity risk from germanium supplements outweighs any benefit.

WARNINGS

Germanium supplements should not be consumed owing to concerns of renal, hepatic, and neurotoxicity. Although acute toxicity studies in animals reveal low potential for toxicity, low-dose chronic toxicity has been demonstrated repeatedly. Renal toxicity is characterized by vacuolar degeneration in renal tubular epithelial cells, without proteinuria or hematuria, in the absence of glomerular changes.[1,2]

MECHANISM OF ACTION

Germanium has chemical properties similar to tin, silicon, and arsenic. It is unknown whether germanium is an essential ultratrace element for humans; no cases of germanium deficiency are known to have occurred. The atomic structure of germanium allows it to act as a free radical scavenger. Neuronal activity may be attributable to suppression of catecholamines and stimulation of serotonin. Spirogermanium has been shown to inhibit deoxyribonucleic acid (DNA) and ribonucleic acid synthesis in HeLa cells.[1,3]

USAGE

Arthritis, cancer treatment, health maintenance, HIV and AIDS.

PHARMACOKINETICS

Absorption: Oral administration of germanium dioxide (GeO_2) to rats demonstrates approximately 95% bioavailability. Organic radiolabeled germanium (Ge-132) has repeatedly been shown to have 30% bioavailability in humans and animal models.

Distribution: Extensive throughout body, but detectable levels in tissue vary based on dose and frequency of administration. Can be detected in blood, lung, and spleen with preferential accumulation in liver and kidneys.

Elimination: Excreted primarily by the kidneys.[4]

ADVERSE REACTIONS

Common: Weight loss, fatigue, nausea, vomiting, anorexia, anemia, muscle weakness, paresthesias, and sensory ataxia.

Rare: Chronic renal failure, elevated liver enzymes, hepatic steatosis, peripheral neuropathies, cerebellar ataxia, and bone marrow hypoplasia.[3,5–7]

DRUG INTERACTIONS

Theoretically, may have additive toxicity with other drugs known to cause renal (eg, aminoglycosides), hepatic, or neurologic toxicity (eg, taxanes) or myelosuppression.

LABORATORY INTERACTIONS

Elevated liver enzymes, increased serum creatinine, decreased blood counts, and elevated creatinine phosphokinase.

CONTRAINDICATIONS

Patients with a history of seizures should not take germanium.

DOSAGE

Normal dietary intake from food ranges from 0.1 to 3.0 mg/d.

Oral: Additional supplementation is not recommended.

LITERATURE SUMMARY AND CRITIQUE

Many clinical trials evaluating spirogermanium for various cancers were conducted in the early 1980s. A significant incidence of renal, hepatic, and neurologic toxicity was documented. To date, 31 case reports of toxicity, including 9 deaths, have been published.

Woolley PV, et al. A phase I trial of spirogermanium administered on a continuous infusion schedule. Invest New Drugs 1984;2:305–9.

Fifteen patients with various oncologic diagnoses (two leukemia; four lymphoma; one Hodgkin's disease; four ovarian, two colon, one lung, one head/neck cancer) and extensive prior chemotherapy were included in this dose-ranging study. Adverse effects were documented at all dosing levels ranging from phlebitis at the lowest dose (up to 200 mg/m²/d) to neurologic effects (at 250 mg/m²/d), including stuttering, confusion, hallucinations, and peripheral phlebitis. Tremors were considered the dose-limiting toxicity at 400 mg/m²/d. Phlebitis was unresponsive to premedication with hydrocortisone. No clinical response was documented during the trial.

Boros L, et al. Phase II Eastern Cooperative Oncology Group study of spirogermanium in previously treated lymphoma. Cancer Treat Rep 1986;70:917–8.
A total of 25 patients with malignant high- or low-grade lymphoma or Hodgkin's disease were evaluated. All patients had received at least one prior chemotherapy regimen. Spirogermanium 80 mg/m² intravenously was administered over 60 to 90 minutes three times a week for 2 weeks. Therapy was continued until evidence of disease progression. Two partial responses were documented, one lasting 90 days (diffuse large cell lymphoma) and another lasting 7 months (diffuse poorly differentiated lymphocytic lymphoma). Two patients had stable disease lasting 4 and 8 months. Median time to disease progression was 19 days, and 23 patients died. Median survival from date of enrolment was 5 months (range of 6 days to 3 years). Toxicity included seizure (the patient had a history of seizures), paresthesia, tinnitus, lethargy, visual disturbances, insomnia, somnolence, vertigo, and headache. The Eastern Cooperative Oncology Group recommended not initiating future studies with spirogermanium.

REFERENCES

1. Schauss AG. Nephrotoxicity and neurotoxicity in humans from organogermanium compounds and germanium dioxide. Biol Trace Elem Res 1991;29:267–79.
2. Boros L, et al. Phase II Eastern Cooperative Oncology Group study of spirogermanium in previously treated lymphoma. Cancer Treat Rep 1986;70:917–8.
3. Goodman S. Therapeutic effects of organic germanium. Med Hypotheses 1988;26:207–15.
4. Tao SH, Bolger PM. Hazard assessment of germanium supplements. Regul Toxicol Pharmacol 1997;25:211–9.
5. Asaka T, et al. Germanium intoxication with sensory ataxia. J Neurol Sci 1995;130:220–3.
6. van der Spoel JI. Dangers of dietary germanium supplements. Lancet 1990;336:117.
7. Krapf R, Schaffner T, Iten PX. Abuse of germanium associated with fatal lactic acidosis. Nephron 1992;62:351–6.

Gerson Regimen

COMMON NAMES
Gerson diet, Gerson therapy, Gerson method, Gerson program, Gerson treatment

CLINICAL SUMMARY
Regimen developed by Max Gerson, MD, involving a strict metabolic diet, coffee enemas, and various supplements, including *l*-mandelonitrile-β-glucuronic acid (Laetrile). Currently available at clinics in Mexico and elsewhere. Patients use this therapy to treat cancer and alleviate cancer-related pain (the Gerson Institute Web site identifies 49 cancers and degenerative conditions that have been "cured" with the Gerson regimen).[1] Clinic fees may be $4,000/wk or more; therapy may last months to years.[2,3] The diet emphasizes fresh fruit and vegetable juice, high carbohydrate and potassium, no sodium or fat, and low animal protein and is sometimes supplemented with exogenous digestive enzymes. This regimen claims to address the cause of cancer by detoxifying the system and stimulating metabolism so that the body can heal itself. Coffee enemas can cause infections, dangerous electrolyte deficiencies, and death. Despite proponents' claims of recovery rates as high as 70 to 90%, case reviews by the National Cancer Institute (NCI) and New York County Medical Society in 1947 found no confirmation of the Gerson diet's benefit in cancer. The only large, retrospective review of patient survival in the literature was conducted by the Gerson Research Organization. It found higher survival rates for melanoma patients treated with the Gerson method. The American Cancer Society (ACS) warns that the Gerson method can be very harmful. Although the Gerson diet is similar to some US Department of Agriculture (USDA) recommendations, dietary changes should be tailored to specific patient needs in combination with conventional cancer care.

CONSTITUENTS
Metabolic Diet: Juice from fresh fruits and vegetables; high-potassium, high-carbohydrate, little animal protein, fat-free, sodium-free diet; prohibited items include coffee, berries, nuts, dairy, tap water, bottled, canned, or processed foods, and aluminum utensils; coffee enemas.

Additional Therapies: Linseed oil, acidophilus-pepsin capsules, potassium solution, Laetrile, Lugol's solution (iodine/potassium iodine), thyroid tablets, niacin, pancreatic enzymes, royal jelly capsules, castor oil, ozone enemas, vaccines, and vitamin B_{12} mixed with liver.

172

WARNINGS
The ACS warns that Gerson therapy can be very harmful to the body.[2]

MECHANISM OF ACTION
Gerson claims that he originally developed the diet to treat his migraines but found it successful as a treatment for skin tuberculosis and stomach cancer. His therapy is based on the theory that cancer is caused by alteration of cell metabolism by toxic environmental substances and food processing, which changes the sodium and potassium content of foods. Gerson's rationale is that cancer patients have low immunity and generalized tissue damage characterized by decreased intracellular potassium-to-sodium (K/Na) ratios, and when their cancer is destroyed, toxic degradation products cause coma and death. His diet increases potassium intake and minimizes sodium consumption in an effort to correct the electrolyte imbalance, repair tissue, and detoxify the liver, whereas coffee enemas reportedly cause dilation of bile ducts and excretion of toxic breakdown products by the liver and through the colon wall. Supplemental potassium and oxidizing thyroid enzymes are given to introduce oxidation to cancer cells and kill them. None of these claims have been substantiated by scientific research. It is possible that metabolism is stimulated by pancreatic enzymes, pepsin, and thyroid capsules, as proponents claim, because such adjuvants are occasionally given by conventional oncologists.

A number of studies affirm that the ratio of intracellular potassium to sodium is negatively correlated to cancer rates, but no evidence supports that the Gerson diet restores a healthy ratio or effectively treats cancer in this manner. Instead, the regimen has resulted in coma-inducing low levels of sodium. Case reports of deaths from repeated administration of coffee enemas indicate that the practice causes a dangerous decrease in serum electrolytes. Coffee enemas have an osmolality of 62 mOsm/kg; repeated administration increases extravascular fluid volume and may cause electrolyte imbalances and subsequent death.

The high levels of phytochemicals and vitamins A and C ingested in the Gerson diet might have immune-stimulating and antioxidant effects. The ease of absorption of the large volumes of raw fruits and vegetables by the cancer patient is questionable, however, especially in patients with gastrointestinal cancers or chemotherapy-induced gastrointestinal disorders. Steaming vegetables allows increased digestive efficacy. Although elements of the Gerson diet are similar to diet recommendations made by the USDA and the ACS, metabolic diets are unsuitable for some patients with disseminated or metastatic disease, particularly of the head, neck, and gut.[2-9]

USAGE
Allergies, arthritis, asthma, atherosclerosis, cancer treatment, cardiovascular disease, chronic fatigue syndrome, detoxification, diabetes, hypertension, infertility, Lou Gehrig's disease, migraine treatment, multiple sclerosis, peptic ulcers, psoriasis, tuberculosis.

PHARMACOKINETICS

No formal pharmacokinetic studies have been performed.

ADVERSE REACTIONS

Common: Flu-like symptoms, loss of appetite, perspiration with foul odor, weakness, dizziness, cold sores, fever blisters, high fever, tumor pain, intestinal cramping, diarrhea, and vomiting. (The Gerson handbook claims that these adverse reactions are indicative of response.)

Common (Metabolic Diet): Nutrient deficiencies (calcium, vitamins D and B_{12}, protein), anemia, and malabsorption may result from metabolic diets.

Reported: Campylobacter fetus sepsis caused by the liver injections was reported in 13 patients using the Gerson therapy between 1980 and 1986; liver injections were subsequently eliminated from the regimen. Coma from low serum sodium (as low as 102 mEq/L) occurred in 5 of these patients. Coffee enemas cause electrolyte imbalance, which has resulted in serious infections, dehydration, colitis, constipation, and death.

Case Reports (Coffee Enemas): Case 1: Multiple seizures and hypokalemia leading to cardiorespiratory arrest, coma, and death were reported after excessive use of coffee enemas (one to four per hour) for a number of days. *Case 2:* Death attributable to fluid and electrolyte imbalance causing pleural and pericardial effusions after use of coffee enemas, four per day for 8 weeks.[2,6,10]

DRUG INTERACTIONS

None known.

DOSAGE

Diet: Juice from approximately 9 kg of freshly crushed fruits and vegetables (about 13 hourly 8 oz glasses/d).

Coffee Enemas: Three to four per day.

Therapies supplemental to diet and enemas vary by patient.

LITERATURE SUMMARY AND CRITIQUE

In 1947, the NCI reviewed 10 "cured" cases, and the New York County Medical Society reviewed 86 medical records and interviewed 10 patients treated with the Gerson therapy. Additionally, the NCI reviewed the 50 cases published in Gerson's book, *A Cancer Therapy: Results of Fifty Cases.* None of these case reviews could find sufficient evidence to show efficacy. In 1989, a best-case review and psychological study was conducted by British researchers. They found that some patients were benefitting from the Gerson regimen but not a clinically significant amount; however, the patients did seem to be helped psychologically by the therapy.

Austin S, Dale EB, Dekadt S. Long-term follow-up of cancer patients using Contreras, Hoxsey and Gerson therapies. J Naturopath Med 1994;5:74–6.
Small prospective evaluation of survival rates at three Tijuana clinics, including the Gerson Institute's La Gloria Hospital (now Centro Hospitalario Internationale). Patients were interviewed at the clinic regarding the location of the primary tumor, presence of metastasis, and whether it was biopsy confirmed. Most patients were unaware of the stage of their cancer, and medical records were not available for review. Patients receiving Gerson therapy ($n = 38$) were queried by mail yearly for 4 to 5 years or until death; the 20 who did not reply were excluded. Of the 18 evaluable patients, one was alive but not disease free at 5 years; mean survival time from the beginning of the study was 9 months. Meaningful statistical analysis and comparison to historic control could not be performed owing to the small sample size for each cancer site. Despite the obvious flaws of this study—the majority of patients lost to follow-up and the lack of access to detailed medical records—the authors concluded that the Gerson therapy does not cure late-stage cancer.

Hildenbrand GL, et al. Five-year survival rates of melanoma patients treated by diet therapy after the manner of Gerson: a retrospective review. Altern Ther Health Med 1995;1:29–37.
A retrospective review of 5-year survival of 153 white adult melanoma patients treated with the Gerson method at a Centro Hospitalario Internacional del Pacifico, SA (CHIPSA), Tijuana, compared with survival rates reported in medical literature. Of 249 patients treated for melanoma between 1975 and 1990, charts of only 153 were assessable for both outcome and stage at admission. Patients followed the Gerson regimen, including diet, coffee enemas, and variable additional therapies, for an unspecified amount of time. Altogether, 45 (29%) patients lived at least 5 years. Of 14 patients with stage I or II melanoma, none had progression of disease, and all remained free from melanoma for up to 17 years. Of 35 stage III patients, 25 (71%) survived 5 years, compared with the survival rates ranging from 27 to 42% in the literature. Of 104 stage IV patients, 18 were admitted presenting only superficial metastatic disease with no internal metastases, of whom 7 (39%) survived 5 to 19 years. This was contrasted to a 6% survival rate in similar cases in a published outcomes analysis by the Eastern Cooperative Oncology Group. None of the 86 patients with advanced metastases survived 5 years. The authors suggest no mechanism of action for the Gerson regimen but admit that the supportive psychosocial environment of the clinics might affect outcomes. A serious flaw in this study is its failure to control for additional variable therapies used by patients and to specify any prior or concurrent conventional treatments used. Because this study follows only 61% of the patients treated at the clinic, there remains the possibility that this is not a comprehensive representation of the therapy's outcomes. The authors claim that the NCI's prior best-case review of the Gerson therapy was flawed in its focus on the outcome of tumor regression, which is not adequately documented at most alternative medical clinics. Although its questionable data are interesting, this study illustrates the need for more comprehensive record keeping at alternative medical clinics. If proponents of such therapies wish them to be evaluated sci-

entifically and considered valid adjuvant treatments, they must provide extensive records (more than simple survival rates) and conduct controlled, prospective studies as evidence.

REFERENCES

1. Gerson Institute Web site. Available at: http://gerson.org (accessed Mar 20, 2002).
2. Gerson therapy. American Cancer Society's guide to complementary and alternative methods. American Cancer Society; 2000. Available at: http://www.cancer.org/docroot/eto/content/eto_5_3x_Gerson_Therapy.ASP?sitearea-eto (accessed March 20, 2002).
3. Hildenbrand GL, et al. Five-year survival rates of melanoma patients treated by diet therapy after the manner of Gerson: a retrospective review. Altern Ther Health Med 1995;1:29–37.
4. Dwyer JT. Unproven nutritional remedies and cancer. Nutr Rev 1992;50:106–9.
5. McCarty MF. Aldosterone and the Gerson diet: a speculation. Med Hypotheses 1981;7:591–7.
6. Cope FW. A medical application of the Ling association-induction hypothesis: the high potassium, low sodium diet of the Gerson cancer therapy. Physiol Chem Phys 1978;10:465.
7. Eisele JW, Reay DT. Deaths related to coffee enemas. JAMA 1980;244:1608–9.
8. Jansson B. Geographic cancer risk and intracellular potassium/sodium ratios. Cancer Detect Prev 1986;9:171–94.
9. Gerson M. The cure of advanced cancer by diet therapy: a summary of 30 years of clinical experimentation. Physiol Chem Phys 1978;10:449–64.
10. American Cancer Society. Questionable methods of cancer management: nutritional therapies. CA Cancer J Clin 1993;43:309–19.

Ginger

COMMON NAMES
Zingiberis rhizoma, zingiberaceae,
ginger root, shen jiang

SCIENTIFIC NAME
Zingiber officinale

KEY WORD
Zingiber officinale

A.DONATO

CLINICAL SUMMARY
Derived from the root and rhizome of the plant. Ginger is used primarily for nausea and vomiting and other gastrointestinal symptoms. Clinical studies suggest that ginger reduces nausea and vomiting postoperatively and during pregnancy and associated with motion sickness. In vitro study suggested that ginger may have therapeutic effects against Alzheimer's disease. Possible adverse effects include heartburn and dermatitis. Consumption of excessive amounts may result in central nervous system depression and arrhythmias. Because ginger can inhibit thromboxane formation and platelet aggregation, concomitant use with anticoagulants is not recommended. Other potential drug interactions include an increased effect of hypoglycemics and antihypertensive agents and decreased efficacy of histamine$_2$ (H$_2$) blockers (eg, ranitidine) and proton pump inhibitors (eg, lansoprazole).

CONSTITUENTS
Carbohydrates: starch (up to 50%); lipids: free fatty acids (6–8%); palmitic acid, oleic acid, linoleic acid; oleo-resin: gingerol homologue (up to 33%); volatile oils: hydrocarbons (1–3%), beta-bisabolene, curcumene, farnesene, sesquiphellandrene, zingiberol, zingiberene; monoterpenes: linalool, borneol, neral, geraniol; amino acids; proteins.[1,2]

MECHANISM OF ACTION

The antiemetic action of ginger is attributed to the shogaol and gingerol constituents found in the rhizome. They are believed to stimulate the flow of saliva, bile, and gastric secretions. Additional activities include the suppression of gastric contractions and improvement of the intestinal muscle tone and peristalsis. Galanolactone is thought to interact with 5-hydroxytryptamine$_3$ receptors and may be partially responsible for antiemetic activity. Ginger has been shown to inhibit thromboxane formation and inhibit platelet aggregation; however, this effect appears to depend on dose and formulation (eg, dried, fresh, or extract). An in vitro study suggested that ginger may have therapeutic effects against Alzheimer's disease by protecting neuronal cells from the beta-amyloid.[3–7]

USAGE

Appetite, colic, diarrhea, drug withdrawal symptoms, indigestion, motion sickness, nausea and vomiting, promotion of urination, rheumatoid arthritis, spasms, stomach and intestinal gas.

ADVERSE REACTIONS

Common: Heartburn and dermatitis.
Toxicity: Central nervous system depression and arrhythmias have occurred following overdose.

DRUG INTERACTIONS

Anticoagulants/Antiplatelets: Ginger may increase the risk of bleeding.
H$_2$ Blockers/Proton Pump Inhibitors: Ginger may antagonize activity by increasing stomach acid production.
Antihypertensives: Ginger may cause additive hypotensive effects.
Hypoglycemics/Insulin: Ginger may cause additive reductions in blood glucose.[8]

DOSAGE

Oral: Nausea and vomiting: Dosage varies between patients. Maximum total daily dose is 4 g/d given in divided doses. *Pregnancy:* Unknown whether ginger is teratogenic; 250 mg of ginger root three times a day after meals and bedtime has been used. *Chemotherapy:* Not recommended owing to inhibition of platelet aggregation; 1 to 4 g of ginger root given in divided doses has been used. *Motion sickness:* 1,000 mg ginger root 30 minutes before travel. *Prevention of postoperative nausea and vomiting:* 1 g of ginger root 1 hour before anesthesia. *Selective serotonin reuptake inhibitor (SSRI) discontinuation syndrome:* Based on a single case report, 500 to 1,000 mg of ginger root three times daily for 2 weeks after discontinuation of the SSRI.[9–11]

LITERATURE SUMMARY AND CRITIQUE

Vutyavanich T, Kraisarin T, Ruangsri R. Ginger for nausea and vomiting in pregnancy: randomized, double-masked, placebo-controlled trial. Obstet Gynecol 2001;97:577–82.
Administration of ginger to women less than 17 weeks pregnant and experiencing related nausea and vomiting. Seventy women (32 ginger, 38 placebo) were enrolled and administered the study medication four times a day for 4 days. All patients had episodes of vomiting 24 hours prior to enrolment. Nausea and vomiting scores were significantly reduced on the fourth day of treatment with ginger compared with placebo. On day 4, 12 of 32 patients receiving ginger compared with 23 of 35 patients on placebo had at least one episode of vomiting. No difference in outcome of pregnancy was noted between the groups. This study suggests that ginger is effective for short-term management of nausea and vomiting associated with pregnancy.

Phillips B, et al. *Zingiber officinale* (ginger)—an antiemetic for day case surgery. Anaesthesia 1993;48:715–7.
The effect of ginger root was compared with metoclopramide and placebo. In a prospective, randomized, double-blind trial, the incidence of postoperative nausea and vomiting was measured in 120 women presenting for laparoscopic surgery on a day-stay basis. The results showed that the incidence of nausea and vomiting was similar for patients given metoclopramide and ginger and less than those who received placebo. No difference in the incidence of side effects was reported.

Bone ME, et al. Ginger root—a new antiemetic. The effect of ginger on postoperative nausea and vomiting after major gynaecological surgery. Anaesthesia 1990;45:669–71.
A double-blind, randomized study of the effectiveness of ginger as an antiemetic compared with placebo and metoclopramide in 60 women who had major gynecologic surgery. Significantly fewer recorded incidences of nausea were recorded in the ginger group compared with the placebo group. The number of incidences of nausea in the groups that received either ginger root or metoclopramide was similar.

REFERENCES

1. Newall CA, et al. Herbal medicines: a guide for health-care professional. London: Pharmaceutical Press; 1996.
2. Fetrow CW, et al. Professional's handbook of complementary and alternative medicines. Philadelphia: Springhouse; 1999.
3. Bisset NG. Herbal drugs and phytopharmaceuticals; a handbook for practice on scientific basis. Boca Raton (FL): Medpharm Publishers; 1994.
4. Lumb AB. Mechanism of antiemetic effect of ginger. Anaesthesia 1993;48:1118.
5. Srivastava KC. Isolation and effects of some ginger components on platelet aggregation and eicosanoid biosynthesis. Prostaglandins Leukot Med 1986;25:187–98.
6. Lumb AB. Effect of dried ginger on human platelet function. Thromb Haemost 1994;71:110–1.
7. Kim DS, Kim DS, Oppel MN. Shogaols from *Zingiber officinale* protect IMR32 human neuroblastoma and normal human umbilical vein endothelial cells from beta-amyloid (25-35) insult. Planta Med 2002;68:375–6.
8. Brinker F. Herb contraindications and drug interactions. 2nd ed. Sandy (OR): Eclectic Medical Publications; 1998.

9. Vutyavanich T, Kraisarin T, Ruangsri R. Ginger for nausea and vomiting in pregnancy: randomized, double-masked, placebo-controlled trial. Obstet Gynecol 2001;97:577–82.
10. Ernst E, Pittler MH. Efficacy of ginger for nausea and vomiting: a systemic review of randomized clinical trials. Br J Anaesth 2000;84:367–71.
11. Schechter JO. Treatment of disequilibrium and nausea in the SRI discontinuation syndrome. J Clin Psychiatry 1998;59:431–2.

Ginkgo

COMMON NAMES
Fossil tree, maidenhair tree, kew tree, bai guo ye, yinhsing

SCIENTIFIC NAME
Ginkgo biloba

A. DONATO

CLINICAL SUMMARY
Derived from the leaf and seed of the tree, *Ginkgo biloba* extract (GBE) is used to treat cerebral circulation, dementia, peripheral vascular disorders, sexual dysfunction resulting from selective serotonin reuptake inhibitors (SSRIs), hearing loss, and more. Although GBE has been extensively studied, there are conflicting results. It may have modest benefit in memory improvement in healthy people and in patients with dementia. The National Cancer Institute and National Center for Complementary and Alternative Medicine are conducting a large randomized trial evaluating efficacy of GBE in older patients with dementia as the primary end point (details are available at <www.clinicaltrials.gov>). Frequently reported adverse events include diarrhea, flatulence, headache, dizziness, and palpitations. There are case reports of spontaneous bleeding and seizures following administration of GBE. It should not be administered to patients receiving anticoagulants or drugs that reduce the seizure threshold or to those with a history of seizures or underlying coagulation disorder. It may potentiate the effect of monoamine oxidase inhibitors (MAOIs) and alter response to insulin. Doses should not exceed 240 mg/d, and GBE should be standardized to contain 24% ginkgo-flavone glycosides and 6% terpenoids. The product label should state that the extract is free of ginkgolic acid as this component is thought to increase the risk of allergic reaction.

CONSTITUENTS

Leaf: Amino acids; flavonoids: dimeric flavones (bilobretinl, ginkgetin, isoginkgetin, sciadopitysin); flavonols: quercetin, kaempferol, and their glycosides; proanthocyanidins; terpenoids: bilobalide, ginkgolides A, B, C, J, and M, which are unique cage molecules. *Seeds:* Alkaloids: ginkgotoxin; cyanogenetic glycosides; phenols.[1]

WARNINGS

GBEs should not contain ginkgolic acid. Discontinue ginkgo biloba at least 36 hours before surgery.

MECHANISM OF ACTION

The active constituents, bilobalide and ginkgolides, improve the tolerance of brain tissue to hypoxia by increasing cerebral blood flow. Ginkgo can increase blood flow to the brain through arterial vasodilatation by stimulating prostaglandin biosynthesis or indirectly stimulating norepinephrine release. Ginkgo has slight anti-inflammatory and spasmolytic activities that are similar to papaverine. It has free radical scavenging activity for hydroxyl, nitric oxide, peroxyl, and superoxide radicals; it is as effective as uric acid. Ginkgo increases tolerance to ischemic conditions and seems to inhibit the platelet activating factor.

Animal studies have shown that ginkgo has a beneficial effect on neurotransmitter disturbance that can restore vascular tone of the smooth muscle cells by maintaining α-adrenergic constrictive and β-adrenergic relaxation vasoregulation. Both in vitro and in vivo tests have shown anti-infective activity for ginkgo.[2]

USAGE

Anxiety, asthma, bronchitis, cardiovascular disease, circulatory disorders, hearing loss, memory loss, Raynaud's disease, sexual dysfunction, stress, tinnitus.

PHARMACOKINETICS

Ginkgolide A: Extent of absorption = 98 to 100%; volume of distribution = 40 to 60 L; time to peak concentration = 1 to 2 hours; half-life after 80 mg = 3.9 hours (oral); clearance = 130 to 200 mL/min; urine excretion unchanged = 70%.

Ginkgolide B: Extent of absorption = 79 to 93%; volume of distribution = 60 to 100 L; time to peak concentration = 1 to 2 hours; half-life after 80 mg = 7.0 hours (oral); clearance = 140 to 250 mL/min; urine excretion unchanged = 50 hours.

Bilobalide: Extent of absorption = > 70%; volume of distribution = 170 L; time to peak concentration = 1 to 2 hours; half-life after 80 mg = 3.2 hours; clearance = 600 mL/min; urine excretion unchanged = 30 hours.[3]

ADVERSE REACTIONS

Common: Headache, dizziness, gastrointestinal upset, flatulence, diarrhea, contact dermatitis, and palpitations.

Case Reports: Seizures have occurred in patients predisposed to seizures or on medications that lower the seizure threshold (eg, prochlorperazine, chlorpromazine, perphenazine). Spontaneous bleeding, including hematomas and hyphema, has been noted in the literature.[4-8]

DRUG INTERACTIONS

MAOIs: Ginkgo may potentiate the effect of MAOIs.

Anticoagulants/Antiplatelets: Ginkgo may induce spontaneous bleeding possibly associated with reduced platelet aggregation resulting from inhibition of platelet activating factor by ginkgolide components.

Antipsychotics/Prochlorperazine: Ginkgo may cause seizures when combined with medications that lower the seizure threshold.

Insulin: Ginkgo can alter insulin secretion and affect blood glucose levels.

Cytochrome P-450: There is preliminary evidence that ginkgo can affect the cytochrome enzymes 1A2, 2D6, and 3A4; however, controversial data exist as to whether it induces or inhibits the individual enzymes.

Trazodone: Ginkgo extract was associated with coma in a woman with Alzheimer's disease who was also taking trazodone.[4,9-12]

LABORATORY INTERACTIONS

Partial thromboplastin time, activated partial thromboplastin time, international normalized ratio.

DOSAGE

Oral: 120 to 240 mg daily in three divided doses standardized to contain 24% ginkgoflavone glycosides and 6% terpenoids. This extract is currently available in the United States under the trade names Ginkgold and Ginkgoba.

LITERATURE SUMMARY AND CRITIQUE

Van Dongen MC, et al. The efficacy of ginkgo for elderly people with dementia and age-associated memory impairment: new results of a randomized clinical trial. J Am Geriatr Soc 2000;48:1183–94.

A 24-week, randomized, double-blind, placebo-controlled, parallel-group, multicenter trial. Two hundred fourteen participants were allocated randomly to treatment with EGb 761, a special extract of ginkgo biloba, two tablets per day, total dosage either 240 mg or 160 mg/d or placebo. The total intervention was 24 weeks. After 12 weeks of treatment, the initial ginkgo users were randomized once again to either continued ginkgo treatment or placebo treatment. Initial placebo use was prolonged after 12 weeks. An intention-to-treat analysis showed no effect on each of the outcome measures for participants who were assigned to ginkgo compared with placebo for the entire 24-week period. After 12 weeks of treatment, the combined high-dose and usual-dose groups performed slightly better with regard to self-reported activities of daily life. No duration of ginkgo treatment was found. No adverse effects were noted. In conclusion, the results suggested that ginkgo was not effective as a treatment for older people with mild to moderate dementia or age-associated memory impairment. These results contrasted sharply with those of previous ginkgo reports.

Le Bars PL, et al. A 26-week analysis of a double-blind, placebo controlled trial of the *Ginkgo biloba* extract Egb 761 in dementia. Dement Geriatr Cogn Disorder 2000; 11:230–7.

This intent-to-treat analysis was performed to provide a realistic image of the efficacy that could be expected after 26 weeks of treatment with a 120 mg dose (40 mg three times a day) of EGb 761. The data were collected during a 52-week, double-blind, placebo-controlled, fixed-dose, parallel-group, multicenter study. Patients were mildly to severely impaired and diagnosed with uncomplicated Alzheimer's disease or multi-infarct dementia. From the 309 patients included in the study, 244 patients (76% for placebo and 73% for EGb) actually reached the twenty-sixth week visit. The placebo group showed a statistically significant worsening in all domains of assessment, whereas the EGb group was considered slightly improved. In the group receiving EGb, 26% of the patients achieved at least a 4-point improvement on the Alzheimer Disease Assessment Scale-Cognitive (ADAS-Cog) compared with 17% with placebo. On the Geriatric Evaluation by Relative's Rating Instrument (GERRI), 30% of the EGb group improved and 17% worsened, whereas the placebo group showed an opposite trend, with 37% of patients worsening and 25% improving. Regarding safety, no differences between ginkgo and placebo were observed.

LeBars PL, et al. A placebo-controlled, double-blind, randomized trial of an extract of *Ginkgo biloba* for dementia. JAMA 1997;278:1327–32.

This placebo-controlled, double-blind study was designed to investigate the effects of a standardized extract in 309 patients with mild to severe dementia associated with either Alzheimer's disease or multi-infarct dementia. Patients were randomized to receive 52 weeks of treatment with placebo or ginkgo extract at a dose of 40 mg three times a day, a total daily dose of 120 mg. At 52 weeks, 202 patients were included in the end-point analysis, which was based on standard tests of cognitive impairment, daily living and social behavior, and general psychopathology. The researchers reported that 27% of patients who received 26 or more weeks of treatment with ginkgo extract experienced at least a 4-point improvement on the 70-point ADAS-Cog subscale compared with 14% in the placebo group. Daily living and social behavior were deemed improved in 37% of ginkgo patients compared with 23% of those taking placebo, as measured by the GERRI. In contrast, the GERRI showed that 40% of patients taking placebo experienced a worsening of their conditions, whereas worsening was seen in only 19% of those taking ginkgo. The researchers concluded that ginkgo appears to stabilize and, in an additional 20% of cases (versus placebo), improves the patient's functioning for periods of 6 months to 1 year. The adverse events associated with ginkgo were no different from those associated with placebo.

Kanowski, S. et al. Proof of efficacy of the *Ginkgo biloba* extract EGb 761 in outpatients suffering from mild to moderate primary degenerative dementia of the Alzheimer type or multi-infract dementia. Pharmacopsychiatry 1996;29:47–56.
This double-blind, placebo-controlled, randomized study investigated the effects of ginkgo extract in 156 patients with either Alzheimer's disease or multi-infarct dementia. A responder rate of 28% for multiple therapeutic effects was observed in patients taking ginkgo extract compared with 10% in the placebo group. A separate analysis of the two different diagnostic subgroups showed that the differences in improvements between ginkgo and placebo after 24 weeks were consistently slightly higher in patients with Alzheimer's disease. The researchers reported that the ginkgo was well tolerated.

REFERENCES

 1. Newall C, et al. Herbal medicines: a guide for health care professionals. London: Pharmaceutical Press; 1996.
 2. Chavez M, et al. Ginkgo: history, use and pharmacologic properties. Hosp Pharm 1998;33:658–72.
 3. Kleijnen J, Knipschild P. *Ginkgo biloba*. Lancet 1992;340:1136–9.
 4. Gregory PJ. Seizure associated with *Ginkgo biloba*? Ann Intern Med 2001;134:344.
 5. Rowin J, Lewis SL. Spontaneous bilateral subdural hematomas associated with chronic *Ginkgo biloba* ingestion. Neurology 1996;46:1775–6.
 6. Matthews MK. Association of *Ginkgo biloba* with intracerebral hemorrhage. Neurology 1998;50:1934.
 7. Gilbert GJ. *Ginkgo biloba*. Neurology 1997;48:1137.
 8. Rosenblatt M, Mindel J. Spontaneous hyphema associated with ingestion of *Ginkgo biloba* extract. N Engl J Med 1997;336:1108.
 9. Brinker F. Herb contraindications and drug interactions. 2nd ed. Sandy (OR): Eclectic Medical Publications; 1998.
10. Kudolo GB. The effect of 3-month ingestion of *Ginkgo biloba* extract on pancreatic beta-cell function in response to glucose loading in normal glucose tolerant individuals. J Clin Pharmacol 2000;40:647.
11. Budzinski JW, et al. An in vitro evaluation of human cytochrome P450 3A4 inhibition by selected commercial extracts and tinctures. Phytomedicine 2000;7:273–82.
12. Scott GN, Elmer GW. Update on natural product-drug interactions. Am J Health Syst Pharm 2002;59:339–47.
13. Tyler V. Herbs of choice, the therapeutical use of phytomedicinals. Binghamton (NY): Pharmaceutical Press; 1994.
14. Solomon PR, et al. Ginkgo for memory enhancement: a randomized controlled trial. JAMA 2002;288:835–40.
15. Lister RE. An open, pilot study to evaluate the potential benefits of coenzyme Q_{10} combined with *Ginkgo biloba* extract in fibromyalgia syndrome. J Int Med Res 2002;30:195–9.
16. Daba MH, et al. Effects of L-carnitine and *Ginkgo biloba* extract (EGb 761) in experimental bleomycin-induced lung fibrosis. Pharmacol Res 2002;45:461–6.
17. Kennedy DO, Scholey AB, Wesnes KA. Modulation of cognition and mood following administration of single doses of *Ginkgo biloba*, ginseng, and a ginkgo/ginseng combination to healthy young adults. Physiol Behav 2002;75:739–51.
18. Ang-lee M, et al. Herbal medicines and perioperative care [review]. JAMA 2001;286:208–16.

Ginseng (American)

COMMON NAMES

Xi yang shen, Tienchi ginseng, Western ginseng, five-fingers

SCIENTIFIC NAME

Panax quinquefolius

CLINICAL SUMMARY

Derived from the root of the plant. Most American ginseng is cultivated in the northwest region of the United States and Canada. Patients take this supplement to improve athletic performance, strength, and stamina and to treat diabetes and cancer. In Chinese herbal formulas, American ginseng is frequently used to nourish "yin." The saponin glycosides, also known as ginsenosides or panaxosides, are thought to be responsible for American ginseng's effects, but there is limited laboratory or clinical research for this species. Ginsenosides have both stimulatory and inhibitory effects on the central nervous system (CNS), alter cardiovascular tone, enhance humoral and cellular-dependent immunity, and may inhibit the growth of cancer in vitro. American ginseng may increase the hypoglycemic effect of insulin and sulfonylureas and possibly antagonize the effects of anticoagulants. Limited data suggest that American ginseng may improve glucose control in diabetics, but additional research is necessary. Further research must be performed to determine the efficacy and optimal dose of American ginseng for all proposed uses.

CONSTITUENTS

Saponin glycosides: panaquilon, ginsenosides; volatile oils; antioxidants; polysaccharides; fatty acids; vitamins; polyacetylenes.[1,2]

MECHANISM OF ACTION

Ginsenosides are thought responsible for American ginseng's activity, although the exact mechanism of action is unknown. American ginseng lowers serum glucose and may affect carbohydrate metabolism. Related species, such as *Panax ginseng*, have been the focus of most laboratory and clinical research. Experiments using extracts from these species indicate that ginsenosides stimulate and inhibit the CNS. The extracts also stimulate tumor necrosis factor-α production by alveolar macrophages. The Rg1 ginsenoside is associated with improvements in humoral and cell-mediated immune response and increases in T helper cells, T lymphocytes, and natural killer cells in mice. Anticancer activity has been shown in vitro for several ginsenosides.[2-7]

USAGE

Cancer prevention, cancer treatment, diabetes, health maintenance, immunostimulation, strength and stamina.

PHARMACOKINETICS

Evaluation of A1, A2, B2, and C ginsenosides in the rabbit suggests one-compartment pharmacokinetics for all ginsenosides following intravenous administration. Elimination half-lives range from 20 to 500 minutes. Ginsenoside A1 is rapidly absorbed after intraperitoneal administration. All ginsenosides are primarily eliminated unchanged in the urine.[1]

ADVERSE REACTIONS

No significant reactions reported.

DRUG INTERACTIONS

Monoamine Oxidase Inhibitors (MAOIs): American ginseng may cause manic-like symptoms when combined with MAOIs.
Insulin and Sulfonylureas: American ginseng may increase the hypoglycemic effect of insulin and sulfonylureas.
Anticoagulants: Theoretically, American ginseng may antagonize the effects of anticoagulants.[8]

LABORATORY INTERACTIONS

Reductions in prothrombin time, partial thromboplastin time, and international normalized ratio may occur. Reductions in blood glucose may occur.[9]

DOSAGE

Oral: No standardized extract is available. *Root powder:* one to three per day have been used.

LITERATURE SUMMARY AND CRITIQUE

Vuksan V, et al. American ginseng (*Panax quinquefolius* L) reduces postprandial glycemia in nondiabetic subjects and subjects with type 2 diabetes mellitus. Arch Intern Med 2000;160:1009–13.

A small open-label evaluation of American ginseng extract on healthy (*n* = 10) and type 2 diabetic (*n* = 9) subjects. Patients were given 3 g of American ginseng extract or placebo prior to a 25 g glucose tolerance test on four separate occasions. Nondiabetic and diabetic subjects had significantly lower glucose concentrations 40 minutes after glucose administration. No adverse effects were noted during the study. The authors suggest that American ginseng extract reduces postprandial glucose concentrations by an unknown mechanism. Additional studies are required to understand the effects of chronic American ginseng administration.

REFERENCES

1. Huang KC. The pharmacology of Chinese herbs. 2nd ed. New York: CRC Press; 1999.
2. Chen SE. American ginseng. III. Pharmacokinetics of ginsenosides in the rabbit. Eur J Drug Metab Pharmacokinet 1980;5:161–8.
3. Vuksan V, et al. American ginseng (*Panax quinquefolius* L) reduces postprandial glycemia in nondiabetic subjects and subjects with type 2 diabetes mellitus. Arch Intern Med 2000;160:1009–13.
4. Shin HR, et al. The cancer-preventive potential of *Panax ginseng*: a review of human and experimental evidence. Cancer Causes Control 2000;11:565–76.
5. Attele AS, Wu JA, Yuan CS. Ginseng pharmacology: multiple constituents and multiple actions. Biochem Pharmacol 1999;58:1685–93.
6. Vuksan V, et al. American ginseng (*Panax quinquefolius* L.) attenuates postprandial glycemia in a time-dependent but not dose-dependent manner in healthy individuals. Am J Clin Nutr 2001;73:753–8.
7. Assinewe VA, et al. Extractable polysaccharides of *Panax quinquefolius* L. (North American ginseng) root stimulate TNFalpha production by alveolar macrophages. Phytomedicine 2002;9:398–404.
8. Brinker F. Herb contraindications and drug interactions. 3rd ed. Sandy (OR): Eclectic Medical Publications; 2001.
9. Vuksan V, et al. American ginseng improves glycemia in individuals with normal glucose tolerance: effect of dose and time escalation. J Am Coll Nutr 2000;6:738–44.

Ginseng (Asian)

COMMON NAMES
Chinese ginseng, panax, ren shen, jintsam, ninjin, Asiatic ginseng, Japanese ginseng, Oriental ginseng, Korean red ginseng

SCIENTIFIC NAME
Panax ginseng

KEY WORDS
Ginsana, *Panax ginseng*

CLINICAL SUMMARY
Derived from the root of the plant. Patients take this supplement to improve athletic performance, strength, and stamina and as an immunostimulant for diabetes, cancer, human immunodeficiency virus/acquired immune deficiency syndrome (HIV/AIDS), and a variety of other conditions. It is also widely used as a "yang" tonic in Chinese herbal formulas. The saponin glycosides, also known as ginsenosides or panaxosides, are thought to be responsible for *Panax ginseng*'s effects. Ginsenosides have both stimulatory and inhibitory effects on the central nervous system (CNS), alter cardiovascular tone, increase humoral and cellular-dependent immunity, and may inhibit the growth of cancer in vitro. *P. ginseng* is usually well tolerated, but insomnia, nausea, vomiting, and diarrhea have been reported. *P. ginseng* may increase the hypoglycemic effect of insulin and sulfonylureas and possibly antagonize the effects of anticoagulants. It may also interact with monoamine oxidase inhibitors (MAOIs). Despite an extensive body of research evaluating it for a variety of uses, *P. ginseng* has not been conclusively demonstrated to benefit any of the conditions studied. *P. ginseng* has been promoted in the treatment of erectile dysfunction, but current studies to support this claim are limited. Most *P. ginseng* extracts are standardized to ginsenoside content, but independent laboratory analysis reveals considerable variation between manufacturers and products. *P. ginseng* does not have significant toxicity and may be safe when used for short periods of time. Adequately designed clinical

studies are needed to establish efficacy and optimal dosage levels. P. ginseng *should not be confused with American ginseng or Siberian ginseng, which have different medicinal properties.*

CONSTITUENTS

Saponin glycosides: ginsenosides (eg, Ra1, Ra2, Rb1, Rd, Re, Rh1, Rh2, Rh3, F1, F2, F3), panaxosides; volatile oils; antioxidants; polysaccharides; fatty acids; vitamins; polyacetylenes.[1,2]

WARNINGS

Discontinue ginseng at least 1 week before surgery.[3]

MECHANISM OF ACTION

Ginsenosides, also known as panaxosides, are thought to be responsible for *P. ginseng*'s activity, although the exact mechanism of action is unknown. Ginsenosides have stimulatory and inhibitory effects on the CNS. Animal studies suggest that ginsenoside Rb1 improves the release of acetylcholine and enhances postsynaptic uptake of choline. Ginsenosides compete for binding sites on γ-aminobutyric acid (GABA)$_A$ and GABA$_B$ receptors in vitro. Rb1, Rb2, and Rc ginsenosides prolong hexobarbital sleeping time in mice and exhibit additional depressant effects on the CNS. Rg1 is associated with improved humoral and cell-mediated immune response and increases in T helper cells, T lymphocytes, and natural killer cells in mice. Anticancer activity has been shown in vitro for several ginsenosides. Differentiation of HL-60 (promyelocytic cells) is induced in Rh2- and Rh3-treated cells. Rh2 appears to cause arrest of B16-BL6 melanoma cells at the G_1 phase along with suppression of cyclin-dependent kinase 2. Studies with Rh2 show inhibited growth of human ovarian cancer xenografts and prolonged survival in nude mice. Use of *P. ginseng* for chemoprevention reduces the incidence of chemically induced lung, liver, skin, and ovarian cancers in mice. Two case-controlled epidemiologic studies of Korean subjects suggest that *P. ginseng* extract consumption reduces the incidence of all cancers (odds ratio = 0.6, 95% CI = 0.5–0.7). Chemopreventive *P. ginseng* also exhibits antioxidant activity. *P. ginseng* may improve nitric oxide synthesis in the endothelium of the heart, lung, and kidneys and in the corpus cavernosum. Ginsenosides administered intrathecally, intraperitoneally, or intracerebroventricularly produce analgesia against capsaicin-induced pain in mice. *P. ginseng* may reduce muscle injury and inflammation following exercise in humans, as demonstrated by reduced levels of creatine kinase, beta-glucuronidase, and glucose-6-phosphate dehydrogenase following oral *P. ginseng* administration. In animal studies with rats and quails, *P. ginseng* lowers total plasma cholesterol and triglyceride levels.[2,4–9]

USAGE
Angina, diabetes, health maintenance, HIV and AIDS, immunostimulation, improvement in clotting, pain, sexual dysfunction, strength and stamina.

ADVERSE REACTIONS
Common: Usually well tolerated.
Reported: Dry mouth, tachycardia, nausea, vomiting, diarrhea, insomnia, and nervousness.
Case Report: A 26-year-old male with no history of mental illness became manic following chronic consumption of 250 mg *P. ginseng* capsules three times a day. Symptoms, including irritability, insomnia, flight of ideas, and rapid speech, resolved following discontinuation of supplement.[2,10]

DRUG INTERACTIONS
MAOIs: P. ginseng may cause manic-like symptoms when combined with MAOIs.
Insulin and Sulfonylureas: P. ginseng may increase the hypoglycemic effect of insulin and sulfonylureas.
Anticoagulants: P. ginseng may antagonize the effects of anticoagulants.[11]

LABORATORY INTERACTIONS
Reductions in prothrombin time, partial thromboplastin time, and international normalized ratio may occur. Reductions in blood glucose may occur.

CONTRAINDICATIONS
P. ginseng may have estrogenic activity, but data are inconsistent. Patients with hormone-sensitive disease should not consume *P. ginseng*.

DOSAGE
P. ginseng extracts are frequently standardized to 2 to 7% ginsenoside content, but variability exists between each manufacturer, their products, and individual lots.
Oral: P. ginseng extract: 100 mg standardized extract once or twice daily. *Root powder:* 1 to 6 g/d (maximum 12 g) have been used. *Decoction:* 1 to 6 g boiled in water and consumed daily. *Dosage used in clinical trials:* Erectile dysfunction: 900 mg/d.[12,13]

LITERATURE SUMMARY AND CRITIQUE
Vogler BK, Pittler MH, Ernst E. The efficacy of ginseng. A systematic review of randomised clinical trials. Eur J Clin Pharmacol 1999;55:567–75.
The authors reviewed all available randomized trials evaluating Asian *P. ginseng*. A total of 57 trials were found in the literature, of which 41 were excluded (8 were not double blind, 30 evaluated *P. ginseng* in combination with other botanicals or supplements, 3 did not

evaluate the extract of *P. ginseng* root). Of the 16 evaluable trials, no definitive conclusions regarding efficacy could be drawn. Seven studies evaluated *P. ginseng*'s effect on physical performance in healthy male volunteers, five reported cognitive effects, two studied immunomodulation, and individual studies reported glucose control in type 2 diabetic patients and severity and duration of type 2 herpes simplex infections. According to Vogler and colleagues, the majority of studies reviewed were poorly designed or biased. Adverse events, including fatigue, sour stomach, and diarrhea, were reported in 2 of the 16 studies. Various manufacturers and types of *P. ginseng* extracts were used. Therefore, results of individual studies cannot be extrapolated to all *P. ginseng* products. Additional, well-designed clinical research must be conducted to determine optimal use of Asian ginseng.

Cho YK, et al. Long-term intake of Korean red ginseng in HIV-1-infected patients: development of resistance mutation to zidovudine is delayed. Int Immunopharmacol 2001;1:1295–305.
A small, prospective evaluation of patients initiated on zidovudine (AZT) for HIV with or without the addition of Korean red ginseng (KRG) containing 5.4 mg ginsenosides. Change in CD4+, resistance to AZT, and viral load were the primary outcomes measured. Each treatment group consisted of nine patients, and treatment continued for at least 24 months. Cho and colleagues suggest that addition of KRG to AZT therapy may maintain CD4+ cell counts and delay the development of resistance, but the effects of KRG when added to highly active antiretroviral therapy remain unknown. Treatment allocation was not randomized. Also, owing to the small sample size, further research is necessary to confirm these data.

Cardinal BJ, Engels HJ. Ginseng does not enhance psychological well-being in healthy, young adults: results of a double-blind, placebo-controlled, randomized clinical trial. J Am Diet Assoc 2001;101:655–60.
A prospective, double-blind, placebo-controlled, randomized clinical trial evaluating 83 adults randomly assigned to one of three experimental conditions: placebo, 200 mg G115 *P. ginseng*, or 400 mg G115 *P. ginseng*. Each participant was given a 60-day allotment of their respective supplement along with written instructions about the proper intake and storage of the capsules during the 8-week study period. Primary outcomes were change in mood and total mood disturbance as measured by the Profile of Mood Status. Following 1 month of *P. ginseng* supplementation, there was no significant improvement in affect or total mood disturbance compared with placebo ($p > .016$). No significant adverse effects are reported. This study suggests that *P. ginseng* does not alter mood in healthy subjects.

Scaglione F, et al. Efficacy and safety of the standardized ginseng extract G115 for potentiating vaccination against common cold and-or influenza syndrome. Drugs Exp Clin Res 1996;22:65–72.
A prospective, randomized, double-blind, placebo-controlled evaluation of G115 ginseng extract on immune response following administration of the influenza vaccine and rate of common cold and flu infections. Patients were randomized to two capsules of placebo ($n = 113$) or G115 ginseng extract ($n = 114$) once daily initiated 4 weeks prior to vaccination and continued for a total of 12 weeks. Between weeks 4 and 12, 37% of patients on

placebo developed infections consistent with the common cold or influenza versus 13% for those receiving G115. Antibody titers and natural killer cell activity were significantly higher for the active treatment arm compared with the placebo group, 200 versus 148 units and 43.6% versus 27%, respectively. Adverse events for the G115 group included insomnia, nausea, vomiting, and epigastric pain. The authors suggest that G115 improves immune response and decreases the frequency of the common cold and/or influenza. It is unknown if effects persist following discontinuation of G115 as patients were not monitored past 12 weeks. Additional research is necessary to understand the short- and long-term effects of ginseng extract supplementation on the immune system.

REFERENCES

1. Baranov AI. Medicinal uses of ginseng and related plants in the Soviet Union: recent trends in the Soviet literature. J Ethnopharmacol 1982;6:339–53.
2. Huang KC. The pharmacology of Chinese herbs. 2nd ed. New York: CRC Press; 1999.
3. Ang-lee M, et al. Herbal medicines and perioperative care. JAMA 2001;286:208–16.
4. Attele AS, Wu JA, Yuan CS. Ginseng pharmacology. multiple constituents and multiple actions. Biochem Pharmacol 1999;58:1685–93.
5. Cheng TO. *Panax (ginseng)* is not a panacea. Arch Intern Med 2000;160:3329.
6. Nah JJ, et al. Effect of ginsenosides, active components of ginseng, on capsaicin-induced pain-related behavior. Neuropharmacology 2000;39:2180–4.
7. Shin HR, et al. The cancer-preventive potential of *Panax ginseng:* a review of human and experimental evidence. Cancer Causes Control 2000;11:565–76.
8. Yun TK, Choi SY. Non-organ specific cancer prevention of ginseng: a prospective study in Korea. Int J Epidemiol 1998;27:359–64.
9. Cabral de Oliveira AC, et al. Protective effects of *Panax ginseng* on muscle injury and inflammation after eccentric exercise. Comp Biochem Physiol C Toxicol Pharmacol 2001;130:369–77.
10. Engelberg D, McCutcheon A, Wiseman S. A case of ginseng-induced mania. J Clin Psychopharmacol 2001;21:535–6.
11. Brinker F. Herb contraindications and drug interactions. 3rd ed. Sandy (OR): Eclectic Medical Publications; 2001.
12. Hall T, et al. Evaluation of consistency of standardized Asian ginseng products in the ginseng evaluation program. Herbalgram 2001;52:31–45.
13. Hong B, et al. A double-blind crossover study evaluating the efficacy of Korean red ginseng in patients with erectile dysfunction: a preliminary report.
14. Lim DS, et al. Anti-septicaemic effect of polysaccharide from *Panax ginseng* by macrophage activation. J Infect 2002;45:32–8.

Ginseng (Siberian)

A. DONATO

COMMON NAMES
Eleuthero, Russian ginseng, devil's shrub, touch-me-not, wild pepper, shigoka, ci wu ja

SCIENTIFIC NAMES
Eleutherococcus senticosus, Acanthopanax senticosus

KEY WORDS
Eleutherococcus senticosus, Acanthopanax senticosus

CLINICAL SUMMARY
Derived from the root of the plant. Siberian ginseng, or eleuthero, has been used traditionally as an adaptogen, a performance enhancer, and an immunostimulant. Active components are thought to include several eleutherosides and polysaccharides. Eleuthero has been shown to bind to estrogen, progestin, and mineralocorticoid receptors and stimulate T-lymphocyte and natural killer cell production. The literature contains conflicting data. Most published information, which suggests efficacy for proposed claims, is from Russia. Large randomized trials have not been conducted and are required. Adverse events include drowsiness, tachycardia, nervousness, and possible hypoglycemia. Theoretical drug interactions include caffeine, insulin, and hypoglycemics. Various types of ginseng exist (eg, American, Asian, Siberian). Siberian ginseng is technically not a species of ginseng but is thought to have activities comparable to Asian and American ginsengs. Product contamination and concerns about potency compared to labeling are reported. Products should be tested for purity and standardized to content.

CONSTITUENTS
Terpenoid: oleanolic acid; glycosides: eleutheroside A (daucosterin), B1, C to G; phytosterol: beta-sitosterol; coumarins: eleutheroside B1 and B3, isofraxidine; polysaccharide:

eleutherans; others: volatile oils, caffeic acid, coniferyl aldehyde, glucose, maltose, sucrose.[1-3]

WARNINGS

Case reports in the literature suggest possible contamination with incorrect botanical. Analysis of the product suggests that labeled concentration differs from listed or assumed contents. Products should be tested and standardized to ensure purity and accuracy of content.[4]

MECHANISM OF ACTION

The exact mechanism of action has not been determined. In vitro studies indicate that eleuthero contains chemicals that bind to estrogen, progestin, mineralocorticoid, and glucocorticoid receptors. Estrogenic activity was suggested in studies of immature female mice. Stimulation of helper/inductor T lymphocytes and natural killer cells also occurs by an unknown mechanism.[1]

USAGE

Chemotherapy side effects, health maintenance, immunostimulation, strength and stamina.

ADVERSE REACTIONS

Reported: Insomnia, drowsiness, nervousness, tachycardia, headache, hypoglycemia.[1,5]

DRUG INTERACTIONS

Insulin/Hypoglycemics: Theoretical additive hypoglycemic effect.
Caffeine: May have an additive effect leading to insomnia or nervousness.
Hexobarbital: Eleuthero inhibits metabolism possibly by inhibition of cytochrome P-450 2C19.
Digoxin: Elevate serum digoxin levels.[1,6-8]

LABORATORY INTERACTIONS

Siberian ginseng may cause falsely elevated digoxin serum assays.

CONTRAINDICATIONS

Patients with hypertension should not consume ginseng.[4]

DOSAGE

Oral: Products vary in content of various eleutherosides. *Crude herb:* 0.6 to 3.0 g daily. *Ethanolic extract:* 2 to 16 mL one to three times a day for up to 60 days. Ginseng should not be used for more than 1 month (up to 3 months according to some references).[1,4]

LITERATURE SUMMARY AND CRITIQUE

Dowling EA, et al. Effect of *Eleutherococcus senticosus* on submaximal and maximal exercise performance. Med Sci Sports Exerc 1996;28:482–9.

A prospective pair evaluation of 6-week supplementation, with either 60 drops of eleuthero extract (eleutherosides B and E) or placebo. Effects on performance, blood chemistry, and personal perception were recorded. Sixteen subjects were paired and analyzed for 6 weeks on therapy and 2 weeks after discontinuation. No significant difference was documented in any of the indices evaluated including heart rate, oxygenation, serum lactate, time to exhaustion, and psychological measurements. No adverse reactions were noted. The authors concluded that the study may have been underpowered or an inadequate dose of eleuthero was studied. Additional studies are required.

REFERENCES

1. Schulz V, et al. Rational phytotherapy: a physician's guide to herbal medicine. 4th ed. New York: Springer; 2001.
2. Newall C, et al. Herbal medicines: a guide for health-care professionals. 1st ed. London: Pharmaceutical Press; 1996.
3. Baranov AI. Medicinal uses of ginseng and related plants in the Soviet Union: recent trends in the Soviet literature. J Ethnopharmacol 1982;6:339–53.
4. Harkey MR, et al. Variability in commercial ginseng products: an analysis of 25 preparations. Am J Clin Nutr 2001;73:1101–6.
5. Huang KC. The pharmacology of Chinese herbs. 2nd ed. New York: CRC Press; 1999.
6. Brinker F. Herb contraindications and drug interactions. 3rd ed. Sandy (OR): Eclectic Medical Publications; 2001.
7. Medon PJ, Ferguson PW, Watson CF. Effects of *Eleutherococcus senticosus* extracts on hexobarbital metabolism in vivo and in vitro. J Ethnopharmacol 1984;10:235–41.
8. McRae S. Elevated serum digoxin levels in a patient taking digoxin and Siberian ginseng. Can Med Assoc J 1996;155:293–5.

Glehnia

COMMON NAMES
Radix glehniae, Adenophora tetraphylla, sha shen, hamabofu, American silvertop root

SCIENTIFIC NAME
Glehnia littoralis

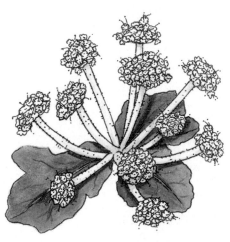

A. DONATO

CLINICAL SUMMARY
Derived from the root of the plant. This supplement is used in traditional Chinese medicine as an expectorant and to treat bronchitis and whooping cough. Its mechanism of action is unknown, but animal models reveal analgesic properties. No adverse reactions are reported, but because photosensitivity may result from the psoralens component, patients receiving radiotherapy should not consume this herb. Theoretically, glehnia may have additive effects with anticoagulants and antiplatelets owing to the coumarin component. Additional research is necessary to determine the safety and efficacy of this botanical.

CONSTITUENTS
Coumarins, psoralens, umbelliferone, ostenol, monoterpenoids, chorchionoside A; volatile oils: alpha-pinene, beta-phellandrene, germacrene B.[1-4]

MECHANISM OF ACTION
The mechanism of action is unknown. It is reported that glehnia root can hemolyze blood cells, stimulate myocardial contractility, and exert antibacterial effects. Various extracts from glehnia root display analgesic effects in a mouse study using acetic acid–induced

writhing tests. Concentrations of 10 to 50 mg/kg polyacetylene and 80 to 100 mg/kg coumarin fractions are necessary to elicit analgesia.[5,6]

USAGE

Bronchitis, chest congestion, whooping cough.

PHARMACOKINETICS

No formal pharmacokinetic studies have been performed.

ADVERSE REACTIONS

No adverse reactions have been reported, but photosensitivity may occur owing to the psoralens component.

DRUG INTERACTIONS

Anticoagulants/Antiplatelets: Theoretically, glehnia root may have additive effects with anticoagulants and antiplatelets owing to the coumarin content.

CONTRAINDICATIONS

Owing to the psoralens content, patients receiving radiation therapy should not consume this herb.

DOSAGE

No dosage has been studied in humans.

LITERATURE SUMMARY AND CRITIQUE

No human trials have been performed with glehnia.

REFERENCES

1. Miyazawa M, et al. Components of the essential oil from *Glehnia littoralis*. Flavour Fragrance J 2001;16:215–8.
2. Kitajima J, et al. Coumarin glycosides of *Glehnia littoralis* root and rhizoma. Chem Pharm Bull 1998;46:1404–7.
3. Ishikawa T, Sega Y, Kitajima J. Water-soluble constituents of *Glehnia littoralis* fruit. Chem Pharm Bull 2001;49:584–8.
4. Kitajima J, et al. New glycosides and furocoumarin from the *Glehnia littoralis* root and rhizoma. Chem Pharm Bull 1998;46:1939–40.
5. Huang KC. The pharmacology of Chinese herbs. 2nd ed. New York: CRC Press; 1999.
6. Okuyama E, et al. Analgesic components of glehnia root (*Glehnia littoralis*). Natural Med 1998;52:491–501.

Glutamine

COMMON NAMES
L-Glutamine, GLN

KEY WORDS
L-Glutamine, GLN

CLINICAL SUMMARY

The most abundant amino acid in the body, synthesized by most body tissues and absorbed from food sources. Patients take glutamine supplements to treat cancer and human immunodeficiency virus/acquired immune deficiency syndrome (HIV/AIDS)-related cachexia or recovery from catabolic states such as surgery, sepsis, and intense exercise. Glutamine is the major fuel source of enterocytes, lymphocytes, and macrophages and is thought to act by enhancing gut integrity, immune function, and protein synthesis. Pilot studies suggest benefit in treating HIV- and cancer-related cachexia when used in combination with β-hydroxy-β-methylbutyrate (HMB) and arginine, but larger long-term studies are needed. Several clinical trials show that parenteral or enteral free glutamine or glutamine-containing dipeptides improve nitrogen balance, preserve intestinal integrity, maintain intracellular glutamine levels, and reduce hospital stay in postsurgical or critically ill patients. Glutamine gargles may ameliorate chemotherapy-induced stomatitis, but further research is necessary. No adverse effects are reported.

MECHANISM OF ACTION

Glutamine is the most abundant amino acid in the body; it is synthesized in most body tissues and absorbed from food sources. It is the major fuel source of enterocytes and colonocytes and is therefore essential for the maintenance of intestinal mucosal integrity and function. It also maintains immune function by serving as the principal metabolic fuel for lymphocytes and macrophages. It acts as a precursor for protein synthesis and, with cysteine and glycine, is involved in glutathione (GSH) synthesis. Intravenous glutamine preserves liver and intestinal GSH stores in animal models of oxidant damage. Glutamine is also involved in nitrogen exchange as it neutralizes and eliminates excess ammonia formed during protein catabolism. As a nitrogen donor, it contributes to the synthesis of other nonessential amino acids, including the purines and pyrimidines, and is therefore essential for the proliferation of most cells. Glutamine plays a supportive role during biochemical

199

stress and sepsis. Although the mechanism in treatment of cachexia is unclear, it is thought that glutamine, a modulator of protein turnover, enhances net protein synthesis.

Glutamine may potentiate the tumoricidal effect of methotrexate (MTX) because polyglutamation of MTX impairs its efflux from tumor cells and may reduce its accumulation in the gut. Rats fed a glutamine-enriched diet while receiving MTX chemotherapy exhibit less enterocolitis, improved hematologic parameters, decreased sepsis, and improved survival. Supplemental intravenous glutamine leads to increases of GSH in the gut, but not in tumors, in a sarcoma-bearing rat model. Clinical evidence suggests that total parenteral nutrition (TPN) supplemented with glutamine improves nitrogen balance, maintains the intracellular glutamine pool, enhances protein synthesis, and prevents deterioration of gut permeability in postsurgery patients.[1-6]

USAGE

Alcoholism, cancer-related cachexia, enhancement of tissue integrity, HIV- and AIDS-associated wasting, immunostimulation, peptic ulcers, recovery from surgery, strength and stamina.

PHARMACOKINETICS

Absorption: Glutamine is taken up by enterocytes from both the gut lumen and the bloodstream. The gut lumen extracts approximately 50 to 80% of free glutamine when administered enterally. After ingestion of 0.1 g/kg glutamine solution, plasma levels increase by at least 50% and peak at 30 minutes before returning to fasting levels after about 2 hours. De novo synthesis occurs in almost all tissues via the enzyme glutamine synthetase, which catalyzes adenosine triphosphate–dependent synthesis from glutamate and ammonia. Glutamine synthetase exists at high concentrations in skeletal muscle, lung, liver, brain, and stomach tissue and is regulated by glutamine levels.

Distribution: Skeletal muscle exhibits the greatest intracellular concentration of glutamine; it contains approximately 60% of total body stores.

Excretion: The pathways of glutamine excretion have not been fully elucidated but probably follow that of other nonessential amino acids.[1,2,5,7,8]

ADVERSE REACTIONS

No significant reactions have been reported. Although concern exists that elevated blood glutamic acid concentration might occur with glutamine supplementation, clinical studies have found no increase in circulating glutamic acid levels.[9]

DRUG INTERACTIONS

Methotrexate (MTX): Glutamine may preferentially increase tumor retention of MTX, thereby increasing its therapeutic efficacy.[6]

DOSAGE

Oral: No Recommended Dietary Allowances or upper safe tolerable levels have been set for glutamine. Various studies have used dosages ranging from 1 to 20 g/d.
Parenteral: 0.23 g/kg body weight has been used.
Enteral: Up to 20 g/d has been used. *Gargle:* 4 g "swish and swallow" twice a day has been used to treat stomatitis.[4,5,10]

LITERATURE SUMMARY AND CRITIQUE

May PE, et al. Reversal of cancer-related wasting using oral supplementation with a combination of beta-hydroxy-beta-methylbutyrate, arginine, and glutamine. Am J Surg 2002;183:471–9.

A randomized, double-blind, nitrogen-controlled, multicenter evaluation of an amino acid nutrient mixture's effect on weight in stage IV cancer patients with solid tumors and weight loss greater than 5%. Chemotherapy and radiotherapy were acceptable during treatment, but other forms of weight maintenance treatments were disallowed. The treatment group (*n* = 24) received Juven powder (3 g HMB, 14 g L-arginine, and 14 g L-glutamine) daily, whereas controls (*n* = 25) received an isonitrogenous and isocaloric mixture of nonessential amino acids. Body weight and composition were measured at baseline and weeks 4, 8, 12, 16, 20, and 24. Only 9 patients (7 HMB/arginine/glutamine, 2 controls) finished the study; 17 withdrew before 4 weeks and 23 withdrew before 24 weeks. At the 4-week evaluation, HMB/arginine/glutamine patients gained 0.95 ± 0.66 kg (1.12 ± 0.68 kg of fat-free mass), whereas controls lost 0.26 ± 0.78 kg (1.34 ± 0.78 kg in fat-free mass). An intent-to-treat analysis showed higher weight gain in HMB/arginine/glutamine patients at 24 weeks than controls (2.27 ± 1.17 kg versus 0.27 ± 1.39 kg, respectively). No changes in quality of life measures were found. Larger trials are necessary.

Clark RH, et al. Nutritional treatment for acquired immunodeficiency virus-associated wasting using beta-hydroxy-beta-methylbutyrate, glutamine, and arginine: a randomized, double-blind, placebo-controlled study. JPEN J Parenter Enteral Nutr 2000;24:133–9.

A prospective, randomized, double-blind evaluation of the effect of HMB, glutamine, and arginine supplementation on weight in patients with HIV exhibiting greater than 5% weight loss over the previous 3 months. Patients were randomized to receive one packet of Juven powder (1.5 g HMB, 7 g glutamine, and 7 g arginine) (*n* = 34) or placebo (*n* = 34) twice daily for 8 weeks. Primary outcomes measured were body weight, lean weight, body fat and muscle content, viral load, and T-cell count. Blood samples were taken to monitor patient compliance. Twenty-two patients withdrew from the study for unknown reasons and three individuals were deemed noncompliant. Final numbers of patients receiving HMB and placebo were 21 and 22, respectively. HMB supplementation significantly improved cumulative and lean weight gain compared with placebo. Although changes in viral load and T-cell subsets were statistically significant, they were not clinically meaningful. HMB appears effective in managing weight loss associated with HIV/AIDS, but long-term studies are required.

Rubio IT, et al. Effect of glutamine on methotrexate efficacy and toxicity. Ann Surg 1998;227:772–80.

A phase I dose-escalation study of oral glutamine supplementation in nine patients with inflammatory breast cancer receiving MTX chemotherapy. Supplementation with 0.5 g/kg/d glutamine began 4 days prior to the start of chemotherapy and continued through 1 week after therapy had finished. Two patients received 40 mg/m³ MTX, three 60 mg/m³ MTX, two 80 mg/m³ MTX, and two 100 mg/m³ MTX for 3 weeks. Toxicity owing to MTX was greatly reduced: no liver or renal toxicities were reported, and no patient required granulocyte colony-stimulating factor for neutropenia. One patient experienced grade I mucositis (at 80 mg/m³). Larger, controlled trials are necessary to evaluate the effect of glutamine on MTX efficacy.

Morlion BJ, et al. Total parenteral nutrition with glutamine dipeptide after major abdominal surgery. A randomized, double-blind, controlled study. Ann Surg 1998;227:302–8.

Twenty-eight patients with elective resection of carcinoma of the colon or rectum were randomized to receive 5 days continuous TPN supplemented with either 1.5 g amino acids/kg/d or 1.3 amino acids plus alanine-glutamine, 0.3 g/kg/d. Urine was collected to measure nitrogen output, and blood samples were obtained before surgery and on days 1, 3, and 6 for routine chemistry and measurement of plasma free amino acids. Nitrogen balances were significantly better in treatment patients than controls on postoperative days 3 and 4 (2.31 ± 0.55 g versus −5.73 ± 0.69 g, $p < .001$) and day 5 (−7.44 ± 4.04 g versus −23.04 ± 2.62 g, $p < .01$). The number of lymphocytes declined in the control group on postoperative day 3 and remained low, whereas normal values were found on days 3 and 6 in treatment patients. Mean hospital stay in the treatment arm was 15.5 days, compared with 21.7 days in the control arm and 22.1 days in historical controls ($p < .05$).

Griffiths RD, et al. Six-month outcome of critically ill patients given glutamine-supplemented parenteral nutrition. Nutrition 1997;13:295–302.

A block-randomized, double-blind, controlled evaluation of parenteral nutrition with ($n = 42$) or without ($n = 42$) glutamine supplementation (median 18 g) in critically ill patients with Acute Physiological and Chronic Health Evaluation (APACHE) II scores of 10 or higher. Treatment groups were comparable at the start of the study. End points were mortality, morbidity, and hospital cost at 6 months postintervention. Mortality rates were similar between groups for the first 20 days. At 6 months, patients receiving glutamine had significantly higher survival rates (24/42 versus 14/42, $p = .049$) and lower hospital cost per survivor. Because the trial was conducted in an intensive care unit (ICU), heterogeneity of primary diagnosis is a limitation of this study.

Jones C, Palmer ET, Griffiths RD. Randomized clinical outcome study of critically ill patients given glutamine supplemented enteral nutrition. Nutrition 1999;15:108–15.

A block-randomized, double-blind, controlled evaluation of enteral nutrition with ($n = 26$) or without ($n = 24$) glutamine supplementation in 50 critically ill patients with APACHE II scores of 11 or higher. End points were mortality, morbidity, and hospital cost at 6 months postintervention. No mortality differences were seen between treatment arms, but median length of ICU stay and postintervention ICU and hospital patient costs were significantly lower in the glutamine group compared with controls (11 days versus 16.5 days and $23,000 versus $30,900, respectively). More control patients developed secondary infections and required supplementation with TPN.

van der Hulst RR, et al. Glutamine and the preservation of gut integrity. Lancet 1993;344:1363–5.

A small randomized, double-blind, controlled evaluation of the effect of parenteral nutrition with ($n = 10$) or without ($n = 10$) glycyl-L-glutamine, for 11 to 14 days, on gut integrity. Treatment arms had the same proportion of patients with inflammatory bowel disease and neoplastic disease. The glutamine/TPN group received TPN supplemented with 0.23 g/kg/d glutamine. Mucosal biopsy specimens were taken from the second part of the duodenum before and 2 weeks after starting TPN. Intestinal permeability, assessed by measuring the ratio of lactulose and mannitol concentrations in the urine, was unchanged in the glutamine/TPN group after 2 weeks and had increased in the standard TPN group. Villus height remained unchanged in the glutamine/TPN group after 2 weeks and had decreased in those receiving standard TPN. Patients receiving glutamine were slightly younger and weighed less than controls, and original diagnoses among all patients were heterogeneous.

REFERENCES

1. Miller AL. Therapeutic considerations of L-glutamine: a review of the literature. Altern Med Rev 1999;4:239–48.
2. Wilmore DW. Metabolic support of the gastrointestinal tract: potential gut protection during intensive cytotoxic therapy. Cancer 1997;79:1794–803.
3. May PE, et al. Reversal of cancer-related wasting using oral supplementation with a combination of beta-hydroxy-beta-methylbutyrate, arginine, and glutamine. Am J Surg 2002;183:471–9.
4. van der Hulst RR, et al. Glutamine and the preservation of gut integrity. Lancet 1993;344:1363–5.
5. Jones C, Palmer TE, Griffiths RD. Randomized clinical outcome study of critically ill patients given glutamine supplemented enteral nutrition. Nutrition 1999;15:108–15.
6. Rubio IT, et al. Effect of glutamine on methotrexate efficacy and toxicity. Ann Surg 1998;227:772–80.
7. Matera M, et al. Pharmacokinetic study of the relative bioavailability and bioequivalence after oral intensive or repeated short term treatment with two polyamino acid formulations. Int J Clin Pharmacol 1993;13:93–105.
8. Castell LM, Newsholme EA. The effects of oral glutamine supplementation on athletes after prolonged, exhaustive exercise. Nutrition 1997;13:738–42.
9. Morlion BJ, et al. Total parenteral nutrition with glutamine dipeptide after major abdominal surgery. A randomized, double-blind, controlled study. Ann Surg 1998;227:302–8.
10. Skubitz KM, Andersen PM. Oral glutamine to prevent chemotherapy induced stomatitis: a pilot study. J Lab Clin Med 1996;127:223–8.

Goldenseal

A.DONATO

COMMON NAMES
Eye root, yellow Indian plant, turmeric root, yellow paint root, orange root, goldenroot

SCIENTIFIC NAME
Hydrastis canadensis

KEY WORD
Hydrastis canadensis

CLINICAL SUMMARY

Derived from the root of the plant. Primary active components are hydrastine, berberine, and canadine. No published clinical studies evaluate its efficacy. Studies have been performed with berberine. Patients who have hypertension or cardiovascular disease or are pregnant should not take this herb. Minimal adverse events have been reported at recommended doses, but nausea, vomiting, hallucinations, or seizures may be signs of toxicity. Potential drug interactions include reduced effect of anticoagulants, inhibition of cytochrome P-450 3A4, and altered response to antihypertensives.

CONSTITUENTS

Alkaloids: hydrastine (1.5–4%), berberine (0.5–6%), canadine, beta-hydrastine, canadaline.[1]

WARNINGS

Berberine-containing botanicals may cause Q–Tc prolongation in patients with severe underlying heart disease.

MECHANISM OF ACTION
Goldenseal is claimed to have anti-inflammatory, astringent, antimicrobial, and laxative properties. The pharmacologic action of goldenseal is attributed to both hydrastine and berberine. The majority of clinical studies are not performed on goldenseal but are focused on berberine and hydrastine. Berberine has been shown to have antimicrobial activity against certain pathogens such as enterotoxigenic *Escherichia coli* and *Vibrio cholerae*. The hydrastine component induces constriction of peripheral blood vessels.[2,3]

USAGE
Anorexia, cancer treatment, cirrhosis, colitis, common cold, conjunctivitis, diabetes, edema, fever, infections, menorrhagia.

ADVERSE REACTIONS
Common: Gastrointestinal complaints.
Rare: Nervousness.
Toxicity: Stomach ulcerations, constipation, convulsions, hallucinations, nausea, vomiting, depression, nervousness, bradycardia, respiratory depression, seizures.[4,5]

DRUG INTERACTIONS
Antihypertensives: Goldenseal may interfere with blood pressure control.
Anticoagulants/Antiplatelets: Berberine may inhibit anticoagulant effects.
Barbiturates: Goldenseal may potentiate effects.
Cytochrome P-450: Goldenseal may inhibit the 3A4 isoenzyme, resulting in increased levels of certain medications.
Vitamin B Complex: Goldenseal may decrease gastric absorption, resulting in possible deficiency.

LABORATORY INTERACTIONS
Berberine may increase bilirubin levels owing to displacement of bilirubin from albumin.
Delta-9-Tetrahydrocannabinol (THC, Marijuana): Goldenseal may interfere with THC detection in urinalysis.
Prothrombin Time/Partial Thromboplastin Time/International Normalized Ratio: Goldenseal may alter anticoagulation test results.[6,7]

CONTRAINDICATIONS
Patients who have hypertension or cardiovascular disease or women who are pregnant or nursing should not consume goldenseal.

DOSAGE

Oral: Capsules: 250 to 500 mg three times a day as an expectorant. *Dried root made into a tea:* 2 to 4 g; *Tincture:* 1:10 w/v (60% ethanol extract) 2 to 4 mg.

LITERATURE SUMMARY AND CRITIQUE

There are no clinical studies reported in MEDLINE using goldenseal. The following studies concern berberine, an active component of goldenseal.

Werbach MR, et al. Botanical influences on illness: a sourcebook of clinical research. Tarzana (CA): Third Line Press; 1994.
Berberine alkaloids produced an average of 91% tumor inhibition against six malignant brain tumor cell lines both in vivo in mice and in vitro against human brain tumors. The berberine alkaloids have shown potent macrophage-activating activity for inducing cytostatic activity against tumor cells.

Zhang RX, et al. Laboratory studies of berberine use alone and in combination with 1,3-bis(2-chloroethyl)-1-nitrosourea to treat malignant brain tumors. Chin Med J 1990;103:658–65.
In vitro studies were performed on a series of human malignant brain tumor cells and rat brain tumor cells. Berberine used alone at a dose of 150 µg/mL had an average cancer cell kill rate of 91%. Carmustine (BCNU) had a cell kill rate of 43%. Rats treated with berberine at 10 mg/kg had an 81% kill rate. The combination of both berberine and BCNU had additive effects on killing cancer cells.

REFERENCES

1. Newall C, et al. Herbal medicines: a guide for health-care professionals. London: Pharmaceutical Press; 1996.
2. Gruenwald J, et al. PDR for herbal medicines. 2nd ed. Montvale (NJ): Medical Economics Company; 1998.
3. Rabbani G, et al. Randomized controlled trial of berberine sulfate therapy for diarrhea due to enterotoxigenic *Escherichia coli* and *Vibrio cholerae*. J Infect Dis 1987;155:979–84.
4. DeSmet PA. Adverse effects of herbal drugs. Vol. 3. Soquel (CA): Springer-Verlag; 1996.
5. Chan E. Displacement of bilirubin from albumin by berberine. Biol Neonate 1993;63:201–8.
6. Mikkelsen SL, Ash KO. Adulterants causing false negatives in illicit drug testing. Clin Chem 1988;34:2333–6.
7. Budzinski JW, et al. An in vitro evaluation of human cytochrome P450 3A4 inhibition by selected commercial herbal extracts and tinctures. Phytomedicine 2000;7:273–82.

Gotu Kola

COMMON NAMES
Indian pennywort, hydrocotyle, mandukaparni, madecassol, TECA, centelase, tsubo-kusa, luei gong gen, idrocotyle, kaki kuda

SCIENTIFIC NAMES
Centella asiatica, Hydrocotyle asiatica

KEY WORDS
Centella asiatica, Hydrocotyle asiatica

A.DONATO

CLINICAL SUMMARY
Extracts from the leaf and the entire plant are used for a variety of conditions, including venous insufficiency, varicose veins, wound healing, scleroderma, and scars. There is a significant amount of in vitro data but few human studies. Several trials demonstrate a reduction in lower-extremity edema with gotu kola compared with placebo for patients with chronic venous insufficiency. It is thought to act on connective tissue, increasing collagen formation and glycosaminoglycan synthesis, and to act as an anti-inflammatory. Possible adverse effects include headache, contact dermatitis, pruritus, and elevations in blood glucose. There are no known drug interactions, but gotu kola theoretically may interact with hypoglycemic agents.

CONSTITUENTS
Amino acids: alanine and serine (major components); terpenoids: triterpenes, asiaticoside, brahmoside and brahminoside (saponin glycosides), aglycones, asiaticentoic acid, centellic acid, centoic acid, madecassic acid; sesquiterpenes: caryophyllene, trans-β-farnesene; volatile oils: germacrene D; alkaloid: hydrocotylin; flavones: quercetin, kaempferol, sesquiterpenes, stigmasterol, sitosterol; other constituents: vallerine, fatty acids, resin, tannins.[1]

WARNINGS

Gotu kola should not be confused with kolanut. Gotu kola does not contain any caffeine and has not been shown to have stimulant properties.

There are wide variations in terpenoid concentrations depending on the location in which gotu kola is grown. Products should be standardized as to asiaticoside, asiatic acid, madecassic acid, and madecassoside content.

MECHANISM OF ACTION

The triterpenoids are considered to be the active constituents in gotu kola. They seem to be involved in wound healing and decreasing venous pressure in venous insufficiency. The glycoside madecassoside has anti-inflammatory properties, whereas asiaticoside appears to stimulate wound healing by stimulating collagen and glycosaminoglycan synthesis. The asiaticosides might also elevate blood glucose and cholesterol levels. There is preliminary evidence that gotu kola might be beneficial in Alzheimer's disease, act as a sedative, and have analgesic properties.[2]

USAGE

Burns, cancer treatment, gastrointestinal disorders, hypertension, memory loss, psoriasis, scars, sedation, varicose veins.

ADVERSE REACTIONS

Reported: Contact dermatitis, pruritus, photosensitization, and headache; reduced fertility may occur in women wishing to become pregnant.
Toxicity: Hyperglycemia, hyperlipidemia, and sedation have occurred following consumption of higher doses.

DRUG INTERACTIONS

Hypoglycemics/Insulin: Theoretically, gotu kola may interfere with blood glucose levels.
Antihyperlipidemics: Theoretically, gotu kola may interfere with cholesterol-lowering agents.

DOSAGE

Oral: Dried leaf capsules (most common formulation): 600 mg three times a day. *European formulations:* Madecassol, TECA, and centelase are standardized to 40% asiaticoside, 29% asiatic acid, 29% madecassic acid, and 2% madecassoside. *Crude plant:* 2 to 4 g given in divided doses three times a day. *Tincture (1:5):* 10 to 20 mL/d given in divided doses three times a day. *Fluid extract (1:1):* 2 to 4 mL/d given in divided doses three times a day. *Venous insufficiency:* 60 to 120 mg of standardized extract daily for 2 months.[3,4]

LITERATURE SUMMARY AND CRITIQUE

Bradwein J, et al. A double-blind placebo-controlled study on the effects of gotu kola (*Centella asiatica*) on acoustic startle response in healthy subjects. J Clin Psychopharmacol 2000;20:680–4.

An evaluation of the effects of gotu kola on the acoustic startle response (ASR) in humans. Subjects were randomly assigned to receive either a single 12 g orally administered dose of gotu kola (*n* = 20) or placebo (*n* = 20). Gotu kola significantly attenuated the peak ASR amplitude 30 and 60 minutes after treatment.

Pointel JP, et al. Titrated extract of *Centella asiatica* (TECA) in the treatment of venous insufficiency of the lower limbs. Angiology 1987;38:46–50.

Ninety-four patients suffering from venous insufficiency of the lower limbs participated in a multicenter, double-blind, placebo-controlled study. After randomization, they were allotted for a treatment period of 2 months to one of three groups: TECA 120 mg/d, TECA 60 mg/d, or placebo. A significant improvement in the symptoms of heaviness in the lower limbs and edema, as well as in the overall evaluation by the patient, was reported for the TECA groups. The venous distensibility measured by mercury strain gauge plethysmograph at three occlusion pressures was improved for the TECA groups but aggravated for the placebo group.[5,6]

REFERENCES

1. Newall CA, et al. Herbal medicines: a guide for health-care professionals. London: The Pharmaceutical Press; 1996.
2. DerMarderosian A, editor. The review of natural products. St. Louis: Facts and Comparisons; 1999.
3. Pointel JP, et al. Titrated extract of *Centella asiatica* (TECA) in the treatment of venous insufficiency of the lower limbs. Angiology 1987;38:46–50.
4. Pizzorno JE, et al. Textbook of natural medicine. 2nd ed. New York: Churchill Livingstone; 1999.
5. Brinkhaus B, et al. Chemical, pharmacological and clinical profile for the East Asian medical plant *Centella asiatica*. Phytomedicine 2000;5:427–48.
6. Bradwein J, et al. A double-blind, placebo-controlled study on the effects of gotu kola *(Centella asiatica)* on acoustic startle response in healthy subjects. J Clin Psychopharmacol 2000;20:680–4.

Green Tea

A. DONATO

COMMON NAMES
Chinese tea, tea, green tea extract, green tea polyphenols, epigallocatechin-3-gallate (EGCG), *Camellia thea, Camellia theifera, Thea sinensis, Thea bohea, Thea viridis*

SCIENTIFIC NAME
Camellia sinensis

KEY WORD
EGCG

CLINICAL SUMMARY
Derived from the leaf of the plant. Patients use this as a dietary beverage and to prevent and treat cancer, hyperlipidemia, hypertension, and atherosclerosis. The principal active constituent in green tea is EGCG, which accounts for 40% of the total polyphenol content of green tea extract. Caffeinated green tea may cause insomnia and nausea. Use of decaffeinated products may be preferred owing to lower incidence of adverse events, but data are inconsistent regarding the relative efficacy of caffeinated versus decaffeinated teas. Tannins in green tea may reduce the absorption and bioavailability of codeine, atropine, and iron supplements. Studies of the chemopreventive activity of green tea indicated some positive results. Green tea polyphenols may reduce the risk of prostate, breast, esophageal, lung, skin, pancreatic, and bladder cancers and oral leukoplakia. Research evaluating the effectiveness of green tea extracts to treat cancer is currently under way. Cardiovascular protection from constituents in green tea is not established in large-scale human studies. Moderate intake of green tea appears safe.

CONSTITUENTS
Caffeine; flavonoids; methylxanthines: theophylline, theobromine, theanine; polyphenols: gallic acid and catechins: gallocatechin (GC), epigallocatechin (EGC), epicatechin

(EC), EGCG; polysaccharides; proanthocyanidins (tannins); vitamins: ascorbic acid, tocopherol; other: fluoride, chlorophyll, organic acids.[1]

WARNINGS

Although the US Food and Drug Administration (FDA) includes tea on their list of "Generally Recognized As Safe" substances, pregnant women and women who breast-feed should limit their intake of green tea because of caffeine content. Because tea can pass into breast milk, it may cause sleep disorders in nursing infants. Green tea ingestion in infants has been linked to impaired iron metabolism and microcytic anemia. Individuals with peptic ulcers may want to avoid drinking green tea because it can stimulate the production of gastric acid.[2]

MECHANISM OF ACTION

The anticancer activity of green tea is thought to be related to its polyphenol content. Its chemopreventive attributes are associated with catechin EGCG, which is thought to induce apoptosis and tumor antiangiogenesis. EGCG may inhibit enzymes involved in cell replication and deoxyribonucleic acid (DNA) synthesis by interfering with cell-to-cell adhesion or via inhibition of intracellular communication pathways required for cell division. In vitro data indicate that concentrations of 30 µg/mL EGCG and (-)-EGC inhibit lipoxygenase-dependent arachidonic acid metabolism by 30 to 75% in normal human colon mucosa and colon cancers. In vitro studies in human colon cancer cell lines suggest that EGCG inhibits topoisomerase I but not topoisomerase II. EGC also inhibits DNA replication in vitro in three leukemia cancer cell lines: Jurkat T, HL-60, and K562. Topical EGCG may be useful as chemoprevention for skin cancer, but additional research and formulation are necessary. Green tea's antioxidant activity may repair oxidative damage to cells, but its role in protection against cancer is unclear. The mechanism of action is not fully known as the biologic activity of its polyphenols may act synergistically with other constituents of the plant. Administration of green tea before and during carcinogen treatment reduces the incidence and number of stomach and esophageal tumors in mice.

The tannins in green tea may have antibacterial properties and can produce antidiarrheal effects. Green tea is thought to confer cardiovascular protection by increasing high-density lipoprotein cholesterol, decreasing low-density lipoprotein cholesterol and triglycerides, and by blocking platelet aggregation. Flavonoids present in green tea may reduce lipoprotein oxidation, although more research on green tea constituents and cardiovascular disease is required. Green tea also contains caffeine, which has stimulatory effects and is responsible for the majority of adverse effects and drug interactions. It is unknown whether removing caffeine alters green tea's activities.[2–19]

USAGE

Cancer prevention, cancer treatment, cardiovascular disease, cognitive improvement, gastrointestinal disorders, hypertension, weight loss.

PHARMACOKINETICS

Catechins from green tea are absorbed rapidly; the addition of milk does not impair the bioavailability of tea catechins in green tea. Following ingestion of steeped green tea leaves or catechin extract, polyphenol can be measured in blood, urine, saliva, and feces. This indicates that ingested polyphenols and their metabolites may provide localized tissue action in addition to indirect gastrointestinal effects.[1,11,20–22]

ADVERSE REACTIONS

Reported (Oral): Nausea and gastrointestinal upset, possibly owing to the tannin content. Insomnia, irritability, and nervousness can occur owing to the caffeine content.

DRUG INTERACTIONS

Adenosine: The caffeine content in green tea may inhibit the hemodynamic effects of adenosine.

Anticoagulants/Antiplatelets: Theoretically, consumption of large amounts of green tea (2–4.5 L/d) may provide enough vitamin K to antagonize the effects of anticoagulants and antiplatelet agents, although this effect has not been reported in humans.

Atropine: The tannin content in green tea may reduce the absorption of atropine.

Iron Supplements: The tannin content in green tea may reduce the bioavailability of iron. Green tea should be taken either 2 hours before or 4 hours following iron administration.

Codeine: The tannin content in green tea may reduce the absorption of codeine.[2,23,24]

LABORATORY INTERACTIONS

Caffeine in green tea may increase the prothrombin time/partial thromboplastin time. Check labels for a caffeine-free product.

DOSAGE

Oral: Highly variable. *Tea:* 3 cups (750 mL) per day of brewed tea (1 tsp or 5 g green tea leaves in 1 cup near boiling water, steeped for 3 minutes). Three cups provides 240 to 320 mg of polyphenols. *EGCG extract capsules/tablets:* 97% polyphenol content is equivalent to drinking 4 cups (1,000 mL) of tea. However, no studies have evaluated the consistency of tablet formulations.[2]

LITERATURE SUMMARY AND CRITIQUE

Pisters KM, et al. Phase I trial of oral green tea extract in adult patients with solid tumors. J Clin Oncol 2001;19:1830–8.

A phase I trial to determine the maximum tolerated dose, toxicity, and pharmacology of oral green tea extract (GTE) administered once or three times daily to patients with refractory solid tumors. Each cohort consisted of three or more adult cancer patients with dose ranges of 0.5 to 5.05 g/m² once daily and 1.0 to 2.2 g/m² three times daily with water after meals for 4 weeks, to a maximum of 6 months. Pharmacokinetic analyses were encouraged but optional. A total of 49 patients were studied. Patient characteristics: median age, 57 years (range 27 to 77 years); 23 patients were women (47%); 21 were diagnosed with non–small cell lung cancer, 19 with head and neck cancer, 3 with mesothelioma, and 6 with other cancers. No major responses were noted. Mild to moderate toxicity was related to caffeine content of GTE and promptly reversed on discontinuation. Dose-limiting toxicities included neurologic and gastrointestinal effects. The maximum tolerated dose was 4.2 g/m² once daily or 1.0 g/m² three times daily (approximately 2.5 L brewed green tea per day). Additional studies are recommended.

Sun CL, et al. Urinary tea polyphenols in relation to gastric and esophageal cancers: a prospective study of men in Shanghai, China. Carcinogenesis 2002;23:1497–503.
A prospective cohort study examining the relationship between tea polyphenols and cancer risk. The Shanghai Cohort consists of 18,244 men aged 45 to 64 with up to 12 years of follow-up. Validated biomarkers of tea polyphenols (ECG, EC, and their metabolites M4 and M6) were measured in urine collected at the introductory interview. Tea intake was not assessed at the interview. One hundred and ninety cases of gastric cancer and 42 cases of esophageal cancer developed; these cases were compared with 772 cohort control subjects matched for age, month/year of sample collection, and neighborhood of residence but not for risk factors. When adjusted for risk factors (smoking, alcohol intake, *Helicobacter pylori* seropositivity, and serum carotene level), tea polyphenols were not associated with a decreased risk of gastric cancer. After exclusion of cases diagnosed under 4 years of follow-up, which the authors justified by proposing that data from patients with advancing disease may have been inappropriate for dietary studies, a protective effect of ECG alone on gastric cancer was found. This effect was primarily seen among subjects with low serum carotenes. It is not likely that a one-time measurement of urine tea polyphenols is an adequate indicator of average long-term tea consumption.

Tsubono Y, et al. Green tea and the risk of gastric cancer in Japan. N Engl J Med 2001;344:632–6.
A prospective population survey conducted in the Miyagi Prefecture of Japan assessing green tea intake and various health habits. A total of 26,311 resident surveys were included equaling nearly 200,000 person-years of follow-up. No association was found between consumption of green tea (range < 1 to > 5 cups per day) and risk of gastric cancer development. Adjustments were made for cigarette and alcohol use, age, health insurance, and other dietary intake. Although the results cannot be extrapolated to other populations, it appears that green tea is not related to an increase or a decrease in the risk of gastric cancer.[25,26]

REFERENCES

1. Yang CS, et al. Blood and urine levels of tea catechins after ingestion of different amounts of green tea by human volunteers. Cancer Epidemiol Biomarkers Prev 1998;7:351–4.

2. LaValle JB, et al. In: Natural therapeutics pocket guide 2000-2001; Hudson (OH):Lexi-comp, Inc.; 2000; p. 452–4.
3. Hamilton-Miller JM. Anti-cariogenic properties of tea (*Camellia sinensis*). J Med Microbiol 2001;50:299–302.
4. Tosetti F, Ferrari N, De Flora S. Angioprevention: angiogenesis is a common and key target for cancer chemopreventive agents. FASEB J 2002;16:2–14.
5. Wang ZY, et al. Inhibitory effect of green tea on the growth of established skin papillomas in mice. Cancer Res 1992;52:6657–65.
6. Kada T, et al. Detection and chemical identification of natural bio-antimutagens. A case of the green tea factor. Mutat Res 1985;150:127–32.
7. Liao S, et al. Growth inhibition and regression of human prostate and breast tumors in athymic mice by tea epigallocatechin gallate. Cancer Lett 1995;96:239–43.
8. Dulloo AG, et al. Efficacy of a green tea extract rich in catechin polyphenols and caffeine in increasing 24-h energy expenditure and fat oxidation in humans. Am J Clin Nutr 1999;70:1040–5.
9. Huang MT, et al. Effects of tea, decaffeinated tea, and caffeine on UVB light-induced complete carcinogenesis in SKH-1 mice: demonstration of caffeine as a biologically important constituent of tea. Cancer Res 1997;57:2623–9.
10. Yang CS, et al. Prevention of carcinogenesis by tea polyphenols. Drug Metab Rev 2001;33:237–53.
11. Yang CS, et al. Human salivary tea catechin levels and catechin esterase activities: implications in human cancer prevention studies. Cancer Epidemiol Biomarkers Prev 1999;8:83–9.
12. Hong J, et al. Effects of purified green and black tea polyphenols on cyclooxygenase- and lipoxygenase-dependent metabolism of arachidonic acid in human colon mucosa and colon tumor tissues. Biochem Pharmacol 2001;62:1175–83.
13. Berger SJ, et al. Green tea constituent (--)-epigallocatechin-3-gallate inhibits topoisomerase I activity in human colon carcinoma cells. Biochem Biophys Res Commun 2001;288:101–5.
14. Smith DM, et al. Green tea polyphenol epigallocatechin inhibits DNA replication and consequently induces leukemia cell apoptosis. Int J Mol Med 2001;7:645–52.
15. Proniuk S, et al. Preformulation study of epigallocatechin gallate, a promising antioxidant for topical skin cancer prevention. J Pharm Sci 2002;91:111–6.
16. Sartippour MR, et al. Green tea inhibits vascular endothelial growth factor (VEGF) induction in human breast cancer cells. J Nutr 2002;132:2307–11.
17. Kinjo J, et al. Activity-guided fractionation of green tea extract with antiproliferative activity against human stomach cancer cells. Biol Pharm Bull 2002;25:1238–40.
18. Hsu SD, et al. Chemoprevention of oral cancer by green tea. Gen Dent 2002;50:140–6.
19. Sun CL, et al. Urinary tea polyphenols in relation to gastric and esophageal cancers: a prospective study of men in Shanghai, China. Carcinogenesis 2002;23:1497–503.
20. Graham HN. Green tea composition, consumption, and polyphenol chemistry. Prev Med 1992;21:334–50.
21. He YH, Kies C. Green and black tea consumption by humans: impact on polyphenol concentrations in feces, blood, and urine. Plant Foods Hum Nutr 1994;46:221–9.
22. van het Hof KH, et al. Bioavailability of catechins from tea: the effect of milk. Eur J Clin Nutr 1998;52:356–9.
23. Brinker F. Herb contraindications and drug interactions. 3rd ed. Sandy (OR): Eclectic Medical Publications; 2001.
24. Taylor JR, Wilt VM. Probable antagonism of warfarin by green tea. Ann Pharmacother 1999;33:426–8.
25. Hoshiyama Y, et al. A prospective study of stomach cancer death in relation to green tea consumption in Japan. Br J Cancer 2002;87:309–13.
26. Chen PC, et al. A green tea-derived polyphenol, epigallocatechin-3-gallate, inhibits IkappaB kinase activation and IL-8 gene expression in respiratory epithelium. Inflammation 2002;26:233–41.

Guarana

COMMON NAMES
Guarana gum, guarana seed, zoom cocoa, Brazilian cocoa

SCIENTIFIC NAME
Paullinia cupana

KEY WORD
Paullinia cupana

CLINICAL SUMMARY
Derived from the seed and gum from the tree. Actions of guarana are attributed primarily to its caffeine content. This product is used mainly as an appetite suppressant and a central nervous system (CNS) stimulant and to alleviate fatigue. Although there are no clinical studies of guarana, there are extensive data regarding caffeine and its activity. Guarana may interact with other medications. It should not be combined with monoamine oxidase inhibitors (eg, tranylcypromine, phenelzine), adenosine, or anxiolytics. Additive effects and potential toxicity may occur when guarana is combined with other caffeine-containing beverages. Guarana has the potential to inhibit platelet activity. Abrupt withdrawal may result in symptoms similar to those seen with caffeine withdrawal.

CONSTITUENTS
Caffeine 2.5 to 7.0%; alkaloids: theophylline and theobromine; tannins: catechutannic acid and catechol; saponins.[1]

MECHANISM OF ACTION

The primary activity of guarana is attributable to its high content of caffeine. Caffeine's actions include CNS stimulation, cardiac stimulation, diuresis, increased blood pressure, inhibition of platelet aggregation, skeletal muscle stimulation, and hyperglycemia.[2,3]

USAGE

Appetite suppression, CNS stimulation, fatigue, sexual performance.[10]

ADVERSE REACTIONS

Common: Diuresis and insomnia.
Toxicity: Anxiety, agitation, headache, irritability, nausea, tachycardia, tremors, vomiting, diarrhea, and premature ventricular contractions.[3–7]

DRUG INTERACTIONS

MAOIs: Guarana may cause hypertensive crisis when combined with isocarboxazid, phenelzine, and tranylcypromine.
Adenosine: Caffeine inhibits the hemodynamic effects of adenosine. Guarana or caffeine should not be consumed for at least 12 hours prior to receiving adenosine.
Clozapine: The effects of clozapine are altered when taken less than 40 minutes after caffeine or guarana administration.
Benzodiazepines: Sedative effects of benzodiazepines may be reduced by caffeine.
Lithium: Serum levels of lithium may be decreased by caffeine.
Aspirin: Absorption and bioavailability of aspirin are increased by caffeine.
Oral Contraceptives, Cimetidine, Verapamil, Disulfiram, Fluconazole, Mexiletine, and Quinolone Antibiotics: Caffeine metabolism is inhibited.
Ephedrine: Ephedrine may increase the stimulatory effects of caffeine.
Acetaminophen (Tylenol): Efficacy of acetaminophen may be increased. Caffeine increases the pain-relieving activity of acetaminophen by 40%.
Terbinafine (Lamisil): Terbinafine decreases the rate of caffeine clearance.[8,9]

LABORATORY INTERACTIONS

Prothrombin time, partial thromboplastin time, and international normalized ratio may be elevated. Blood pressure may be elevated.[9]

DOSAGE

Oral: 200 to 800 mg daily in divided doses. Maximum dose is 3,000 mg.

LITERATURE SUMMARY AND CRITIQUE

No clinical studies were found on the therapeutic effects of guarana. The caffeine content is thought to be responsible for its effects.

REFERENCES

1. McGuffin M. A botanical safety handbook. Boca Raton (FL): CRC Press; 1997.
2. Gruenwald J, et al. PDR for herbal medicines. 2nd ed. Montvale (NJ): Medical Economics Company; 1998.
3. Schulz V, et al. Rational phytotherapy: a physician's guide to the use of herbs and related remedies. 3rd ed. Berlin: Springer; 1998.
4. Fetrow CW, et al. Professional's handbook of complementary and alternative medicines. Philadelphia: Springhouse; 1999.
5. McEvoy GK, et al. AHFS drug information. Bethesda (MD): American Society of Health-System Pharmacists; 1998.
6. Brinker F. Herb contraindications and drug interactions. 2nd ed. Sandy (OR): Eclectic Medical Publications; 1998.
7. Cannon ME, Cooke CT, McCarthy JS. Caffeine-induced cardiac arrhythmia: an unrecognized danger of healthfood products. Med J Aust 2001;174:520–1.
8. Robbers JE. Tyler's herbs of choice: the therapeutic use of phytomedicinals. New York: Haworth Herbal Press; 1999.
9. Wallach J. Interpretation of diagnostic tests: a synopsis of laboratory medicine. Boston: Little, Brown, & Company; 1992.
10. Boozer CN, et al. An herbal supplement containing ma huang-guarana for weight loss: a randomized, double-blind trial. Int J Obes Related Metab Disord 2001;25:316–24.

Hawthorn

COMMON NAMES
Mayflower, quickthorn, whitehorn

SCIENTIFIC NAME
Crataegus monogyna

KEY WORDS
Crataegus monogyna, Shan Zha

CLINICAL SUMMARY

Derived from the flower, leaves, and fruits of the plant. Hawthorn has been used as a digestive aid in traditional Chinese medicine for centuries. Today, hawthorn is used primarily to treat heart failure. Placebo-controlled clinical studies suggest significant improvement in cardiac function, dyspnea, and palpitations for patients with ischemic or hypertensive heart diseases. Frequently reported adverse events include nausea, sweating, and fatigue. Signs of overdose include hypotension and arrhythmias. An initial reduction in digoxin dose may be required if used concomitantly with hawthorn. Other drug interactions include enhanced response to central nervous system (CNS) depressants and antihypertensive agents.

CONSTITUENTS

Amines: phenyletylamine, tyramine, O-methoxyphenethylamine; flavonoids: flavonol (kaempferol, quercetin) and flavone (apigenin, luteolin) derivatives, rutin, vitexin glycosides, oligomeric procyanidins; tannins: condensed proanthocyanidins; other constituents: saponins, cyanogenetic glycosides.[1]

MECHANISM OF ACTION

It is thought that hawthorn causes direct dilation of smooth muscle in coronary vessels, thereby lowering their resistance and increasing blood flow. Hawthorn is also characterized as having positive inotropic effects leading to an increase in heart rate, nerve conductivity, and heart muscle irritability.[1–9]

USAGE

Angina, atherosclerosis, congestive heart failure, hypertension, indigestion.

ADVERSE REACTIONS

Common: Nausea, fatigue, sedation, and sweating.
Toxicity: Hypotension, arrhythmia.[7]

DRUG INTERACTIONS

Digoxin: Hawthorn enhances the action of digoxin. The dose of digoxin may need to be lowered if hawthorn is added. Conversely, an increase in digoxin dose may be required if hawthorn is discontinued.
Hypertensives: Hawthorn may potentiate activity.
Antiarrhythmics: Hawthorn may potentiate or interfere with their activity.
CNS Depressants: Hawthorn may have additive effects.[10]

CONTRAINDICATIONS

Should not be taken by women who are pregnant or breast-feeding.

DOSAGE

Oral: Many different formulations exist; dosages vary between products. *New York Heart Association (NYHA) stage II cardiac insufficiency:* 160 to 900 mg extract (standardized 4 to 20 mg flavonoids/30 to 160 mg oligomeric procyanidins) daily in divided doses for 6 weeks or 120 to 240 mg extract (standardized to 1.8% vitexin rhamnoside/10% procyanidins) three times a day for 6 weeks.

LITERATURE SUMMARY AND CRITIQUE

Hawthorn has been extensively studied in Europe. Few studies to date have been performed in the United States.

Werbach MR, et al. Botanical influences on illness: a sourcebook of clinical research. Tarzana (CA): Third Line Press; 1994.
A controlled, double-blind study of hawthorn versus placebo on patients with ischemic or hypertensive heart disease in NYHA's functional class II or III. The hawthorn group

had significant improvements in cardiac edema, dyspnea, and palpitations. No differences in electrocardiograms were seen between treatment groups. The authors did not report any adverse events.

Iwamoto M, Sato T, Ishizaki T. Klinische Wirkung von Crataegutt bei Herzerkrankungen ischasemischer und/oder hypertensiver Genese. Planta Med 1981;42:1–16.
A hawthorn preparation containing 30 mg hawthorn extract, standardized to 1 mg procyanidins, was used in a double-blind, controlled study of 80 patients (35 active, 45 placebo). The hawthorn group reported a greater overall improvement of cardiac function, dyspnea, and palpitations. Improvements in electrocardiograms were not found to differ. Nausea, fatigue, and sweating were reported in the hawthorn group.

Schmidt U, et al. Efficacy of the hawthorn preparation in 78 patients with chronic congestive heart failure defined as NYHA functional class II. Phytomedicine 1994;1:17–24.
Seventy-eight patients were administered hawthorn extract 600 mg/d or a placebo. After a 1-week washout, patients were treated for 8 weeks. An ergometer bicycle was used to determine working capacity at baseline and during treatment. Between day 0 and day 56, the working capacity of those taking hawthorn increased by 28 watts compared with 5 watts in those receiving placebo. There was a significant decrease in systolic blood pressure and heart rate compared with placebo.

REFERENCES
1. Newall C, et al. Herbal medicines: a guide for health care professionals. London: Pharmaceutical Press; 1996.
2. Tyler V. Herbs of choice, the therapeutic use of phytomedicinals. Binghamton (NY): Pharmaceutical Press; 1994.
3. Gildor A. *Crataegus oxyacantha* and heart failure. Circulation 1998;98:2098.
4. Schussler M, Holzl J, Fricke U. Myocardial effects of flavonoids from *Crataegus* species. Arzneimittelforschung 1995;45:843–5.
5. Upton R, et al. Hawthorn leaf with flower: quality control, analytical and therapeutical monograph. Belmont (CA): American Herbal Pharmacopoeia; 1999.
6. Blumenthal M, et al. The complete German Commission E monographs: therapeutic guide to herbal medicines. Austin (TX): American Botanical Council; 1998.
7. Iwamoto M, Sato T, Ishizaki T. Klinische Wirkung von Crataegutt bei Herzerkrankungen ischasemischer und/oder hypertensiver Genese. Planta Med 1981;42:1–16.
8. Walker AF, et al. Promising hypotensive effect of hawthorn extract: a randomized double-blind pilot study of mild, essential hypertension. Phytother Res 2002;16:48–54.
9. Rigelsky JM, Sweet BV. Hawthorn: pharmacology and therapeutic uses. Am J Health Syst Pharm 2002;59:417–22.
10. Brinker F. Herb contraindications and drug interactions. 2nd ed. Sandy (OR): Eclectic Medical Publications; 1998.

HMB

COMMON NAMES
β-Hydroxymethylbutyrate, β-hydroxy-β-methylbutyrate monohydrate

SCIENTIFIC NAME
β-Hydroxy-β-methylbutyrate

KEY WORDS
Juven, β-hydroxymethylbutyrate

CLINICAL SUMMARY
A metabolite of the amino acid leucine. Patients use β-hydroxy-β-methylbutyrate (HMB) for body strength, muscle gain, human immunodeficiency virus/acquired immune deficiency syndrome (HIV/AIDS) wasting, and cancer-related cachexia. The mechanism of action is unknown. Clinical studies suggest that HMB increases lean weight gain and reduces adipose tissue. HMB does not increase muscle strength or affect plasma levels of androgens, cortisol, or insulin. Of note, most published clinical trials were sponsored by Metabolic Technologies Inc. (Ames, IA), the manufacturer of Juven (proprietary blend of arginine, glutamine, and HMB). No side effects or drug interactions have been reported. The usual dose is 3 g/d administered in divided doses. HMB may be of benefit in HIV wasting, but additional research is necessary concerning use for cancer-related cachexia.

CONSTITUENTS
β-Hydroxy-β-methylbutyrate.

MECHANISM OF ACTION
The mechanism of action is unknown. Theoretically, HMB reduces skeletal muscle proteolysis. HMB may be metabolized to HMB coenzyme A, which can elevate cholesterol and androgen synthesis. HMB does not affect circulating plasma levels of testosterone, cortisol, insulin-like growth factor-1, or insulin. In animal studies, HMB causes a decrease in total subcutaneous fat content and a reduction in low-density lipoprotein cholesterol.[1–5]

USAGE

Cancer-related cachexia, HIV- and AIDS-associated wasting, strength and stamina, weight gain.

PHARMACOKINETICS

Following single-dose administration of 3 g of HMB to healthy volunteers, peak plasma levels of nearly 480 nmol/L occur in about 1 hour. Concomitant administration of HMB and 75 g of glucose appears to reduce the rate but not the extent of HMB absorption. The biologic half-life is approximately 2.4 hours, with less than 30% of the parent compound excreted in the urine. Animal studies indicate that there is no toxicity with doses up to 5,000 mg/kg/dose for up to 16 weeks.[5,6]

ADVERSE REACTIONS

None reported.

DRUG INTERACTIONS

None known.

LABORATORY INTERACTIONS

May reduce low-density lipoprotein.[1]

DOSAGE

Oral: 3 g/d administered in split doses either two or three times daily.

LITERATURE SUMMARY AND CRITIQUE

Vukovich MD, et al. Body composition in 70-year-old adults responds to dietary β-hydroxy-β-methylbutyrate similarly to that of young adults. J Nutr 2001;131: 2049–52.

A prospective, randomized, double-blind study evaluating the effect of 3 g/d HMB ($n = 14$) or placebo ($n = 17$) supplementation on muscle gain and weight loss in healthy subjects 70 years or older. Patients took four 250 mg capsules of HMB or placebo three times a day and completed an 8-week program of exercise and resistance training. Blood samples monitored patient compliance. Primary outcome was change in body composition as determined by skinfold measurements, computed tomographic scans, and dual x-ray absorptiometry. Compared with those who received placebo, patients receiving HMB showed a statistically significant decrease in total body fat. There was no significant difference in fat-free mass gain or improvement in strength. No adverse effects from supplementation were noted. This study does not address the effect of HMB in older patients without exercise or resistance training, nor did it study changes in fat or muscle composition following discontinuation of HMB.

May PE, et al. Reversal of cancer-related wasting using oral supplementation with a combination of β-hydroxy-β-methylbutyrate, arginine, and glutamine. Am J Surg 2002;183:471–9.
A randomized, double-blind, nitrogen-controlled, multicenter trial of the effects of an amino acid nutrient mixture in stage IV cancer patients with solid tumors and weight loss greater than 5%. Chemotherapy and radiotherapy were acceptable during treatment, but other forms of weight maintenance treatments were disallowed. The treatment group ($n = 24$) received Juven powder (3 g of HMB, 14 g of L-arginine, and 14 g of L-glutamine) daily, whereas controls ($n = 25$) received an isonitrogenous and isocaloric mixture of nonessential amino acids. Body weight and composition were measured at baseline and weeks 4, 8, 12, 16, 20, and 24. Only nine patients (7 HMB/arginine/glutamine, 2 control) finished the study; 17 withdrew before 4 weeks and 23 withdrew before 24 weeks. At the 4-week evaluation, HMB/arginine/glutamine patients gained 0.95 ± 0.66 kg (1.12 ± 0.68 kg of fat-free mass), whereas controls lost 0.26 ± 0.78 kg (1.34 ± 0.78 kg in fat-free mass). An intent-to-treat analysis showed higher weight gain in HMB/arginine/glutamine patients at 24 weeks than controls (2.27 ± 1.17 kg versus 0.27 ± 1.39 kg, respectively). No changes in quality of life measures were found. Larger trials are necessary.

Clark RH, et al. Nutritional treatment for acquired immunodeficiency virus-associated wasting using β-hydroxy-β-methylbutyrate, glutamine, and arginine: a randomized, double-blind, placebo-controlled study. JPEN J Parenter Enteral Nutr 2000;24:133–9.
A prospective, randomized, double-blind evaluation of HMB, glutamine, and arginine supplementation on weight in patients with HIV exhibiting greater than 5% weight loss over the previous 3 months. Patients were randomized to receive one packet of Juven powder (1.5 g of HMB, 7 g of glutamine, and 7 g of arginine) ($n = 34$) or placebo ($n = 34$) twice daily for 8 weeks. Primary outcomes measured were body weight, lean weight, body fat and muscle content, viral load, and T-cell count. Blood samples were taken to monitor patient compliance. Twenty-two patients withdrew from the study for unknown reasons and three individuals were deemed noncompliant. The final number of patients receiving HMB and placebo was 21 and 22, respectively. HMB supplementation significantly improved cumulative and lean weight gain compared with placebo. Although changes in viral load and T-cell subsets were statistically significant, they were not clinically meaningful. HMB appears to be effective in managing weight loss associated with HIV/AIDS, but long-term studies are required.

REFERENCES

1. Slater GJ, Jenkins D. β-Hydroxy-β-methylbutyrate (HMB) supplementation and the promotion of muscle growth and strength. Sports Med 2000;30:105–16.
2. Nissen S, et al. β-Hydroxy-β-methylbutyrate (HMB) supplementation in humans is safe and may decrease cardiovascular risk. J Nutr 2000;130:1937–45.

3. Gallagher PM, et al. β-Hydroxy-β-methylbutyrate ingestion, part II: effects on hematology, hepatic and renal function. Med Sci Sports Exerc 2000;32:2116–9.
4. Gallagher PM, et al. β-Hydroxy-β-methylbutyrate ingestion, part I: effects on strength and fat free mass. Med Sci Sports Exerc 2000;32:2109–15.
5. Slater GJ, et al. β-Hydroxy β-methylbutyrate (HMB) supplementation does not influence the urinary testosterone: epitestosterone ratio in healthy males. J Sci Med Sport 2000;3:79–83.
6. Vukovich MD, et al. β-Hydroxy-β-methylbutyrate (HMB) kinetics and the influence of glucose ingestion in humans. J Nutr Biochem 2001;12:631–9.

Horse Chestnut

COMMON NAMES
Chestnut, marron europeen, escine, aescin

SCIENTIFIC NAME
Aesculus hippocastanum

KEY WORD
Aesculus hippocastanum

A. DONATO

CLINICAL SUMMARY
Derived from the seeds of the tree. This herb contains several active components. Commercial products should be standardized to 50 mg of aescin and free from aesculin, a hydroxycoumarin. Studies have shown clinical efficacy in chronic venous insufficiency, but no data support the reversal of varicose veins. At recommended doses, no significant adverse reactions are reported. Patients with compromised renal or hepatic function should not consume horse chestnut products. Horse chestnut extracts that contain aesculin may interact with anticoagulants and increase the risk of bleeding.

CONSTITUENTS
Coumarins: aesculetin, fraxin, scopolin; flavonoids: flavonol (kaempferol, quercetin), glycosides including astragalin, isoquercetrin, rutin, leucocyanidin; saponins: several saponins collectively referred to as aescin; tannins; other constituents: allantoin, amino acids, choline, citric acid, phytosterol.[1]

WARNINGS

Horse chestnut seed is classified by the US Food and Drug Administration as an unsafe herb. Many of the constituents are considered toxic, such as the glycosides and the saponins. Should not be consumed by patients with hepatic or renal insufficiency.[2]

MECHANISM OF ACTION

Anti-inflammatory actions have been documented for the saponins (aescin). Aescin reduces transcapillary filtration of water and protein and increases venous tone related to increased prostaglandin $F_{2\alpha}$ (vasoconstrictor). It stabilizes cholesterol-containing membranes of lysosomes and limits the release of the enzymes. Usually, the release of the enzymes is increased in chronic pathologic conditions of the vein. It also improves vascular resistance and aids toning of vein walls. Aesculetin (esculin) is a hydroxycoumarin, which may increase bleeding time. The triterpene glycosides and steroid saponins decrease venous capillary permeability and appear to have a tonic effect on the circulatory system.[3,4]

USAGE

Circulatory disorders, diarrhea, hemorrhoids, phlebitis, varicose veins.

PHARMACOKINETICS

Orally administered aescin has an absorption half-life of about 1 hour and an elimination half-life of about 20 hours.[5]

ADVERSE REACTIONS

Common: Gastrointestinal upset, nausea, and vomiting.
Toxicity: Chestnut poisoning: Diarrhea, muscle twitching, dilated pupils, depression, and paralysis.

DRUG INTERACTIONS

Anticoagulants/Antiplatelets: Horse chestnut may have an additive anticoagulant effect owing to aesculin, a hydroxycoumarin. No reported interactions with Venastat (does not contain aesculin) have been reported (D. Morrison, Boehringer-Ingelheim, personal communication, August 17, 2001).

LABORATORY INTERACTIONS

May prolong activated partial thromboplastin time, partial thromboplastin time, international normalized ratio.

DOSAGE

Oral: One capsule, standardized to 50 mg aescin, taken once or twice a day.
Intravenous: Not available in the United States.

LITERATURE SUMMARY AND CRITIQUE

Pittler MH, et al. Horse-chestnut seed extract for chronic venous insufficiency. A criteria-based systematic review. Arch Dermatol 1998;134:1356–60.
A criteria-based systematic review of double-blind, randomized, controlled trials of oral horse chestnut extract for patients with chronic venous insufficiency. Thirteen studies (eight placebo controlled) with a total of 1,083 patients were reviewed. Trial length ranged from 4 to 12 weeks, with a total of 63 dropouts. Use of horse chestnut seed extract was associated with a statistically significant decrease in lower-leg volume and reduction of leg circumference at the calf and ankle compared with placebo. Symptoms such as leg pain, pruritus, fatigue, and tenseness were also reduced. Adverse effects were mild and comparable to placebo. It was the authors' conclusion that short-term, symptomatic use of horse chestnut appears to be safe, but long-term studies are necessary.

Diehm C, et al. Comparison of leg compression stocking and oral horse-chestnut seed extract therapy in patients with chronic venous insufficiency. Lancet 1996;347:292–4.
Comparison of therapies in 240 patients with chronic venous insufficiency. Patients were treated over a period of 12 weeks in a randomized, partially blinded, placebo-controlled, parallel-study design. Lower-leg volume of the more severely affected limb decreased on average by 43.8 mL with horse chestnut and 46.7 mL with compression therapy, whereas it increased by 9.8 mL with placebo after 12 weeks of therapy. These results indicate that compression stocking therapy and horse chestnut therapy are alternative therapies for the effective treatment of patients with edema resulting from chronic venous insufficiency.

REFERENCES

1. Newall C, et al. Herbal medicines: a guide for health-care professionals. London: Pharmaceutical Press; 1996.
2. Tyler V. Herbs of choice, the therapeutic use of phytomedicinals. Binghamton (NY): Pharmaceutical Press; 1994.
3. Fetrow CW, et al. Professional's handbook of complementary and alternative medicines. Philadelphia: Springhouse; 1999.
4. Brinker F. Herb contraindications and drug interactions. 2nd ed. Sandy (OR): Eclectic Medical Publications; 1998.
5. Schulz V, et al. Rational phytotherapy: a physician's guide to herbal medicine. 3rd ed. Berlin: Springer; 1998.

Hoxsey Herbal Therapy

COMMON NAMES
Hoxsey herbs, Hoxsey formula, Hoxsey method

CLINICAL SUMMARY
Alternative therapy composed of herbal tonics and a restrictive diet that supposedly cures cancer. The Hoxsey treatment, illegal in the United States, is available at the Bio-Medical Center and other clinics in Tijuana, Mexico. According to inventor Harry Hoxsey (1901–1974), a self-taught healer, the principal "brown" tonic contains potassium iodide, licorice, red clover, burdock root, stillingia root, barberry, cascara, pokeroot, prickly ash bark, and buckthorn bark at unknown concentrations (see individual monographs at http://www.mskcc.org/aboutherbs). The diet eliminates pork, vinegar, tomatoes, pickles, carbonated drinks, alcohol, bleached flour, sugar, and salt and emphasizes iron, calcium, vitamin C, yeast supplements, and grape juice. Hoxsey claimed that the treatment detoxifies the body, strengthens the immune system, balances body chemistry, and allows the body to digest and excrete tumors. Superoxide dismutase (SOD), vitamin B_{12}, Gerovital (a mixture of procaine hydrochloride and vitamins), "Prolobin liver," TST-100, rosette cactus, Koch Antitoxins, bacille Calmette-Guérin vaccine, and Shulte's medications sometimes are included in the regimen. Hoxsey was convicted numerous times for practicing medicine without a license; the US government reported that the 400 patients Hoxsey claimed to have cured never had cancer and were cured before receiving his treatment, still had cancer, or had died from the disease. The National Cancer Institute (NCI) evaluated 137 case reports submitted by Hoxsey and concluded that none showed efficacy. Although in vitro and animal data suggest that some tonics may have antitumor or immunostimulant properties, no clinical data support the value of this therapy. Patients should be urged not to use the Hoxsey method.

CONSTITUENTS
Formulae have varied with time and by clinic.

Brown Tonic (per 5 cc): Potassium iodide, 150 mg; licorice (*Glycyrrhiza glabra*), 20 mg; red clover (*Trifolium pratense*), 20 mg; burdock root (*Arctium lappa*), 10 mg; stillingia root (*Stillingia sylvatica*), 10 mg; barberry (*Berberis vulgaris*), 10 mg; cascara (*Cascara sagrada*), 5 mg; prickly ash bark (*Zanthoxylum americanum*), 5 mg; buckthorn bark (*Rhamnus catharticus*), 20 mg; pokeroot (*Phytolacca americana*), 10 mg.

Pink Tonic: Potassium iodide, elixir lactate of pepsin.

External Paste: Antimony trisulfide, zinc chloride, bloodroot.
External Powder: Arsenic sulfide, sulfur, talc.
Topical Liquid: Trichloroacetic acid.[1,2]

WARNINGS

The American Cancer Society (ACS) strongly urges cancer patients not to use the Hoxsey treatment as no objective evidence exists to support its efficacy.[2]

MECHANISM OF ACTION

Hoxsey claimed that the internal formulation "stimulates the elimination of toxins that poison the system, thereby correcting the abnormal blood chemistry and normalizing cell metabolism." His head nurse added that it restores acid/base balance, normal metabolism, and immune function and "deals with the [deoxyribonucleic acid] DNA." None of these claims are substantiated by scientific data. The herbal tonic was developed by Hoxsey's great grandfather, whose horse was reportedly cured of a leg tumor after eating wild herbs growing nearby. Hoxsey combined these herbs with home cancer remedies to create the brown tonic. In vitro and animal studies conducted with individual components (eg, licorice, red clover, burdock, pokeroot, stillingia, barberry) indicate possible antitumor and immunostimulant properties, but their concentrations and activity in the tonic have not been determined. Despite claims of selective cytotoxicity, topical preparations used in the Hoxsey treatment contain caustic ingredients that do not differentiate between cancerous and healthy tissue.[1,2]

USAGE

Cancer treatment.

PHARMACOKINETICS

No formal pharmacokinetics studies have been conducted.

ADVERSE REACTIONS

External Paste and Powder: Severe burns, scars, and disfigurement can occur with use of the external treatments.
Iodine Toxicity: "Iodisms" can result from intake as low as 60 mg/d or long-term use, causing pimples, excessive secretion of the eyes or nose, impotence, and inflammation of salivary glands.
Buckthorn: A violent laxative, causing abdominal pain, dehydration, anxiety, decreased respirations, diarrhea, nausea, trembling, and vomiting.

Cascara: Only approved for short-term use. Laxative effects can cause abdominal pain, cramping, diarrhea, discoloration of urine, fluid and electrolyte imbalance, osteomalacia, steatorrhea, vitamin and mineral deficiencies, vomiting.

Licorice: Hypertension, lethargy, muscle pain, cardiac arrhythmias, sodium retention, hypokalemia, hypermineralcorticoidism, pseudohyperaldosteronism, decreased libido in men, and suppression of scalp sebum secretion.

Pokeweed: Nausea, vomiting, diarrhea, abdominal cramps. Ingestion has been associated with illnesses requiring hospitalization and has caused deaths in children and heart block.[2–5]

DRUG INTERACTIONS

Potassium iodine has been found to interact with the following medications:

Lithium: Concomitant use has been found to cause hyperthyroidism.

Anticoagulants: Decreased effectiveness (however, this may be counteracted by the coumarin derivatives in prickly ash).[4]

Please see individual monographs at the above Web site for drug interactions.

DOSAGE

Oral: Hoxsey recommended that the tonic be diluted with water before ingested, taken "when [patients] feel like they need some."

The flat fee for treatment at the Bio-Medical Center is $3,500, not including costs of additional laboratory tests, imaging, or other prescribed medications.[2]

LITERATURE SUMMARY AND CRITIQUE

No clinical trials, only retrospective reviews, evaluate the Hoxsey treatment. In the 1940s and 1950s, the NCI evaluated 137 case reports of patients Hoxsey claimed to have cured with his internal herbal tonic. The NCI found no evidence that the tonic is more effective than no treatment at all. Researchers from the University of British Columbia followed up on 71 of Hoxsey's patients in 1957 and also found inadequate evidence for the treatment's effectiveness. Subsequent reviews of the available literature and cases by the ACS have reached the same conclusion.[1,2]

Austin S, Dale EB, DeKadt S. Long term follow-up of cancer patients using Contreras, Hoxsey and Gerson therapies. J Naturopath Med 1994;5:74–6.

A small, prospective evaluation of patient survival at three Tijuana clinics, including the Biomedical Center. Patients were interviewed at the clinic regarding location of primary tumor, presence of metastasis, and whether it was biopsy confirmed. Most patients were unaware of the stage of their cancer, and medical records were not available for review. Patients receiving Hoxsey treatment (*n* = 39) were queried by mail yearly for 4 to 5 years or until death; the 23 who did not reply were excluded. Of the 16 evaluable patients, 10 died with an average survival from the beginning of the study of 15.4 months. The 6 remaining patients claimed to be disease free with an average follow-up of 58 months.

Meaningful statistical analysis and comparison with historical controls could not be performed owing to the small sample size for each cancer site. Because of the obvious flaws of this study—the majority of patients lost to follow-up, lack of access to detailed medical records, and reliance on patients for disease stage information—the authors claim that their results are uncertain but should provoke interest in further investigation of the Hoxsey treatment.

Richardson MA, et al. Assessment of outcomes at alternative medicine cancer clinics: a feasibility study. J Altern Complement Med 2001;7:19–32.
A recent evaluation of record keeping at the Bio-Medical Center found that only 43.6% of patients treated for cancer had pathologic confirmation, data needed for follow-up on outcomes were not available, and 60 to 90% of patients had received prior conventional therapy. The authors concluded that a retrospective study of survival to evaluate the efficacy of this clinic's treatment is not feasible.

REFERENCES

1. American Cancer Society. Questionable methods of cancer management: "nutritional" therapies. CA Cancer J Clin 1993;43:309–19.
2. American Cancer Society. Hoxsey Method/Bio-Medical Center. CA Cancer J Clin 1990;40:51–5.
3. Smith M, Boon HS. Counseling cancer patients about herbal medicine. Pat Educ Couns 1999;38:109–20.
4. Fetrow CW, et al. Professional's handbook of complementary and alternative medicines. Philadelphia: Springhouse; 1999.
5. Hoxsey herbal treatment. American Cancer Society's guide to complementary and alternative methods. American Cancer Society. Available at: http://www.cancer.org/docroot/eto/content/eto_5_3x_ hoxsey-herbal-treatment.asp?Sitearea-eto (accessed April 2, 2003).
6. Janssen WF. Cancer quackery: past and present. FDA Consumer 1977;11:27–32.

Huanglian

COMMON NAMES
Goldthread, *Coptis chinese, Coptis deltoidea, Coptis teetoides*

SCIENTIFIC NAME
Coptis chinensis

KEY WORD
Coptis chinensis

CLINICAL SUMMARY

Derived from the root of the plant. This supplement is used in traditional Chinese medicine primarily for gastrointestinal complaints, diarrhea, hypertension, and bacterial and viral infections. Berberine and berberine-like alkaloids are thought to be responsible for its activity. Laboratory studies indicate that berberine induces morphologic changes and internucleosomal deoxyribonucleic acid (DNA) fragmentation in hepatoma cancer cells. Preliminary data support the hypothesis that huanglian suppresses cyclin B_1 protein and causes cell-cycle arrest at G_2. It also interacts with acetylcholine and muscarinic receptors and inhibits cholinesterase. Possible adverse effects include nausea and vomiting. There are no known drug interactions. Theoretically, huanglian may have additive hypotensive effects with antihypertensive agents. A phase I dose-ranging study of huanglian in solid tumors is currently under way at the Memorial Sloan-Kettering Cancer Center (MSKCC) based on promising in vitro results.

CONSTITUENTS

Alkaloids: berberine (7–9%), coptisine, urbenine, worenine, palmaline, jatrorrhizine, columbamine.[1]

MECHANISM OF ACTION

The berberine and berberine-like compounds in huanglian are thought to be responsible for its activity. Berberine inhibits human hep-62 hepatoma cell growth owing to morphologic changes and internucleosomal DNA fragmentation. Huanglian also inhibits topoisomerase I and is thought to suppress cyclin B_1 protein and cause cancer cell arrest at the G_2 phase. Berberine interferes with gastric peristalsis, resulting in antidiarrheal activity, and with the bacterial metabolism of carbohydrates, protein synthesis, and complex nucleic acids, resulting in growth inhibition. Hypotensive effects are thought to be mediated by muscarinic stimulation and inhibition of cholinesterase. In dogs, berberine shows positive inotropic effects and lowers peripheral vascular resistance. Berberine also inhibits platelet aggregation and can antagonize thromboxane B_2. Berberine can cause potassium channel blockade, resulting in prolongation of the action potential in cat ventricular monocytes.[1-3,5]

USAGE

Cancer treatment, diarrhea, car infections, hypertension, microbial infection, respiratory infections.

ADVERSE REACTIONS

Common (Oral): Nausea, vomiting, and dyspnea.
Toxicity (Oral): Seizures, hepatic toxicity, and cardiac toxicity.[1]

DRUG INTERACTIONS

Antihypertensives: Theoretically, huanglian may cause additive hypotension.

CONTRAINDICATIONS

Huanglian displaces bilirubin and should not be administered to jaundiced neonates. Berberine-containing botanicals may cause Q–Tc prolongation in patients with severe underlying heart disease.[4]

DOSAGE

Oral: Tea: Up to 30 g/d brewed as a tea has been used, but the taste is quite bitter.
Topical: 20% huanglian extract solution directly applied to skin.

LITERATURE SUMMARY AND CRITIQUE

There are no published trials evaluating the efficacy of huanglian for any of its traditional applications. However, a phase I trial evaluating huanglian capsules on solid tumors is being conducted at MSKCC as in vitro studies conducted here suggest potential activity.

REFERENCES

1. Huang KC. The pharmacology of Chinese herbs. 2nd ed. New York: CRC Press; 1999.
2. Kobayashi Y, et al. Inhibitors of DNA topoisomerase I and II isolated from the *Coptis* rhizomes. Planta Med 1995;61:414–8.
3. Lin HL, et al. Up-regulation of multidrug resistance transporter expression by berberine in human and murine hepatoma cells. Cancer 1999;85:1937–42.
4. Brinker F. Herb contraindications and drug interactions. 3rd ed. Sandy (OR): Eclectic Medical Publications; 2001.
5. Li XK, et al. Huanglian, a Chinese herbal extract, inhibits cell growth by suppressing the expression of cyclin B1 and inhibiting CDC2 kinase activity in human cancer cells. Mol Pharmacol 2000;58:1287–93.

Hydrazine Sulfate

COMMON NAMES
Sehydrin, hydrazine, hydrazine monosulfate, HS

CLINICAL SUMMARY
A synthetic chemical (H_4N_2-H_2SO_4) primarily used in industrial manufacturing (eg, agricultural chemicals, rocket fuel). Patients use hydrazine sulfate to treat cancer, maintain or gain weight, and ameliorate cancer-related cachexia. It is thought to interfere with gluconeogenesis via the inhibition of phospho*enol*pyruvate carboxykinase. It has moderate monoamine oxidase inhibitor (MAOI) activity. Several large randomized clinical trials failed to show overall significant benefit from hydrazine supplementation. Animal studies suggest that hydrazine is carcinogenic, although it is not established in humans. Potential adverse effects include nausea, pruritus, dizziness, peripheral neuropathies, hypoglycemia, and insomnia. Case reports detailing fatal hepatorenal failure and encephalopathy exist in the literature. Potential drug interactions include increased hydrazine toxicity when combined with benzodiazepines, barbiturates, and alcohol. Theoretically, foods high in tyramine content, meperidine, sympathomimetics, and dextromethorphan should be avoided owing to MAOI activity. Hydrazine sulfate has not been proven to alleviate cancer-related cachexia or to improve cancer survival.

CONSTITUENTS
Chemical formula: H_4N_2-H_2SO_4; molecular weight: 130 daltons.

WARNINGS
Hydrazine is classified as a carcinogen.

MECHANISM OF ACTION
Hydrazine sulfate is thought to inhibit phospho*enol*pyruvate carboxykinase, an enzyme involved with the Cori cycle for gluconeogenesis from anaerobically metabolized lactic acid. Hydrazine therapy is used to antagonize the inappropriate activation of gluconeogenesis pathways, reduce excessive gluconeogenesis, and improve glucose tolerance particularly in patients with cancer and cancer-related cachexia. Hydrazine also has been shown to be a weak MAOI. Inhibition and stabilization of glioblastoma cell growth have

been seen in vitro and in animal models, but the significance in humans is unknown. Hydrazine sulfate appears to have no effect on prostate cancer cell lines in vitro.[1-4]

USAGE
Cancer treatment, cancer-related cachexia, weight gain, weight maintenance.

ADVERSE REACTIONS
Common: Nausea, pruritus, dizziness, sedation, peripheral neuropathies, hypoglycemia, insomnia.
Case Reports: Hepatorenal failure, encephalopathy.
Food Interactions: Foods containing high amounts of tyramine (red wine, aged cheeses, etc) should be avoided.[4-6]

DRUG INTERACTIONS
Barbiturates: Increased toxicity of hydrazine has been suggested.
Alcohol: Increased toxicity of hydrazine has been suggested.
Benzodiazepines: Increased toxicity of hydrazine has been suggested.
Meperidine: Theoretical interaction owing to monoamine oxidase inhibition caused by hydrazine. Potential for hypertensive crisis.
Dextromethorphan: Theoretical interaction owing to monoamine oxidase inhibition caused by hydrazine. Potential for hypertensive crisis.
Sympathomimetics: Theoretical interaction owing to monoamine oxidase inhibition caused by hydrazine. Potential for hypertensive crisis.[1,3,4]

CONTRAINDICATIONS
Patients with diabetes should use this product with caution owing to potential hypoglycemia.

DOSAGE
Oral: 60 mg three times a day, administered with meals, continuously or in cycles of 30 to 45 days on followed by 2 to 6 weeks off.

LITERATURE SUMMARY AND CRITIQUE
Kosty MP, et al. Cisplatin, vinblastine, and hydrazine sulfate in advanced, non-small-cell lung cancer: a randomized placebo-controlled, double-blind phase III study of the cancer and leukemia group B. J Clin Oncol 1994;12:1113–20.
A prospective evaluation of 266 patients with primary non–small cell lung cancer (NSCLC) randomized to receive placebo or 60 mg hydrazine sulfate orally three times

daily in combination with standard chemotherapy. Primary outcomes included toxicity and response. Survival was calculated and estimated using Kaplan-Meier. There were no significant differences between treatment groups at baseline. No difference in response rates or survival was noted. Sensory and motor neuropathies were seen more frequently in patients receiving hydrazine sulfate ($p < .05$). No improvements in albumin or weight were noted between treatment groups. The use of hydrazine sulfate with cisplatin and vinblastine for NSCLC appeared to have no significant advantage over placebo.

Loprinzi CL, et al. Placebo-controlled trial of hydrazine sulfate in patients with newly diagnosed non-small cell lung cancer. J Clin Oncol 1994;12:1126–9.
A prospective evaluation of 237 patients randomized to receive either placebo or 60 mg of hydrazine sulfate orally three times daily in combination with cisplatin and etoposide. Primary outcomes were survival and quality of life; response and weight were secondary outcomes. There was no significant difference between treatment groups with the addition of hydrazine sulfate. Additional central nervous system toxicity was noted in the hydrazine sulfate group, including dizziness and headache. No improvement in weight or albumin was noted between treatment groups, but it should be noted that cancer-related cachexia may not have been an issue in newly diagnosed NSCLC patients.

Loprinzi CL, et al. Randomized placebo-controlled evaluation of hydrazine sulfate in patients with advanced colorectal cancer. J Clin Oncol 1994;12:1121–5.
A prospective evaluation of 127 patients not receiving chemotherapy, randomized to either placebo or 60 mg hydrazine sulfate orally three times a day indefinitely. A Cox proportional hazards model was used to assess the effects of stratification by electrocorticographic performance status, sex, weight, number of previous chemotherapy regimens, and measurable disease. Inferior survival was shown repeatedly for hydrazine compared with placebo. Hydrazine appeared to offer no improvement in weight gain or improvement compared with placebo. Toxicity appeared to be similar between treatment arms. Hydrazine sulfate appears to be worse than placebo for the management of advanced colorectal cancer.

Chlebowski RT, et al. Hydrazine sulfate in cancer patients with weight loss. A placebo-controlled clinical experience. Cancer 1987;59:406–10.
A randomized clinical observation of placebo versus 60 mg orally three times daily hydrazine sulfate on body weight, albumin, caloric intake, and toxicity. Seventy-one patients received hydrazine and 30 received placebo. Only 58 patients completed repeat evaluations after 30 days; the results indicate a short-term benefit associated with hydrazine sulfate with respect to weight maintained, improvement in appetite, and caloric intake. The authors do not disclose the reason for patient discontinuation in either the placebo or the hydrazine group. Adverse events associated with hydrazine included light-headedness, nausea and vomiting, and "toxic effects" not otherwise specified. The authors conclude that hydrazine leads to short-term improvement in appetite and caloric intake. However, the study does not address long-term effects, nor does it reveal important information needed to interpret study results.

REFERENCES

1. Kaegi E. Unconventional therapies for cancer: 4. Hydrazine sulfate. The Task Force on Alternative Therapies of the Canadian Breast Cancer Research Initiative. Can Med Assoc J 1998;158:1327–30.
2. Kamradt JM, Pienta KJ. The effect of hydrazine sulfate on prostate cancer growth. Oncol Rep 1998;5:919–21.
3. Chlebowski RT, et al. Hydrazine sulfate: clinical pharmacokinetics and influence on in vitro growth of human glioblastoma cell lines. Proc Am Assoc Cancer Res 1985;26:1002.
4. Hydrazine sulfate (pdq). Available at: http://cancernet.nci.nih.gov/cam/hydrazine.htm (accessed Nov 20, 2001).
5. Hainer MI, et al. Fatal hepatorenal failure associated with hydrazine sulfate. Ann Intern Med 2000;133:877–80.
6. Nagappan R, Riddel T. Pyridoxine therapy in a patient with severe hydrazine sulfate toxicity. Crit Care Med 2000;28:2116–8.

Inositol Hexaphosphate

COMMON NAMES

IP$_6$, InsP$_6$, NA-InsP$_6$, phytic acid, inositol hexakisphosphate, *myo*-inositol hexaphosphate, inositol 1,2,3,4,5,6-hexakis-phosphate, phytate

KEY WORD

IP$_6$

A. DONATO

CLINICAL SUMMARY

Ubiquitous intracellular molecule present in mammalian cells obtained from various dietary sources. Inositol hexaphosphate (IP$_6$) is used to prevent and treat cancer and heart disease. Metabolites of IP$_6$ enter the inositol phosphates' pool and perform secondary messenger roles, extracellular signaling, and additional cellular signal transduction. IP$_6$ is absorbed in the upper gastrointestinal tract and exhibits saturable absorption. It is extensively distributed in the body and eliminated primarily in the urine. Several published in vitro and animal studies suggest the efficacy of IP$_6$ in various cancer cell lines, but human data remain to be obtained. No adverse events have been reported. A theoretical drug interaction may occur when IP$_6$ is combined with anticoagulants such as heparin, aspirin, or warfarin. Additional studies are needed to establish the proper dosage and safety of IP$_6$.

CONSTITUENTS

Phosphorylated hexacarbon carbohydrate.

MECHANISM OF ACTION

IP_6 can be synthesized from inositol or obtained from the diet. Metabolites and derivations of IP_6 perform secondary messenger roles, including mobilization of intracellular calcium for mitosis. Extracellular signaling also has been demonstrated. IP_6 interacts with both tyrosine kinase and phospholipase C–coupled growth factor receptors. IP_6 also enters the inositol phosphates' pool, is subsequently dephosphorylated, and contributes to additional cellular signal transduction and intracellular functions. In vitro and animal studies suggest that IP_6 reduces initiation and/or promotion, inhibits proliferation by chelation of metalloproteins, causes G_0/G_1 arrest, and induces differentiation of various cancer cell lines. IP_6 also may inhibit in vitro platelet activation with adenosine diphosphate, collagen, and thrombin by interacting with platelet cytoskeletal reorganization, P13-K activity, or agonist-induced platelet aggregation.[1-4]

USAGE

Cancer prevention, cancer treatment, cardiovascular disease, depression, kidney stones.

PHARMACOKINETICS

Absorption: IP_6 appears to have rapid absorption in the upper gastrointestinal track following oral administration according to studies performed in rats. IP_6 also can be synthesized from inositol. Studies in humans suggest that there is saturable absorption of IP_6 with escalating doses that results in elimination of unabsorbed doses in the feces. The chemical used in formulating IP_6 (ie, sodium, magnesium, calcium) may also influence the rate and extent of absorption.

Distribution: IP_6 and its metabolites are widely distributed throughout the body to all sites, including skeletal muscle and skin. Active transport across cellular membranes has been attributed to various binding proteins (clathrin adaptor complex AP2, AP180, coatomer of COP I coat).

Metabolism/Excretion: IP_6 may be dephosphorylated to IP_{1-5} as it is passes through mucosal cells. There are multiple pathways for IP_6 metabolism, including dietary phytase. IP_6 can be metabolized to IP_{1-5} as well as inositol. Primary route of excretion is in urine, although saturable excretion also occurs. Measured urinary levels of IP_6 can be directly correlated to serum levels.[1,5,6]

ADVERSE REACTIONS

Common: Flatulence, gastrointestinal distress.

DRUG INTERACTIONS

Anticoagulants/Aspirin: Theoretically, IP_6 may have an additive effect owing to inhibition of platelet aggregation.

Supplements/Diet: IP_6 has been reported to bind calcium, iron, magnesium, zinc, and copper in the stomach and reduce their bioavailability, although conflicting data exist.[2]

DOSAGE

Oral: Capsules: Optimal or safe dosage has not been defined; 500 mg to 8 g in split doses have been used.

LITERATURE SUMMARY AND CRITIQUE

Although in vitro and animal data regarding IP_6 have been published, no human studies evaluate IP_6 for any of its proposed uses.

REFFRENCES

1. Shamsuddin AM, Vucenik I, Cole KE, IP_6: a novel anti-cancer agent. Life Sci 1997;61:343–54.
2. Vucenik I, Podczasy JJ, Shamsuddin AM. Antiplatelet activity of inositol hexaphosphate (IP_6). Anticancer Res 1999;19:3689–94.
3. Shamsuddin AM. Metabolism and cellular functions of IP_6: a review. Anticancer Res 1999;19:3733–6.
4. El-Sherbiny YM, et al. G0/G1 arrest and S phase inhibition of human cancer cell lines by inositol hexaphosphate (IP_6). Anticancer Res 2001;21:2393–403.
5. Grases F, et al. Absorption and excretion of orally administered inositol hexaphosphate (IP_6 or phytate) in humans. Biofactors 2001;15:53–61.
6. Sakamoto K, Vucenik I, Shamsuddin AM. [3H] Phytic acid (inositol hexaphosphate) is absorbed and distributed to various tissues in rats. J Nutr 1993;123:713–20.

Kava

COMMON NAMES
Kava kava, kawa, kavain, rauschpfeffer, intoxicating long pepper, tonga, yagona, yaqona

SCIENTIFIC NAME
Piper methysticum

KEY WORD
Piper methysticum

A. DONATO

CLINICAL SUMMARY

Derived from the rhizome, or root, of the plant. Kava is from the Pacific Rim and Hawaiian Islands. It is used for anxiety, stress, and insomnia. The Canadian, French, and British governments have warned consumers not to consume kava-containing products owing to concerns of hepatotoxicity. The US Food and Drug Administration is asking all physicians to report any cases of hepatotoxicity possibly linked to the consumption of kava. The kava pyrones, thought to be responsible for activity, produce skeletal muscle relaxation, nonnarcotic anesthesia, and local anesthetic effects. Clinical trials repeatedly suggest that kava is more effective than placebo in reducing anxiety. Also, because dependency and addiction have not been shown following prolonged administration, kava has been suggested as a viable alternative to benzodiazepines, but this is not confirmed adequately in clinical trials. Chronic administration can result in specific adverse effects, including kava dermopathy, thrombocytopenia, leukopenia, and hepatotoxicity, which appear to be reversible following discontinuation. Other common adverse effects include headache, restlessness, tiredness, stomach complaints, visual disturbances, tremor, and a hangover effect. Additive effects may occur when combined with benzodiazepines, barbiturates, alcohol, and other centrally acting depressants. Patients should be warned that kava may reduce reaction time and affect driving ability. Although kava may provide short-term relief for anxiety, the risk of hepatotoxicity may outweigh any benefits obtained.

CONSTITUENTS

Kava pyrones: kawain, dihydrokavain, methysticin, dihydromethysticin, demethoxy-yangonin, yangonin; other: starch.[1,2]

WARNINGS

Kava may cause hepatotoxicity. The British, French, and Swiss governments have requested that kava be removed from the market. The Canadian government has warned consumers not to use kava-containing products.

Prolonged use may produce kava dermopathy. See "Toxicity" under "Adverse Reactions." It may interact with anesthetics; discontinue kava use before surgery. Kava may impair the ability to drive or operate heavy machinery.[3-6]

MECHANISM OF ACTION

Kava pyrones are centrally acting skeletal muscle relaxants, anticonvulsants, and peripherally acting local anesthetics. They induce anesthesia via non-narcotic pathways. Animal studies suggest interaction with γ-aminobutyric acid $(GABA)_A$ receptors and inhibition of monoamine oxidase B (MAO-B). There are conflicting data concerning whether kava pyrones increase or have no effect on central nervous system levels of dopamine and serotonin.[1]

USAGE

Anxiety, insomnia, restlessness, stress.

PHARMACOKINETICS

Absorption: The kava pyrones kawain and dihydrokawain were well absorbed following oral administration in mice. Plasma levels of 2 µg/mL were detected 30 minutes after an initial oral dose of 100 mg/kg kava extract (standardized to 70% kava pyrones). It should be noted that extraction and preparation of dosage form could affect bioavailability.
Distribution: Dihydrokawain, kawain, desmethoxy-yangonin, and yangonin have been shown to cross the blood-brain barrier in mice.
Elimination: Plasma half-life of kava pyrones ranges from 90 minutes to several hours.[7,8]

ADVERSE REACTIONS

Common: Headache, impaired reflexes or judgment, visual disturbances, sedation, restlessness, tremor, hangover effect.
Rare: Hepatotoxicity.
Toxicity: Thrombocytopenia; leukopenia; reversible ichthyosiform eruption (kava dermopathy characterized dry, flaking skin); yellowish discoloration to the skin, sclerae, fingernails, and toenails; anorexia; respiratory problems; and hearing impairment.[9,10]

DRUG INTERACTIONS

Benzodiazepines: Kava may enhance sedation when adminstered concurrently. Avoid concomitant administration. Kava indirectly increases the affinity of GABA receptor binding sites (in vitro).

Alcohol: Kava may enhance the hypnotic and sedative effects of alcohol. Avoid concomitant administration.

Barbiturates: Theoretically, kava may have an additive effect on sedation and muscle relaxant activity. The effect has been demonstrated only in animals.

Sedatives: Theoretically, kava may have an additive effect with any centrally acting medication that can potentially cause sedation.[11,12]

LABORATORY INTERACTIONS

Increased aspartate transaminase/alanine transaminase, lowered blood pressure.

DOSAGE

Oral: Herb and preparations equivalent to 60 to 120 mg kava pyrones given three times a day. Maximum dose is 480 mg kava pyrones per day.[13]

LITERATURE SUMMARY AND CRITIQUE

Pittler MH, Ernst E. Efficacy of kava extract for treating anxiety: systematic review and meta-analysis. J Clin Psychopharmacol 2000;20:84–9.

A systematic analysis of all randomized, double-blind, placebo-controlled trials using preparations of kava for the treatment of anxiety. Seven trials were found that met criteria, all of which used Hamilton Rating Scale for Anxiety (HAM-A) scores as an outcome. All trials showed a significant advantage of kava compared with placebo in the reduction of anxiety of HAM-A scores (95% CI = 3.54–15.83 points). Five of seven trials reported adverse events, including stomach complaints, restlessness, drowsiness, tremor, headache, and tiredness. Although no trial was flawless, with problems ranging from inadequate power analysis to poor randomization, the weighted mean difference of the meta-analysis favored kava when compared with placebo.

De Leo V, et al. Evaluation of combining kava extract with hormone replacement therapy in the treatment of postmenopausal anxiety. Maturitas 2001;39:185–8.

A prospective, randomized evaluation of 40 women experiencing anxiety associated with physiologic or surgically induced menopause. Patients had anxiety scores greater than 19 based on the HAM-A. Patients were randomized to standard hormone treatment either with or without kava extract 100 mg/d (55% kavain). Treatments were continued for 6 months with HAM-A scores measured at 3-month intervals. There were no dropouts during the study. Patients receiving combined therapy (hormones plus kava) demonstrated significantly lower HAM-A scores, indicating lower anxiety. No adverse effects were reported. The authors concluded that kava extract is effective in managing anxiety associated with menopause but did not report adverse effects that occurred during treatment or following discontinuation.

REFERENCES

1. Robbers JE, et al. Pharmacognosy and pharmacobiotechnology. Baltimore: Williams & Wilkins; 1996.
2. Foster S, et al. Tyler's honest herbal: a sensible guide to the use of herbs and related remedies. New York: Haworth Herbal Press; 1999.
3. Norton SA, Ruze P. Kava dermopathy. J Am Acad Dermatol 1994;31:89–97.
4. Advisory: Health Canada is advising consumers not to use any products containing kava [on-line]. http://www.hc-sc.gc.ca/english/protection/warnings/2002/2002_02e.htm (accessed Nov 1, 2001).
5. Burros M. Eating well; new questions about kava's safety. The New York Times 2002 Jan 16; Sect. F:(col. 2).
6. Ang-lee M, et al. Herbal medicines and perioperative care. JAMA 2001;286:208–16.
7. Schulz V, et al. Rational phytotherapy: a physician's guide to herbal medicine. 4th ed. New York: Springer; 2001.
8. Keledjian J, et al. Uptake into mouse brain of four compounds present in the psychoactive beverage kava. J Pharm Sci 1988;77:1003–6.
9. Escher M, et al. Hepatitis associated with kava, a herbal remedy for anxiety. BMJ 2001;322:139.
10. Pittler MH, Ernst E. Efficacy of kava extract for treating anxiety: systematic review and meta-analysis. J Clin Psychopharmacol 2000;20:84–9.
11. Brinker F. Herb contraindications and drug interactions. 3rd ed. Sandy (OR): Eclectic Medical Publishers; 2001.
12. Almeida JC, Grimsley EW. Coma from the health food store: interaction between kava and alprazolam. Ann Intern Med 1996;125:940–1.
13. Blumenthal M. The complete German Commission E monographs: therapeutic guide to herbal medicines. 1st ed. Austin (TX): American Botanical Council; 1998.

Lentinan

COMMON NAMES
Shiitake, Hua Gu, snake butter, forest mushroom, pasania fungus

CLINICAL SUMMARY
The polysaccharide lentinan is derived from the mycelium of the shiitake mushroom body. It is considered a biologic response modifier. In other countries, parenteral lentinan is classified as an antineoplastic polysaccharide and is available for clinical use. Only oral formulations and extracts, which are considered dietary supplements, are available for use in the United States. Although efficacy data are limited regarding oral administration, it appears to be safe as there are no frequently reported adverse effects.

CONSTITUENTS
Polysaccharide: water-soluble 1,3-β-glucan polysaccharide characterized by 1,6-β-glucan branched linkage; at least five additional polysaccharides.[1]

MECHANISM OF ACTION
Lentinan's active polysaccharide 1,3-β-glucan is not cytotoxic but seems to enhance T helper (Th) cell function and increase stimulation of interleukin (IL), interferon (IFN), and normal killer cells. In addition to antitumor activity, it also possesses immunoregulatory effects, antiviral activity, antimicrobial properties, and cholesterol-lowering effects.[2–4]

USAGE
Cancer prevention, cancer treatment, high cholesterol, immunostimulation, infections.

ADVERSE REACTIONS
Case Report: Single case report of chest tightness when injected parenterally.[5]

DRUG INTERACTIONS
Zidovudine (AZT): Lentinan may enhance activity when used in combination.

Didanosine (ddI, Videx): Lentinan may increase CD4 levels in patients with human immunodeficiency virus (HIV) when used in combination.[6,7]

LABORATORY INTERACTIONS
CD4 counts may be altered.

DOSAGE
No typical dosage is recommended for mycelium extract.
Parenteral: 1 to 4 mg intravenously or intramuscularly administered weekly or every other week. Not available in the United States.

LITERATURE SUMMARY AND CRITIQUE
A MEDLINE search displayed over 300 case reports and foreign studies using lentinan as a single agent or in combination against many tumor types. Lentinan was administered intravenously or intramuscularly in a majority of these reports.

Yoshino S, et al. Immunoregulatory effects of the antitumor polysaccharide lentinan on Th1/Th2 balances in patients with digestive cancers. Anticancer Res 2000;20: 4707–11.
Studies have demonstrated that patients with advanced cancer may have impaired cell-mediated immunity caused by an imbalance between Th1 and Th2 responses. The study evaluated the ability of lentinan to modulate Th1 and Th2 responses in patients with digestive cancers. After lentinan treatment, CD4+ IFN-γ+ T-cell percentages increased significantly ($p < .05\%$), whereas CD4+ IL-4+ T-cell and CD4+ IL-6 T-cell percentages decreased significantly ($p < .02$). Lentinan apparently can cancel a Th2-dominant condition in patients with digestive cancers and may improve the balance between Th1 and Th2.

Nakano H, et al. A multi-institutional prospective study of lentinan in advanced gastric cancer patients with unresectable and recurrent diseases: effect on prolongation of survival and improvement of quality of life. Hepatogastroenterology 1999;46: 2662–8.
A randomized, prospective evaluation of 45 patients who received treatment consisting of tegafur 600 mg/d plus 20 mg/m² and cisplatin intravenously weekly with or without 2 mg/wk intravenous lentinan, with quality of life (QOL) and survival as the primary outcomes. Twenty-two patients were in the control group (18 unresectable and 4 recurrent disease), and 23 patients received lentinan (17 unresectable and 6 recurrent disease). Total QOL scores after 12 weeks of treatment were significantly improved in all patients receiving lentinan compared with the control group. One-year survival for patients with either unresectable or recurrent disease receiving lentinan was statistically better compared with control patients, although the sample size may have been inadequate to detect actual difference. No difference in performance status was documented, but patients who

received lentinan appeared to maintain body weight compared with controls. Intravenous lentinan appears to improve QOL and possibly survival, but additional studies are needed.

Tari K, et al. Effect of lentinan for advanced prostate carcinoma. Hinyokika Kiyo 1994;40:119–23.
A prospective, randomized, multicenter study assessing the clinical effectiveness of lentinan in 69 patients with metastatic prostate cancer. All patients received hormonal therapy and chemotherapy using oral tegafur at a dose of 400 to 800 mg/d. Although 33 patients received lentinan intramuscularly for at least 3 months, the other 36 did not. The dose of lentinan was 2 mg weekly for inpatients and 4 mg every other week for outpatients. The median survival rates of treated and control patients were 48 and 35 months, respectively. The 5-year survival rate of treated patients was 43% according to the Kaplan-Meier method, whereas that of control patients was 29% ($p < .05$). The authors concluded that lentinan is effective in metastatic prostate cancer when incorporated into hormonochemotherapy.

Ochiai T, et al. Effect of immunotherapy with lentinan on patients' survival and immunological parameters in patients with advanced gastric cancer: results of a multicenter randomized controlled study. Int J Immunother 1992;8:161–9.
The clinical effectiveness of immunotherapy with lentinan was assessed in a study involving 89 patients with inoperable or recurrent gastric cancer. Patients were randomly assigned to two treatment groups receiving chemotherapy alone or lentinan plus chemotherapy. Among the 64 completely evaluable patients, a statistically significant difference in the survival curve was observed between the two treatment groups. Chemotherapy with lentinan prolonged the life span when compared with chemotherapy alone. The results emphasized the effectiveness of lentinan as an immunotherapeutic agent in advanced gastric cancer.

Taguchi T. Clinical efficacy of lentinan on patients with stomach cancer: end point results of a four-year follow-up survey. Cancer Detect Prev Suppl 1987;1:333–49.
Sixty-eight eligible patients in control groups were administered tegafur 600 mg/d, and 96 eligible patients in the treated group were administered lentinan in combination with tegafur. Lentinan was injected intravenously 2 mg weekly. Life span prolongation effects of lentinan were observed both at the end of the control trial and at the end of the follow-up survey. Survival at 1, 2, and 3 years was observed in the treated group using life-table analysis. The author suggests that lentinan should be effective in combination with tegafur for patients with stomach cancer.

REFERENCES

1. Hobbs C. Medicinal mushrooms. 3rd ed. Loveland (CO): Interweave Press; 1996.
2. Chihara G, et al. Inhibition of mouse sarcoma 180 by polysaccharides from *Lentinus edodes*. Nature 1969;222:637–88.

3. Hamuro J, Rollinghoff M, Wagner H. Induction of cytotoxic peritoneal exudate cells by T-cell immune adjuvants of the β (1 leads to 3) glucan-type lentinan and its analogues. Immunology 1980;39:551.

4. Reed FC, et al. Immunomodulating and antitumor activity of lentinan. Int J Immunopharmacol 1982;4:264.

5. Wada T, et al. A comparative clinical trial with tegafur plus lentinan treatment at two different doses in advanced cancer. Gan To Kagaku Ryoho 1987;14:2509–11.

6. Tochikura T, et al. Suppression of human immunodeficiency virus replication by 3'-azido-3'-deoxythymidine in various human hematopoietic cell lines in vitro: augmentation of the effect by lentinan. Jpn J Cancer Res 1987;78:583–9.

7. Gordon M, et al. A phase II controlled study of a combination of the immune modulator, lentinan, with didanosine (ddI) in HIV patients with CD4 cells of 200-500/MM3. J Med 1995;26:193–207.

Licorice

A.DONATO

COMMON NAMES
Gan Cao, sweet root, glycyrrhiza, *Radix liquiritiae*, liquorice

SCIENTIFIC NAMES
Glycyrrhiza glabra, Glycyrrhiza uralensis

KEY WORDS
Glycyrrhiza glabra, Glycyrrhiza uralensis, Gan Cao

CLINICAL SUMMARY

Derived from the root of the plant. Licorice is used extensively in traditional Chinese medicine for a variety of conditions and ailments. Almost all clinical studies on licorice have been performed in combination with other herbs. Alone, licorice is used primarily to manage gastric complaints. A number of active chemicals are thought to account for its biologic activity. Owing to the adverse reaction profile of licorice, many studies have been performed using the deglycyrrhizinated licorice (DGL) extract, which is free of glycyrrhizin and has had no significant reported adverse effects. Adverse effects from glycyrrhizin are primarily related to possible changes in electrolytes causing hypokalemia, hypernatremia, pseudohyperaldosteronism, and decreased libido in men. Drugs that interact with licorice containing glycyrrhizin include diuretics, cardiac glycosides, insulin, and corticosteroids, all of which are related to changes in electrolytes. Other possible drug interactions with any licorice product include potentiation of anticoagulants and possible interference with hormonal therapy owing to the estrogenic activity of licorice.

CONSTITUENTS

Triterpenoid saponins: glycyrrhizin (metabolized in vivo to glycyrrhetinic acid and glycyrrhizinic); flavonoids: liquiritin, chalcones; isoflavone: formononetin; amines: asparagines, betaine and choline; amino acids; polysaccharides; sterols: β-sitosterol; coumarins.[1]

WARNINGS

Owing to the adverse reaction profile of licorice, many studies have been performed using the DGL extract. DGL is free of glycyrrhizin and has had no reported significant adverse effects.

MECHANISM OF ACTION

Glycyrrhizin has been reported to bind to glucocorticoid and mineralocorticoid receptors with moderate affinity and to estrogen receptors, sex hormone–binding globulin, and corticosteroid-binding globulin with very weak affinity. The antiestrogenic action documented for glycyrrhizin at high concentration has been associated with glycyrrhizin binding at estrogen receptors. However, estrogenic activity has also been reported for licorice and is attributed to its isoflavone constituents.

It has been suggested that glycyrrhizin may exert its mineralocorticoid effect via an inhibition of 11-β-hydroxysteroid dehydrogenase. The coumarin constituent has antiplatelet activity. Anti-inflammatory action is exhibited by glycyrrhetinic acid against ultraviolet erythema. Antimicrobial activity is attributed to the isoflavonoid constituents. Carbenoxolone, an ester derivative of glycyrrhetinic acid, has been used in the treatment of gastric and esophageal ulcers; it is thought to exhibit a mucosal protectant effect by beneficially interfering with gastric prostanoid synthesis and increasing both mucous production and regional blood flow. Data show suppression of both plasma rennin activity and aldosterone secretion. Also, a decrease in serum testosterone and an increase in 17-hydroxyprogesterone have been shown.[2,3]

USAGE

Bronchitis, chest congestion, constipation, gastrointestinal disorders, hepatitis, inflammation, menopausal symptoms, microbial infection, peptic ulcers, primary adrenocortical insufficiency, prostate cancer.

PHARMACOKINETICS

Administration of licorice after meals delays the time (T_{max}) to peak concentration but does not affect maximum concentration (C_{max}) or area under the curve. Elimination half-life is approximately 5 hours following intravenous administration. The primary route of excretion is in bile.[4–6]

ADVERSE REACTIONS

Hypertension, lethargy, muscle pain, cardiac arrhythmias, sodium retention, hypokalemia, hypermineralocorticoidism, pseudohyperaldosteronism, decreased libido in men, and suppression of scalp sebum secretion.[7]

DRUG INTERACTIONS

Cardiac Glycosides: Licorice may potentiate toxicity.

Stimulant Laxatives: Chronic use of licorice may increase loss of potassium.
Diuretics: Chronic use of licorice may increase loss of potassium.
Spironolactone/Amiloride: Licorice should not be used simultaneously owing to effects on sodium and potassium excretion.
Corticosteroids: Concomitant use with licorice might potentiate the duration of activity.
Aspirin: Licorice may reduce ulcer formation from aspirin and possibly provide protection from gastric mucosal damage.
Insulin: Licorice may have a synergistic effect, possibly causing hypokalemia and sodium retention with concomitant use.
Hormonal Therapy: Licorice may interfere with the activity of hormonal therapy owing to its estrogenic or antiestrogenic properties.
Anticoagulant/Antiplatelet Drugs: Licorice may potentiate activity owing to its coumarin constituent.
Monoamine Oxidase Inhibitors: Licorice may potentiate the activity of MAOIs.[2,8]

LABORATORY INTERACTIONS
Blood pressure may be increased. Potassium levels may be decreased. Sodium levels may be elevated. Testosterone levels may be decreased.

CONTRAINDICATIONS
Licorice should not be consumed by those with renal or liver dysfunction or women who are pregnant or breast-feeding.

DOSAGE
Oral: 200 to 600 mg for no more than 4 to 6 weeks.[1]

LITERATURE SUMMARY AND CRITIQUE
The only studies in humans showing positive results have used DGL as a single agent in peptic ulcers. Studies of licorice in combination with other herbs have shown favorable results, such as PC-SPES for prostate cancer.[9–12]

REFERENCES
1. Blumenthal M, et al. Herbal medicine, expanded Commission E monographs. Austin (TX): American Botanical Council; 2000.
2. Newall C, et al. Herbal medicines: a guide for health-care professionals. London: Pharmaceutical Press; 1996.
3. Tyler V. Herbs of choice, the therapeutical use of phytomedicinals. Binghamton (NY): Pharmaceutical Press; 1994.
4. Miyamura M, et al. Properties of glycyrrhizin in Kampo extracts including licorice root and changes in the blood concentration of glycyrrhetic acid after oral administration of Kampo extracts. Yakugaku Zasshi 1996;116:209–16.

5. Ichikawa T, et al. Biliary excretion and enterohepatic cycling of glycyrrhizin in rats. J Pharm Sci 1986;75:672–5.
6. Stormer FC, Reistad R, Alexander J. Glycyrrhizic acid in licorice—evaluation of health hazard. Food Chem Toxicol 1993;31:303–12.
7. De Smet K, et al. Adverse effects of herbal drugs. Vol 3. New York: Springer; 1997.
8. Brinker F. Herb contraindications and drug interactions. 2nd ed. Sandy (OR): Eclectic Medical Publications; 1998.
9. Schulz V, et al. Rational phytotherapy: a physician's guide to the use of herbs and related remedies. 3rd ed. Berlin: Springer; 1998.
10. Takahara T, Watanabe A, Shiraki K. Effects of glycyrrhizin on hepatitis B surface antigen: a biochemical and morphological study. J Hepatol 1994;21:601–9.
11. Amato P, Christophe S, Mellon PL. Estrogenic activity of herbs commonly used as remedies for menopausal symptoms. Menopause 2002;9:145–50.
12. Budzinski JW, et al. An in vitro evaluation of human cytochrome P450 3A4 inhibition by selected commercial herbal extracts and tinctures. Phytomedicine 2000;7:273–82.

D-Limonene

A. DONATO

COMMON NAMES
R-limonene, orange peel oil, citrus peel oil, citrene

SCIENTIFIC NAME
p-Mentha-1,8-diene

KEY WORD
Limonene

CLINICAL SUMMARY

Derived from the peels of citrus fruits. Patients use this supplement to prevent and treat cancer. D-Limonene is a cyclic monoterpene that causes G_1 cell-cycle arrest, induces apoptosis, and inhibits post-translational modification of signal transduction proteins. Following oral administration, D-limonene is rapidly metabolized to limonene-1,2-diol, perillic acid, dihydroperillic acid, and uroterpenol. D-Limonene has a biologic half-life of approximately 24 hours, whereas its metabolites exhibit relatively short biologic half-lives of approximately 2 hours. Side effects include nausea, vomiting, and diarrhea. In vitro and animal data suggest the potential efficacy of D-limonene in treating cancer, but human data are lacking. Further research is necessary to determine if D-limonene has a role in the prevention or treatment of cancer.

CONSTITUENTS

Monocyclic monoterpene.

MECHANISM OF ACTION

The exact mechanism of action is unknown. D-Limonene and its metabolites, perillic acid, dihydroperillic acid, uroterpenol, and limonene-1,2-diol, may inhibit tumor growth

254

via inhibition of p21-dependent signaling and apoptosis resulting from induction of the transforming growth factor-β signaling pathway. D-Limonene metabolites also cause G_1 cell-cycle arrest, inhibit post-translational modification of signal transduction proteins, and cause differential expression of cell cycle– and apoptosis-related genes. Animal studies show activity of D-limonene against pancreatic, stomach, colon, skin, and liver cancers. Data also indicate that D-limonene slows the promotion/progression stage of carcinogen-induced tumors in rats.[1–10]

USAGE
Cancer prevention, cancer treatment.

PHARMACOKINETICS
Following oral administration, D-limonene is absorbed rapidly and metabolized to perillic acid, dihydroperillic acid, limonene-1,2-diol, and uroterpenol. D-Limonene metabolites distribute throughout the body to all sites, including adipose tissue, and are eliminated as glucuronide metabolites in the urine.[1,2,11]

ADVERSE REACTIONS
Reported: Nausea, vomiting, diarrhea.[1]

DRUG INTERACTIONS
None known.

DOSAGE
Oral: A phase I study in cancer patients used doses up to 12,000 mg/m²/d. Optimal dosage is yet to be established.[1]

LITERATURE SUMMARY AND CRITIQUE
Vigushin DM, et al. Phase I and pharmacokinetic study of D-limonene in patients with advanced cancer. Cancer Research Campaign Phase I/II Clinical Trials Committee. Cancer Chemother Pharmacol 1998;42:111–7.
A phase I pharmacokinetic study was conducted with doses ranging from 500 to 12,000 mg/m²/d. A single tumor response was documented in a breast cancer patient at the 8,000 mg/m²/d dose level. The investigators conducted a small phase II study with 10 additional breast cancer patients, but no additional tumor response was noted. Side effects include nausea, vomiting, and diarrhea. Additional studies are necessary to establish the efficacy of D-limonene.

REFERENCES

1. Vigushin DM, et al. Phase I and pharmacokinetic study of D-limonene in patients with advanced cancer. Cancer Research Campaign Phase I/II Clinical Trials Committee. Cancer Chemother Pharmacol 1998;42:111–7.
2. Hardcastle IR, et al. Inhibition of protein prenylation by metabolites of limonene. Biochem Pharmacol 1999;57:801–9.
3. Belanger JT. Perillyl alcohol: applications in oncology. Altern Med Rev 1998;3:448–57.
4. Hudes GR, et al. Phase I pharmacokinetic trial of perillyl alcohol (NSC 641066) in patients with refractory solid malignancies. Clin Cancer Res 2000;6:3071–80.
5. Ripple GH. Phase I clinical and pharmacokinetic study of perillyl alcohol administered four times a day. Clin Cancer Res 2000;6:390–6.
6. Reddy BS, et al. Chemoprevention of colon carcinogenesis by dietary perillyl alcohol. Cancer Res 1997;57:420–5.
7. Low-Baselli A, et al. Failure to demonstrate chemoprevention by the monoterpene perillyl alcohol during early rat hepatocarcinogenesis: a cautionary note. Carcinogenesis 2000; 21:1869–77.
8. Kaji I, et al. Inhibition by D-limonene of experimental hepatocarcinogenesis in Sprague-Dawley rats does not involve p21(ras) plasma membrane association. Int J Cancer 2001;93: 441–4.
9. Uedo N, et al. Inhibition by D-limonene of gastric carcinogenesis induced by N-methyl-N'-nitro-N-nitrosoguanidine in Wistar rats. Cancer Lett 1999;137:131–6.
10. Crowell PL, et al. Human metabolism of the experimental cancer therapeutic agent d-limonene. Cancer Chemother Pharmacol 1994;35:31–7.
11. Asamoto M, et al. Mammary carcinomas induced in human c-Ha-ras proto-oncogene transgenic rats are estrogen-independent, but responsive to D-limonene treatment. Jpn J Cancer Res 2002;93:32–5.

Livingston-Wheeler Therapy

COMMON NAME
Livingston therapy

CLINICAL SUMMARY
Metabolic treatment available at the Livingston-Wheeler Clinic in San Diego, CA; involves a strict vegetarian diet, bacille Calmette-Guérin (BCG) vaccine, coffee enemas, an autogenous vaccine, vitamins, antibiotics, antioxidants, nutritional counseling, and support groups/counseling. Patients use this therapy to treat cancer, arthritis, allergies, and acquired immune deficiency syndrome (AIDS). The regimen is based on a theory, discarded in the early twentieth century, that cancer is caused by the bacterium *Progenitor cryptocides*, which Virginia Livingston-Wheeler, MD, claims to have isolated in a wide variety of cancer tissues. A weakened immune system supposedly allows the bacterium to grow; consequently, the therapy's focus is immune stimulation. Although clinic activities are illegal under California's 1959 Cancer Act, no legal action has been taken by the state. Metabolic diets may result in nutrient deficiencies. Repeated use of coffee enemas is linked to several deaths from serious infection and electrolyte imbalance. A self-selected, matched-cohort, prospective comparison of patients at the Livingston-Wheeler Clinic and a conventional cancer center found no difference in survival times between groups and consistently lower quality of life in the Livingston-Wheeler cohort. Although the Livingston-Wheeler diet has some similarities to the recommendations made by the American Cancer Society, dietary changes should be tailored to the specific needs of the cancer patient. The American Cancer Society strongly urges cancer patients not to seek treatment at the Livingston-Wheeler Clinic.

CONSTITUENTS
Diet, BCG vaccine, autogenous vaccine, nonspecific vaccines, antibiotics (penicillin, erythromycin, cephalexin, tetracycline, furazolidone, methenamine); injections: gammaglobulin (1/wk), sheep spleen extract (1–2/wk), crude liver extract (1+/wk), vitamin B_{12} (1+/wk); adjuvant therapy: levamisole (50 mg 3/d, alternate weeks); fresh whole-blood transfusions; enemas with coffee, lemon juice, or hot water; lactic acid bacillus; digestive enzymes to help maintain an acidic blood and urine pH (to kill *P. cryptocides*); megadoses of vitamins; abscisic acid, a derivative of vitamin A and carotene from plants.[1]

WARNINGS

The American Cancer Society strongly urges cancer patients not to seek treatment at the Livingston-Wheeler Clinic as no evidence has supported the efficacy of the treatments offered there. A number of deaths related to coffee enemas have been reported.[1,2]

MECHANISM OF ACTION

Livingston-Wheeler claimed that the bacterium *P. cryptocides* (family Mycobacterium, order Actinomycetales) is ubiquitous, but a weakened immune system allows it to become pathogenic and cause cancer. She described it as an intermittently acid-fast, pleomorphic bacterium capable of producing large amounts of human chorionic gonadotropin (HCG), which accounts for the rapid growth of cancer cells and cancer-related cachexia. Furthermore, *P. cryptocides* reportedly induces neoplastic changes when injected into animals. Livingston-Wheeler and her husband claimed to consistently find *P. cryptocides* in the fresh and cultured blood of cancer patients visualized by dark- and light-field microscopy but failed to specify the criteria by which they distinguished *P. cryptocides* from other bodies present in the bloodstream. The number and forms of the bacterium present in a patient's culture allegedly can be used to determine the stage of the disease. The presence of the bacterium in healthy subjects is explained by claims that the bacterium is "ubiquitous" and "latent." Although the presence of *P. cryptocides* reportedly decreased as patients were treated with antibiotics, it is curious that Livingston-Wheeler did not simply use antibiotic therapy to treat cancer. Independent analyses of cultures provided by Livingston-Wheeler identified the bacteria as *Staphylococcus epidermis*, *Streptococcus faecalis*, *Staphylococcus faecalis*, and other unrelated bacteria and found that many of them produced HCG. A cancer-causing bacterium has never been isolated.

Although the Livingston-Wheeler diet has similarities to the recommendations made by the American Cancer Society, its nutrient deficits (calcium, iron, vitamins D and B_{12}) are unsuitable for some patients with disseminated or metastatic disease, particularly of the head, neck, and gut. The elimination of eggs, dairy, and poultry in the Livingston-Wheeler diet, which is based on the faulty premise that they are contaminated with the *P. cryptocides* bacterium, removes important sources of protein for some cancer patients and is not necessary.[1,3-5]

USAGE

Allergies, arthritis, cancer treatment, human immunodeficiency virus (HIV) and AIDS.

PHARMACOKINETICS

No formal pharmacokinetic studies have been performed.

ADVERSE REACTIONS

Common (Metabolic Diet): Nutrient deficiencies (calcium, vitamin B_{12}, protein), anemia, and malabsorption may result from metabolic diets.

Reported (Autogenous Vaccine): Malaise, aching, slight fever, and tenderness at the injection site.

Case Reports (Coffee Enemas): Case 1: Multiple seizures and hypokalemia leading to cardiorespiratory arrest, coma, and death were reported after excessive use of coffee enemas (1–4/h) for a number of days. *Case 2:* Death attributable to fluid and electrolyte imbalance causing pleural and pericardial effusions after use of coffee enemas, four per day for 8 weeks.[1,2]

DRUG INTERACTIONS
None known.

DOSAGE
Patients receive initial therapy at a clinic and are trained to continue the regimen at home.

Oral/Injection: Autogenous vaccine (made from bacteria in patient's urine, blood, or tissue) is administered two times a week, alternating between oral and injection, indefinitely.

LITERATURE SUMMARY AND CRITIQUE
Cassileth BR, et al. Survival and quality of life among patients receiving unproven as compared with conventional cancer therapy. N Engl J Med 1991;324:1180–5.

A matched-cohort study of 156 end-stage cancer patients at the Livingston-Wheeler Medical Clinic in San Diego, CA (treatment group, $n = 78$), and at the University of Pennsylvania Cancer Center (control group, $n = 78$). Most control patients received standard chemotherapy agents, but six receiving experimental agents were also included in the analysis because their survival times and demographics did not differ from the others. Patients too ill to participate (24% at the University of Pennsylvania and 27% at the Livingston-Wheeler Medical Clinic) did not differ demographically. Medical records were obtained for all study subjects. Patients were matched by sex, race, age (< 59 or ≥ 60 years), diagnosis, and date of metastatic or recurrent disease; unmatched patients were included in a second analysis. Follow-up contact, consisting of interview by telephone assessing performance status (Eastern Cooperative Oncology Group) and quality of life (Functional Living Index), occurred every 2 months until death or the end of the study. For both groups, median survival was 15 months. Quality of life deteriorated at an equal rate for both cohorts, although University of Pennsylvania patients reported significantly better quality of life at all times, including enrolment ($p = .002$). More Livingston-Wheeler patients reported adverse effects. Patient self-selection and lack of investigator blinding are admitted design flaws of this study. Because this study failed to consider cohorts with less extensive disease, its findings cannot be extrapolated to these populations.

Richardson MA, et al. Assessment of outcomes at alternative medicine cancer clinics: a feasibility study. J Altern Complement Med 2001;7:19–32.

Prospective study assessing the feasibility of obtaining data and records from complementary and alternative medicine clinics and comparing 5-year survival to that of conventional therapies. Records were available for all 167 new American patients at the Livingston Foundation Medical Center, previously the Livingston-Wheeler Medical Clinic, in San Diego, CA. Follow-up was possible in 166 (99.4%) patients. Five-year survival from the time of treatment at the clinic (not diagnosis) was found to be 18.9% for all cancer types, 12% for breast (3 of 25), 25% for prostate (2 of 9), 1 of 18 for lung, and 0 of 12 for colon cancer. Evaluation was incomplete because the clinic does not assess stage of disease at arrival or keep records of conventional therapies that the patients may have had after leaving the clinic. Meaningful statistical analysis and comparison with historical controls could not be performed owing to the small number of patients in each stage- and site-specific group. The authors call for improvements in record keeping at such clinics so that evidence-based evaluation of their methods may occur.

REFERENCES

1. American Cancer Society. Livingston-Wheeler therapy. CA Cancer J Clin 1990;40:103–8.
2. Eisele JW, Reay DT. Deaths related to coffee enemas. JAMA 1980;244:1608–9.
3. Livingston VW, Livingston AM. Demonstration of *Progenitor cryptocides* in the blood of patients with collagen and neoplastic diseases. Trans N Y Acad Sci 1972;34:433–53.
4. Livingston VW, Livingston AM. Some cultural, immunological, and biochemical properties of *Progenitor cryptocides*. Trans N Y Acad Sci 1974;36:569–82.
5. Dwyer JT. Unproven nutritional remedies and cancer. Nutr Rev 1992;50:106–9.

Lobelia

COMMON NAMES
Lobelia, asthma weed, eyebright, gagroot, Indian pink, Indian tobacco, pukeweed, vomit weed, *Lobelia berlandieri, Lobelia cardinalis*

SCIENTIFIC NAME
Lobelia inflata

A.DONATO

CLINICAL SUMMARY
Derived from the aerial parts of the plant. Patients use this supplement for smoking cessation and to treat asthma and depression. The piperidine alkaloids (eg, lobeline) are thought to be responsible for the activity of this botanical. Animal and in vitro studies show that lobeline crosses the blood-brain barrier, has similar activity to nicotine, and stimulates the release of dopamine and norepinephrine. At low doses, lobelia has stimulant effects, but higher doses result in central nervous system (CNS) depression. Significant toxicity has occurred following use, including vomiting, seizures, cardiovascular collapse, and coma. Lobelia may have additive toxicity when combined with nicotine. Clinical studies evaluating lobelia for smoking cessation do not support its use. Doses greater than 20 mg are considered to be toxic. Patients should be warned not to use this supplement.

CONSTITUENTS
Alkaloids: lobeline, lobelanine, lobelanidine; β-amyrin palmitate.[1,2]

MECHANISM OF ACTION

Animal studies report that lobeline has anxiolytic and cardiovascular effects and increases cognitive performance. Lobelia has central stimulant activity, dilates bronchioles, and increases respiration rate at low doses, but higher doses cause CNS and respiratory depression. In rat and mouse models, lobeline increases dopamine release from striatal synaptosomes, increases norepinephrine release from the hippocampus, and binds extensively to nicotinic receptors both centrally and peripherally. In vitro, lobeline redistributes dopamine pools in presynaptic vesicles and antagonizes their release following amphetamine stimulation. Lobeline can have both antagonistic and synergistic effects when combined with nicotine and does not induce receptor up-regulation, as seen with nicotine. Intravenous administration of approximately 12 µg/kg lobeline to healthy human subjects resulted in cough, apnea, prolonged inspiration and expiratory pause, the feeling of choking, and pressure in the throat and chest. Animal studies suggest that β-amyrin palmitate stimulates the release of norepinephrine in the brain, possibly leading to an antidepressant effect.[1,3–11]

USAGE

Asthma, depression, drug withdrawal symptoms, inducement of vomiting, inflammation, smoking cessation.

PHARMACOKINETICS

Lobeline, an extract from *L. inflata*, has high lipophilicity, crosses the blood-brain barrier, and distributes widely throughout the body. Additional pharmacokinetic data are not available.[12]

ADVERSE REACTIONS

Reported: Nausea, vomiting, sweating, cough, dizziness, bradycardia, hypertension, seizures, respiratory stimulation (low doses), or depression (high doses).
Toxicity: Sinus arrhythmia, bundle branch block, diaphoresis, cardiovascular collapse, seizures, coma.[2]

DRUG INTERACTIONS

Nicotine: Lobelia may have additive effects when combined with nicotine-containing products, resulting in toxicity.[13]

CONTRAINDICATIONS

Lobelia is known to cross into breast milk and should not be consumed by pregnant or nursing mothers.

DOSAGE

Oral: No dosage is recommended. Adverse effects have been reported for doses as low as 0.5 mg and toxicity at doses of 8 to 20 mg. *Smoking cessation:* 0.5 to 2 mg capsules and lozenges have been used. Sublingual tablets, patches, nasal sprays, and transbuccal patches also exist.

LITERATURE SUMMARY AND CRITIQUE

Stead LF, Hughes JR. Lobeline for smoking cessation. Cochrane Database Syst Rev 2002;2:CD000124.

Although 16 studies have been performed evaluating lobelia for smoking cessation, none met the inclusion criteria set by Stead and Hughes. Trials evaluated only short-term efficacy (up to 14 days) of lobelia use, with no long-term follow-up performed. Reduction in the number of cigarettes, not abstinence, was the primary outcome for a majority of the studies reviewed. No evidence supports the hypothesis that lobelia is effective for smoking cessation.

REFERENCES

1. Subarnas A, et al. A possible mechanism of antidepressant activity of β-amyrin palmitate isolated from *Lobelia inflata* leaves in the forced swimming test. Life Sci 1993;52:289–96.
2. Fetrow CW, et al. Professional's handbook of complementary and alternative medicines. Philadelphia: Springhouse; 1999.
3. Foster S, et al. Tyler's honest herbal: a sensible guide to the use of herbs and related remedies. New York: Haworth Herbal Press; 1999.
4. Damaj MI, et al. Pharmacology of lobeline, a nicotinic receptor ligand. J Pharmacol Exp Ther 1997;282:410–9.
5. Santha E, et al. Multiple cellular mechanisms mediate the effect of lobeline on the release of norepinephrine. J Pharmacol Exp Ther 2000;294:302–7.
6. Miller DK, et al. Lobeline inhibits the neurochemical and behavioral effects of amphetamine. J Pharmacol Exp Ther 2001;296:1023–34.
7. Decker MW, Majchrzak MJ, Arneric SP. Effects of lobeline, a nicotinic receptor agonist, on learning and memory. Pharmacol Biochem Behav 1993;45:571–6.
8. Subarnas A, et al. An antidepressant principle of *Lobelia inflata* L. (Campanulaceae). J Pharm Sci 1992;81:620–1.
9. Raj H, et al. Sensory origin of lobeline-induced sensations: a correlative study in man and cat. J Physiol 1995;482:235–46.
10. Terry AV Jr, et al. Lobeline and structurally simplified analogs exhibit differential agonist activity and sensitivity to antagonist blockade when compared to nicotine. Neuropharmacology 1998;37:93–102.
11. Dwoskin LP, Crooks PA. A novel mechanism of action and potential use for lobeline as a treatment for psychostimulant abuse. Biochem Pharmacol 2002;63:89–98.
12. Reavill C, et al. Behavioural and pharmacokinetic studies on nicotine, cytisine and lobeline. Neuropharmacology 1990;29:619–24.
13. Brinker F. Herb contraindications and drug interactions. 3rd ed. Sandy (OR): Eclectic Medical Publications; 2001.

Lutein

COMMON NAMES
Xanthophyll, dihydroxycarotenoid, nonprovitamin A carotenoid

KEY WORD
Xanthophyll

CLINICAL SUMMARY

A natural pigment synthesized by plants and microorganisms. Lutein is used primarily as an antioxidant and also to prevent and treat cancer, heart disease, and macular degeneration. Lutein has antioxidant activity and is classified as a nonprovitamin A carotenoid, which also includes lycopene and zeaxanthin. Alpha-carotene, beta-carotene, and β-cryptoxanthin are classified as provitamin A carotenoids because they can be converted into retinol. Epidemiologic studies suggest an inverse relationship between increased lutein consumption and decreased incidence of atherosclerosis, macular degeneration, and possibly colon cancer. No significant adverse effects or drug interactions have been reported.

MECHANISM OF ACTION

Lutein is a natural pigment synthesized by plants and microorganisms. Lutein has been associated with a decreased risk of macular degeneration and cataracts. The physiologic function of lutein in the macular membranes is not known at this time. Referred to as a nonprovitamin A carotenoid, it is not known to have any vitamin A activity. Other possible actions for carotenoids are as an antioxidant, immunoenhancement, inhibition of mutagenesis and transformation, and inhibition of premalignant lesions. Lutein has been associated with decreased risk of colon cancer and atherosclerosis.[1–5]

USAGE
Cancer prevention, cataracts, macular degeneration, visual acuity.

PHARMACOKINETICS
Absorption: Intestinal absorption of carotenoids, including lutein, is facilitated by the formation of bile acid micelles containing carotenoids. The presence of fat in the small intestine stimulates the secretion of bile acids from the gallbladder and improves the absorption of carotenoids by increasing the size and stability of the micelles, thus allowing more carotenoids to be solubilized. The bioavailability of lutein is affected by the dose and presence of other carotenoids, such as beta-carotene. The bioavailability of lutein from vegetables is approximately 70%.

Distribution: The concentrations of various carotenoids in human serum and tissues are highly variable and depend on food sources, efficiency of absorption, and the amount of fat in the diet. Lutein is transported by high-density lipoprotein and, to a lesser extent, by very-low-density lipoprotein. The serum concentration of carotenoids after a single dose peaks at 24 to 48 hours postdose. The average lutein concentration in human serum is 280 nM. Lutein is primarily stored in adipose and the liver. Of all of the carotenoids circulating in the body, only two polar species, lutein and zeaxanthin, are contained in the macula.

Metabolism/Excretion: It is assumed that lutein is excreted through the bile and kidneys.[1–3,6]

ADVERSE REACTIONS
No adverse effects have been reported at normal doses.[1]

Toxicity: Carotenodermia is a harmless biologic effect of high carotenoid intake. Characterized by a yellowish discoloration of the skin, it results from chronically elevated serum concentrations of carotenes.

DRUG INTERACTIONS
No known drug interactions at this time.[7]

DOSAGE
Oral: No standard dosing exists. *Tolerable upper intake level:* None set.[1]

LITERATURE SUMMARY AND CRITIQUE
Dagnelie G, Zorge IS, McDonald TM. Lutein improves visual function in some patients with retinal degeneration: a pilot study via the Internet. Optometry 2000;71:147–64.
A small prospective evaluation of Internet-recruited patients with either retinal pigmentation ($n = 13$) or macular degeneration ($n = 3$) given 9 weeks of lutein 40 mg/d. Patients performed biweekly self-evaluation of visual acuity and central visual field extent.

Although patients who received supplementation with lutein did report improvements over those who did not, randomized trials are necessary to validate findings.

REFERENCES

1. Dietary Reference Intakes for vitamin C, vitamin E, selenium, and carotenoids. Washington (DC): National Academy Press; 2000.
2. Khachik F, Beecher GR, Smith JC. Lutein, lycopene, and their oxidative metabolites in chemo-prevention of cancer. J Cell Biochem Suppl 1995;22:236–46.
3. van het Hof KH, et al. Bioavailability of lutein from vegetables is 5 times higher than that of beta-carotene. Am J Clin Nutr 1999;70:261–8.
4. Dwyer JH, et al. Oxygenated carotenoid lutein and progression of early atherosclerosis: the Los Angeles atherosclerosis study. Circulation 2001;103:2922–7.
5. Slattery ML, et al. Carotenoids and colon cancer. Am J Clin Nutr 2000;71:575–82.
6. Olmedilla B, et al. A European multicentre, placebo-controlled supplementation study with α-tocopherol, carotene-rich palm oil, lutein or lycopene; analysis of serum responses. Clin Sci (Lond) 2002;102:447–56.
7. Elinder LS, et al. Probucol treatment decreases serum concentrations of diet-derived anti-oxidants. Arterioscler Thromb Vasc Biol 1995;15:1057–63.

Lycopene

COMMON NAME
Nonprovitamin A carotenoid

CLINICAL SUMMARY

A natural pigment synthesized by plants and microorganisms. Lycopene is used primarily as an antioxidant and also to prevent and treat cancer, heart disease, and macular degeneration. Lycopene has antioxidant activity and is classified as a nonprovitamin A carotenoid, which also includes lutein and zeaxanthin. Alpha-carotene, beta-carotene, and β-cryptoxanthin are classified as provitamin A carotenoids because they can be converted into retinol. Epidemiologic studies suggest an inverse relationship between increased lycopene consumption and reduced risk of cancer, particularly lung, prostate, and stomach. Small clinical trials suggest possible benefit in cancer and exercise-induced asthma (EIA), but no optimal dosage has been established, and larger clinical trials are needed. No adverse effects or drug interactions are known for lycopene. A recent analysis of six commercially available brands revealed actual lycopene content to vary considerably from the labeled dosage by as much as 43%.

WARNINGS

A recent analysis of six commercially available brands revealed actual lycopene content to vary considerably from the labeled dosage, from 62 to 143% of the stated amount.[1]

MECHANISM OF ACTION

Lycopene is a natural pigment synthesized by plants and microorganisms. Referred to as a nonprovitamin A carotenoid, it is not known to have any vitamin A activity. Biologic actions include antioxidant activity via singlet oxygen quenching and peroxyl radical scavenging, induction of cell-to-cell communication, and growth control, although less efficiently than beta-carotene. Proposed mechanisms of action in cancer prevention include inhibition of cancer growth, induction of differentiation by modulation of cell-cycle regulatory proteins, alterations in insulin-like growth factor-1, prevention of oxidative DNA damage, and possible enhancement of carcinogen-metabolizing enzymes. Other possible actions for all carotenoids include immunoenhancement, inhibition of mutagenesis and transformation, and inhibition of premalignant lesions. Carotenoids have also been associated with decreased risk of macular degeneration and cataracts, decreased risk for some types of cancers, and decreased risk of some cardiovascular events.[2-5]

USAGE

Asthma, cancer prevention, cancer treatment, cardiovascular disease, macular degeneration.

PHARMACOKINETICS

Absorption: Intestinal absorption of carotenoids, including lycopene, is facilitated by the formation of bile acid micelles containing carotenoids. The presence of fat in the small intestine stimulates the secretion of bile acids from the gallbladder and improves the absorption of carotenoids by increasing the size and stability of the micelles, thus allowing more carotenoids to be solubilized. The bioavailability of lycopene is affected by the dose and presence of other carotenoids, such as beta-carotene.

Distribution: Concentrations of lycopene in serum and body tissues are highly variable and are dependent on food source, efficiency of absorption, and the amount of fat in the diet. The serum concentration after a single dose peaks at 24 to 48 hours postdose. Lycopene is primarily stored in adipose and liver. In both serum and tissue storage, lycopene *cis*-isomers constitute greater than 50% of the total lycopene present.

Metabolism/Excretion: It is assumed that lycopene is excreted through the bile and kidneys.[3,6]

ADVERSE REACTIONS

No adverse effects have been reported at normal doses.[3]

Toxicity: Lycopenodermia has resulted following chronic ingestion of large quantities of lycopene-rich foods (ie, tomato products) and is characterized by a deep orange discoloration of the skin.

DRUG INTERACTIONS

One large-scale prospective cohort study in the Netherlands suggested that alcohol comsumption may affect the chemopreventive properties of vitamin A.[5]

DOSAGE

Oral: No standard dosing exists. Supplementation for the general population is not recommended. *Tolerable upper intake level:* None set.[3]

LITERATURE SUMMARY AND CRITIQUE

Kucuk O, et al. Phase II randomized clinical trial of lycopene supplementation before radical prostatectomy. Cancer Epidemiol Biomarkers Prev 2001;10:861–8.

A prospective evaluation of 15 mg of lycopene ($n = 15$) or placebo ($n = 11$), administered twice daily, in patients with localized prostate cancer undergoing radical prostatectomy 3 weeks following supplementation. Study end points included cell growth and differentiation, plasma levels of IGF-1 and prostate-specific antigen, and tumor pathology. There was no difference in baseline demographics between treatment groups. Following surgery and analysis of data, it was shown that serum levels of IGF-1 and involvement of surgical margins and/or extraprostatic tissues with cancer were significantly lower in the lycopene group. No adverse events were noted. Although beneficial trends were seen for patients supplemented with lycopene, larger randomized studies are required to validate results.

Neuman I, Nahum H, Ben-Amotz A. Reduction of exercise-induced asthma oxidative stress by lycopene, a natural antioxidant. Allergy 2000;55:1184–9.

A small randomized, double-blind evaluation of lycopene (LYC-O-MATO) supplementation on airway hyperreactivity in 20 patients with EIA. The test was based on the following sequence: measurement of baseline pulmonary function; a 7-minute exercise session on a motorized treadmill, 8-minute rest, and again measurement of pulmonary function; 1-week, oral, randomly administered, double-blind supplementation of placebo or 30 mg/d of lycopene; measurement of pulmonary function at rest, a 7-minute exercise session, and 8-minute rest and again measurement of pulmonary function. A 4-week washout interval was allowed between each protocol. All patients given placebo showed significant postexercise reduction of more than 15% in their forced expiratory volume in 1 second. After receiving a daily dose of 30 mg of lycopene for 1 week, 11 (55%) patients were significantly protected against EIA. These results must be substantiated by a larger trial.[6–10]

REFERENCES

1. Feifer AH, Fleshner NE, Klotz L. Analytical accuracy and reliability of commonly used nutritional supplements in prostate disease. J Urol 2002;168:150–4.
2. Stahl W, Sies H. Lycopene: a biologically important carotenoid for humans? Arch Biochem Biophys 1996;336:1–9.

3. Dietary Reference Intakes for vitamin C, vitamin E, selenium, and carotenoids. Washington (DC): National Academy Press; 2000.
4. Kucuk O, et al. Phase II randomized clinical trial of lycopene supplementation before radical prostatectomy. Cancer Epidemiol Biomarkers Prev 2001;10:861–8.
5. Schuurman A, et al. A prospective cohort study on intake of retinol, vitamins C and E, and carotenoids and prostate cancer risk (Netherlands). Cancer Causes Control 2002;13:573–82.
6. Stahl W, Sies H. Uptake of lycopene and its geometrical isomers is greater from heat processed than from unprocessed tomato juice in humans. J Nutr 1992;122:2161–6.
7. Gartner C, Stahl W, Sies H. Lycopene is more bioavailable from tomato paste than from fresh tomatoes. Am J Clin Nutr 1997;66:116–22.
8. Agarwal S, Rao AV. Role of antioxidant lycopene in cancer and heart disease. J Am Coll Nutr 2000;19:563–9.
9. Giovannucci E. Tomatoes, tomato-based products, lycopene, and cancer: review of the epidemiologic literature. J Natl Cancer Inst 1999;91:317–31.
10. Olmedilla B, et al. A European multicentre, placebo-controlled supplementation study with α-tocopherol, carotene-rich palm oil, lutein or lycopene; analysis of serum responses. Clin Sci (Lond) 2002;102:447–56.

Magnesium

COMMON NAMES

Magnesium chloride, magnesium citrate, magnesium pyrrolidone carboxylic acid, magnesium gluconate

A.DONATO

CLINICAL SUMMARY

An essential mineral obtained from various foods. Patients take this supplement to prevent and treat fatigue, migraines, premenstrual syndrome, and heart disease. Magnesium is obtained from nuts, grains, vegetables, and meats. This mineral is essential for numerous biochemical processes, including the formation of adenosine triphosphate (ATP), cellular signal transduction, synthesis of deoxyribonucleic acid (DNA), ribonucleic acid (RNA) and protein, and formation of bone. Following oral absorption, the bioavailability varies because of active transport uptake and nonuniform dosage formulations. Clinical data suggest that supplementation may benefit premenstrual syndrome (PMS), some heart conditions, diabetes, chronic fatigue, and, in conjunction with calcium, osteoporosis. Additional research is under way for migraine prophylaxis. Diarrhea is the primary reported adverse event. Patients with renal insufficiency or heart block should not self-medicate with magnesium supplements. The daily recommended allowance from food for men and women over 30 years is 400 mg and 320 mg, respectively, with a tolerable upper intake of 350 mg from supplements.

MECHANISM OF ACTION

Magnesium is a necessary mineral for many biochemical processes. Magnesium is required for approximately 300 enzyme systems, for anaerobic and aerobic pathways, and for forming the Mg-ATP complex. Magnesium is essential in the synthesizing of DNA, RNA, and protein. Various enzymes that participate in the synthesis of carbohydrates and lipids use ionized magnesium. Magnesium ions play a structural role, where they are bound to phospholipid membranes, ribosomes, and chromatin. Enzymes that are used in transmitting signals within cells also require magnesium ions. These enzymes include adenylate cyclase, which catalyzes the synthesis of cyclic adenosine monophosphate, and protein kinase C, which catalyzes the phosphorylation of a number of proteins. Magnesium is used by muscle proteins, including creatinine kinase, actin, sodium-potassium ATPase, and calcium pumps. Magnesium is vital for energy production, as it is required by the F1 protein, the ATP-synthesizing protein in the mitochondrion.[1,2]

USAGE
Asthma, cardiovascular disease, chronic fatigue syndrome, diabetes, fatigue, glaucoma, hypertension, muscle pain, osteoporosis, perinatal care, premenstrual syndrome.

PHARMACOKINETICS
Absorption: Magnesium is absorbed primarily in the distal small intestines or colon. Active uptake is required involving various transport systems such as the vitamin D–sensitive transport system. Because magnesium is not passively absorbed, it demonstrates saturable absorption resulting in variable bioavailability, averaging 35 to 40% of administered dose. Magnesium levels in the body and the presence of calcium, phosphate, phytate, and protein can affect the rate of absorption.

Distribution: Normal plasma levels of magnesium range from about 1.6 to 2.1 nM. Magnesium rapidly distributes throughout the body following absorption. About half of the plasma Mg occurs as the free ion, with about one-third bound to albumin and the remainder occurring in complexes with phosphate, citrate, and other anions. The non–protein-bound Mg (70% of total Mg) in the plasma can enter the glomerular filtrate. Nearly all of the Mg entering the filtrate is reabsorbed by the renal tubule. About 60 to 65% of the body's Mg is in bone, 27% in muscle, 6% in other cells, and about 1% in extracellular fluids. About 20 to 30% of bone magnesium is freely exchangeable and is in rapid equilibrium with serum. The remaining bone magnesium is intimately associated with the apatite crystal of the bone and is called nonexchangeable magnesium.

Metabolism/Excretion: Magnesium is regulated and excreted primarily by the kidneys, where various ATPase enzymes are responsible for maintaining homeostasis. Magnesium also undergoes efficient enterohepatic circulation.[1,3,4]

ADVERSE REACTIONS
Common: Elevated doses of magnesium can cause osmotic diarrhea, nausea, vomiting, cramps, and a chalky taste in the mouth.

Toxicity: Hypermagnesemia is relatively rare. Cardiac and neurologic symptoms of hypermagnesemia generally do not occur until serum levels exceed 2 to 4 mmol/L. Common symptoms of severe hypermagnesemia include nausea, vomiting, lethargy, confusion, respiratory depression, hypotension, bradycardia, heart block, and cardiac arrest. The most frequent cause of death from hypermagnesemia is respiratory arrest. Severe symptomatic hypermagnesemia predominantly occurs in patients with renal insufficiency.[5,6]

DRUG INTERACTIONS

Digoxin: Magnesium supplements may reduce the bioavailability of digoxin when taken concomitantly.

Tetracyclines: Magnesium may reduce the absorption and serum levels of tetracycline antibiotics.

Nitrofurantoin: Magnesium may adsorb to nitrofurantoin, reducing its bioavailability.

Neuromuscular Blockers: Magnesium supplements may potentiate the effects of neuro-muscular blockers (eg, vecuronium, succinylcholine).[7]

NUTRIENT INTERACTIONS

Folate or iron supplements should be taken separately by 2 hours. Magnesium should also not be taken with high-phytate food.[5]

CONTRAINDICATIONS

Patients with renal insufficiency or end-stage renal disease should not consume magnesium supplements. Patients with heart block should not consume magnesium supplements.

DOSAGE

Oral: 250 to 1,000 mg/d given in divided doses has been used.

Recommended Dietary Allowances: Tolerable upper intake level: 350 mg from nonfood sources.

Men
    19 to 30 years: 400 mg
    31 to 70 years: 420 mg
Women
    9 to 30 years: 310 mg
    31 to 70 years: 320 mg
Pregnancy
    14 to 18 years: 400 mg
    19 to 30 years: 350 mg
    31 to 50 years: 360 mg

Lactation
    14 to 18 years: 360 mg
    19 to 30 years: 310 mg
    31 to 50 years: 320 mg[2]

LITERATURE SUMMARY AND CRITIQUE

Witteman JC, et al. Reduction of blood pressure with oral magnesium supplementation in women with mild to moderate hypertension. Am J Clin Nutr 1994;60:129–35.

A prospective, randomized, double-blind evaluation of magnesium supplementation for reduction of blood pressure in 91 women ages 35 to 77 years with mild to moderate hypertension not currently receiving pharmacologic therapy. Patients were randomized to 485 mg/d elemental magnesium or placebo for 6 months. Change in blood pressure was the primary outcome measured. Rates of adverse effects were similar between treatment groups. Although the study results suggest that supplementation may lower blood pressure, it is not a clinically meaningful change. Additional studies in homogeneous populations are necessary.

Facchinetti F, et al. Oral magnesium successfully relieves premenstrual mood changes. Obstet Gynecol 1991;78:177–81.

A prospective, randomized, double-blind evaluation of magnesium supplementation from the fifteenth day of the cycle until menstruation on 32 women suffering from chronic PMS. Following a 2-month baseline period, subjects were randomized to receive magnesium pyrrolidine carboxylic acid containing 360 mg elemental magnesium ($n = 14$) or placebo ($n = 14$) for two menstrual cycles; all subjects subsequently received magnesium supplements for an additional two cycles. Primary outcomes measured were the Menstrual Distress Questionnaire and magnesium and hormone serum levels. Four patients withdrew from the study, one from the magnesium group owing to diarrhea. Questionnaire total scores were significantly lower after 2 months of magnesium supplementation. Cellular concentration of magnesium was significantly elevated, whereas hormone levels were unchanged. The data suggest that magnesium supplementation reduces cluster pain and overall menstrual distress, although additional studies are required to determine long-term effects.[8,9]

REFERENCES

1. Brody T. Nutritional biochemistry. San Diego (CA): Academic Press; 1999.
2. Dietary Reference Intakes for calcium, phosphorus, magnesium, vitamin D, and fluoride. Washington (DC): National Academy Press; 2000.
3. Dengel JL, et al. Magnesium homeostasis: conservation mechanism in lactating women consuming controlled-magnesium diet. Am J Clin Nutr 1994;59:990–4.
4. Ranade VV, Somberg JC. Bioavailability and pharmacokinetics of magnesium after administration of magnesium salts to humans. Am J Ther 2001;8:347–57.
5. Pronsky ZM. Power's and Moore's food-medication interactions. 11th ed. Pottstown (PA): Food Medication Interactions; 2000.
6. Schelling JR. Fatal hypermagnesemia. Clin Nephrol 2000;53:61–5.

7. Drugs: facts and comparisons. St. Louis (MO): Lippincott Williams and Wilkins; 2001.
8. Whitney EN, et al. Understanding normal & clinical nutrition. 4th ed. Belmont (CA): West Publishing; 1994.
9. Finstad EW, et al. The effects of magnesium supplementation on exercise performance. Med Sci Sports Exerc 2001;33:493–8.

Magnet Therapy

COMMON NAMES
Biomagnetic therapy, electromagnetic field therapy

KEY WORD
Electromagnetic field therapy

CLINICAL SUMMARY
Unconventional therapy available in alternative clinics in Mexico, Germany, and elsewhere. Magnetic therapies are promoted to diagnose and treat cancer, human immunodeficiency virus (HIV), psychiatric disorders, stress, multiple sclerosis, and infections; increase energy; prolong life; and stimulate the immune system. Magnetic fields are administered by application of magnets to certain parts of the body, by magnetic field–generating machines, or with magnetic mattresses or blankets. Treatment can last minutes to weeks. Evidence supporting the use of magnetic therapies for the above conditions is limited. State consumer protection agencies and the US Food and Drug Administration have prosecuted various marketers of magnetized devices and therapies, forcing them to halt unsubstantiated claims of health benefits. In vitro studies show that static magnetic fields may modulate ion transport and related cell and neuronal activity, but no anticancer activity is demonstrated. Patients also use magnetized braces and mattresses to treat pain associated with fibromyalgia, diabetic neuropathy, sciatica, and arthritis. Clinical studies of these devices are small and flawed. Although some show improvements in pain associated with conditions such as diabetic neuropathy, fibromyalgia, and arthritis, the results are often indistinguishable from placebo effects. Larger, placebo-controlled studies are needed to evaluate the therapeutic effects of magnets.

MECHANISM OF ACTION
Marketers make varying unsubstantiated claims for how magnets work, such as magnets "act upon the body's energy field" or correct "magnetic field deficiency syndrome," a condition said to result from decreases in the earth's magnetic field over the past 1,000 years. It is purported that the positive (south) pole of the magnet has a "stress effect," which interferes with metabolic functioning, produces acidity, reduces cellular oxygen supply, and encourages the replication of latent microorganisms. The negative (north) pole is said to have a "calming effect" and helps to normalize metabolic functioning, promote

oxygenation, and treat neurologic/psychiatric disorders. No evidence supports these claims, and no anticancer activity is seen for magnetic fields in laboratory or human studies. Most anecdotes of magnetic "healing" involve symptoms that may be psychosomatic, associated with stress, or subjective measures such as pain or depression.

Theoretically, static magnetic fields (SMFs) may alter ion flow, cellular potential, membrane configuration, ion pump activity, or neurotransmitter release. Most of the biologic phenomena associated with SMFs may be caused by changes in cellular calcium. SMFs of 1,000 to 4,000 G are found to alter protein and enzyme structure and the kinetics of reactions involving free radicals. Reduced action potential firing in cultured neurons and permeability changes in synthetic liposome vesicles are observed after application of an SMF. It may not be legitimate to extrapolate in vitro data, in which cells are directly exposed to magnetic fields, to their effect in a complex biologic system. Moreover, many in vitro studies have not been replicated. Although some authors refer to documented effects of pulsed electromagnetic fields in attempting to explain a mechanism of action for static magnets, SMFs do not generate an electric field and therefore cannot confer the claimed physiologic effects. It is suggested that positive reports of magnet use reflect placebo effects.[1,11]

USAGE
Antiaging, arthritis, cancer treatment, circulatory disorders, diabetic neuropathy, fatigue, fibromyalgia, HIV and acquired immune deficiency syndrome (AIDS), immunostimulation, infections, inflammation, insomnia, multiple sclerosis, muscle pain, nausea and vomiting, neuralgia, pain, peripheral neuropathy, rheumatoid arthritis, strength and stamina, stress, wound healing.

ADVERSE REACTIONS
Regular use of low-intensity magnets appears to be safe. The World Health Organization reports that the available evidence indicates the absence of adverse effects on human health with exposure to magnetic fields up to 2 Tesla (20,000 G).
Reported: Pain, nausea, and dizziness. Symptoms ceased on removal of the magnets.
Case Report: Bullous pemphigoid associated with magnetic mattress use.[2,12,13]

DRUG INTERACTIONS
None known.

CONTRAINDICATIONS
Patients with a cardiac pacemaker and pregnant women should avoid use of magnetic devices.

DOSAGE

No specific dosage is recommended. Clinical trials have evaluated permanent magnets with strengths from 300 to 1,100 G. The duration of magnet application varies from minutes to weeks.

Manufacturers claim to design magnets so that 300 to 600 G reach the skin. The magnetic field decreases most rapidly with distance from bipolar magnets, whereas multipolar magnets generate the deepest field gradient penetration.

Independent analysis of five commercially available magnets found surface flux densities to be significantly less than manufacturer claims; flux densities 2.5 cm above the surface varied from 0 to 200 G.[14,15]

LITERATURE SUMMARY AND CRITIQUE

No clinical studies evaluate magnetic field therapy for any proposed claim other than pain relief.

Segal NA, et al. Two configurations of static magnetic fields for treating rheumatoid arthritis of the knee: a double-blind clinical trial. Arch Phys Med Rehabil 2001;82:1453–60.

A randomized, double-blind, controlled, multicenter trial evaluated magnetic pads in 64 patients with rheumatoid arthritis and persistent knee pain rated $> 40/100$ mm. Patients were randomized to wear MagnaBloc quadrapolar 1,900 G magnets, measured to penetrate 5 cm into cadaveric tissue ($n = 38$), or a unipolar 720 G control device containing one functional and three sham magnets ($n = 26$). Rheumatologist's Global Assessment of Disease Activity (R-GADA), erythrocyte sedimentation rate and/or C-reactive protein, knee range of motion (ROM), examination for tenderness and swelling, patients' assessment of physical function, 100 mm Visual Analog Scale (VAS) score for pain, Subjects' Global Assessment of Disease Activity (S-GADA), and the Modified Health Assessment Questionnaire (MHAQ) were measured at baseline, 1 hour, 1 day, and 1 week after placement of devices. Patients were asked to keep a pain diary. Both treatment arms showed a significant reduction in pain from baseline at 1 day and 1 week post-treatment ($p < .0001$). Although the MagnaBloc group showed a greater reduction in pain, the difference was not statistically significant ($p < .23$). S-GADA decreased significantly at 1 week in the MagnaBloc group (33%) while declining only 2% in controls. At 1 week, 68% of the MagnaBloc patients and 27% of the controls reported feeling better or much better ($c2 = 10.64, p = .001$). No other outcome changed significantly. No power analysis was performed to assess adequate sample size, and the length of the intervention may be too short.

Collacott EA, et al. Bipolar permanent magnets for the treatment of chronic low back pain. JAMA 2000;283:1322–5.

A small, randomized, double-blind, placebo-controlled, crossover pilot study of the use of bipolar magnetic devices in 20 patients with low back pain. Subjects were randomized to receive 1 week of 282 to 330 G magnets and 1 week of sham magnets, or vice versa, with

1 week washout between. Subjects applied devices 6 h/d, Monday, Wednesday, and Friday. Outcomes measured were pre- and post-treatment pain on the VAS, Pain Rating Index (PRI) of the McGill Pain Questionnaire, and ROM of the lumbosacral spine. No significant differences were noted in any outcome for real or sham magnets; post-treatment pain declined slightly for both groups. Subjects reported no adverse effects. This study has been criticized for sex bias (95% of subjects were male), selection bias (55% subjects were disabled, 85% were retired), and a weak intervention compared with other studies requiring 24 h/d use of stronger magnets.

Colbert AP, et al. Magnetic mattress pad use in patients with fibromyalgia: a randomized double-blind pilot study. J Back Musculoskel Rehabil 1999;13:19–31.
A small, randomized, double-blind evaluation of 16 weeks magnetized mattress pad use on 25 female patients with fibromyalgia. Thirteen patients received unipolar magnetized (1,100 ± 50 G) and 12 received nonmagnetized mattress pads. Magnetic field intensity and penetration were not measured independently before mattress use. Study group demographics did not differ significantly, but control subjects were heavier and had higher use of anxiolytic and narcotic medications for pain management. Outcomes measured related to quality of life: VAS for global well-being, pain, sleep disturbance, fatigue, and tiredness on awakening; Total Myalgic Score; Pain Distribution Drawings; and a modified Fibromyalgia Impact Questionnaire. The experimental group experienced statistically significant improvements in all outcomes, whereas the control group had smaller improvements in pain, sleep, fatigue, and tiredness. No power analysis was performed to ensure adequate sample size, and improvements in both groups may be attributable to use of the better mattress pad.

Vallbona C, Hazlewood CF, Jurida G. Response of pain to static magnetic fields in postpolio patients: a double-blind pilot study. Arch Phys Med Rehabil 1997;78:1200–3.
A prospective double-blind study of bipolar 300 to 500 G Bioflex magnets versus sham magnets in 50 patients with postpolio syndrome experiencing muscular or arthritic pain for at least 4 weeks. No significant differences in demographics or location of pain existed between the study groups. However, a higher prevalence of muscular pain (compared with arthritic) and a higher female-to-male ratio were present in the experimental group. Only the most sensitive area of pain was evaluated per patient. Four different magnet sizes were used, depending on the site of pain, applied to the skin with adhesive tape. Patients wore the device for 45 minutes; position or activity during this time was not monitored. Outcomes measured were the McGill Pain Questionnaire and pain as assessed by palpation of a trigger point pre- and post-treatment. Both outcomes improved significantly for the treatment group compared with the control, but pressure of palpation was not measured, so consistency is questionable. This study does not address the efficacy of long-term magnet use for chronic pain relief. Additional, larger studies are necessary and should control for magnet size between groups, female-to-male ratio, position during treatment, and source of pain.

Caselli MA, et al. Evaluation of magnetic foil and PPT Insoles in the treatment of heel pain. J Am Podiatr Med Assoc 1997;87:11–6.
Prospective, randomized evaluation of the effect of insoles with or without magnetic foil on 34 otherwise healthy patients with medial plantar calcaneal heel pain. The primary outcome was foot function index, measured before and after 4 weeks of constant insole use. Eleven of 19 (58%) patients in the treatment group and 9 of 15 (60%) controls reported improvement, and no significant difference in the percentage improvement was measured. The authors concluded that the molded insole alone was effective in treating heel pain.

REFERENCES
1. Hong CZ, et al. Magnetic necklace: its therapeutic effectiveness on neck and shoulder pain. Arch Phys Med Rehabil 1982;63:462–6.
2. Colbert AP, et al. Magnetic mattress pad use in patients with fibromyalgia: a randomized double-blind pilot study. J Back Musculoskel Rehabil 1999;13:19–31.
3. Macklis RM. Magnetic healing, quackery, and the debate about the health effects of electromagnetic fields. Ann Intern Med 1993;118:376–83.
4. Burkhart CG, Burkhart CN. Are magnets effective for pain control? JAMA 2000;284:564–5.
5. Man D, Man B, Plosker H. The influence of permanent magnetic field therapy on wound healing in suction lipectomy patients: a double-blind study. Plast Reconstr Surg 1999;104:2261–6.
6. Szor JK, Topp R. Use of magnet therapy to heal an abdominal wound: a case study. Ostomy Wound Manage 1998;44:24–9.
7. Repacholi MH, Greenebaum B. Interaction of static and extremely low frequency electric and magnetic fields with living systems: health effects and research needs. Bioelectromagnetics 1999;20:133–60.
8. Flipo D, et al. Increased apoptosis, changes in intracellular Ca2+, and functional alterations in lymphocytes and macrophages after in vitro exposure to static magnetic field. J Toxicol Environ Health 1998;54:63–76.
9. Atef MM, et al. Effects of a static magnetic field on haemoglobin structure and function. Int J Biol Macromol 1995;17:105–11.
10. Rosen AD. Threshold and limits of magnetic field action at the presynaptic membrane. Biochim Biophys Acta 1994;1193:62–6.
11. Carter R, et al. The effectiveness of magnet therapy for treatment of wrist pain attributed to carpal tunnel syndrome. J Fam Pract 2002;51:38–40.
12. Ohkubo C, Xu S. Acute effects of static magnetic fields on cutaneous microcirculation in rabbits. In Vivo 1997;11:221–6.
13. Vallbona C, Richards T. Evolution of magnetic therapy from alternative to traditional medicine. Phys Med Rehabil Clin North Am 1999;10:729–54.
14. Weintraub MI. Are magnets effective for pain control? JAMA 2000;284:565.
15. Blechman AM. Discrepancy between claimed field flux density of some commercially available magnets and actual gaussmeter measurements. Altern Ther Health Med 2001;7:92–5.

Maitake

COMMON NAMES
King of mushrooms, dancing mushroom, cloud mushroom, MD-fraction, hen of woods

A. DONATO

SCIENTIFIC NAME
Grifola frondosa

KEY WORD
Grifola frondosa

CLINICAL SUMMARY
Derived from the cap and stem of the mushroom. The active constituent is thought to be a β-glucan polysaccharide. The whole mushroom is used primarily as a dietary element, but extracts and supplements are sold as immune stimulants for patients with human immunodeficiency virus (HIV) or cancer. Although no adverse effects have been reported, animal studies reveal a hypoglycemic effect following administration of maitake extract. In a small noncontrolled study, tumor regression or significant symptom improvements were observed in half of the subjects using maitake extract. Research is under way to test maitake's anticancer effects in human.

CONSTITUENTS
Polysaccharides: 1,3- and 1,6-β-glucan appears to be the most active ingredient; α-glucan is also present; lipids: octadecanoic and octadecadienoic acids; phospholipids: phosphatidylethanolamine, phosphatidylcholine, phosphatidylinositol, phosphatidylserine, phosphatidic acid; ergosterol (vitamin D_2).[1]

MECHANISM OF ACTION

Maitake is thought to exert its effects through its ability to activate various effector cells, such as macrophages, natural killer cells, T cells, interleukin-1, and superoxide anions, all of which have anticancer activity. Animal studies suggest possible hypoglycemic activity.[2–4]

USAGE

Cancer prevention, diabetes, high cholesterol, hypertension, immunostimulation, weight loss.

ADVERSE REACTIONS

None reported.

DRUG INTERACTIONS

None reported.

DOSAGE

Oral: 0.5 to 1 mg/kg/d of β-glucan from maitake extract, given in divided doses. Note that products vary in β-glucan content. Maitake is available as raw mushroom and in capsules, tablets, and liquid extract formulations.

LITERATURE SUMMARY AND CRITIQUE

Adachi K, Nanba H, Kuroda H. Potentiation of host-mediated antitumor activity by β glucan obtained from *Grifola frondosa*. Chem Pharm Bull 1987;35:262–70.

A polysaccharide (3-branched 1,6-β-glucan membrane type 2) extracted from maitake showed an antitumor effect against syngeneic tumors (MM-46 carcinoma and IMC carcinoma cell lines). It directly activates various effector cells (macrophages, natural killer cells, and killer T cells) to attack tumor cells and potentiates the activities of various mediators, including lymphokines and interleukin-1. Thus, it acts to potentiate cellular functions and at the same time prevents a decrease in immune functions of the tumor-bearing host.

Yamada Y, et al. Antitumor effect of orally administered extracts from fruit body of *Grifola frondosa* (maitake). Chemotherapy 1990;38:790–6.

A footpad swelling test to assess whether a delayed-type hypersensitivity (DTH) reaction against tumor antigen was potentiated by oral administration of maitake mushroom. When the antigen was injected into tumor-bearing mice administered maitake extract, footpad swelling was observed, suggesting that a DTH reaction against the tumor antigen was potentiated by oral administration of maitake extract. The authors hypothesized that the DTH reaction manifested by the action of DTH T cells and macrophages was potentiated by oral administration of maitake. Even when cytotoxic T cells were absent, there was a high degree of tumor involution.

REFERENCES

1. Hobbs C. Medicinal mushrooms. 3rd ed. Loveland (CO): Interweave Press; 1996.
2. Adachi K, Nanba H, Kuroda H. Potentiation of host-mediated antitumor activity by β glucan obtained from *Grifola frondosa* (maitake). Chem Pharm Bull 1987;35:262–70.
3. Kubo K, Aoki H. Nanba H. Anti-diabetic activity present in the fruit body of *Grifola frondosa* (maitake). Biol Pharm Bull 1994;17:1106–10.
4. Horio H, Ohtsuru M. Maitake (*Grifola frondosa*) improve glucose tolerance of experimental diabetic rats. J Nutr Sci Vitaminol 2001;47:57–63.
5. Kodama N, Komuta K, Nanba H. Can maitake MD-fraction aid cancer patients? Altern Med Rev 2002;7:236–9.
6. Miura NN. Blood clearance of (1—>3)-β-D-glucan in MRL *lpr/lpr* mice. FEMS Immunol Med Microbiol 1996;13:51–7.
7. Ohno N, et al. Characterization of the antitumor glucan obtained from liquid-cultured *Grifola frondosa*. Chem Pharm Bull 1986;34:1709–15.
8. Nanba H, Kubo K. Maitake D-fraction: healing and preventive potential for cancer. J Orthomol Med 1997;12:43–9.

Maté

A. DONATO

COMMON NAMES
Yerba maté, St. Bartholomew's tea, Jesuit's tea, ilex, hervea, guyaki Paraguay tea

SCIENTIFIC NAME
Ilex paraguariensis

KEY WORDS
Ilex paraguariensis, yerba maté

CLINICAL SUMMARY

Derived from the leaf of the plant. Yerba maté contains caffeine, theophylline, and theobromine, which are responsible for the stimulant activity of this herb. No clinical studies have evaluated its efficacy, although there is extensive experience with each of the previously mentioned chemicals. Epidemiologic studies conducted in the past decade indicate that chronic maté drinkers are at an increased risk of bladder, oral, esophageal, and lung cancer. Frequently reported adverse effects include insomnia, restlessness, agitation, nausea, vomiting, and headache. Yerba maté may interact with many prescription medications. Increased or altered activity of β-adrenergic agonists, central nervous system (CNS) stimulants, theophylline, diuretics, and caffeine-containing beverages may occur with concomitant administration. Patients with hypertension, cardiac disorders, or anxiety or women who are pregnant or breast-feeding, should not consume yerba maté.

CONSTITUENTS

Xanthene alkaloids: 1 to 2% caffeine, 0.45 to 0.9% theobromine, 0.05% theophylline; tannins: 4 to 16% caffeic and chlorogenic acids; amines: choline and trigonelline; amino acids; flavonoids: kaemferol, quercetin, rutin; volatile oils; other constituents: ursolic acid (antitumor agent); vitamins B_2, B_6, and C; niacin; pantothenic acid.[1]

WARNINGS

High doses and prolonged consumption of maté tea are associated with an increased risk of certain cancers.

MECHANISM OF ACTION

Maté's action is attributable to its caffeine, theophylline, and theobromine activities, which are well documented.

USAGE

Appetite suppression, CNS stimulation, depression, fatigue, headaches, pain, promotion of urination.

ADVERSE REACTIONS

Reported: Insomnia, anxiety, tremor, restlessness, agitation, nausea and vomiting, palpitations, and headache.[2]

DRUG INTERACTIONS

Aspirin: Maté may increase absorption and bioavailability.
Acetaminophen: Pain relief of acetaminophen is increased owing to the caffeine content in maté.
Benzodiazepines: The effects of benzodiazepines are reduced by the caffeine content in maté.
β-Adrenergic Agonists: The effects of β-adrenergic agonists are increased by maté.
Clozapine: Maté may alter effects.
CNS Stimulants: Maté may increase effects.
Monoamine Oxidase Inhibitors: Maté can cause hypertensive crisis.
Theophylline: Maté may increase effects and lead to possible toxicity.
Diuretics: Maté may cause an additive effect.[3]

LABORATORY INTERACTIONS

Owing to the caffeine content in maté, the following laboratory tests may be altered: blood pressure, catecholamine levels, and bleeding time as measured by prothrombin time, activated partial thromboplastin time, or international normalized ratio.

CONTRAINDICATIONS

Warnings associated with caffeine apply to maté. Patients with hypertension, cardiac disorders, and anxiety should not consume maté. Women who are pregnant or breastfeeding should not consume maté.

DOSAGE

Oral: Tea: 2 to 4 g dried leaf three times a day. *Liquid extract:* 1:1 in 25% alcohol 2 to 4 mL three times a day.[4]

LITERATURE SUMMARY AND CRITIQUE

Pintos J, et al. Maté, coffee, and tea consumption and risk of cancers of the upper aerodigestive tract in southern Brazil. Epidemiology 1994;5:583–90.

To test the hypothesis that maté drinkers have high risks of upper aerodigestive tract cancers, data were analyzed from a case-control study in southern Brazil. The unadjusted relative risk for all upper aerodigestive tract cancers was 2.1. After controlling for tobacco use, and alcohol and coffee or tea drinking, the relative risk was 1.6. Most of the excess risk for maté drinkers was for oral and laryngeal cancers. There was no evidence of associations with coffee and tea drinking. The author concluded that owing to a high prevalence of maté drinking in South America, maté tea might be linked to as many as 20% of all cases occurring in this region.

De Stefani E, et al. Maté drinking and risk of lung cancer in males: a case control study from Uruguay. Cancer Epidemiol Biomarkers Prev 1996;5:515–9.

Maté drinking has been associated with the risk of most upper aerodigestive tract cancers. After adjusting for pack-years of cigarette smoking, the amount of maté was associated with a 1.6-fold increase in risk for heavy drinkers, compared with light drinkers, with a significant dose-response pattern. Small cell lung cancer showed a significant increase in relative risk for maté amount and maté duration. On the other hand, pulmonary adenocarcinoma was not associated with maté drinking.

De Stefani E, et al. Black tobacco, maté and bladder cancer. A case-control study from Uruguay. Cancer 1991;67:536–40.

After adjustments for age, tobacco smoking, and social class, a sevenfold increase in the risk of bladder cancer was seen among the heavy maté tea drinkers.

McGee J, et al. A case of veno-occlusive disease of the liver in Britain associated with herbal tea consumption. J Clin Pathol 1976;29:788–94.

Small amounts of pyrrolizidine alkaloids were recovered from a sample of maté tea, to which the patient was addicted. It seems probable that the consumption of large amounts of maté tea over a period of years was the cause of the hepatic disease.

REFERENCES

1. Bisset N. Herbal drugs and phytopharmaceuticals. Stuttgart (Germany): CRC Press; 1994.
2. Schulz V, et al. Rational phytotherapy: a physician's guide to herbal medicine. Berlin: Springer; 1998.
3. Brinker F. Herb contraindications and drug interactions. 2nd ed. Sandy (OR): Eclectic Medical Publications; 1998.
4. Blumenthal, et al. Herbal medicine, expanded Commission E monographs. Austin (TX): American Botanical Council; 2000.

5. DerMarderosian A, editor. The review of natural products. St. Louis: Facts and Comparisons; 1999.
6 Newall C, et al. Herbal medicines: a guide for health-care professionals. Binghamton (NY): Pharmaceutical Press; 1996.
7. Goldenberg D. Maté: a risk factor for oral and oropharyngeal cancer. Oral Oncol 2002;38:646.

Melatonin

COMMON NAMES
MLT, pineal hormone

SCIENTIFIC NAME
N-Acetylmethoxytryptamine

CLINICAL SUMMARY
Hormonal supplement primarily of synthetic origin but occasionally derived from animal sources. Patients use melatonin to treat insomnia, jet lag, and cancer. Melatonin is produced endogenously in humans by the pineal gland. Exogenous melatonin is absorbed poorly following oral administration and is metabolized rapidly by the liver. The exact mechanism of action is unknown, but melatonin is thought to control the circadian pacemaker and promote sleep. Melatonin demonstrates antiproliferative effects on cancer cell lines in both in vitro and animal models. Clinical studies suggest that doses of 0.3 to 5 mg 30 minutes to 5 hours before bedtime may decrease sleep latency and improve overall sleep. Melatonin may be effective for jet lag, but data are inconsistent. Clinical trials evaluate melatonin as monotherapy and in combination with other agents in patients with solid tumors. Results suggest improvements in quality of life and survival, but complete response is not documented. Reported adverse effects are rare but include drowsiness, headache, hypothermia, pruritus, abdominal cramps, and tachycardia. Melatonin may interact with nifedipine (Procardia XL), resulting in elevated blood pressure and heart rate. Optimal dose, length of therapy, and effect on endogenous melatonin are unknown; thus, additional research is necessary.

WARNINGS
Melatonin may cause drowsiness; patients should not drive or operate heavy machinery until familiar with the effects of melatonin.

MECHANISM OF ACTION
Melatonin is an endogenously produced indolamine hormone secreted by the pineal glands in humans. Nocturnal secretion is regulated by circadian rhythms and nighttime darkness. Its exact mechanism of action is unknown, but melatonin is thought to control

the circadian pacemaker and promote sleep. Ironically, melatonin is associated with wakefulness and activity in nocturnal animals. As levels of melatonin increase, an associated drop in core body temperature occurs. Both elderly and depressed patients tend to have lower basal levels of melatonin. Melatonin appears to be a potent free radical scavenger, interacts with cytosolic calmodulin, and stimulates the production of interleukin-4 in bone marrow T lymphocytes. In vitro and animal studies suggest antitumor effects exerted through antimitotic or immunomodulatory activity. In vitro studies demonstrate that melatonin has antiproliferative effects on human breast cancer (HS578T) and mouse melanoma (B16BL6, PG19). Melatonin reduces the proliferation of PC-3 and LNCaP in mice but has no effect on apoptosis.[1-8]

USAGE

Alzheimer's disease, antiaging, cancer treatment, depression, drug withdrawal symptoms, human immunodeficiency virus (HIV) and acquired immune deficiency syndrome (AIDS), insomnia, jet lag, seasonal affective disorder.

PHARMACOKINETICS

Doses of 1 to 2,000 mg melatonin given to healthy volunteers cause no significant toxicity. Intravenous administration of melatonin displays one-compartment pharmacokinetics. Tablets are absorbed following oral administration but appear to undergo extensive first-pass metabolism. Melatonin is metabolized rapidly in the liver to hydroxy metabolites, possibly by cytochrome P-450 isoenzymes 1A2 and 2C19. Oral bioavailability is estimated to be 15% for the parent compound. Elimination half-life is approximately 45 minutes, with a total-body clearance of 10 hours for a 3 mg dose.[1,9,10]

ADVERSE REACTIONS

Reported: Drowsiness, alterations in sleep patterns, altered mental status, disorientation, tachycardia, flushing, pruritus, abdominal cramps, headache, hypothermia.[1-3,11]

DRUG INTERACTIONS

Nifedipine: Concomitant administration of melatonin and nifedipine has resulted in elevations in blood pressure and heart rate.
Fluvoxamine: Fluvoxamine may increase circulating plasma levels of melatonin resulting in sedation.[9,12,13]

DOSAGE

Oral/Sublingual: Optimal dose and length of therapy are unknown. Melatonin formulation is immediate release or sublingual unless otherwise noted.
Insomnia: 0.3 to 5 mg at bedtime in adults have been used.

Tardive Dyskinesia: 10 mg controlled-release melatonin once a day have been used.
Cancer: 10 to 50 mg once a day have been used.
Jet Lag: Eastward flights: 5 mg at 6 pm for 3 nights prior to flight and at 10 to 11 pm (local time) for 4 days after arrival. *Westward flights:* 5 mg at 11 pm (local time) for 4 nights after arrival.
Cluster Headaches: 10 mg controlled-release melatonin once a day has been used.
Benzodiazepine Withdrawal: 2 mg controlled-release melatonin nightly for 6 weeks where benzodiazepine dosage is reduce 50% during week 2, 75% during weeks 3 and 4, and discontinued during weeks 5 to 6.[2,3,10–12,14–17]

LITERATURE SUMMARY AND CRITIQUE

Ghielmini M, et al. Double-blind randomized study on the myeloprotective effect of melatonin in combination with carboplatin and etoposide in advanced lung cancer. Br J Cancer 1999;80:1058–61.

A prospective, randomized, double-blind, crossover design study evaluating the effect of 40 mg oral melatonin supplementation on hematologic indices. Twenty previously untreated patients with inoperable lung cancer (16 non–small cell and 4 small cell) received two cycles of carboplatin (area under the curve = 5, Calvert formula) on day 1 and 150 mg/m^2 intravenous etoposide on days 1 to 3 every 4 weeks. Melatonin or placebo was given once daily, initiated 2 days before chemotherapy and continued for 21 days. Patients were randomized to receive melatonin with either the first or the second cycle. The median age of the cohort was 60 years. Multivariate analysis including age, sex, diagnosis, stage, performance status, doses of carboplatin and etoposide, and concomitant treatment of melatonin or placebo indicates no difference in hematologic indices between treatment arms. No significant adverse effects related to melatonin were reported. Ghielmini and colleagues concluded that 40 mg of oral melatonin does not improve hematologic status in lung cancer patients receiving carboplatin and etoposide.

Lissoni P, et al. A phase II study of tamoxifen plus melatonin in metastatic solid tumour patients. Br J Cancer 1996;74:1466–8.

A prospective, open-label evaluation of 20 mg of melatonin and 20 mg of tamoxifen in patients with metastatic solid tumors other than breast or prostate tumors. Subjects were refractory to previous treatment, had poor performance status, or had no alternate treatment option. Twenty-five patients (male-to-female ratio = 10:15, ages 38 to 81, 6 unknown primary, 4 melanoma, 4 uterine cervical, 5 pancreatic, 3 hepatocarcinoma, 2 ovarian, 1 non–small cell lung) were administered melatonin at bedtime and tamoxifen at noon, regardless of estrogen receptor status, until progression of disease or death. Patients received computed tomography or magnetic resonance imaging every 3 months and routine laboratory tests every 14 days. No complete response was documented. Three partial responses (12%) ranging from 5 to 8 months were recorded (melanoma, uterine cervical, and unknown primary). Stable disease, average duration of 6 months, was noted in 13 patients (52%), whereas the remaining 9 patients (36%) had progressive disease. No toxicity related to melatonin was reported. Lissoni and colleagues suggest that neuroendocrine treatment with 20 mg of melatonin and tamoxifen may be feasible for refractory solid tumors other than breast or prostate tumors, but additional research is necessary.

Lissoni P, et al. A randomized study with the pineal hormone melatonin versus supportive care alone in patients with brain metastases due to solid neoplasms. Cancer 1994;73:699–701.
A prospective, randomized, open-label evaluation of patients with brain metastases from solid tumors refractory to radiation and nitrosourea-based chemotherapy. Patients were randomized to supportive care ($n = 26$) or supportive care plus 20 mg of melatonin once daily ($n = 24$). Primary outcome was time to progression of disease and survival. Baseline characteristics and demographics did not differ significantly between groups. One-year survival, progression of brain disease, and mean survival were significantly better in patients receiving melatonin compared with placebo, 37% versus 12%, 5.9 versus 2.7 months, and 9.2 versus 5.5 months, respectively ($p < .05$). No adverse events related to melatonin were noted. Lissoni and colleagues suggest that melatonin reduces the frequency of hyperglycemia and steroid-related infective complications and improves performance status. Additional research in controlled patient populations must be conducted to determine optimal dose for melatonin.

REFERENCES

1. Sack RL, Lewy AJ, Hughes RJ. Use of melatonin for sleep and circadian rhythm disorders. Ann Med 1998;30:115–21.
2. Avery D, Lenz M, Landis C. Guidelines for prescribing melatonin. Ann Med 1998;30:122–30.
3. Brzezinski A. Melatonin in humans. N Engl J Med 1997;336:186–95.
4. Xi SC, et al. Inhibition of androgen-sensitive LNCaP prostate cancer growth in vivo by melatonin: association of antiproliferative action of the pineal hormone with mt1 receptor protein expression. Prostate 2001;46:52–61.
5. Cos S, Garcia-Bolado A, Sanchez-Barcelo EJ. Direct antiproliferative effects of melatonin on two metastatic cell sublines of mouse melanoma (B18BL6 and PG19). Melanoma Res 2001;11:197–201.
6. Blask E, Wilson ST, Zalatan F. Physiological melatonin inhibition of human breast cancer cell growth in vitro: evidence for a glutathione-mediated pathway. Cancer Res 1997;57:1909–14.
7. Karbownik M, Reiter RJ. Antioxidative effects of melatonin in protection against cellular damage caused by ionizing radiation. Proc Soc Exp Biol Med 2000;225:9–22.
8. Reppert SM, Weaver DR. Melatonin madness. Cell 1995;83:1059–62.
9. Hartter S, et al. Increased bioavailability of oral melatonin after fluvoxamine coadministration. Clin Pharmacol Ther 2000;67:1–6.
10. DeMuro RL, et al. The absolute bioavailability of oral melatonin. J Clin Pharmacol 2000;40:781–4.
11. Shamir E, et al. Melatonin treatment for tardive dyskinesia: a double-blind, placebo-controlled, crossover study. Arch Gen Psychiatry 2001;58:1049–52.
12. Lusordi P, Piazza E, Fogari R. Cardiovascular effects of melatonin in hypertensive patients well controlled by nifedipine: a 24-hour study. Br J Clin Pharmacol 2000;49:423.
13. Von Bahr C, et al. Fluvoxamine but not citalopram increases serum melatonin in healthy subjects—an indication that cytochrome P450 CYP1A2 and CYP2C19 hydroxylate melatonin. Eur J Clin Pharmacol 2000;56:123–7.

14. Zhdanova IV, Wurtman RJ, Regan MM, et al. Melatonin treatment for age-related insomnia. J Clin Endocrinol Metab 2001;86:4727–30.
15. Leone M, et al. Melatonin versus placebo in the prophylaxis of cluster headache: a double-blind pilot study with parallel groups. Cephalalgia 1996;16:494–6.
16. Garfinkel D, et al. Facilitation of benzodiazepine discontinuation by melatonin: a new clinical approach. Arch Intern Med 1999;159:2456–60.
17. Zhdanova IV, et al. Melatonin treatment for age-related insomnia. J Clin Endocrinol Metab 2001;86:4727–30.

Metabolic Therapies

COMMON NAMES
Nutritional therapies, Gerson regimen, Kelley therapy, Gonzalez regimen, Contreras therapy, Manner therapy

KEY WORDS
Nutritional therapies, Gerson regimen, Kelley metabolic therapy, Gonzalez metabolic therapy, Contreras metabolic therapy, Manner metabolic therapy

CLINICAL SUMMARY
Strict dietary and detoxification regimens touted to prevent and treat cancer and degenerative diseases. Metabolic therapies, offered in the United States and at Mexican border clinics, are based on the theory that cancer and other diseases are caused by an accumulation of toxic substances in the body. Advocates claim that a healthful diet, detoxification practices (eg, coffee enemas, herbal laxatives), and immune augmentation detoxify the body and allow it to heal naturally. Therapies such as the Gerson, Kelley, Contreras, Manner, and Gonzalez regimens share this ideology but differ in modality. Diet is often tailored to the individual, based on whole foods and fresh fruits and vegetables, and is supplemented by digestive enzymes, glandular extracts, megadose vitamins, minerals, or herbal products. Agents such as bacille Calmette-Guérin (BCG), gammaglobulins, interleukins, hydrazine sulphate, hydrogen peroxide, or l-mandelonitrile-β-glucuronic acid (Laetrile) may also be administered. Weekly costs at Mexican border clinics are typically $3,000 to $5,000. Although dietary remedies provide a strong sense of personal control, the strict dietary recommendations of some metabolic therapies can cause nutritional deficiencies, whereas some entail potentially toxic doses of supplements or agents. Excessive use of coffee enemas can cause sepsis, dangerous electrolyte deficiencies, and death. Retrospective reviews of the Gerson, Kelley, and Contreras metabolic therapies show no evidence of efficacy. An open-label trial sponsored by the National Institutes of Health National Center for Complementary and Alternative Medicine of the Gonzalez regimen in patients with stage II to IV pancreatic adenocarcinoma is under way after promising results from a small pilot study. The American Cancer Society strongly urges cancer patients not to seek treatment with metabolic therapies at Mexican border clinics.

CONSTITUENTS

Therapy components vary between regimen and clinic. Typical regimens may contain an assortment of the following:

- *Restricted "Natural" Diet:* no processed foods.
- *Detoxification:* enemas, coffee enemas, hydrogen peroxide enemas, herbal laxatives, and/or fasting.
- *Nutritional Supplements:* high-dose vitamin C, vitamin A, B complex vitamins, magnesium, zinc, selenium, animal glandular extracts, digestive enzymes, para-aminobenzoic acid (PABA), carnitine, lecithin, inositol hexaphosphate, amino acids, and/or herbal products.
- *Other Agents:* Laetrile, hydrazine sulfate, gerovital, cesium chloride, BCG vaccine, interleukins, gammaglobulins, germanium sesquioxide, hydrogen peroxide, low-dose chemotherapy.

WARNINGS

The American Cancer Society strongly urges cancer patients not to seek treatment with costly and potentially hazardous metabolic/nutritional therapies, including the Gerson, Manner, and Contreras regimens, in Mexican border clinics. Excessive use of coffee enemas can cause infections, dangerous electrolyte deficiencies, and death, especially when combined with fasting.[1]

MECHANISM OF ACTION

Advocates of metabolic therapies claim that cancer and other diseases result from an accumulation of toxins in the body from food additives, preservatives, pesticides, and industrial pollution that disrupt the immune system and cell metabolism. The removal of these toxins through bowel purging and a healthful diet, they claim, allows the body to heal naturally. Although diet may play a role in cancer prevention and some cancers are associated with environmental exposures, no evidence shows that removal of such toxins or changing the diet can impede the course of cancer once it has been established. Furthermore, strict dietary restrictions, as in the Gerson regimen, cause nutritional deficiencies. Supplements are purported to normalize metabolism, strengthen the immune system, and destroy tumors, but oversupplementation has caused toxicity, requiring hospitalization. Glandular extracts are likely rendered ineffective when hydrolyzed in the gut, and animal extracts have been found to be contaminated. Experimental drugs such as interleukins and immunoglobulins may be used improperly. Overall, patients risk abandoning effective treatment by pursuing metabolic therapies.

Caffeine in coffee enemas is purported to cause dilation of bile ducts, bile production, glutathione S-transferase (GST) activation, and excretion of toxic breakdown products by the liver and through the colon wall. No published evidence supports these claims, and no human studies examine the clinical efficacy or physiologic effects of coffee enema administration. Kahweol and cafestol are constituents of green coffee that stimulate GST activation, but their activity is destroyed with roasting. Repeated administration of coffee enemas increases extravascular fluid volume and can cause serum electrolyte imbalances. The significant loss of bile salts associated with repeated long-term administration of enemas can result in malabsorption of fat, fat-soluble vitamins, and calcium.[2–4]

USAGE
Cancer prevention, cancer treatment, detoxification.

PHARMACOKINETICS
No formal pharmacokinetic studies have been performed with metabolic diets or coffee enema administration.

ADVERSE REACTIONS
Common: Flu-like symptoms, nausea, vomiting, diarrhea, weakness, dizziness, intestinal cramping, fever, muscle aches and pains, rashes. Nutrient deficiencies (calcium, vitamins D and B_{12}, protein), anemia, and malabsorption may result from metabolic diets.
Reported (Coffee Enemas): Electrolyte imbalance, which has resulted in serious infections (eg, *Campylobacter* sepsis and amebiasis), dehydration, colitis, constipation, and death. Perforation or rupture of the colon from hard insertion devices and transfer of pathogenic microorganisms by contaminated devices are also reported.
Case Reports (Coffee Enemas): Case 1: Multiple seizures and hypokalemia leading to cardiorespiratory arrest, coma, and death were reported after excessive use of coffee enemas (1–4/h) for a number of days. *Case 2:* Death attributable to fluid and electrolyte imbalance causing pleural and pericardial effusions after use of coffee enemas, four per day for 8 weeks.[1,2,4]

DRUG INTERACTIONS
None known.

DOSAGE
Dietary recommendations and supplement administration vary by regimen.
Coffee Enemas: 2 to 3 tablespoons of ground coffee boiled with 1 L of water and cooled to body temperature. The fluid is held for 10 to 15 minutes before being expelled. Coffee enemas are administered from once a day to every 4 hours in a typical clinic regimen.[5]

LITERATURE SUMMARY AND CRITIQUE
Retrospective analyses of the Gerson and Kelley therapies show no evidence of therapeutic efficacy. Laetrile, which the Contreras and Manner metabolic therapies employ, has been found ineffective in treating cancer. An NCI-sponsored open-label trial of Gonzalez's

nutritional therapy versus gemcitabine in patients with stage II to IV adenocarcinoma of the pancreas is under way.[7]

Gonzalez NJ, Isaacs LL. Evaluation of pancreatic proteolytic enzyme treatment of adenocarcinoma of the pancreas, with nutrition and detoxification support. Nutr Cancer 1999;33:117–24.
A small, unblinded, one-treatment pilot prospective case study assessing survival in 11 patients with inoperable stage II to IV pancreatic adenocarcinoma treated with high doses (25–40 g) of oral pancreatic enzymes, nutritional supplements (vitamins, minerals, organ concentrates), detoxification procedures (coffee enemas), and an organic diet. Patients had not undergone previous chemo- or radiation therapy. Nine patients survived 1 year, five survived 2 years, and four had survived 3 years at the time of publication. Median survival was 17 months. Results were compared with statistics from the National Cancer Data Base from 1995: 25% survival at 1 year and 10% survival at 2 years for all stages of pancreatic carcinoma; median survival, 6 months. A criticism of this study is that its eligibility criteria select for a subset of "good-prognosis" pancreatic cancer patients. A large-scale, randomized, controlled trial comparing this nutritional therapy to gemcitabine is under way.

Austin S, Dale EB, Dekadt S. Longterm followup of cancer patients using Contreras, Hoxsey and Gerson therapies. J Naturopath Med 1994;5:74–6.
Small prospective evaluation of survival rates in advanced cancer patients at three Tijuana clinics, including Dr. Ernesto Contreras's Clinica Del Mar. Patients were interviewed at the clinic regarding the location of the primary tumor, the presence of metastasis, and whether it was biopsy confirmed. Most patients were unaware of the stage of their cancer, and medical records were not available for review. Patients receiving Contreras therapy ($n = 31$), including Laetrile, a modified vegan diet, proteolytic enzymes, and antioxidant supplements, were queried by mail yearly for 4 to 5 years or until death. Of 22 evaluable patients, mean survival time from the beginning of the study was 7 months. Despite the obvious flaws of this study—small sample size, majority of patients lost to follow-up, and lack of access to detailed medical records—it can be concluded that the Contreras therapy is ineffective in treating late-stage cancer patients.

REFERENCES
1. American Cancer Society. Questionable methods of cancer management: questionable cancer practices in Tijuana and other Mexican border clinics. CA Cancer J Clin 1991;41:310–9.
2. Eisele JW, Reay DT. Deaths related to coffee enemas. JAMA 1980;244:1608–9.
3. Josefson D. US cancer institute funds trial of complementary therapy. West J Med 2000;173:153–4.
4. Green S. A critique of the rationale for cancer treatment with coffee enemas and diet. JAMA 1992;268:3224–7.
5. American Cancer Society. Questionable methods of cancer management: "nutritional" therapies. CA Cancer J Clin 1993;43:309–19.
6. Reed A, James N, Sikora K. Juices, coffee enemas, and cancer. Lancet 1990;336:677–8.

7. Phase III study of gemcitabine versus intensive pancreatic proteolytic enzyme therapy with ancillary nutritional support in patients with stage II, III, or IV adenocarcinoma of the pancreas [clinical trial PDQ, NCI Web site]. Available at: http://www.nci.nih.gov/clinical_trials/view_clinicaltrials.aspx?version=health+professional&args=1;0b7d9c21-ff5f-449a-bb68-b894f5ba1dfb (accessed Jul 15, 2002).

MGN-3

A. DONATO

KEY WORD
Biobran

CLINICAL SUMMARY

Proprietary product derived from rice bran. Promoters claim that this product improves immune function against cancer and human immunodeficiency virus/acquired immune deficiency syndrome (HIV/AIDS). Polysaccharides are the primary ingredient and are thought to increase the level of tumor necrosis (TNF)-α and interferon (IFN)-γ secretion and augment natural killer (NK) cell cytotoxic function in vitro. The product developer, Mamdooh H. Ghoneum, PhD, has performed all of the clinical studies. Although improved immune function is demonstrated, clinical significance remains to be seen. No adverse effects have been reported. There are no known drug interactions with this product.

CONSTITUENTS

Main Ingredients: Rice bran, enzymatically treated with extracts from shiitake *(Lentinus edodes),* kawaratake *(Coriolus versicolor),* and suehirotake *(Schizophyllum commune)* mushrooms.
Other Ingredients: Beet root fiber, calcium phosphate, silica, magnesium stearate.

WARNINGS
The US Food and Drug Administration (FDA) previously filed a lawsuit against Lane Labs for making unsubstantiated claims of effectiveness against cancer, HIV/AIDS, and other diseases.[1]

MECHANISM OF ACTION
MGN-3 is an arabinoxylane from rice bran made using enzymes from the mycelia of shiitake, kawaratake, and suehirotake mushrooms. MGN-3 is claimed to cause an overall increase of the immune system, such as NK cell activity, to increase IFN-γ and TNF-α, and to act synergistically with interleukin-2, which also increases NK cell activity.[1,2]

USAGE
Cancer treatment, chemotherapy side effects, HIV and AIDS, immunostimulation.

ADVERSE REACTIONS
None reported.

DRUG INTERACTIONS
None reported.

DOSAGE
Oral: Available in 250 mg capsules. *Cancer and AIDS:* Four capsules three times a day is the dosage printed on the product label.

LITERATURE SUMMARY AND CRITIQUE
All of the clinical findings performed on humans were conducted and reported by Ghoneum, the developer of this product.

Ghoneum M. Production of tumor necrosis factor-α and interferon-gamma from human peripheral blood lymphocytes by MGN-3, and its synergy with interleukin-2 in vitro. Cancer Detect Prev 2000;24:314.
The mechanism by which MGN-3 elevates NK cytotoxic activity was examined. The effect of MGN-3 on the levels of TNF-α and IFN-γ secretions was measured, as was the expression of key cell-surface receptors. Results suggest that MGN-3 is a potent TNF-α inducer. Treating highly purified NK cells with MGN-3 also resulted in increased levels of TNF-α and IFN-γ secretion in conjunction with augmentation of NK cell cytotoxic function. Furthermore, addition of MGN-3 to interleukin-2–activated NK cells resulted in a synergistic induction of TNF-α and IFN-γ secretion.

Ghoneum M. Anti-HIV activity in vitro of MGN-3, an activated arabinoxylane from rice bran. Biochem Biophys Res Commun 1998;243:25.
MGN-3 activity against HIV-1 was examined in primary cultures of peripheral blood mononuclear cells. MGN-3 inhibited HIV-1 replication via inhibition of HIV-1p24 antigen production in a dose-dependent manner and via inhibition of syncytia formation. Further studies showed that ingestion of MGN-3 at a concentration of 15 mg/kg/d resulted in a significant increase in T- and B-cell mitogen response at 2 months after treatment. The author claims that MGN-3 possesses potent anti-HIV activity without notable side effects.

Ghoneum M. NK immunomodulatory function in 27 cancer patients by MGN-3 [abstract]. Proceedings of the 87th Annual Meeting of the American Association for Cancer Research Washington, DC; 1996 Apr 20–24.
Patients had different types of advanced malignancies: seven breast cancer, seven prostate, eight multiple myeloma, three leukemia, and two cervical. All patients were under treatment with conventional therapy and were also given 3 g of MGN-3 daily. Results showed that patients who had a low level of basal NK activity treated with MGN-3 had a significant increase in NK activity in 2 weeks. The enhancement of NK activity continued to rise at 3 and 6 months after treatment.

REFERENCES

1. FDA takes action against firm marketing unapproved drugs [talk paper online]. 1999 Dec 10 [cited 2001 August 15]. Available at: http://www.fda.gov/bbs/topics/ANSWERS/ANS00988.html. (accessed Oct 8, 2001)
2. Ghoneum MH, Maeda H. Immunopotentiator and method of manufacturing the same (Arabinoxylane Compound). US patent 5560914. 1995 July 12.

MICOM

COMMON NAMES

O$_2$ MYGA III, Sundance Nachez mineral water, SNMW

CLINICAL SUMMARY

Mineral solution advertised to prevent and treat cancer and other degenerative diseases by raising cellular oxygen levels. This supplement is available in the United States, Mexico, Canada, Europe, China, South Korea, and Australia. Also called O$_2$ MYGA III and Sundance Nachez mineral water, MICOM was created by Bob Simpson, purported molecular physicist and son of a Native American medicine man. The product is said to simulate natural spring mineral water and is prepared with igneous rock, iron pyrite, weak acids, and weak bases. Its supposed efficacy is based on the assumption that a high-oxygen environment is lethal to cancer cells and that its minerals "tag" cancer cells for recognition and elimination by the immune system. An oral formulation is promoted for treating stage I and II cancers and an intravenous preparation for treating late-stage disease. Simpson's Web site claims years of testing and over 1,000 trials performed in eight countries and provides testimonials, but no clinical results are published in peer-reviewed journals.[1] In February 2002, a Washington nurse was indicted for manslaughter after administering intravenous MICOM to a cancer patient who subsequently died from kidney and heart failure. A physician testified that high levels of potassium in MICOM caused the man's death. Of note, the product was also found to be contaminated with bacteria.

CONSTITUENTS

Said to be prepared with igneous rock, iron pyrite, weak acids and weak bases; water.[2]

WARNINGS

Intravenous preparations of MICOM have been found contaminated with bacteria, possibly leading to the death of at least one patient. Patients should be warned not to use this product.

MECHANISM OF ACTION

The inventor personally offers no mechanism of action for his mineral water. His Web site claims that conditions of low cellular oxygen cause and are indicative of cancer and that MICOM raises cellular oxygen levels to 10 to 13 ppm, allowing detoxification and reduced organ burden.[1] No evidence shows that MICOM raises cellular oxygen levels. Additionally, research shows that oxygen neither prevents nor inhibits cancer growth, tumors grow rapidly in tissues that are well supplied with oxygenated blood, and absence of oxygen does not stimulate tumor growth in vitro or in vivo. The Web site also claims that the mineral water will "tag" cancer cells so that they might be recognized and eliminated by the immune system, a mechanism not supported by current knowledge of immune response to cancer.[1]

USAGE

Alcoholism, antidote, asthma, cancer prevention, cancer treatment, circulatory disorders, cognitive improvement, detoxification, drug withdrawal symptoms, hepatitis, HIV and AIDS, leukemia, strength and stamina.

PHARMACOKINETICS

No formal pharmacokinetic studies have been performed with MICOM.

ADVERSE REACTIONS

Case Report: A 52-year-old man with colon and liver cancer experienced kidney and heart failure leading to death after intravenous infusion of MICOM found to be contaminated with bacteria. A physician testified that high levels of potassium in MICOM caused the man's death. A second patient with brain cancer experienced infection, pneumonia, and kidney failure after infusion with the same contaminated product.[2]

DRUG INTERACTIONS

None known.

DOSAGE

No dosage is recommended.
Oral: 3.8 L of MICOM costs $250. *Stage I and II cancers:* 230 mL/d for at least 15 days when results of diagnostic tests are satisfactory. Next 30 days: 57 to 114 mL/d. Maintenance dosage: 28 to 57 mL/d.
Intravenous: One intravenous preparation of MICOM costs $2,700.[1]

LITERATURE SUMMARY AND CRITIQUE

No evaluations of MICOM are reported in peer-reviewed journals.

REFERENCES

1. Simpson Advanced Sciences Web site. Available at: http://www.simpsonadvancedsciences.com (accessed May 7, 2002).
2. Sunde S. Cancer "cure" ended in death. Seattle Post-Intelligencer 2001 May 14. Available at: http://seattlepi. nwsource.com/local/22927_cancer14.shtml (accessed Feb 19, 2002).

Milk Thistle

A. DONATO

COMMON NAMES
Holy thistle, lady's thistle, Mary thistle, Marian thistle

SCIENTIFIC NAMES
Silybum marianum, Carduus marianum

KEY WORD
Silybum marianum

CLINICAL SUMMARY

Derived from the seed, pod, or fruit of the plant. Milk thistle is used primarily to manage various liver diseases. Placebo-controlled clinical studies show efficacy in reducing aminotransferases in alcoholic liver disease, but studies in other types of hepatic disease have been flawed. Animal models suggest that flavonoids in milk thistle have antioxidant and anticancer effects. To date, there is no evaluation of survival or quality of life. Side effects such as sweating, nausea, vomiting, and weakness have been reported.[1] Milk thistle inhibits cytochrome P-450 3A4. Therefore, increased levels of medications metabolized via this enzyme may occur.

CONSTITUENTS

Flavolignan: 1.5% silymarin; a mixture of three compounds, silybinin, silidyanin, silychristin; also dehydrosilybin, siliandrin, silybinome, silyhermin; tocopherol sterols: cholesterol, capesterol, stigmasterol, sitosterol; other constituents: taxifolin, quercetin, dihydrokaempferol, kaempferol, apigenin, naringin, eriodyctiol, chrysoeriol, linoleic acid, palmitic acid.[2]

MECHANISM OF ACTION

Milk thistle provides hepatocellular protection by stabilizing hepatic cell membranes. It alters the structure of the outer cell membrane of the hepatocytes in such a way as to prevent the penetration of the liver toxins into the interior of the cell. The stimulation effect on nucleolar polymerase A results in an increase in ribosomal protein synthesis and thus increases the regenerative ability of the liver and the formation of new hepatocytes. Other actions include interruption of enterohepatic recirculation of toxins and regeneration of damaged hepatocytes. An animal study performed in rats demonstrated a reduction in kidney damage following administration of cisplatin without diminished antitumor activity. Other animal studies indicate that the antioxidant flavonoids in milk thistle have anticancer effects. Anecdotal data suggest that milk thistle may prevent liver damage from hepatotoxic medications, including butyrophenones, phenothiazines, and phenytoin.[3–6]

USAGE

Alcoholism, cancer prevention, cirrhosis, drug-induced hepatotoxicity, food poisoning, hepatitis, indigestion, liver disease.

PHARMACOKINETICS

Following oral administration, milk thistle is poorly absorbed from the gastrointestinal tract with a bioavailability of approximately 23 to 47%. Peak plasma concentrations occur within 2 to 4 hours. Milk thistle inhibits cytochrome P-450 isoenzyme 3A4 and has an elimination half-life of approximately 4 hours. Thirty to 40 percent of the administered dose is recoverable from the bile as both glucuronide or sulfate conjugates and 2 to 5% is excreted in the urine.[7,8]

ADVERSE REACTIONS

Common: Diarrhea caused by a mild laxative effect, uterine and menstrual stimulation.
Case Report: One report of a patient who experienced intermittent episodes of sweating, nausea, vomiting, diarrhea, abdominal pain, weakness, and collapse that resolved after discontinuation of supplement.[1]

DRUG INTERACTIONS

Cytochrome P-450 3A4: Milk thistle has been shown to inhibit cytochrome P-450 3A4. Although no interactions have been reported, inhibition of drug metabolism may occur for several agents (eg, ketoconazole, itraconazole, erythromycin, triazolam).[7]

LABORATORY INTERACTIONS

Liver function tests may be altered. Reduced aminotransferases.

DOSAGE

Oral: 200 to 800 mg silymarin per day given in split doses has been used in clinical studies. Tablets or capsules should be standardized to content of silymarin based on silibinin component.

LITERATURE SUMMARY AND CRITIQUE

The majority of human studies with milk thistle have been performed for the treatment of alcoholic hepatitis.

Feher J, et al. Liver-protective action of silymarin therapy in chronic alcoholic liver diseases. Orv Hetil 1989;130:2723–7.
The effects of silymarin therapy on liver function tests, serum procollagen III, peptide level, and liver disease were studied in 36 patients with chronic alcoholic liver disease in a 6-month double-blind clinical trial. During silymarin treatment, serum bilirubin, aspartate aminotransferase (AST), and alanine aminotransferase (ALT) values were normalized, whereas γ-glutamyltransferase activity and procollagen III peptide levels decreased. The changes were significant, and there was a significant difference between post-treatment values of the two groups as well. The histologic alterations showed an improvement in the silymarin group while remaining unchanged in the placebo group. These results suggest that silymarin exerts hepatoprotective activity and is able to improve liver function in alcoholic patients.

Salmi HA, et al. Effect of silymarin on chemical, functional, and morphological alterations of the liver: a double blind study. Scand J Gastroenterol 1982;17:517–21.
Ninety-seven patients with alcoholic liver disease and persistently abnormal liver function tests following at least 1 month of abstinence from alcohol were enrolled in a placebo-controlled trial. After 4 months of treatment, AST and ALT levels decreased by 30% and 41% with silymarin and increased 5% and 3% with placebo, respectively. The study did not monitor abstinence from alcohol. No changes in bilirubin were noted.

Ferenci P, et al. Randomized controlled trial of silymarin treatment in patients with cirrhosis of the liver. J Hepatol 1989;1:105–13.
To determine the effect of silymarin on the outcome of patients with cirrhosis, a double-blind, prospective, randomized study was performed on 170 patients with cirrhosis. Eighty-seven received 140 mg silymarin three times a day and 83 received placebo. Analysis of subgroups indicated that treatment was effective in patients with alcoholic cirrhosis.

REFERENCES

1. Adverse Drug Reactions Advisory Committee. An adverse reaction to the herbal medication milk thistle (*Silybum marianum*). Med J Aust 1999;170:218–9.
2. Bissett N, et al. Herbal drugs and phytopharmaceuticals. New York: Medpharm, CRC Press; 1994.
3. Blumenthal M. Herbal medicine, expanded Commission E monographs. 1st ed. Austin (TX): American Botanical Council; 2000.

4. Brinker F. Herb contraindications and drug interactions. 2nd ed. Sandy (OR): Eclectic Medical Publications; 1998.
5. Kohno H, et al. Silymarin, a naturally occurring polyphenolic antioxidant flavonoid, inhibits azoxymethane-induced colon carcinogenesis in male F344 rats. Int J Cancer 2002;101:461–8.
6. Tyagi A, et al. Antiproliferative and apoptotic effects of silibinin in rat prostate cancer cells. Prostate 2002;53:211–7.
7. Schandalik R, Perucca E. Pharmacokinetics of silybin following oral administration of silipide in patients with extrahepatic biliary obstruction. Drugs Exp Clin Res 1994;20:37–42.
8. Venkataramanan R, et al. Milk thistle, a herbal supplement, decreases the activity of CYP3A4 and uridine diphosphoglucoronosyl transferase in human hepatocyte cultures. Drug Metab Dispos 2000;28:1270–3.

Mistletoe (European)

A. DONATO

COMMON NAMES
Viscum, all-heal, birdlime

SCIENTIFIC NAMES
Viscum album, Viscum coloratum

KEY WORDS
Viscum album, Helixor, Iscador, Eurixor

CLINICAL SUMMARY

Derived from the aerial parts, except berries, of the plant. Patients use mistletoe preparations for a variety of conditions, including cancer, human immunodeficiency virus (HIV), hepatitis, and degenerative joint disease. Polypeptides, including lectins and viscotoxins, are thought to be responsible for in vitro immune stimulant and tumor inhibition activity. Although orally administered products are available, all research reported in the literature has evaluated parenteral formulations of mistletoe, which are not approved for use in the United States by the Food and Drug Administration. The body of published research suggesting efficacy for the treatment of cancer lacks well-designed randomized trials. Data are available only from small, uncontrolled trials and case reports. A meta-analysis by Kleijnen and colleagues analyzed 11 of these clinical trials conducted before 1994 and showed no benefit from mistletoe.[1] A recent epidemiologic study suggested a possible survival advantage following treatment with mistletoe, but this has not been confirmed in controlled trials. Confirmed efficacy for any other proposed claims is also lacking. Possible adverse effects from treatment include injection site reactions, chills, fever, headache, leukocytosis, chest pain, orthostatic hypotension, bradycardia, diarrhea, and vomiting. Toxic doses of mistletoe can produce coma, seizures, and death. Possible drug interactions include additive hypotensive effect from antihypertensives and antagonism of cardiac glycosides or antiarrhythmics.

CONSTITUENTS

Acids: oleic, palmitic, anisic, caffeic, para-coumaric, quinic, vanillic; amines: acetyl-choline, choline, histamine, tyramine; flavonoid: quercetin; lectins: I, II, III (high-molecular-weight polypeptides); terpenoids: β-amyrin, resin acids, β-sitosterol, stigmasterol, sterol A; viscotoxins: A2, A3, B (low-molecular-weight polypeptides); others: mucilage, mannitol, inositol, fructose, glucose, starch, syringin, tannin.[2]

WARNINGS

Mistletoe berries and leaves are highly poisonous; more than two berries or three leaves can produce toxic effects.[3]

MECHANISM OF ACTION

The immunologic action of mistletoe is attributed to lectins. Lectins induce macrophage cytotoxicity, stimulate phagocytosis of immune cells, increase cytokine secretion (tumor necrosis factor-α, interleukin [IL]-1, IL-2, IL-6), and enhance cytotoxicity effects on various cell lines in vitro. Its hypotensive effect is thought to be mediated by acetylcholine, histamine, γ-aminobutyric acid (GABA), tyramine, and flavones, although the exact mechanism of action is unknown. Lectins and alkaloids have produced conflicting data about in vitro and animal model inhibition of cancer cell growth with mouse and human cell lines.[3]

USAGE

Arthritis, cancer treatment, hepatitis, HIV and acquired immune deficiency syndrome (AIDS), hypertension, immunostimulation, sedation, spasms.

ADVERSE REACTIONS

Common: Chills, fever, headache, leukocytosis, chest pain, orthostatic hypotension, bradycardia, diarrhea, vomiting, hypersensitivity, subcutaneous infiltrates.
Toxicity: Hypotension, coma, seizures, myosis, death.[2–4]

DRUG INTERACTIONS

Antihypertensives: Theoretically, mistletoe may have an additive hypotensive effect.
Digoxin: Theoretically, mistletoe may have antagonizing effects owing to its negative inotropic property.
Antiarrhythmics: Theoretically, mistletoe may have antagonizing effects owing to its negative inotropic property.

CONTRAINDICATIONS

Pregnant women should not consume mistletoe owing to uterine stimulant activity of tyramine and unidentified constituents.

DOSAGE

Intramuscular, Subcutaneous, or Intravenous: Products should be standardized based on lectin and viscotoxin content.

Eurixor: Standardized to lectin-I content. Doses at 1 ng/kg lectin-I administered subcutaneously twice a week for 12-week cycles followed by a 4-week break.

Iscador: 5 mg administered subcutaneously two to three times a week.

LITERATURE SUMMARY AND CRITIQUE

Literature about mistletoe preparations consists primarily of uncontrolled trials, case report series, or studies with questionable designs. Several recent publications indicate possible survival advantage with various effects on quality of life.

Steuer-Vogt MK, et al. The effect of an adjuvant mistletoe treatment programme in resected head and neck cancer patients: a randomized controlled clinical trial. Eur J Cancer 2001;37:23–31.

A prospective evaluation of head and neck cancer patients stratified based on intervention (surgery with or without radiotherapy) and randomized to receive either placebo or mistletoe 1 ng/kg Eurixor subcutaneously twice a week for up to 60 weeks. A total of 447 patients were enrolled: group A consisted of 105 patients receiving surgery alone compared with 97 receiving surgery and mistletoe; group B contained 137 patients receiving surgery and radiotherapy compared with 138 receiving concomitant mistletoe. The study did not demonstrate any difference in lymphocyte subsets, quality of life, efficacy, or survival for either group A or B. Injection site reactions were noted in 45% of all patients receiving mistletoe. Other reactions noted included myalgia, mild fever, fatigue, and sneezing. Sixteen percent of patients in group A and 20% in group B discontinued mistletoe owing to adverse events. The authors failed to find any benefit for mistletoe injections for head and neck cancer.

Grossarth-Maticek R, et al. Use of Iscador, an extract of European mistletoe (*Viscum album*) in cancer treatment: prospective nonrandomized and randomized matched-pair studies nested within a cohort study. Altern Ther Health Med 2001;7:57–78.

A large epidemiologic matched-pair evaluation of survival in patients receiving standard chemotherapy with or without mistletoe for the treatment of various oncologic diagnoses. Patients received treatment between 1971 and 1988 throughout Germany. A total of 1,668 patients received Iscador brand mistletoe injections in combination with standard chemotherapy. The authors matched patients for comparison in an unblinded fashion allowing no more than two minor deviations in criteria between patients. Final data analysis revealed a statistically significant survival advantage for patients receiving

Iscador. All types of cancer appeared to benefit, with added survival ranging from 0.48 to 1.72 years. The authors make no mention of adverse events or toxicity. The authors also did not match for the type or number of previous chemotherapy regimens that patients received.

Tusenius KJ, Spoek JM, Kramers CW. Iscador Qu for chronic hepaptis C: an exploratory study. Complement Ther Med 2001;9:12–6.
A case report series of five patients administered 5 mg Iscador subcutaneously three times a week for 12 months. All patients had serologically confirmed hepatitis C. Changes in viral load and improvement in liver function tests were noted in two patients, but elevated viral load and stable or elevated liver functions tests were noted in another three patients. The only side effect reported was injection site reaction. Improvements in quality of life were shown after treatment and persisted up to 6 months following treatment. Additional studies are needed to confirm this effect.

Goebell P, et al. Evaluation of an unconventional treatment modality with mistletoe lectin to prevent recurrence of superficial bladder cancer: a randomized phase II trial J Urol 2002;168:72 5.
A randomized phase II trial consisting of 45 subjects with bladder cancer treated with transurethral resection during a 3-year period. The patients were randomly divided into two cohorts. One group received adjuvant therapy with mistletoe lectin. The standard extract was applied subcutaneously twice weekly for 3 months, followed by a 3-month drug-free interval. The placebo group received no additional treatment. After 18 months, the recurrence-free interval and the total number of recurrences were similar in both groups. The authors concluded that subcutaneous application of mistletoe lectin has no effect on preventing the recurrence of superficial bladder cancer.

REFERENCES
1. Foster S, et al. Tyler's honest herbal: a sensible guide to the use of herbs and related remedies. 4th ed. New York: Hawthorn Herbal Press; 1999.
2. Newall CA, et al. Herbal medicines: a guide for health care professionals. London: Pharmaceutical Press; 1996.
3. Schulz V, et al. Rational phytotherapy: a physician's guide to herbal medicine. 4th ed. New York: Springer; 2001.
4. Gorter RW, et al. Subcutaneous infiltrates induced by injection of mistletoe extracts (Iscador). Am J Ther 1998;5:181–7.

N-Acetylcysteine

COMMON NAMES
Acetylcysteine, NAC

SCIENTIFIC NAME
N-Acetylcysteine

CLINICAL SUMMARY

Endogenous antioxidant and precursor to intracellular glutathione. N-acetylcysteine (NAC) is used to prevent exacerbations of chronic bronchitis, treat drug-induced hepatotoxicity, and prevent and treat conditions of oxidative stress and reduced glutathione levels, such as human immunodeficiency virus/acquired immune deficiency syndrome (HIV/AIDS), cancer, and toxicity from chemo- or radiotherapy. NAC increases plasma levels of cysteine and glutathione and has antioxidant, nucleophilic, mucolytic, and possibly chemopreventive properties. Animal models suggest anticarcinogenic, antimetastatic, and antiangiogenic activities. Oral bioavailability is low. Studies in smokers and patients with a history of adenomatous colonic polyps show an inhibition of cancer biomarker development, although NAC did not inhibit formation of secondary head and neck or lung tumors in a EUROSCAN trial. Dosages of 400 to 1,200 mg/d NAC reduce the number of acute exacerbations in patients with chronic bronchopulmonary disease. Human studies evaluating the role of NAC in the prevention of chemotherapy- or radiotherapy-induced toxicities are inconclusive. Gastrointestinal side effects are most often reported.

MECHANISM OF ACTION

NAC is a precursor to intracellular glutathione. It is a known nucleophile and free radical scavenger, either directly or as a source of cysteine and glutathione. In rodent models, NAC inhibits a variety of mutagen/carcinogen-induced cancer biomarkers, interferes with the promotion phase of multistage carcinogenesis, and produces a decrease in the incidence of carcinogen-induced tumors of the lung, colon, and bladder. This activity may be attributable to its ability to enhance glutathione S-transferases, glutathione peroxidase, glutathione reductase, and reduced nicotinamide adenine dinucleotide and reduced nicotinamide adenine dinucleotide phosphate quinone reductase. In in vitro and animal models, NAC exhibits anti-invasive, antimetastatic, and antiangiogenic properties. NAC can also be employed as a mucolytic agent in the treatment of respiratory diseases and as an antidote to acetaminophen poisoning. Animal studies report that NAC may also protect against doxorubicin toxicity and bladder cystitis induced by ifosfamide and cyclophosphamide.[1-5]

USAGE

Bronchitis, cancer prevention, chronic obstructive pulmonary disorders, cirrhosis, cystic fibrosis, HIV and AIDS, Lou Gehrig's disease.

PHARMACOKINETICS

Absorption: Orally administered NAC reaches peak plasma concentrations (C_{max}) in 1 to 2 hours. Bioavailability is estimated to be between 4 and 10%, depending on whether the drug is in its reduced or total form. In plasma, NAC may be found in intact, reduced, or various oxidized forms. Low bioavailability is most likely attributable to extensive first-pass metabolism and not to incomplete absorption.

Distribution: Studies show that volume distribution for total NAC ranges from 0.33 to 0.47 L/kg. Two hours after administration, tissue distribution is as follows in descending order: kidney, liver, adrenal gland, lung, spleen, blood, brain, and urine.

Metabolism/Excretion: Animal and human studies show the major metabolites of NAC to be cysteine and cystine. Inorganic sulphate is the primary urinary excretion product together with small amounts of taurine and unchanged NAC.[1-3]

ADVERSE REACTIONS

Common (Oral): Gastrointestinal disturbance, diarrhea, nausea, vomiting, fatigue, conjunctival irritation, skin rash.

Reported: Hypotension, anaphylaxis, asthma attacks, headache.[1,6,7]

DRUG INTERACTIONS

Paracetamol: NAC can reduce the hepatotoxicity of paracetamol by forming conjugates with the reactive metabolites.

Contrast Agents (eg, Iopromide): NAC is shown to prevent the reduction of renal function in patients with chronic renal failure who receive contrast agents such as iopromide.

Doxorubicin: NAC may be of value in preventing the cardiotoxicity associated with doxorubicin.[1,6,8]

DOSAGE

Oral: No Recommended Dietary Allowances have been set for NAC. Various studies have used dosages ranging from 400 to 1,800 mg/d.

LITERATURE SUMMARY AND CRITIQUE

Van Schooten FJ, et al. Effects of oral administration of N-acetyl-L-cysteine: a multi-biomarker study in smokers. Cancer Epidemiol Biomarkers Prev 2002;11:167–75.

A double-blind, controlled evaluation of NAC supplementation ($n = 21$) versus placebo ($n = 20$) in healthy smokers. Internal dose markers (plasma and bronchoalveolar lavage (BAL) fluid cotinine and urine mutagenicity), biologically effective dose markers (smoking-related deoxyribonucleic acid [DNA] adducts, oxidative DNA damage, and hemoglobin adducts), and biologic response markers (frequency of micronuclei and antioxidants scavenging capacity) were assessed pre- and postintervention. Patients were randomized to receive 600 mg NAC or placebo twice daily for 6 months. NAC administration significantly inhibited formation of lipophilic-DNA adducts and 8-OH-dG adducts in BAL cells but had no effect on MFC/BMC PAH-DNA adducts, PBL lipophilic-DNA adducts, and 4-ABP-Hb adducts. Further studies, possibly with development of lung cancer as an outcome, should be conducted.

Van Zandwijk N, et al. EUROSCAN, a randomized trial of vitamin A and N-acetyl-cysteine in patients with head and neck cancer or lung cancer. J Natl Cancer Inst 2000;92: 977-86.

A prospective, open-label, randomized evaluation of vitamin A (300,000 IU daily for 1 year followed by 150,000 IU daily for 1 year), NAC (600 mg once daily for 2 years), both agents, or placebo in patients with non–small cell lung cancer (NSCLC), laryngeal cancer, or cancer of the oral cavity. A total of 2,573 patients were randomized to vitamin A ($n = 647$), NAC ($n = 642$), both agents ($n = 643$), or placebo ($n = 641$). Demographics appear to be similar between treatment arms, but no statistical tests were reported. Five-year survival, event-free survival, and development of secondary tumors were not significantly different between treatment arms. Nearly 18% of patients receiving NAC alone reported adverse occurrences related to gastric events and skin rash. The authors concluded that vitamin A alone, in combination with NAC, or NAC alone, is no better than placebo in improving survival or decreasing second tumors for patients with primary NSCLC or head and neck cancers.

Tepel M, et al. Prevention of radiographic-contrast-agent-induced reductions in renal function by acetylcysteine. N Engl J Med 2000;343:180–4.

A prospective, randomized, controlled trial of acetylcysteine in 83 patients with chronic renal insufficiency undergoing computed tomography with iopromide. Patients were randomized to receive 600 mg twice-daily oral acetylcysteine or placebo plus intravenous saline before and after administration of 75 mL iopromide. Serum creatinine and urea nitrogen were measured before, 48 hours after, and 6 days after administration of iopromide. An acute iopromide-induced reduction in renal function was defined as an increase in serum creatinine of at least 0.5 mg/dL, which occurred in one treatment patient and nine controls. At the 48-hour reading, mean serum creatinine had increased slightly in the control group but decreased significantly in the acetylcysteine group ($p < .001$). Mean serum urea nitrogen also decreased significantly in the treatment arm while increasing slightly in the control group ($p < .001$). Patient diagnoses were heterogeneous, which may have influenced the efficacy of acetylcysteine treatment.

Grandjean EM, et al. Efficacy of oral long-term *N*-acetylcysteine in chronic bronchopulmonary disease: a meta-analysis of published double-blind, placebo-controlled clinical trials. Clin Ther 2000;22:209–21.
Meta-analysis of eight double-blind, placebo-controlled trials from 1980 to 1995 evaluating prolonged prophylactic treatment (2–6 months) with NAC in patients with chronic bronchitis. Oral NAC was given in doses of 400 mg/d (one study), 600 mg/d (five studies), 1,200 mg/d (one study), or 600 mg three times per week (one study). Results showed a statistically significant effect size of -1.37 (95% CI = 1.5 to -1.25) for NAC compared with placebo. For trials with number of acute exacerbations as an end point, a 23% decrease was found for NAC compared with placebo. A prolonged course of NAC appears to be effective as prophylaxis for acute exacerbations of chronic bronchitis.

Estensen RD, et al. *N*-Acetylcysteine suppression of the proliferative index in the colon of patients with previous adenomatous colonic polyps. Cancer Lett 1999;147:109–14.
A double-blind, randomized, controlled trial of the effect of NAC supplementation on the proliferative index (PI) in patients with previous adenomatous colonic polyps. PI was identified by immunostaining with proliferating cell nuclear antigen. Patients were randomized to receive 800 mg/d NAC ($n = 34$) or placebo ($n = 30$). Age, sex, diet, and compliance were comparable between groups. Rectal biopsy was performed pre- and post-intervention. Mean percentage of all cells labeled for the NAC group decreased from 7.06 pretreatment to 6.20 post-treatment ($p < .02$), whereas the control group increased from 6.34 pretreatment to 6.70 post-treatment. PI did not change significantly in either group. Larger trials, possibly using development of adenocarcinoma as an end point, should be conducted.

Wagdi P, et al. Cardioprotection in patients undergoing chemo- and/or radiotherapy for neoplastic disease. A pilot study. Jpn Heart J 1996;37:353–9.
A double-blind, randomized, placebo-controlled trial of 600 mg of vitamin E, 1 g of vitamin C, and 200 mg of NAC versus placebo in 32 patients undergoing chemo- and/or radiotherapy with no prior cardiovascular abnormalities. Patients received antioxidant mixture or placebo on days of therapy. Left ventricular ejection fraction was determined by radionucleotide ventriculography before and within 3 weeks of termination of therapy. In the treatment group, left ventricular ejection fraction did not change, whereas it decreased in the placebo group ($p = .03$). However, randomization did not include the chemo- or radiotherapy scheme or dose, and placebo patients received mean higher doses of radiation and chemotherapy than treatment patients. Alteration of chemo- or radiotherapy efficacy was not addressed.

Akerlund B, et al. Effect of *N*-acetylcysteine (NAC) treatment on HIV-1 infection: a double-blind placebo controlled trial. Eur J Clin Pharmacol 1996;50:457–61.
A double-blind, placebo-controlled evaluation of 4 months of 800 mg of NAC supplementation on CD4+ cell count, plasma cysteine and glutathione levels, and immune

parameters in 45 HIV-positive patients. Patients had CD4+ counts over $200 \times 106\,l^{-1}$ and had no previous treatment with antiretroviral drugs. Plasma cysteine levels, initially low, were normalized in the NAC group. The decrease in CD4+ count was less in the NAC group that in controls, but no effect on radical production by neutrophils was seen in either group. Gastrointestinal complaints were reported in two subjects. It is unclear whether NAC exerts a beneficial effect on asymptomatic HIV-positive patients; further research is necessary.

REFERENCES

1. Holdiness MR. Clinical pharmacokinetics of *N*-acetylcysteine. Clin Pharmacokinet 1991;20:123–34.
2. Olsson B, et al. Pharmacokinetics and bioavailability of reduced and oxidized *N*-acetylcysteine. Eur J Clin Pharmacol 1988;34:77–82.
3. Morgan LR, Holdiness MR, Gillen LE. *N*-Acetylcysteine: its bioavailability and interaction with ifosfamide metabolites. Semin Oncol 1983;10 Suppl:56–61.
4. Van Schooten FJ, et al. Effects of oral administration of *N*-acetyl-L-cysteine: a multi-biomarker study in smokers. Cancer Epidemiol Biomarkers Prev 2002;11:167–75.
5. Estensen RD, et al. *N*-Acetylcysteine suppression of the proliferative index in the colon of patients with previous adenomatous colonic polyps. Cancer Lett 1999;147:109–14.
6. Herr SM. Herb-drug interaction handbook. 2nd ed. Nassau (NY): Church Street Books; 2002.
7. Pendyala L, et al. Phase I/pharmacodynamic study of *N*-acetylcysteine/Oltipraz in smokers: early termination due to excessive toxicity. Cancer Epidemiol Biomarkers Prev 2001;10:269–72.
8. Tepel M, et al. Prevention of radiographic-contrast-agent-induced reductions in renal function by acetylcysteine. N Engl J Med 2000;343:180–4.

Nettle

COMMON NAMES
Stinging nettle, common nettle, greater nettle

SCIENTIFIC NAME
Urtica dioica

KEY WORD
Urtica dioica

A. DONATO

CLINICAL SUMMARY
Derived from the root of the plant. Nettle is used to treat benign prostatic hypertrophy (BPH), allergies, and inflammation. Several components appear to account for its activity, although the precise mechanism of action is unknown. Nettle is usually combined with other herbs, such as saw palmetto. To date, no clinical study supports the use of nettle for proposed claims. An in vitro study indicates that nettle extract may have an antiproliferative effect on human prostate cancer cells.[1] Adverse effects include gastrointestinal upset, sweating, and contact dermatitis. Enhanced activity of diclofenac has been reported when combined with nettle, but this is of unknown clinical significance. Theoretically, nettle may have an additive effect with diuretics.

CONSTITUENTS
Acids: carbonic, formic, silicic, citric, fumaric, glyceric, malic, oxalic, phosphoric, quinic, succinic, threonic; amines: acetylcholine, betaine, choline, lecithin, histamine, serotonin; flavonoids: flavonol glycosides (isorhamnetin, kaempferol, quercetin); other constituents: choline acetyltransferase, scopoletin, β-sitosterol, tannin.[2]

WARNINGS

Nature's Way Products, Inc. (Springville, UT) has recalled four lots of its 100-count net-tle capsules owing to lead contamination. The pertinent lot numbers are 131237, 131238, 140738, and 215229. More information is available at <http://www.fda.gov/oc/po/firmrecalls/ nettle06_02.html>.

MECHANISM OF ACTION

The mechanism of action remains unknown. It has been postulated that the herb may have an effect on the amount of free (active) testosterone circulating in the blood, or it may inhibit one of the key enzymes, aromatase, responsible for testosterone synthesis. Another, more recent theory attributes the activity to the presence of a lectin (protein) mixture designated UDA (*Urtica dioica* agglutinin) and several polysaccharides. None of these various postulates regarding its activity are conclusively proven. Nettle also acts as a diuretic and decreases systolic blood pressure. Scopoletin as an active ingredient has anti-inflammatory activity.[3]

USAGE

Allergies, arthritis, BPH, chest congestion, dysuria, inflammation, oily skin, promotion of urination, spasms, urinary tract disorders.

ADVERSE REACTIONS

Reported: Gastrointestinal upset, skin irritation, sweating, hypersensitivity, skin rash.[4]

DRUG INTERACTIONS

Diclofenac: The action of diclofenac was enhanced by nettle extract. This may be owing in part to inhibition of cyclooxygenase products and possibly to inhibition of cytokine release, as evidenced by a reduction in whole blood of induced tumor necrosis factor-α and interleukin-1β.

Diuretics: Theoretically, nettle may have an additive effect owing to diuretic activity.[5]

DOSAGE

Oral: Nettle extract: 150 to 300 mg/d have been used for allergies and BPH. *Dried herb:* Reported dose varies from 4 to 12 g/d. *Tea:* May be prepared using 1 to 2 teaspoons of dried herb.[6]

LITERATURE SUMMARY AND CRITIQUE

Human clinical studies using nettle as a single agent are limited, with inconclusive results. Nettle, in combination with other herbs, has had fair results in BPH. The majority of studies have been performed in animals.

REFERENCES

1. Konrad L, et al. Antiproliferative effect on human prostate cancer cells by a stinging nettle root (*Urtica dioica*) extract. Planta Med 2000;66:44–7.
2. Newall C, et al. Herbal medicines: a guide for health-care professionals. 2nd ed. London: Pharmaceutical Press; 1998.
3. Tyler V. Herbs of choice, the therapeutical use of phytomedicinals. Binghamton (NY): Pharmaceutical Press; 1994.
4. Schulz V, et al. Rational phytotherapy: a physician's guide to herbal medicine. 3rd ed. Berlin: Springer; 1998.
5. Brinker F. Herb contraindications and drug interactions. 2nd ed. Sandy (OR): Eclectic Medical Publishing; 1997.
6. Blumenthal M, et al. Herbal medicine, expanded Commission E monographs. 1st ed. Austin (TX): American Botanical Council; 2000.

Noni

A. DONATO

COMMON NAMES
Lada, Indian mulberry, nono, och plant, cheese fruit, hog apple, mora de la India, wild pine

SCIENTIFIC NAME
Morinda citrifolia

KEY WORDS
Morinda citrifolia, Morinda

CLINICAL SUMMARY
Derived from the fruit, leaves, and roots of the tree. Noni is a traditional Polynesian remedy for a variety of conditions, including cancer, hypertension, and diabetes. Several polysaccharides, anthraquinones, and alkaloids are thought to be responsible for its activity. Animal studies show antitumor and immunomodulatory activity of noni juice extracts. No human clinical trials evaluating noni for any proposed claims are published. No serious adverse events or drug interactions have been noted.

CONSTITUENTS
Acids: caproic, caprylic; anthraquinone: damnacanthal; polysaccharides: noni-ppt, galactose, arabinose, rhamnose, glucuronic acid; glycosides: rutin, 6-0-(β-D-glucopyranosyl)-1-0-octanoyl-β-D-glucopyranose, asperulosidic acid; terpenes; alkaloids.[1-3]

MECHANISM OF ACTION
The exact mechanism of action is unknown. The fruit juice contains noni-ppt, a polysaccharide-rich substance, which significantly enhances survival of inbred Lewis lung carcinoma (LLC)-bearing mice. Noni-ppt is thought to act by an immunomodulatory mechanism. It increases nitric oxide production from murine peritoneal macrophages

and stimulates the release of cytokines, interleukin-1β, and tumor necrosis factor-α from human peripheral mononuclear cells. When combined with suboptimal doses of standard chemotherapeutic agents such as doxorubicin (Adriamycin), cisplatin, 5-fluorouracil, and vincristine, noni-ppt improved survival time and curative effects in an LLC mouse model. Two glycosides isolated from noni juice inhibit activator protein-1 transactivation and cell transformation in the mouse epidermal JB6 cell line. Oral noni juice reduces 7,12-dimethylbenz[a]-anthracene adduct formation by 50 to 90% in the organs of C57 BL-6 mice and shows antioxidant activity in vitro. Aqueous extract of noni root produced a central analgesic effect in Swiss mice that was antagonized by naloxone.[3-7]

USAGE

Cancer treatment, chronic fatigue syndrome, diabetes, health maintenance, hypertension, immunostimulation, menstrual cramps, pain.

ADVERSE REACTIONS

Common: Constipation.
Case Report: Hyperkalemia in a patient with renal failure.[8]

CONTRAINDICATIONS

Owing to potassium content, patients with renal failure should not consume noni.

DOSAGE

Oral: Usually taken on an empty stomach between meals. Dosage varies based on product formulation. *Juice:* 4 oz (approximately 120 mL) once daily. *Capsules/tablets:* 500 to 1,000 mg daily. *Liquid concentrate:* 30 mL daily.[9]

LITERATURE SUMMARY AND CRITIQUE

No human clinical trials have been conducted evaluating the efficacy of noni for any of its proposed claims.

Hirazumi A, et al. Anticancer activity of *Morinda citrifolia* (noni) on intraperitoneally implanted Lewis lung carcinoma in syngeneic mice. Proc West Pharmacol Soc 1994;37:145–6.
Noni fruit was prepared from fruit stored in glass jars in direct sunlight for up to 3 days. The juice was removed and processed to remove the ethanol fractions. LLC was injected intraperitoneally into C57BL/6 mice. Twenty-four hours later, noni extract was injected intraperitoneally either daily or every other day for 5 days. The results of the study showed that mice treated with 15 mg of noni juice extract survived 20 days longer than control mice. Additive toxicity was demonstrated when noni extract was combined with

conventional chemotherapy such as vincristine, 5-fluorouracil, and doxorubicin. Additional animal and human studies are needed to confirm this report.

REFERENCES

1. Levand O, Larson HO. Some chemical constituents of *Morinda citrifolia*. Planta Med 1979;36:186–7.
2. Wang M, et al. Novel trisaccharide fatty acid ester identified from the fruits of *Morinda citrifolia* (noni). J Agric Food Chem 1999;47:4880–2.
3. Liu G, et al. Two novel glycosides from the fruits of *Morinda citrifolia* (noni) inhibit AP-1 transactivation and cell transformation in the mouse epidermal JB6 cell line. Cancer Res 2001;61:5749–56.
4. Hirazumi A, et al. Immunomodulation contributes to the anticancer activity of *Morinda citrifolia* (noni) fruit juice. Proc West Pharmacol Soc 1996;39:7–9.
5. Hirazumi A, Furusawa E. An immunomodulatory polysaccharide-rich substance from the fruit juice of *Morinda citrifolia* (noni) with antitumour activity. Phytother Res 1999;13:380–7.
6. Wang MY, Su C. Cancer preventative effect of *Morinda citrifolia* (noni). Ann N Y Acad Sci 2001;952:161–8.
7. Younos C, et al. Analgesic and behavioural effects of *Morinda citrifolia*. Planta Med 1990;56:430–4.
8. Mueller BA, et al. Noni juice (*Morinda citrifolia*): hidden potential for hyperkalemia? Am J Kidney Dis 2000;35:310–2.
9. Horowitz S. Traditional Hawaiian healing arts enrich conventional medical practices. Altern Complement Ther 2001;7:68–73.

Oxygen Therapies

COMMON NAMES
Oxymedicine, bio-oxidative therapy, oxidative therapy, oxidology, hydrogen peroxide therapy, ozone therapy, ozonolysis, hyperoxygenation therapies, hyperoxygenated water, O_3AHT

KEY WORDS
Hydrogen peroxide therapy, ozone therapy, hyperoxygenated water

CLINICAL SUMMARY
Unproven alternative therapies and products offered over the Internet and at clinics in Mexico, the United States, and Europe. The term "oxygen therapy" refers to any product or treatment based on the false theory that cancer, infections, human immunodeficiency virus (HIV), and degenerative diseases are caused by oxygen deficiency. Such therapies purport to deliver high levels of oxygen to tissues and thereby kill cancer cells, eliminate pathogens, stimulate metabolism, and produce "oxidative detoxification." They include hydrogen peroxide therapy, involving intravenous infusion, ingestion, colonic administration, or soaking in hydrogen peroxide solution; ozone colonics and ozone autohemotherapy, in which blood is bubbled with ozone and reinjected; hyperbaric oxygen chambers; and "oxygenated" water, pills, and solutions. No scientific evidence supports their marketing claims; studies show that oxygen neither prevents nor inhibits cancer growth, and tumors grow rapidly in tissues that are well supplied with oxygen. Even if "oxygenated" products contain the oxygen levels that they claim, oxygen is not likely to be absorbed through the gastrointestinal tract. Ingestion or use of hydrogen peroxide enemas can cause lethal gas embolism and colitis-induced sepsis and gangrene, whereas its intravenous injection has led to acute hemolytic crisis and death. Transmission of bloodborne viruses such as hepatitis C and HIV is reported after treatment with contaminated autohemotherapy devices. Oxygen radicals released by ozone and hydrogen peroxide may be mutagenic. The American Cancer Society urges cancer patients not to seek treatment with hydrogen peroxide, ozone therapy, or other "hyperoxygenation" therapies. Oxygen therapies should not be recommended.

WARNINGS

The American Cancer Society strongly urges cancer patients not to seek treatment with ozone therapy, hydrogen peroxide, or other "hyperoxygenation" therapies. Transmission of bloodborne viruses such as hepatitis C and HIV is reported after treatment with contaminated autohemotherapy devices.[1]

MECHANISM OF ACTION

Oxygen therapies are based on the false concept that cancer and other degenerative diseases are caused by oxygen deficiency resulting from air pollution, processed foods, toxin buildup, emotional distress, and water fluoridation. Proponents cite Otto Warburg's finding of lower metabolism rates in cancer cells to conclude that cancer cells operate on an anaerobic level and therefore will be selectively destroyed by the oxygen liberated by hydrogen peroxide, ozone, and "oxygenated" products. Laboratory studies show that oxygen neither prevents nor inhibits cancer growth, that tumors grow rapidly in tissues that are well supplied with oxygenated blood, and that the absence of oxygen does not stimulate tumor growth in vitro or in vivo.

Exogenous hydrogen peroxide undergoes an exothermic decomposition reaction on contact with catalase in human blood, liberating oxygen and water. It shows no antitumor effects at nonlethal concentrations in animal models. Intravenous administration of hydrogen peroxide results in no decrease in *Escherichia coli* bacteremia in rabbits or free human blood. Typical intra-arterial administration produces only 2.9 mL of oxygen per 100 mL of blood per minute, an insignificant addition considering that normal adult metabolism requires between 200 and 250 mL of oxygen each minute.

Ozone exhibits broad antiviral activity via peroxidation of phospholipids and lipoproteins in the viral envelope. Although ozone effectively kills HIV in vitro, it does not reduce viral load in human studies. Ozone incubation of free human blood has been recorded to result in immunomodulatory effects, but it is unknown whether these effects occur in vivo.[2–15]

USAGE

Alzheimer's disease, angina, antiaging, arthritis, asthma, cancer prevention, cancer treatment, chronic fatigue syndrome, circulatory disorders, cirrhosis, detoxification, emphysema, fungal infections, hepatitis, HIV and acquired immune deficiency syndrome (AIDS), hypertension, infections, influenza, microbial infection, migraine treatment, multiple sclerosis, parasitic infections, Parkinson's disease, psoriasis, viral infections.

PHARMACOKINETICS

Absorption: Hydrogen peroxide has a half-life of 0.75 to 2 seconds in human blood, at which point it dissociates into oxygen and water and possibly hydroxy radicals. Sodium clearance studies in dogs and rats show that blood levels of 0.007 volume percent and above result in oxygen supersaturation and formation of gas emboli, causing capillary blockage, possible tissue necrosis, gangrene, and death. Studies reproducing 0.75 to 3% hydrogen peroxide solution enemas in dogs observe that the bowel wall and surrounding mesenteric vessels blanch white as blood is replaced by gas; bubbles appear in the mesenteric lymphatics, veins, arteries, and lymph nodes and then in the portal vein. Mesenteric and portal vein blood is completely replaced by gas but is restored on the removal of hydrogen peroxide. With higher concentrations, fibrin plugging of capillaries, venous thrombosis, and infarction of tissue are described.

Ozone gas has a half-life of about 40 minutes in dry air at 22°C. In blood, ozone decomposes quickly into a cascade of organic radicals such as ozonides, aldehydes, hydroxyhydroperoxides, hydrogen peroxide, isoprostanes, and lipid hydroperoxides. Colorectal insufflation of oxygen ozone in rabbits causes a slight increase in pO_2 values in both portal and peripheral venous blood.[6,9,16,17]

ADVERSE REACTIONS

Common (Intrarectal Hydrogen Peroxide): Colonic irrigation with hydrogen peroxide solution can cause gas embolism in the portal venous system, which is associated with gangrenous and perforated bowel. Numerous cases of hydrogen peroxide–induced ulcerative colitis and sepsis have been reported.

Reported (Intravenous Hydrogen Peroxide): Discomfort at the site of infusion; a stinging, burning sensation during infusion that disappears 6 to 8 hours later.

Case Report (Intrarectal Hydrogen Peroxide): One infant experienced rupture of the colon and two others died from gram-negative sepsis following evacuation of meconium with peroxide lavage.

Case Reports (Intravenous Hydrogen Peroxide): In a 51-year-old AIDS patient, injection of 35% hydrogen peroxide into the subclavian vein catheter caused Heinz body hemolytic anemia, subsequent hemoglobinuria, and death from progressive renal insufficiency with multiple electrolyte abnormalities. A 39-year-old man with metastatic cancer experienced acute hemolytic crisis leading to death after intravenous injection of hydrogen peroxide.

Case Reports (Oral Hydrogen Peroxide): Ingestion of an unknown amount of 3% hydrogen peroxide solution caused vomiting and reversible portal venous gas embolism in a 2-year-old boy. Ingestion of 30 to 40% hydrogen peroxide solution resulted in three adult deaths from gas embolism and circulatory collapse. Two cases of cerebral embolism are reported after 30 to 40% hydrogen peroxide ingestion: a 33-year-old woman experienced seizures, respiratory arrest, transmucosal emphysema, diffuse hemorrhages and edema of the gastric mucosa, brain edema, and residual motor deficits; an 84-year-old man sustained infarcts in the right anterior, middle, and posterior cerebral arteries and left frontal and multiple cerebellar arteries from gas embolization.[4,9,16,18–21]

Common (Subcutaneous Ozone): Local pain, burning, erythema, edema, and hematoma.

Reported (Colonic Ozone Insufflation): Mild to moderate discomfort during administration.

Reported (Intravenous Ozone): Fever, weakness, a bitter taste in the mouth.

Reported (Ozone Inhalation): At 0.01 ppm, ozone is irritating to the nose and throat mucous membranes. At 1 to 10 ppm, ozone may cause headaches, respiratory irritation, and possibly coma.[22–24]

DRUG INTERACTIONS
Oxygen may potentiate the pulmonary toxicity of bleomycin.[25,26]

DOSAGE
No dosage recommended.

LITERATURE SUMMARY AND CRITIQUE
No clinical studies evaluate use of intravenous or oral hydrogen peroxide or "oxygenated" products in humans.[27]

Carpendale MT, Freeberg J, Griffiss JM. Does ozone alleviate AIDS diarrhea? J Clin Gastroenterol 1993;17:142–5.
A small, open-label pilot study of daily colonic ozone/oxygen insufflations for 21 days in five male HIV+ patients with intractable diarrhea of unknown etiology. A medical ozone generator produced mixtures of 6 to 35 μg ozone/mL oxygen, which was administered through the rectum until the entire colon and cecum were filled; doses varied between patients. Outcomes measured were proportion of formed bowel movements per week, as recorded by the patient and corroborated by a nurse, and physical examination and laboratory studies evaluated on treatment days 1, 8, 15, and 22 and weeks 1, 2, and 3 post-treatment. Patients reported mild to moderate discomfort during administration. By 3 weeks, four of five patients reported resolved or markedly improved symptoms, which lasted 3 weeks post-therapy. No consistent change was found in CD4 count or another parameter. Larger, controlled studies are required to substantiate the efficacy of ozone/oxygen colonics in treating AIDS-related diarrhea.

Garber GE, et al. The use of ozone-treated blood in the therapy of HIV infection and immune disease: a pilot study of safety and efficacy. AIDS 1991;5:981–4.
A phase I open-label evaluation of ozone blood treatments in 10 HIV+ patients with CD4 counts between 50 and 500 cells/μL undergoing no other antiretroviral or opportunistic infection treatment. Ten cubic centimeters of heparinized blood were drawn, ozone was bubbled through the sample for 5 minutes, 2 cc of lidocaine were added, and the sample was injected intramuscularly, three times per week for 8 weeks. As no hematologic or biochemical toxicity was reported and three patients showed improvement in CD4 counts, a randomized, double-blind, phase II trial using the same protocol was initiated in 14 patients with CD4 counts between 200 and 400 cells/μL (treatment $n = 9$, placebo $n = 5$). Placebo patients' blood was drawn, sham processed, and reinjected with lidocaine. Blood parameters were measured at weeks 0, 1, 3, 5, 8, and 12. CD4 count decreased in the ozone group but rebounded after discontinuation of therapy, whereas interleukin-2,

interferon-γ, β_2-microglobulin, neopterin, and P24 antigen were unaffected in both treatment arms. Ozone content of blood was not measured before injection, so actual doses received are unknown. This study does not support the use of ozone blood therapy in HIV patients.

REFERENCES

1. Daschner FD. Hepatitis C and human immunodeficiency virus infection following ozone autohemotherapy. Eur J Clin Microbiol Infect Dis 1997;16:620.
2. Rackoff WR, Merton DF. Gas embolism after ingestion of hydrogen peroxide. Pediatrics 1990;85:593–4.
3. Shenep JL, Stokes DC, Hughes WT. Lack of antibacterial activity after intravenous hydrogen peroxide infusion in experimental *Escherichia coli* sepsis. Infect Immun 1985;48:607–10.
4. Meyer CT, et al. Hydrogen peroxide colitis: a report of three patients. J Clin Gastroenterol 1981;3:31–5.
5. American Cancer Society. Questionable methods of cancer management: hydrogen peroxide and other 'hyperoxygenation' therapies. CA Cancer J Clin 1993;43:47–56.
6. Johnson RJR, Froese G. Hydrogen peroxide and radiotherapy. Bubble formation in blood. Br J Radiol 1968;41:749–54.
7. Green HN, Westrop IW. Hydrogen peroxide and tumor therapy. Nature 1958;181:128–9.
8. Mallams JT, Finney JW, Balla GA. The use of hydrogen peroxide as a source of oxygen in a regional intra-arterial infusion system. South Med J 1962;55:230–2.
9. Farr CH. Physiological and biochemical responses to intravenous hydrogen peroxide in man. J Adv Med 1988;1:113–29.
10. Wells KH, et al. Inactivation of human immunodeficiency virus type 1 by ozone in vitro. Blood 1991;78:1882–90.
11. Garber GE, et al. The use of ozone-treated blood in the therapy of HIV infection and immune disease: a pilot study of safety and efficacy. AIDS 1991;5:981–4.
12. Bocci V, et al. Studies on the biological effects of ozone: 7. Generation of reactive oxygen species (ROS) after exposure of human blood to ozone. J Biol Regul Homeost Agents 1998;12:67–75.
13. Valacchi G, Bocci V. Studies on the biological effects of ozone: 10. Release of factors from ozonated human platelets. Mediators Inflamm 1999;8:205–9.
14. Valacchi G, Bocci V. Studies on the biological effects of ozone: 11. Release of factors from human endothelial cells. Mediators Inflamm 2000;9:271–6.
15. Green S. Oxygenation therapy: unproven treatments for cancer and AIDS. Available at: http://www.quackwatch.com/01QuackeryRelatedTopics/Cancer/oxygen.html (accessed Jun 26, 2002).
16. Shaw A, Cooperman A, Fusco J. Gas embolism produced by hydrogen peroxide. N Engl J Med 1967;277:238–41.
17. Bocci V, et al. Systemic effects after colorectal insufflation of oxygen-ozone in rabbits. Int J Med Biol Environ 2000;28:109–13.
18. Hirschtick RE, Dyrda SE, Peterson LC. Death from an unconventional therapy for AIDS. Ann Intern Med 1994;120:694.
19. Giberson TP, et al. Near-fatal hydrogen peroxide ingestion. Ann Emerg Med 1989;18:778–9.
20. Sherman SJ, Boyer LV, Sibley WA. Cerebral infarction immediately after ingestion of hydrogen peroxide solution. Stroke 1994;25:1065–7.
21. Jordan KS, Mackey D, Garvey E. Case review: a 39-year-old man with acute hemolytic crisis secondary to intravenous injection of hydrogen peroxide. J Emerg Nurs 1991;17:8–10.
22. Carpendale MT, Freeberg J, Griffiss JM. Does ozone alleviate AIDS diarrhea? J Clin Gastroenterol 1993;17:142–5.

23. Franzini M, et al. Subcutaneous oxygen-ozone therapy in indurative hypodermatitis and in localized lipodystrophies: a clinical study of efficacy and tolerability. Acta Toxicol Ther 1993;14:273–88.
24. Tylicki L, et al. Beneficial clinical effects of ozonated autohemotherapy in chronically dialysed patients with atherosclerotic ischemia of the lower limbs—pilot study. Int J Artif Organs 2001;24:79–82.
25. Ingrassia T, et al. Oxygen-exacerbated bleomycin pulmonary toxicity [review]. Mayo Clin Proc 1991;66:173–8.
26. Cersosimo R, et al. Bleomycin pneumonitis potentiated by oxygen administration. Drug Intell Clin Pharm 1985;19:921–3.
27. Bren L. Oxygen bars: is a breath of fresh air worth it? FDA Consumer Magazine 2002;36:Nov-Dec. http://www.fda.gov/fdac/features/2002/602_air.html (accessed Dec 5, 2002).

Passionflower

COMMON NAMES

Maypop, apricot vine, passion vine, purple passion flower, fleur de la passion, passiflore, corona de cristo, maracuja

SCIENTIFIC NAME

Passiflora incarnata

A.DONATO

CLINICAL SUMMARY

Derived from the aerial parts of the plant. Patients use this herb to treat insomnia, anxiety, epilepsy, neuralgia, and withdrawal syndromes from opiates or benzodiazepines. The active component of passionflower is unknown. The alkaloid components (eg, harman, harmaline) are thought to produce monoamine oxidase inhibition, whereas the maltol and γ-pyrone derivatives cause activation of γ-aminobutyric acid (GABA) receptors. Reported adverse events include sedation, dizziness, impaired cognitive function, and one case report of nausea, vomiting, and electrocardiographic (ECG) changes. All adverse events subside following discontinuation of passionflower. Theoretically, passionflower may potentiate the sedative effect of centrally acting substances (eg, benzodiazepines, barbiturates, alcohol). A small pilot study evaluated passionflower for generalized anxiety and showed comparable efficacy to oxazepam, but larger studies are necessary to evaluate safety and determine optimal dose. Passionflower may be of use in combination with clonidine for opiate detoxification, but additional research is required. No standardization exists for passionflower extract; therefore, dosages and activities may vary.

CONSTITUENTS

Alkaloids: harman, harmaline, harmalol, harmol, harmine; flavonoids: vitexin, isovitexin, apigenin, luteolin glycosides (orientin, homoorientin, lucenin), kaempferol, quercetin, rutin; others: carbohydrates, benzopyrones, fatty acids, γ-pyrone derivatives (maltol, ethylmaltol), passicol.[1-3]

MECHANISM OF ACTION

The exact mechanism of action is unknown. Activation of GABA receptors by maltol and γ-pyrone derivatives may mediate passionflower's anxiolytic and sedative properties. It is suggested that the harman alkaloids have monoamine oxidase inhibitor activity. Passionflower exhibits mild anti-inflammatory activity. An ethanolic extract of passionflower reduced carrageenan-induced edema, leukocyte migration, and granuloma formation in mice, although the effect was less than that seen with aspirin.[4-6]

USAGE

Anxiety, benzodiazepine withdrawal, drug withdrawal symptoms, epilepsy, insomnia, neuralgia.

PHARMACOKINETICS

No formal pharmacokinetic studies have been performed.

ADVERSE REACTIONS

Reported: Dizziness, sedation, ataxia, allergic reaction, and impaired cognitive function.
Case Report: Nausea, vomiting, bradycardia, and ECG changes including nonsustained ventricular tachycardia, Q–Tc prolongation, and nonspecific ST-T wave changes. The patient recovered following discontinuation of supplement.[7,8]

DRUG INTERACTIONS

Pentobarbital: Passionflower may potentiate the effects of pentobarbital.
Benzodiazepines: Theoretically, passionflower may increase the sedative effects of benzodiazepines.
Anticoagulant: Passionflower may have an additive anticoagulant effect.
Alcohol: Theoretically, passionflower may increase the sedative effects of alcohol.[9,10]

DOSAGE

Various extracts and formulations exist.
Oral: 1:1 Passionflower 25% alcohol liquid extract: 0.5 to 1 mL three times a day. *1:8 Passionflower 45% alcohol tincture:* 0.5 to 2 mL three times a day. *Tea:* 0.25 to 1 g dried aerial parts steeped in hot water three times a day.[1]

LITERATURE SUMMARY AND CRITIQUE

Akhondzadeh S, et al. Passionflower in the treatment of generalized anxiety: a pilot double-blind randomized controlled trial with oxazepam. J Clin Pharm Ther 2001;26:363–7.

A prospective, randomized, placebo-controlled evaluation of 45 drops/d of passionflower extract liquid (Passipay) plus placebo capsule (*n* = 18) compared with 30 mg/d oxazepam capsule plus placebo liquid (*n* = 18) on patients with generalized anxiety disorder and a Hamilton Anxiety Rating greater than 14. The primary outcome was change in the Hamilton Anxiety Rating scale from baseline as evaluated by a psychiatrist. The authors state that passionflower was as effective as oxazepam after 4 weeks of therapy, but average scores at day 28 are not reported. Adverse effects were similar between groups, including sedation, dizziness, and confusion, although more patients on oxazepam reported impaired job performance. Passionflower appears to be as effective as oxazepam, but larger studies are necessary.

Akhondzadeh S, et al. Passionflower in the treatment of opiates withdrawal: a double-blind randomized controlled trial. J Clin Pharm Ther 2001;26:369–73.

A prospective, randomized, double-blind evaluation of 0.3 to 0.8 mg/d clonidine with or without 60 drops/d passionflower extract for 14 days in male opiate addicts who agreed to detoxification. Primary outcome measure was the Short Opiate Withdrawal Scale, consisting of both physical and mental scores. Following randomization, a total of 30 evaluable patients remained in each arm. No significant difference in efficacy was documented between groups. The authors suggest that passionflower may be of use in opiate withdrawal, but additional studies are required.

REFERENCES

1. Newall C, et al. Herbal medicines: a guide for health-care professionals. 1st ed. London: Pharmaceutical Press; 1996.
2. Dhawan K, Kumar S, Sharma A. Anxiolytic activity of aerial and underground parts of *Passiflora incarnata*. Fitoterapia 2001;72:922–6
3. Grice ID, Ferreira LA, Griffiths LR. Identification and simultaneous analysis of harmane, harmine, harmol, isovitexin, and vitexin in *Passiflora incarnata* extracts with a novel hplc method. J Liq Chrom Rel Technol 2001;24:2513–23.
4. Dhawan K, Kumar S, Sharma A. Anti-anxiety studies on extracts of *Passiflora incarnata* linneaus. J Ethnopharmacol 2001;78:165–70.
5. Borrelli F, et al. Anti-inflammatory activity of *Passiflora incarnata* l. in rats. Phytother Res 1996;10:S104–6.
6. Soulimani R, et al. Behavioural effects of *Passiflora incarnata* l. and its indole alkaloid and flavonoid derivatives and maltol in the mouse. J Ethnopharmacol 1997;57:11–20.
7. Fisher A, Purcell P, Le Couteur DG. Toxicity of *Passiflora incarnata* L. J Toxicol Clin Toxicol 2000;38:63–6.
8. Akhondzadeh S, et al. Passionflower in the treatment of generalized anxiety: a pilot double-blind randomized controlled trial with oxazepam. J Clin Pharm Ther 2001;26:363–7.
9. Brinker F. Herb contraindications and drug interactions. 3rd ed. Sandy (OR): Eclectic Medical Publications; 2001.
10. Speroni E, et al. Sedative effects of crude extract of *Passiflora incarnata* after oral administration. Phytother Res 1996;10:S92–4.

Pau D'arco

A.DONATO

COMMON NAMES
Ipe, lapacho, purple lapacho, trumpet bush, taheebo

SCIENTIFIC NAMES
Tabebuia impetiginosa, Tabebuia avellanedae, Tabebuia heptaphylla

KEY WORDS
Tabebuia impetiginosa, lapacho

CLINICAL SUMMARY

Derived from the bark of the tree. This herb has been used traditionally to treat cancer and infections. No clinical studies support its use for these claims. The quinone compounds are known to possess toxic effects; therefore, this product should not be recommended. Reported adverse events include nausea, vomiting, dizziness, and anemia. Use of this product may increase the activity of anticoagulants.

CONSTITUENTS

Quinone compounds: lapachol, β-lapachone, xyloidone (naphthoquinones), and tabebuin (anthroquinone) are considered to be the active ingredients; flavonoid: quercetin; alkaloids: tecomine, hydroxybenzoic acid, steroidal saponins.[1,2]

WARNINGS

Quinone compounds are known to possess toxic effects. The effectiveness of pau d'arco for the treatment of cancer or any other condition remains unproven and must not be recommended.

MECHANISM OF ACTION

Unknown. Lapachol and β-lapachone have demonstrated antibacterial, antifungal (fungistatic), and antimalarial activity.[2,3]

USAGE

Cancer treatment, *Candida* yeast infection, parasitic infections, respiratory infections.

ADVERSE REACTIONS

Reported: Nausea, vomiting, dizziness, anemia, bleeding, and discoloration of urine.[4]

DRUG INTERACTIONS

Anticoagulants/Antiplatelets: Pau d'arco may potentiate effects.[5]

LABORATORY INTERACTIONS

May increase prothrombin time/activated partial thromboplastin time/international normalized ratio.

DOSAGE

Not recommended.
Oral: Use of up to nine 300 mg powdered lapacho inner bark capsules per day has been reported.[2]

LITERATURE SUMMARY AND CRITIQUE

Adequate clinical studies have not been performed on pau d'arco to confirm efficacy for any claim.

Block JB, et al. Early clinical studies with lapachol. Cancer Chemother Rep 1974; 4:27–8. A phase I clinical trial in 21 patients with nonleukemic tumors or chronic myelocytic leukemia who had relapsed. Pau d'arco did not demonstrate any clinical efficacy. Lapacho was given to 19 patients with nonleukemic tumors and 2 patients with chronic myelogenous at a dose range of 250 to 3,750 mg daily for 5 days and up to 3,000 mg daily for 21 days. Results showed the status of the patients to be neither unchanged nor worse.

REFERENCES

1. Willard T. A textbook of natural medicine. Edinburgh (UK): Churchill Livingstone; 1998.
2. Oswald EH. Lapacho. Br J Phytoth 1994;3:112–7.
3. Guiraud P, et al. Comparison of antibacterial and antifungal activities of lapachol and β-lapachone. Planta Med 1994;60:373–4.
4. Foster S, et al. Tyler's honest herbal: a sensible guide to the use of herbs and related remedies. New York: Haworth Herbal Press; 1999.
5. Brinker F. Herb contraindications and drug interactions. 2nd ed. Sandy (OR): Eclectic Medical Publications; 1998.

PC-SPES

KEY WORD
SPES

CLINICAL SUMMARY

PC-SPES is a natural product composed of eight herbs: reishi mushroom, baikal skullcap, rabdosia, dyer's woad, chrysanthemum, saw palmetto, *Panax ginseng*, and licorice. Patients use this supplement to treat prostate cancer. Published studies document the efficacy of PC-SPES. In vitro testing reveals suppression of human tumor cell lines, including androgen-sensitive and -insensitive prostate cancer. Use of PC-SPES brings about significant decreases in androgen and prostate-specific antigen (PSA) levels in humans. It is thought that PC-SPES contains phytoestrogens and other undefined components that contribute to its activity. Recent concerns about product contamination with warfarin and alprazolam resulted in a voluntary recall by Botanic Labs, the manufacturer of PC-SPES. This product is not available in United States at this time.

CONSTITUENTS

Chrysanthemum mori folium, flower (mum, ju hua); *Ganoderma lucidum*, stem (reishi mushroom, ling zhi); *Glycyrrhiza uralensis*, root (licorice, gan cao); *Isatis indigotica*, leaf (dyers woad, da qing ye); *Panax notoginseng*, root (san qi); *Rabdosia rubescens*, leaf (rubescens, dong ling cao); *Scutellaria baicalensis*, root (baikal skullcap, huang qin); *Serenoa repens*, berry (saw palmetto).[1]

WARNINGS

Recent concerns about product contamination with warfarin and alprazolam resulted in a voluntary recall by Botanic Labs, the manufacturer of PC-SPES. This product is not available in the United States at this time.

PC-SPES should not be confused with SPES, a different product sold by Botanic Labs, which is an immunostimulant that contains 15 botanicals. SPES was also recalled for contamination on February 8, 2002.

MECHANISM OF ACTION

The active components of PC-SPES are unknown. Laboratory analysis of PC-SPES by high-performance liquid chromatography, gas chromatography, and mass spectrometry indicates the presence of estrogenic organic compounds different from diethylstilbestrol (DES), estrone, and estradiol. In vitro testing of this extract shows suppressed cell proliferation and reduced clonogenicity in human tumor cell lines, including prostrate, breast, and colon. The predominant cell-cycle effect induced by PC-SPES is prolongation of the G_1 phase; however, apoptosis was observed after exposure of tumor cells to PC-SPES for 48 hours or longer. PC-SPES also inhibits proliferation of LNCaP prostate cell lines, associated with a 60 to 70% down-regulation of the proliferating cell nuclear antigen. Preliminary studies evaluating the viability of prostate cancer cell lines LNCaP, LNCaP apoptosis-resistant derivative, LNCaP-bcl-2, PC3, and DU145 at three concentrations of PC-SPES show inhibited growth at concentrations of 4 µg/mL or less. Another recent in vitro study indicates that its cytotoxicity may be attributable to alteration of expression of specific genes involved in regulating the cell cycle, cell structure, and androgen response. No single botanical or chemical extract appears to be responsible for the overall effects of this product.[7–9]

USAGE

Prostate cancer.

PHARMACOKINETICS

No data.

ADVERSE REACTIONS

Common: Mastalgia, gynecomastia, sexual dysfunction, decreased libido, transient gastrointestinal symptoms, diarrhea, and dyspepsia.
Infrequent: Pulmonary embolism, deep vein thrombosis, phlebitis, edema, and allergic reactions.
Case Report: Retroperitoneal hemorrhage.[10–12]

DRUG INTERACTIONS

All herbal and dietary supplements should be discontinued while using PC-SPES. Avoid concomitant use of all medications.
Antihypertensives: PC-SPES may antagonize the effect of antihypertensives.
Corticosteroids: PC-SPES may potentiate the effect of steroids.
Diuretics: PC-SPES may antagonize the effect of diuretics.
Digoxin: PC-SPES may increase the risk of cardiac toxicity owing to loss of potassium.
Monoamine Oxidase Inhibitors (MAOIs): PC-SPES may increase the effects of MAOIs.
Hormones: PC-SPES may alter response owing to possible estrogenic activity.
CYP450: PC-SPES may inhibit the 3A4 enzyme, thereby increasing levels of drugs metabolized by CYP450 3A4.

Grapefruit Juice: Grapefruit juice may increase the mineralocorticoid activities of the licorice component owing to inhibition of CYP450 3A4.[13]

LABORATORY INTERACTIONS
Decreased testosterone and hormone levels, reduced PSA levels, lowered blood pressure, decreased serum potassium.[2,12]

CONTRAINDICATIONS
Patients with a history of uncontrolled hypertension, unstable angina, deep venous thrombosis, coagulopathies, history of biliary colic, or untreated cholelithiasis should not take PC-SPES.

DOSAGE
Oral: Each capsule of PC-SPES contains 320 mg of the eight herbs. Dosage varies between patients. PC-SPES should be taken on an empty stomach. *Prostate cancer:* The initial dose is one capsule three times a day during the first week and two capsules three times a day during the second week. If the dose is tolerated, it may be increased to three capsules three times a day.[1]

LITERATURE SUMMARY AND CRITIQUE
Small EJ, et al. Prospective trial of the herbal supplement PC-SPES in patients with progressive prostate cancer. J Clin Oncol 2000;18:3595–603.
A prospective phase II study to assess the efficacy and toxicity of PC-SPES in androgen-dependent or -independent prostate cancer. Thirty-three patients with androgen-dependent prostate cancer (ADPCa) and 37 patients with androgen-independent (AIPCa) were treated with PC-SPES at a dose of nine capsules daily. Clinical outcomes were assessed with serial serum PSA level measurement and imaging studies. One hundred percent of ADPCa patients experienced a PSA decline of $\geq$ 80%, with a median duration of 57+ weeks. No patient developed PSA progression. In 31 patients (97%), testosterone levels dropped to the anorchid range. Two ADPCa patients had positive bone scans; both improved. One patient with a bladder mass measurable on computed tomographic (CT) scan experienced disappearance of this mass. Nineteen (54%) of 35 AIPCa patients had a PSA decline of $\geq$ 50%, including 8 (50%) of 16 patients who had received prior ketoconazole therapy. Severe toxicities included thromboembolic events ($n = 3$) and allergic reactions ($n = 3$). Other frequent toxicities included gynecomastia, leg cramps, and grade 1 or 2 diarrhea.

De la Taille A, et al. Herbal therapy PC-SPES: in vitro effects and evaluation of its efficacy in 69 patients with prostate cancer. J Urol 2000;164:1229–34.
Of the 69 prostate cancer patients, 82% had decreased serum PSA at 2 months, 78% at 6 months, and 88% at 12 months after treatment with PC-SPES. Side effects in the treated

population included nipple tenderness in 42% and phlebitis requiring heparinization in 2%. PC-SPES was effective in inducing apoptosis of hormone-sensitive and -insensitive prostate cancer cells in vitro and in suppressing the growth rate of hormone-insensitive prostate cancer cell lines in vivo.

Pfeifer BL, et al. PC-SPES, a dietary supplement for the treatment of hormone-refractory prostate cancer. BJU Int 2000;85:481–5.

Sixteen men previously treated for advanced metastatic prostate cancer (stage D3) who were refractory to hormonal therapy had 3 consecutive months of increasing PSA and progression of disease by magnetic resonance imaging or CT scan were enrolled. Fourteen patients received concurrent therapy with a luteinizing hormone–releasing hormone agonist ± antiandrogen and two received orchiectomy. Patients were given three capsules of PC-SPES three times a day for 20 weeks. The trial assessed toxicity and response to PC-SPES. Following 20 weeks of treatment, there was a significant improvement in quality of life parameters and greater than 50% reduction in PSA levels. Adverse events were reported and included breast tenderness in eight patients and one report of dyspepsia. The authors reported a decline in the number of bone lesions and pelvic lymphadenopathy, but these data are not delineated. No information regarding progression of disease was provided.

Porterfield H. Survey of UsToo members and other prostate cancer patients to evaluate the efficacy and safety of PC-SPES. Mol Urol 1999;3:333–6.

A survey of UsToo members and other prostate cancer patients was conducted to evaluate the safety and efficacy of PC-SPES. Of 82 patients, beneficial effects were reported in 77% of the respondents, the other 23% reporting more limited or marginal results. Reductions in PSA, as much as 70 ng/mL, were reported and were sustained for the duration of PC-SPES therapy, approaching 2 years in some cases. No significant adverse effects were reported.

In Vitro/Animal Studies
DiPaola R, et al. Clinical and biologic activity of an estrogenic herbal combination (PC-SPES) in prostate cancer. N Engl J Med 1998;339:785–91.

The estrogenic activity of PC-SPES was measured by means of transcriptional activation assays in yeast and a biologic assay in mice. The clinical activity of PC-SPES was assessed in eight patients with hormone-sensitive prostate cancer by measuring serum PSA and testosterone concentrations during and after treatment. The yeast assays showed an estrogenic activity similar to estradiol. In six of six men with prostate cancer, PC-SPES decreased serum testosterone concentrations, and in eight of eight patients, it decreased serum concentrations of PSA. All eight patients had breast tenderness and loss of libido, and one had venous thrombosis. High-performance liquid and gas chromatography and mass spectrometry showed that PC-SPES contains estrogen organic compounds that are distinct from DES, estrone, and estradiol.

Bonham M, et al. Molecular effects of the herbal compound PC-SPES: identification of activity pathways in prostate carcinoma. Cancer Res 2002;62:3920–4.

LNCaP prostate carcinoma cells were exposed to PC-SPES and other estrogenic agents, such as DES. PC-SPES was shown to alter the expression of 156 genes after 24 hours of exposure. Alpha- and β-tubulins and androgen receptors were down-regulated. Comparative analysis between PC-SPES and DES on cytotoxicity and gene expression changes shows that PC-SPES may have effects on prostate cancer cells other than its antiestrogenic activities.

REFERENCES

1. PC SPES® for prostate health: product information. Brea (CA): Botanic Labs; 2000.
2. De la Taille A, et al. Effects of a phytotherapeutic agent, PC-SPES, on prostate cancer: a preliminary investigation on human cell lines and patients. BJU Int 1999;84:845–50.
3. Tiwari RK, et al. Anti-tumor effects of PC-SPES, an herbal formulation in prostate cancer. Int J Oncol 1999;14:713–9.
4. Chenn S. In vitro mechanism of PC SPES. Urology 2001;58:28–35.
5. Kubota T, et al. PC-SPES: a unique inhibitor of proliferation of prostate cancer cells in vitro and in vivo. Prostate 2000;42:163–71.
6. Hsieh TC, Wu JM. Mechanism of action of herbal supplement PC-SPES: elucidation of effects of individual herbs of PC-SPES on cell proliferation and prostate specific gene expression in androgen-dependent LNCaP cells. Int J Oncol 2002;20:583–8.
7. DiPaola R, et al. Clinical and biologic activity of an estrogenic herbal combination (PC-SPES) in prostate cancer. N Engl J Med 1998;339:785–91.
8. Bonham M, et al. Molecular effects of the herbal compound PC-SPES: identification of activity pathways in prostate carcinoma. Cancer Res 2002;62:3920–4.
9. Hsu MJ, Lee SS, Lin WW. Polysaccharide purified from *Ganoderma lucidum* inhibits spontaneous and Fas-mediated apoptosis in human neutrophils through activation of the phosphatidylinositol 3 kinase/Akt signaling pathway. J Leukoc Biol 2002;72:207–16.
10. Pfeifer BL, et al. PC-SPES, a dietary supplement for the treatment of hormone-refractory prostate cancer. BJU Int 2000;85:481–5.
11. Weinrobe MC, Montgomery B. Acquired bleeding diathesis in a patient taking PC-SPES. N Engl J Med 2001;345:1213–4.
12. Small EJ, et al. Prospective trial of the herbal supplement PC-SPES in patients with progressive prostate cancer. J Clin Oncol 2000;18:3595–603.
13. Brinker F. Herb contraindications and drug interactions. 3rd ed. Sandy (OR): Eclectic Medical Publications; 2001.

Pennyroyal

COMMON NAMES
Squaw mint, mosquito plant, American pennyroyal, European pennyroyal, mock pennyroyal, squaw balm, tickweed

SCIENTIFIC NAMES
Mentha pulegium, Hedeoma pulegioides

A. DONATO

CLINICAL SUMMARY
A herbal extract oil or tea derived from the leaves and flowering tops of the plant. This supplement is used in folklore medicine to induce abortion and menses and to treat inflammatory conditions, chronic bronchitis, minor ailments, and colic in infants. Small amounts of the oil are approved by the US Food and Drug Administration for use as a flavoring agent. Pennyroyal oil contains several monoterpenes, principally pulegone, which has known toxic effects on the liver and lungs. Oxidative metabolites of pugelone, such as menthofuran, are oxidized further by cytochrome P-450 to reactive intermediates that form adducts with cellular proteins and cause organ damage. Ingestion of pennyroyal oil in adults or tea in children causes severe toxicity, including hepatic failure, acute renal failure, coagulopathies, metabolic acidosis, gastrointestinal hemorrhage, pulmonary congestion with consolidation, cerebral edema, seizures, disseminated intravascular coagulation, and death. This is a dangerous herb and should not be used.

CONSTITUENTS
Volatile oils: monoterpenes (eg, pulegone, 3-octanone, 3-methylcyclohexanone, α-pinene, β-pinene, *p*-cymene, limonene, *p*-mentha-1,4[8]-diene, pulegol, menthone, isomenthone, menthofuran, isopulegone, pulegone epoxides, piperitone, piperitenone);

monomeric flavonoids; others: 3-octylacetate, 3-octanol, 1-octen-3-ol, hedeomal, tannins, paraffins.[1,2]

WARNINGS
Analysis of commercially available pennyroyal leaves found contamination with low levels of bacteria, fungi, and yeast species.[3]

MECHANISM OF ACTION
The exact mechanism of action is unknown. Pennyroyal's abortifacient properties are thought to be attributable to irritation of the uterus, causing contractions, but lethal doses are necessary for this to occur, and the effect is inconsistent. Pennyroyal's mint properties, attributable to the menthol component, theoretically may act in dilating respiratory passages in bronchitis or asthma when consumed as a tea. European and American pennyroyal oils consist of 80 to 90% and 16 to 30% (R)-$(+)$-pulegone, respectively, which is oxidized by cytochrome P-450 to menthofuran (about 50%) and other toxic metabolites. Animal and human studies show that pulegone is directly neurotoxic. Menthofuran decreases glucose-6-phosphatase activity in rat models, causing hypoglycemia.[1,4,5]

USAGE
Amenorrhea, asthma, bronchitis, cancer treatment, colic, common cold, headaches, inducement of abortion, inflammation, influenza, insect repellent, premenstrual syndrome, stomach and intestinal gas, toothache.

PHARMACOKINETICS
Absorption: Studies in rats show that a single 150 mg/kg intraperitoneal dose of pulegone produces peak plasma levels of 13.5 ± 3.0 mg/mL after about 15 minutes and a half-life of approximately 1 hour. Menthofuran levels peak at 7.0 ± 1.2 mg/mL 1 hour after pulegone administration, with a half-life of about 2 hours.

Distribution: Pulegone is oxidized by cytochrome P-450 2E1, 1A2, and 2C19 to its proximate toxic metabolite menthofuran (about 50%) and other reactive metabolites. Menthofuran is thought to be responsible for less than half of the toxicity attributable to pennyroyal oil. Studies identify 2-Z-(2′-keto-4′-methylcyclohexylidene) propanal, an unsaturated keto aldehyde that forms adducts with cellular proteins, as the ultimate chemically reactive metabolite. Menthofuran also is metabolized to 4-hydroxy-4-methyl-2-cyclohexenone and *p*-cresol, a known liver and lung toxin. End products of cytochrome P-450 oxidation of menthofuran include hydroxymenthofuran and its nontoxic tautomers mintlactone and isomintlactone. Pugelone may be metabolized by P-450 via two other pathways to as yet unidentified electrophilic reactive species, which, together with pulegone, deplete glutathione (GSH) in liver and plasma by forming covalent adducts with its nucleophilic cysteinyl sulfhydryl group. Depletion of GSH further increases the hepatotoxicity induced by pulegone in rat models. Pennyroyal oil causes centrilobular liver necrosis in a dose-dependent manner.

Excretion: At least 14 pulegone metabolites, including menthofuran, are excreted in the urine and at least 10 phase II metabolites are found conjugated to GSH and glucuronide in bile.[6–12]

ADVERSE REACTIONS

Reported: Dizziness, weakness, syncope, hallucinations, abdominal cramps, nausea, gastrointestinal upset, pupillary changes, hepatotoxicity, renal injury.

Toxicity: At least 24 cases of pennyroyal toxicity are in the literature, reporting fulminant hepatic failure, acute renal failure, hypoglycemia, coagulopathy, metabolic acidosis, gastrointestinal hemorrhage, pulmonary congestion with consolidation, mental status changes, cerebral edema, seizures, disseminated intravascular coagulation, and death. Pennyroyal oil ingestion is treated with gastric lavage, activated charcoal, and *N*-acetylcysteine in patients evaluated soon after ingestion.

Case Reports (Oil): A 24-year-old woman ingested pennyroyal extract for over 2 weeks and, after acute ingestion, developed abdominal cramps, chills, vomiting, syncope, cardiopulmonary arrest, and multiorgan failure leading to coma and death. Exploratory laparotomy showed a hemorrhagic ectopic pregnancy. An 18 year old ingested 30 mL of pennyroyal oil and developed abdominal pain, vomiting, and coagulopathy, and died 1 week later from cardiopulmonary arrest and multiple organ failure.

Case Reports (Tea): An 8-week-old boy, after ingesting 120 mL of homegrown pennyroyal mint tea to treat a suspected infection, experienced multiple organ failure, including confluent hepatocellular necrosis, kidney hemorrhage and necrosis, bilateral lung consolidation with diffuse alveolar damage and hemorrhage, and diffuse cerebral edema with acute ischemic necrosis and isolated vacuolation of the midbrain. The infant died 4 days after admission. A 6-month-old boy developed acute hepatic injury, seizures, and sinus hemorrhage after regular consumption of pennyroyal tea and recovered after 2 months of hospitalization.[4,5,13]

DRUG INTERACTIONS

Iron Supplements: Monomeric flavonoids in pennyroyal may complex with iron in the intestinal lumen and reduce bioavailability by 50% or more.[14]

LABORATORY INTERACTIONS

Elevated liver function tests (alanine transaminase, aspartate transaminase, alkaline phosphatase, bilirubin), metabolic acidosis (low pH, low bicarbonate level, increased anion gap), and increased partial thromboplastin time, prothrombin time, and international normalized ratio, indicating coagulopathy.

CONTRAINDICATIONS

Owing to its abortifacient effects, pennyroyal should not be consumed by pregnant or breast-feeding women. Owing to its toxic effects, pennyroyal should not be consumed under any circumstances.

DOSAGE

Oral: No dose is recommended owing to toxicity. *Oil:* 5 mL have been associated with coma and seizures, whereas doses of 10 mL or greater have been fatal. One to eight drops have been used topically as an insect repellant. *Tea:* 1 to 2 teaspoons of pennyroyal leaves in 1 cup of boiling water, steeped for 10 to 15 minutes, or 1 tablespoon of dried herb with 1 cup of water. Two cups daily.[2]

LITERATURE SUMMARY AND CRITIQUE

No clinical studies of pennyroyal have been performed.

REFERENCES

1. Gordon WP, et al. Hepatotoxicity and pulmonary toxicity of pennyroyal oil and its constituent terpenes in the mouse. Toxicol Appl Pharmacol 1982;65:413–24.
2. Fetrow CW, et al. Professional's handbook of complementary and alternative medicines. Philadelphia: Springhouse; 1999.
3. Martins HM, et al. Evaluation of microbiological quality of medicinal plants used in natural infusions. Int J Food Microbiol 2001;68:149–53.
4. Bakerink JA, et al. Multiple organ failure after ingestion of pennyroyal oil from herbal tea in two infants. Pediatrics 1996;98:944–7.
5. Sullivan JB, et al. Pennyroyal oil poisoning and hepatotoxicity. JAMA 1979;242:2873–4.
6. Chen LJ, Lebetkin EH, Burka LT. Metabolism of (R)-(+)-pulegone in F344 rats. Drug Metab Dispos 2001;29:1567–77.
7. Khojasteh-Bakht SC, Nelson SD, Atkins WM. Glutathione S-transferase catalyzes the isomerization of (R)-2-hydroxymenthofuran to mintlactones. Arch Biochem Biophys 1999;370:59–65.
8. Gordon WP, et al. The metabolism of the abortifacient terpene, (R)-(+)-pulegone, to a proximate toxin, menthofuran. Drug Metab Dispos 1987;15:589–94.
9. Thomassen D, Slattery JT, Nelson SD. Menthofuran-dependent and independent aspects of pulegone hepatotoxicity: roles of glutathione. J Pharmacol Exp Ther 1990;253:567–72.
10. Thomassen D, Slattery JT, Nelson SD. Contribution of menthofuran to the hepatotoxicity of pulegone: assessment based on matched area under the curve and on matched time course. J Pharmacol Exp Ther 1988;244:825–9.
11. Khojasteh-Bakht SC, et al. Metabolism of (R)-(+)-pulegone and (R)-(+)-menthofuran by human liver cytochrome P-450s: evidence for formation of a furan epoxide. Drug Metab Dispos 1999;27:574–80.
12. Madyastha KM, Raj CP. Evidence for the formation of a known toxin, p-cresol, from menthofuran. Biochem Biophys Res Commun 1991;177:440–5.
13. Anderson IB, et al. Pennyroyal toxicity: measurement of toxic metabolite levels in two cases and review of the literature. Ann Intern Med 1996;124:726–34.
14. Hurrell RF, Reddy M, Cook JD. Inhibition of non-haem iron absorption in man by polyphenolic-containing beverages. Br J Nutr 1999;81:289–95.
15. Brinker F. Herb contraindications and drug interactions. 3rd ed. Sandy (OR): Eclectic Medical Publications; 2001.

Perillyl Alcohol

COMMON NAMES

Perillyl, POH, p-metha,1,7-diene-6-ol, 4-isopropenyl-cyclohexene-carbinol

A. DONATO

CLINICAL SUMMARY

Derived from essential oils in various botanicals, including lavender, peppermint, cherries, sage, and lemongrass. Patients use this supplement to prevent and treat cancer. Perillyl alcohol is a cyclic monoterpene that causes G_1 cell-cycle arrest, induces apoptosis, and inhibits post-translational modification of signal transduction proteins. Following oral administration, perillyl alcohol is rapidly metabolized to perillic acid (PA) and dihydroperillic acid (DPA). Both metabolites exhibit a relatively short biologic half-life of approximately 2 hours. Phase I studies indicate that doses of 800 to 1,600 mg/m² given three times a day are best tolerated. Tumor response is unimpressive. Side effects include nausea, early satiety, and fatigue. Dose-limiting toxicities, reported at levels of 2,800 mg/m²/dose, included stomatitis, hypokalemia, nausea, and fatigue. In vitro and animal data suggest a potential use for perillyl alcohol in cancer treatment, but no human efficacy data are available. Further research is necessary to determine if perillyl alcohol has a role in preventing or treating cancer.

CONSTITUENTS

Hydroxylated monocyclic monoterpene.

MECHANISM OF ACTION

The exact mechanism of action is unknown. Metabolites of perillyl alcohol, PA, and DPA may inhibit tumor growth through inhibition of p21-dependent signaling and apoptosis resulting from induction of the transforming growth factor-β signaling pathway. Perillyl alcohol metabolites also appear to cause G_1 cell-cycle arrest, inhibit posttranslational modification of signal transduction proteins, and cause differential expression of cell cycle– and apoptosis-related genes. Activity of perillyl alcohol was demonstrated in animal models with pancreatic, stomach, colon, skin, and liver cancers. The role of perillyl alcohol for chemoprevention remains unknown as efficacy data are inconsistent.[1–5]

USAGE

Cancer prevention, cancer treatment.

PHARMACOKINETICS

Following oral administration, perillyl alcohol is rapidly absorbed and subsequently metabolized to PA and DPA. Peak plasma levels of the PA and DPA occur within approximately 2 hours and 4 hours, respectively, with an estimated biologic half-life of 2 hours. Continuous doses of 1,600 to 2,800 mg/m^2/d perillyl alcohol result in PA and DPA plasma levels from 390 to 480 µmol and 11 to 57 µmol, respectively. Administration with food appears to reduce the rate and extent of perillyl alcohol absorption. Approximately 10% of PA and 2% of DPA are eliminated in the urine.[1,6]

ADVERSE REACTIONS

Common (1,600 mg/m²/d): Nausea, unpleasant taste, early satiety, and fatigue.
Toxicity (Doses > 2,800 mg/m²/d): Nausea, fatigue, diarrhea, hypokalemia, stomatitis, and anorexia.[2,3]

DRUG INTERACTIONS

No known drug interactions exist.

DOSAGE

Oral: Phase I studies suggest 800 to 1,200 mg/m^2/dose given three times daily. Dose may be escalated to 1,600 mg/m^2 as tolerated.[2,3]

LITERATURE SUMMARY AND CRITIQUE

Only phase I clinical studies have been performed. Additional studies to establish the efficacy of perillyl alcohol are required.

REFERENCES

1. Belanger JT. Perillyl alcohol: applications in oncology. Altern Med Rev 1998;3:448–57.
2. Hudes GR, et al. Phase I pharmacokinetic trial of perillyl alcohol (NSC 641066) in patients with refractory solid malignancies. Clin Cancer Res 2000;6:3071–80.
3. Ripple GH. Phase I clinical and pharmacokinetic study of perillyl alcohol administered four times a day. Clin Cancer Res 2000;6:390–6.
4. Reddy BS, et al. Chemoprevention of colon carcinogenesis by dietary perillyl alcohol. Cancer Res 1997;57:420–5.
5. Low-Baselli A, et al. Failure to demonstrate chemoprevention by the monoterpene perillyl alcohol during early rat hepatocarcinogenesis: a cautionary note. Carcinogenesis 2000;21:1869–77.
6. Murren JR, et al. Phase I study of perillyl alcohol in patients with refractory malignancies. Cancer Biol Ther 2002;1:130–5.

Phenylbutyrate

COMMON NAMES
Sodium phenylbutyrate, 4-phenylbutyric acid, sodium 4-phenylbutyrate

KEY WORDS
Sodium phenylbutyrate, Buphenyl, TriButyrate

CLINICAL SUMMARY
Phenylbutyrate is a prodrug of phenylacetate, an aromatic fatty acid. Patients are prescribed phenylbutyrate off-label to treat cancer. Sodium phenylbutyrate is classified by the US Food and Drug Administration as an orphan drug for the treatment of urea cycle disorders. Several phase I trials are under way to evaluate phenylbutyrate for leukemias and for refractory solid tumors. Published phase I studies indicate low toxicity and possible activity in these cancers. A number of patients experienced disease stabilization in these trials, although disease regression was not observed. The optimal dose and place in therapy are yet to be defined, but oral doses up to 36 g/d have been used with minimal toxicity. Reported adverse events include fatigue, dyspepsia, nausea, vomiting, body odor, anorexia, menstrual cycle irregularities, hypocalcemia, edema, skin rash, liver toxicity, and renal tubular acidosis. Each 500 mg tablet contains approximately 62 mg of sodium. Studies point to a potential role for phenylbutyrate in treating refractory cancers, but additional clinical research is required.

WARNINGS
Each 500 mg tablet of sodium phenylbutyrate contains approximately 62 mg of sodium.[1]

MECHANISM OF ACTION
Phenylbutyrate is a prodrug of phenylacetate, an aromatic fatty acid. In urea cycle disorders, phenylacetate reduces or normalizes serum ammonium and glutamate levels. Phenylbutyrate and its metabolites have also been shown to increase fetal hemoglobin production in patients with thalassemia and sickle cell disease. In vitro studies suggest that phenylbutyrate causes cancer cell cytostasis, differentiation, and apoptosis. Animal studies indicate that phenylbutyrate, when combined with 12-*cis* retinoic acid, inhibits angiogenesis and causes apoptosis of prostate cancer cells. Other studies show that

phenylbutyrate and its metabolites up-regulate numerous lipid-metabolizing genes via human peroxisome transcription factors, inhibit p21 ras prenylation, resulting in G_1 arrest and apoptosis in myeloid cells, and down-regulate Bcl-2 in MCF7 ras breast cancer cells. In vitro studies with HT-29 colon cancer cells indicate that phenylbutyrate also inactivates nuclear factor-κB, resulting in apoptosis.[1–6]

USAGE
Cancer treatment, cystic fibrosis, sickle cell disease, thalassemia, urea cycle disorders.

PHARMACOKINETICS
Following oral administration, phenylbutyrate tablets are roughly 80% bioavailable. Phenylbutyrate has an approximate distribution of 0.3 L/kg. C_{max} increases linearly following oral doses of 18, 27, and 36 g, with blood concentrations of approximately 1,670, 2,327, and 3,508 mM/L, respectively. Following oral or parenteral administration, phenylbutyrate is metabolized rapidly by β-oxidation in the kidneys and liver to phenylacetate and phenylacetylglutamine. The biologic half-life is around 1 hour for the parent compound and approximately 1.8 and 2.8 hours for phenylacetate and phenylacetylglutamine, respectively. Metabolites are eliminated primarily via the kidneys.[3]

ADVERSE REACTIONS
Common: Fatigue, dyspepsia, nausea, vomiting, body odor, anorexia, menstrual cycle irregularities, amenorrhea.
Reported: Hypocalcemia, edema (possibly related to sodium content), skin rash.
Rare: Liver toxicity (elevations in aspartate transaminase, alanine transaminase, bilirubin, and alkaline phosphatase), renal tubular acidosis.[1,3]

DRUG INTERACTIONS
No interactions of clinical significance.[1]

LABORATORY INTERACTIONS
The following should be monitored: liver function, body weight, blood pressure, renal function, serum calcium, serum electrolytes, complete blood count, and menstruation cycle (if applicable).

DOSAGE
Several phase I trials are under way to evaluate phenylbutyrate for leukemias, including acute myelogenous leukemia and acute promyelocytic leukemia, and for refractory solid tumors. The optimal dose and place in therapy are yet to be defined. Phase II studies are required.

Oral: Doses up to 36 g/d have been applied with minimal toxicity.
Intravenous: 410 mg/kg/d continually infused for 5 days were recommended as a phase II dose in a clinical study.[3,7]

LITERATURE SUMMARY AND CRITIQUE

The available literature consists only of phase I studies, which suggest relative safety of both parenterally and orally administered sodium phenylbutyrate in cancer patients.

Gilbert J, et al. A phase I dose escalation and bioavailability study of oral sodium phenylbutyrate in patients with refractory solid tumor malignancies. Clin Cancer Res 2001;7:2292–2300.
A phase I dose-escalation study in 28 patients with refractory solid tumors receiving 9 to 45 g/d oral sodium phenylbutyrate. The most common toxicities were grade 1 to 2 dyspepsia and fatigue, whereas dose-limiting toxicities of nausea/vomiting and hypocalcemia were seen at 36 g/d. No partial or complete remission was reported in patients receiving phenylbutyrate, but 7 of 23 evaluable patients had stable disease for over 6 months while using the drug. The authors recommend 27 g/d as a phase II dose.

Carducci MA, et al. A phase I clinical and pharmacological evaluation of sodium phenylbutyrate on an 120-h infusion schedule. Clin Cancer Res 2001;7:3047–55.
A phase I and pharmacokinetic study of parenteral phenylbutyrate in 24 patients with refractory solid tumors. Patients were treated with a 120-hour infusion every 21 days, escalated from 150 to 515 mg/kg/d. Dose-limiting toxicity was neurocortical and was experienced by 2 patients at 515 and 345 mg/kg/d. Fatigue and nausea were the most common side effects. Two patients remained on therapy with clinically stable disease for 168 days, and three other patients remained on therapy for a total of six cycles, but no complete responses were reported. The recommended parenteral dose is 410 mg/kg/d.

REFERENCES

1. Buphenyl®, sodium phenylbutyrate [package insert]. Hunt Valley (MD): Ucyclyd Pharma; 1996.
2. Witzig TE, et al. Induction of apoptosis in malignant B cells by phenylbutyrate or phenylacetate in combination with chemotherapeutic agents. Clin Cancer Res 2000;6:681–92.
3. Gilbert J, et al. A phase I dose escalation and bioavailability study of oral sodium phenylbutyrate in patients with refractory solid tumor malignancies. Clin Cancer Res 2001;2292–300.
4. DiGiuseppe JA, et al. Phenylbutyrate-induced G1 arrest and apoptosis in myeloid leukemia cells: structure function analysis. Leukemia 1999;13:1243–53.
5. Pili R, et al. Combination of phenylbutyrate and 12-*cis* retinoic acid inhibits prostate tumor growth and angiogenesis. Cancer Res 2001;61:1477–85.
6. Feinman R, Clarke KO, Harrison LE. Phenylbutyrate-induced apoptosis is associated with inactivation of NF-κB in HT-29 colon cancer cells. Cancer Chemother Pharmacol 2002; 49:27–34.
7. Carducci MA, et al. A phase I clinical and pharmacological evaluation of sodium phenylbutyrate on an 120-h infusion schedule. Clin Cancer Res 2001;7:3047–55.

Pokeweed

COMMON NAMES
Poke root, pocan, red plant,
Phytolacca decandra

SCIENTIFIC NAME
Phytolacca americana

KEY WORD
Poke root

A. DONATO

CLINICAL SUMMARY
Derived from various parts of the plant, including the root, leaf, and berry. Patients use this herb to treat rheumatoid arthritis, infections, and cancer (as part of the Hoxsey herbal tonic). Pokeweed causes significant toxicity following oral or topical administration. Reported adverse effects include nausea, diarrhea, protracted vomiting, hypotension, convulsions, dyspnea, and death. Owing to the toxic nature of this herb, it should not be consumed.

CONSTITUENTS
Alkaloids: betanidine, betanine, phytolaccine, prebetanine; lectins: pokeweed mitogen glycoproteins (Pa^1–Pa^5); saponins: phytolaccosides (A1, D$_2$, and O), jaligonic acid, phytolaccagenic acid, aesculentic acid; other: isoamericanin A, pokeweed antiviral protein (PAP), α-spinasterol, histamine, γ-aminobutyric acid (GABA).[1,2]

WARNINGS
Significant toxicity results from oral or topical administration of pokeweed. The US Herb Trade Association recommends that pokeweed not be sold.

MECHANISM OF ACTION

Pokeweed mitogens and glycosidic saponins are known toxins that possess mitogenic and irritant properties. PAP shows broad antiviral activity in vitro and inhibits replication of herpes simplex, influenza, and poliovirus, possibly via inactivation of eukaryotic ribosomes. Saponin extracts from pokeweed, chiefly phytolaccagenin, exhibit anti-inflammatory activity as demonstrated by carrageenan rat paw edema tests. Pokeweed's histamine and GABA content may have hypotensive effects. Pokeweed Anti Fungal Peptide-s (PAFP-s), an antifungal peptide extract from pokeweed, displays fungistatic effects against a variety of species in vitro.[1,3,4]

USAGE

Cancer treatment, fungal infections, inducement of vomiting, infections, mastitis, rheumatoid arthritis, tonsillitis.

ADVERSE REACTIONS

Reported: Nausea, vomiting, stomach cramps, diarrhea, weakness, hematemesis, hypotension, tachycardia.
Toxicity: Protracted vomiting, bloody diarrhea, dyspnea, muscle spasms, convulsions, death.

DOSAGE

Owing to toxicity, no dosage should be recommended.

LITERATURE SUMMARY AND CRITIQUE

No study supports the use of pokeweed for any proposed claim.

REFERENCES

1. Newall C, et al. Herbal medicines: a guide for health-care professionals. 1st ed. London: Pharmaceutical Press; 1996.
2. Takahashi H, et al. Triterpene glycosides from the cultures of *Phytolacca americana*. Chem Pharm Bull 2001;49:246–8.
3. Irvin JD. Pokeweed antiviral protein. Pharmacol Ther 1983;21:371–87.
4. Shao F, et al. A new antifungal peptide from the seeds of *Phytolacca americana*: characterization, amino acid sequence and cDNA cloning. Biochim Biophys Acta 1999;1430:262–8.

Polydox

COMMON NAMES
LAPd, lipoic acid–palladium complex

CLINICAL SUMMARY
A synthetic product containing lipoic acid–palladium complex and B complex vitamins. Patients use this supplement to treat cancer, human immunodeficiency virus/acquired immune deficiency syndrome (HIV/AIDS), chronic fatigue syndrome, psoriasis, and other degenerative disorders. The inventor asserts that Polydox is a nucleotide reductase that repairs damaged DNA and is selectively cytotoxic to cancer cells. No in vitro, animal, or human data in the literature support the manufacturer's claims regarding product efficacy or safety.

CONSTITUENTS
Lipoic acid complexed with palladium; vitamins: B_{12}, B complex.[1]

MECHANISM OF ACTION
The inventor claims that Polydox is a metallovitamin with antioxidant activity capable of repairing damaged genes. Polydox is said to have deoxyribonucleic acid (DNA) reductase and electroactive properties that alter electron flow in cancer cells at the mitochondrial level, resulting in cytotoxicity. The manufacturer also reports benefits for cancer patients, such as increases in energy and appetite, reduction in cancer-related pain, and retardation of the aging process, but no independent scientific data support these claims.[1,2]

USAGE
Asthma, cancer treatment, chronic fatigue syndrome, HIV and AIDS, psoriasis, systemic lupus erythematosus.

PHARMACOKINETICS
The manufacturer claims that Polydox distributes throughout the body to all sites, including adipose tissue and the central nervous system. No formal pharmacokinetics studies have been performed.[1]

ADVERSE REACTIONS
Unknown.

DRUG INTERACTIONS
Unknown.

DOSAGE
Oral: Cancer treatment: The manufacturer suggests 2 teaspoons 4 times a day for 1 week, 2 teaspoons 2 times a day for 12 weeks, and then 1 teaspoon 2 times a day if no sign of the cancer or degenerative disease remains. (The cost is approximately $1,000 per month.) *Cancer prevention:* The manufacturer suggests half to 1 teaspoon each day for prevention and maintenance. (The cost is approximately $300 per month.)[1]

LITERATURE SUMMARY AND CRITIQUE
No human studies, case reports, animal studies, or in vitro data have been published.

REFERENCES
1. Polymva. American Medicine and Research Center Web site. Available at: http://www.polymva.com (accessed Feb 20, 2002).
2. Garnett M. Palladium complexes and methods for using same in the treatment of tumors. Garnett McKeen Laboratory, Inc. US patent 5,679,697. 1997 Oct 21.

Pygeum

COMMON NAME
African plum tree

SCIENTIFIC NAMES
Pygeum africanum, Prunus africana

KEY WORD
Tadenan

CLINICAL SUMMARY
Derived from the bark of the tree. Traditionally used to manage benign prostatic hypertrophy (BPH). Several chemicals contribute to the action of this product. Clinical studies have suggested improvement in urinary symptoms associated with BPH with adverse events comparable to those of placebo, such as headache and gastrointestinal symptoms. Oral preparations should be standardized to 14% triterpenes and 0.5% n-docosanol. Doses range between 50 and 200 mg daily. Clinical improvement may take several weeks to occur.

CONSTITUENTS
Triterpenes (14%): oleanolic, crataegolic, and ursolic acids; ferulic acid; phytosterols: β-sitosterol, β-sitosterone, campesterol; tannins.[1]

MECHANISM OF ACTION
The phytosterols compete with androgen precursors and also inhibit prostaglandin biosynthesis, thereby reducing inflammation. The triterpenes exhibit anti-inflammatory activity in vitro. The ferulic acid esters reduce the level of cholesterol in the prostate,

thereby limiting androgen synthesis. The phytosterols and the triterpenes appear to work synergistically to improve the symptoms of BPH.[2]

USAGE
BPH, inflammation, sexual performance.

ADVERSE REACTIONS
Reported: Nausea and gastrointestinal upset.

DRUG INTERACTIONS
None reported.

DOSAGE
Oral: 100 to 200 mg (standardized extract 14% triterpenes, 0.5% n-docosanol) per day in 6- to 8-week cycles for functional symptoms of BPH. Some researchers suggest 50 mg twice a day to start.

LITERATURE SUMMARY AND CRITIQUE
Ishani A, et al. *Pygeum africanum* for the treatment of patients with benign prostatic hyperplasia: a systematic review and quantitative meta-analysis. Am J Med 2000;109: 654–64.
A total of 18 randomized, controlled trials involving 1,562 men were analyzed. Seventeen of the studies were double blind. The mean study duration was 64 days. Compared with placebo in 6 studies, *P. africanum* provided a moderately large improvement in the combined outcome of urologic symptoms and flow measures. Nocturia was reduced by 19% and residual urine volume by 24%; peak urine flow increased by 23%. Adverse effects owing to *P. africanum* were similar to those of placebo.

Brackman F, et al. Comparison of once and twice daily dosage forms of *Pygeum africanum* extract in patients with benign prostatic hyperplasia: a randomized, double-blind study, with long-term open label extension. Urology 1999;54:473–8.
In a randomized, double-blind, placebo-controlled study of 209 men with BPH, once- and twice-daily dosages of *Pygeum* were evaluated. The results showed that both dosages significantly decreased International Prostate Symptom Scores, nocturia, and improved quality of life by approximately 44%, 12%, and 36%, respectively. No differences in clinical efficacy were observed.

Barlet A, et al. Efficacy of *Pygeum africanum* extract in the medical therapy of urination disorders due to benign prostatic hyperplasia: evaluation of objective and subjective parameters. A placebo-controlled double-blind multicenter study. Wien Klin Wochenschr 1990;102:667–73.

A multicenter, randomized, double-blind, placebo-controlled study of 263 patients with baseline uroflow of 13.5 to 14 cc/s. Results showed that *Pygeum* 50 mg twice a day for 60 days produced a significant improvement in both quantitative and qualitative parameters. Micturition improved in 66% of patients taking *Pygeum* and in 31% of the placebo group.

REFERENCES

1. Foster S, et al. Tyler's honest herbal: a sensible guide to the use of herbs and related remedies. New York: Haworth Herbal Press; 1999.
2. Schulz V, et al. Rational phytotherapy: a physician's guide to the use of herbs and related remedies. 3rd ed. Berlin: Springer; 1998.
3. Fagelman E, Lowe FC. Herbal medications in the treatment of benign prostatic hyperplasia (BPH). Urol Clin North Am 2002;29:23–9.

Quercetin

COMMON NAME
Polyphenolic flavonoid

SCIENTIFIC NAME
3,3',4',5,7-Pentapentahydroxyflavone

CLINICAL SUMMARY
Quercetin is a flavonol that constitutes the major bioflavonoid sources in the human diet. The glycoside form is readily available in dietary plants such as teas, onions, apples, and buckwheat. Quercetin is thought to have antioxidant, anti-inflammatory, and antiallergy properties. In vitro data suggest that quercetin may have anticancer effects, but more clinical study is needed to explore this potential. No significant adverse events have been reported for this product.

MECHANISM OF ACTION
Quercetin constitutes the major bioflavonoid in the human diet. Its antioxidant activity is attributable to the reactivity of its phenolic group, which reacts with free radicals to form the more stable phenoxy radicals. Quercetin is thought to have anti-inflammatory and antiallergy properties. The proposed mechanism of action is inhibition of lipoxygenase and cyclooxygenase, resulting in reduced production of inflammatory mediators (eg, leukotrienes and histamine). Quercetin appears to inhibit cyclooxygenase to a greater degree than lipoxygenase. It also has been shown to have membrane-stabilizing capabilities and to inhibit aldose reductase and low-density lipoprotein oxidation. Significant antiviral activity has been shown in vitro and in vivo. Proposed anticancer mechanisms of action include down-regulation of mutant p53 proteins, G_1 phase arrest, tyrosine kinase inhibition, estrogen receptor binding, inhibition of heat shock proteins, and ras protein expression inhibition. Presently, considerable in vitro data support the concept of quercetin as an anticancer compound. However, clinical studies that support these uses are few, and the results are mixed.[1–7]

USAGE
Allergies, cancer prevention, cancer treatment, cardiovascular disease, inflammation.

PHARMACOKINETICS

Absorption: Following oral administration, quercetin glycosides are absorbed from the gut. These glycosides may then undergo hydrolysis in the enterocyte via β-glucosidases before draining into the portal vein. Absorption rate from dietary sources is influenced by the position and chemical nature of the glycoside in combination with the various compounds in the food matrix.

Distribution: Quercetin is found predominantly in plasma in the form of its conjugates (eg, quercetin glucuronides and/or sulfates) and small amounts of unconjugated quercetin aglycone. Maximum plasma concentrations are achieved within the first 2 hours of administration. This suggests that the absorption site is in the upper gut compartment and may rule out intestinal bacteria degradation.

Excretion: Previous pharmacokinetic studies using intravenous administration suggest that quercetin is quickly eliminated in humans, with an approximate elimination half-life of less than 2 hours. Several studies report that quercetin is present in urine as conjugates of glucuronic acid and sulfate groups.[1,2,8]

ADVERSE REACTIONS

No adverse effects have been reported with single oral doses up to 4 g.

DRUG INTERACTIONS

Papain and Bromelain: May assist the absorption of quercetin in the intestine.

Quinolone Antibiotic: Quercetin may compete for deoxyribonucleic acid (DNA) gyrase binding sites on bacteria.[3,9]

DOSAGE

No Recommended Dietary Allowances have been set for quercetin. Study doses range from 1.4 to 4,000 mg. The commonly prescribed oral dose is 500 mg twice daily.[3,6,7]

LITERATURE SUMMARY AND CRITIQUE

Shoskes D, et al. Quercetin in men with category III chronic prostatitis: a preliminary prospective, double-blind, placebo-controlled trial. Urology 1999;54:960–3.
Thirty men with chronic pelvic pain syndrome received either placebo or 500 mg of quercetin orally twice a day for 1 month. Sixty-seven percent of the patients taking quercetin compared with 20% of patients from the placebo group had an at least 25% improvement of symptoms. A follow-up unblinded, open-label study suggested that bromelain and papain can enhance the absorption of quercetin.

Beatty E, et al. Effect of dietary quercetin on oxidative DNA damage in healthy human subjects. Br J Nutr 2000;84:919–25.
Thirty-six subjects participated in this randomized crossover study. They were given either a low-flavonol or a high-flavonol diet for 14 days. The study was designed to detect

a change of 20% in DNA damage products ($p < .05$). Although the plasma quercetin levels were higher in the high-flavonol group, no significant difference in oxidative damage in leukocytes was found between groups.

REFERENCES

1. Lamson DW, Brignall MS. Antioxidant and cancer III: quercetin. Altern Med Rev 2000;5:196–208.
2. Graefe EU, et al. Pharmacokinetics and bioavailability of the flavonol quercetin in humans. Int J Clin Pharm Ther 1999;37:219–33.
3. Shoskes D, et al. Quercetin in men with category III chronic prostatitis: a preliminary prospective, double-blind, placebo-controlled trial. Urology 1999;54:960–3.
4. Janssen K, et al. Effects of the flavonoids quercetin and apigenin on hemostasis in healthy volunteers: results from an in vitro and dietary supplement study. Am J Clin Nutr 1998;67:255–62.
5. Chopra M, et al. Nonalcoholic red wine extract and quercetin inhibit LDL oxidation without affecting plasma antioxidant vitamin and carotenoid concentrations. Clin Chem 2000;46: 1162–70.
6. Beatty ER, et al. Effect of dietary quercetin on oxidative DNA damage in healthy human subjects. Br J Nutr 2000;84:919–25.
7. Ferry DR, et al. Phase I clinical trial of the flavonoid quercetin: pharmacokinetics and evidence for in vivo tyrosine kinase inhibition. Clin Cancer Res 1996;2:659–68.
8. Erlund I, et al. Pharmacokinetics of quercetin aglycone and rutin in healthy volunteers. Eur J Clin Pharmacol 2000;56:545–53.
9. Herr SM. Herb-drug interaction handbook. 2nd ed. Nassau (NY): Chuch Street Books; 2002.

Red Clover

COMMON NAMES
Trifolium pratense, cow clover, wild clover, purple clover

SCIENTIFIC NAME
Trifolium pratense

KEY WORDS
Trifolium pratense, Promensil

A. DONATO

CLINICAL SUMMARY
Derived from the aerial parts of the plant including the flowering top. Red clover contains several isoflavones, including biochanin, daidzein, formononetin, and genistein. Anecdotal data from Novogen, the manufacturer of Promensil red clover, have found the product effective in managing menopausal symptoms. Red clover may have estrogenic activity and should therefore be avoided or used cautiously by patients with hormone-sensitive disease. No significant adverse events have been reported. Owing to coumarin content, the potential to enhance anticoagulant effects exists.

CONSTITUENTS
Isoflavones: biochanin, daidzein, formononetin, genistein; coumarins: coumarin, medicagol; other constituents: various flavonoids, saponins, salicylic acid, coumaric acid, minerals, carbohydrates, and fats.[1]

MECHANISM OF ACTION
The isoflavones from red clover are demonstrated to have both cardioprotective and estrogenic effects. Arterial compliance was significantly improved in a study of 17 menopausal women. Red clover extract stimulates cell proliferation of estrogen

receptor–positive breast cancer cells in vitro and acts as an estrogen agonist. Its effect on the endometrium is inconclusive.[2–4]

USAGE

Chest congestion, menopausal symptoms, spasms.

PHARMACOKINETICS

All four isoflavones are metabolized by the liver. Liver demethylation converts biochanin to genistein and formononetin to daidzein. Peak plasma levels of the isoflavones occur within 4 to 6 hours. Reported serum half-lives of isoflavones range from 9 to 16 hours. Isoflavones are primarily metabolized either in the gut or by the liver to active metabolites.[5]

ADVERSE REACTIONS

None reported.

DRUG INTERACTIONS

Anticoagulants/Antiplatelets: Red clover may potentiate effects owing to its coumarin component.

CONTRAINDICATIONS

Red clover may have estrogenic activity and should be avoided or used cautiously by patients with hormone-sensitive disease.

DOSAGE

Oral: Dosages vary based on the manufacturer, usually one tablet or capsule once daily. *Promensil:* 500 mg tablet, administered once daily, contains 200 to 230 mg dried red clover extract with 40 mg total isoflavones.

LITERATURE SUMMARY AND CRITIQUE

There is anecdotal and insufficient reliable information on the effectiveness of red clover. Larger controlled trials are needed to prove its efficacy.

REFERENCES

1. Newall C, et al. Herbal medicines: a guide for health-care professionals. London: Pharmaceutical Press; 1996.
2. Nestel PJ, et al. Isoflavones from red clover improves systemic arterial compliance but not plasma lipids in menopausal women. J Clin Endocrinol Metab 1999;84:895.

3. Le Bail JC, et al. Effects of phytoestrogens on aromatase, 3β and 17β-hydroxysteroid dehydro-genase activities and human breast cancer cells. Life Sci 2000;66:281.
4. Hale GE, et al. A double-blind randomized study on the effects of red clover isoflavones on the endometrium. Menopause 2001;8:338–46.
5. Promensil [scientific brochure]. North Ryde (Australia): Novogen; 1999.

Reishi Mushroom

COMMON NAMES
Ling Zhi, Ling Chi, Lin Zi,
mushroom of immortality

SCIENTIFIC NAME
Ganoderma lucidum

KEY WORD
Ganoderma lucidum

CLINICAL SUMMARY

Derived from the cap and stem of the mushroom. The active constituents are thought to include both β-glucan polysaccharides and triterpenes. It is used primarily as an immune stimulant by patients with human immunodeficiency virus (HIV) or cancer. Reported adverse events include dry nose and throat, nausea, vomiting, and other gastrointestinal symptoms. No clinical trials have been performed evaluating its efficacy for proposed claims. Supplements should be standardized to contain 10 to 12.5% polysaccharides and 4% triterpenes per dose.

CONSTITUENTS

Polysaccharide: β-D-glucan; sterol: ergosterol; fungal lysozyme; proteinase; triterpenes: ganoderic acids; lipids; alkaloids; glucosides; coumarins; volatile oil; other constituents: riboflavin, ascorbic acid, amino acids.[1]

MECHANISM OF ACTION

The triterpenes and polysaccharides seem to have the most biologic activity. A number of its polysaccharides have demonstrated antitumor and immunostimulating activities. For instance, β-D-glucan, also known as G-I, shows potent antitumor activity. It has demonstrated the ability to stimulate macrophages to produce increased levels of tumor necrosis factor and interleukin-10. The steroids are reported to act as hormone precursors, and the triterpenes are reported to have adaptogenic and antihypertensive, as well as antiallergic, effects. The adenosine in reishi is thought to be responsible for the inhibition of platelet aggregation.[2-5]

USAGE

Fatigue, high cholesterol, HIV and acquired immune deficiency syndrome (AIDS), hypertension, immunostimulation, inflammation, strength and stamina, viral infections.

ADVERSE REACTIONS

Reported: Dry throat and nose, gastrointestinal upset, itchiness, nausea, vomiting.

DRUG INTERACTIONS

Anticoagulant/Antiplatelets: Reishi may increase the risk of bleeding.
Antihypertensives: Reishi may cause additive hypotensive effects.

LABORATORY INTERACTIONS

May prolong international normalized ratio, prothrombin time, and activated partial thromboplastin time.

DOSAGE

Oral: 150 to 300 mg three or four times a day, standardized to contain 10 to 12.5% polysaccharides and 4% triterpenes per dose.

LITERATURE SUMMARY AND CRITIQUE

In animal studies, reishi has demonstrated immunomodulatory, antitumor, antihypertensive, antihistamine, and antineoplastic activity. However, no human studies have been conducted.[6,7]

REFERENCES

1. Huang K. The pharmacology of Chinese herbs. 2nd ed. New York: CRC Press; 1999.
2. Hobbs C. Medicinal mushrooms. 3rd ed. Loveland (CO): Interweave Press; 1996.
3. Mao T, et al. Two mushrooms, *Grifola frondosa* and *Ganoderma lucidum*, can stimulate cytokine gene expression and proliferation in human T lymphocytes. Int J Immunother 1999;15:13–22.
4. Shiao MS, et al. Natural products and biological activities of *Ganoderma lucidum*. Am Chem Soc 1994;342–54.
5. Hsu MJ, Lee SS, Lin WW. Polysaccharide purified for *Ganoderma lucidum* inhibits spontaneous and Fas-mediated apoptosis in human neutrophils through activation of the phosphatidyl-inositol 3 kinase/Akt signaling pathway. J Leukoc Biol 2002;72:207–16.

6. van der Hem LG, et al. Ling Zhi-8: studies of a new immunomodulating agent. Transplantation 1995;60:438–43.
7. Furusawa E, et al. Antitumor activity of *Ganoderma lucidum*, on intraperitoneally implant Lewis lung carcinoma in synergistic mice. Phytother Res 1992;6:300–4.

Rhubarb

COMMON NAMES
Turkish rhubarb, turkey rhubarb, rhubarb, Chinese rhubarb, tai-huang, da-huang

SCIENTIFIC NAMES
Rheum palmatum, Rheum officinale

KEY WORDS
Rheum officinale, turkey rhubarb, da-huang

A.DONATO

CLINICAL SUMMARY
Derived from the root of the plant. Rhubarb has been used for a variety of conditions, including cancer, immunosuppression, constipation, diarrhea, gastrointestinal ulcers, and chronic renal failure. The anthraquinone and tannins are thought to be responsible for the laxative and constipating effects, respectively. Limited human clinical data are available for any claims made. Animal data show antitumor effects in mice, but this has not been studied in humans. Adverse effects are primarily gastrointestinal in nature. Chronic consumption can cause hypokalemia owing to diarrhea, possible renal and hepatic damage from oxalates, theoretical hypokalemia when combined with diuretics, and altered response to digoxin. Rhubarb should be used only under medical supervision.

CONSTITUENTS
Anthraquinones: rhein, physcion, aloe-emodin, emodin, chrysophenol, sennosides A to F; tannins: rheum tannic acid, gallic acid, glucogallin, catechin, epicatechin; others: calcium oxalate, lindeyin, fatty acids, rutin, starch, trace volatile oils.[1-3]

WARNINGS

Stimulant laxative products such as rhubarb should not be used for prolonged periods (ie, greater than 7 days) without medical supervision.[3-5]

MECHANISM OF ACTION

When used in very small doses, the tannin content has a constipating effect. At increased doses, however, the hydrolyzed metabolites of emodin and sennidin cause stimulation of the gastrointestinal tract and produce a laxative effect. In vitro tests show suppression of tumor necrosis factor, interleukin (IL)-1, and IL-6 production. Reductions in blood pressure and cholesterol have been seen but are attributable to unknown mechanisms. Anthraquinone extracts have been shown to induce tumor necrosis in mice (sarcoma 37, mammary, and Ehrlich), although this has not been demonstrated in humans. Lindeyin, a phenolic gallylglucoside, exhibits analgesic and anti-inflammatory activity in animal models. Catechin, epicatechin, procyanidins, and gallylglucose inhibit hyaluronidase in vitro.[2,4,6,7]

USAGE

Cancer treatment, constipation, fever, hypertension, immunosuppression, inflammation, microbial infection, peptic ulcers.

ADVERSE REACTIONS

Reported: Abdominal cramps, nausea, vomiting, diarrhea leading to possible hypokalemia, anaphylaxis, renal and hepatic damage.[3]

DRUG INTERACTIONS

Chronic Use of Rhubarb: Diuretics: Potassium loss owing to stimulant laxative effect can increase the potential risk for hypokalemia. *Digoxin:* Potassium loss owing to stimulant laxative effect can increase the potential risk for hypokalemia.[5]

LABORATORY INTERACTIONS

Anthraquinones can cause discoloration of the urine interfering with urinalysis.

CONTRAINDICATIONS

Patients with arthritis, kidney or hepatic dysfunction, a history of kidney stones, inflammatory bowel disease, or intestinal obstruction should not take this herb. Rhubarb may cause uterine stimulation and therefore should not be consumed by women who are pregnant.

DOSAGE
Oral: No standard dosage exists.

LITERATURE SUMMARY AND CRITIQUE
Zhang JH, Li LS, Zhang M. Clinical effects of rheum and captopril on preventing progression of chronic renal failure. Chin Med J 1990;103:788–93.

A prospective evaluation of 30 patients receiving either rheum (rhubarb) ($n = 11$), rheum and captopril ($n = 9$), or captopril alone ($n = 10$) compared with historical controls ($n = 12$). Patients receiving rheum were started on 1 g/d and titrated up to 6 to 9 g/d as tolerated; no information describing final doses achieved was provided. Anecdotal quality of life information stated that uremic symptoms disappeared, and patients had a more active lifestyle regardless of intervention. Rheum with or without captopril appeared to slow the progression of disease compared with controls over a 10-month period. Two-thirds of patients receiving rheum reported diarrhea, but no other adverse reactions were noted. Additional randomized studies are needed to confirm the results found in this study.

REFERENCES
1. Huang KC. The pharmacology of Chinese herbs. 2nd ed. New York: CRC Press; 1999.
2. Tamayo C, et al. The chemistry and biological activity of herbs use in Flor-essence herbal tonic and Essiac. Phytother Res 2000;14:1–14.
3. Newall CA, et al. Herbal medicines: a guide for health-care professionals. London: Pharmaceutical Press; 1996.
4. Blumenthal M, et al. The complete German Commission E monographs: therapeutic guide to herbal medicines. Austin (TX): American Botanical Council; 1998.
5. Brinker F. Herb contraindications and drug interactions. 3rd ed. Sandy (OR): Eclectic Medical Publishing; 2001.
6. Peigen X, Liyi II, Liwei W. Ethnopharmacologic study of chinese rhubarb. J Ethnopharmacol 1984;10:275–93.
7. Mantani N, et al. Rhubarb use in patients treated with Kampo medicine—a risk for gastric cancer? Yakugaku Zasshi 2002;122:403–5.

SAM-e

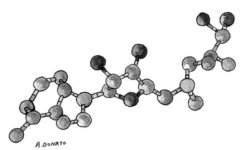

A.DONATO

COMMON NAMES
SAM-e, S-adenosyl-L-methionine

SCIENTIFIC NAME
S-Adenosylmethionine

KEY WORD
S-Adenosylmethionine

CLINICAL SUMMARY

An endogenously produced chemical in the human body, SAM-e is produced from adenosine triphosphate and methionine. In the United States, oral supplementation is used primarily to treat depression and arthritis, although efficacy studies produce conflicting data. Because it is poorly absorbed, enteric-coated tablets are preferred. Outside the United States, parenteral formulations are used to treat fibromyalgia, osteoarthritis, and tendonitis, as well as depression. Minimal adverse effects, such as nausea and diarrhea, are reported following initiation of oral therapy. Dosage should be titrated up over at least 1 to 2 weeks. Patients who are diagnosed with bipolar disorder should not take this supplement. There may be a risk of serotonin syndrome when administered with prescription antidepressants (eg, selective serotonin reuptake inhibitors [SSRIs], monoamine oxidase inhibitors [MAOIs], or tricyclics).

CONSTITUENTS

S-Adenosylmethionine; sulfur-containing compound to stabilize molecule: tosylate, disulfate tosylate, disulfate ditosylate, or 1,4-butanedisulfonate.[1]

MECHANISM OF ACTION

SAM-e is endogenously produced from adenosine triphosphate and the amino acid methionine. It is a major, ubiquitous methyl donor to a wide variety of molecules, including catecholamines and other biogenic amines, fatty acids, neurotransmitters, nucleic acids, polysaccharides, porphyrins, proteins, and membrane phospholipids. Homocysteine is formed through the transsulfuration pathway and is catabolized to cysteine and indirectly to glutathione. The mechanism by which SAM-e treats depression is unknown. However, some researchers believe that it increases the synthesis of neurotransmitters such as serotonin, norepinephrine, and dopamine, thus increasing the responsiveness of neurotransmitter receptors and increasing the fluidity of cell membranes through the production of phospholipids.[2–4]

USAGE

Acquired immune deficiency syndrome (AIDS)-related myelopathy, Alzheimer's disease, bursitis, cirrhosis, depression, muscle pain, osteoarthritis.

PHARMACOKINETICS

Following oral administration of enteric-coated tablets, peak plasma concentrations were obtained within 3 to 6 hours. There is extensive first-pass hepatic metabolism, and the elimination half-life has been reported to be 1.7 hours. Volume of distribution has been calculated to be 0.4 L/kg, and there is no significant protein binding. S-Adenosylmethionine crosses the blood-brain barrier as well as the placenta. Sixteen percent of a dose is excreted in the urine in 48 hours, and 24% is excreted in feces in 72 hours.[3–5]

ADVERSE REACTIONS

Reported: Headache, mild gastrointestinal upset, flatulence, nausea, vomiting. Patients with bipolar disorder may develop a manic phase.[6]

DRUG INTERACTIONS

SSRIs: SAM-e may increase the risk of serotonin syndrome when administered concomitantly.

MAOIs: SAM-e may increase the risk of serotonin syndrome when administered concomitantly.

Tricyclics: SAM-e may increase the risk of serotonin syndrome when administered concomitantly.

Clomipramine: A case report of serotonin syndrome developing in a woman after concomitant clomipramine and intramuscular SAM-e administration.[7]

DOSAGE

Oral: Because of reduced bioavailability, enteric formulations are preferred. To reduce possible gastrointestinal distress, SAM-e should be started at an initial dose of 200 mg twice a day and then titrated to a target dose over 1 to 2 weeks. *Osteoarthritis:* 400 to 1,600 mg/d. *Depression:* Doses up to 1,600 mg/d may be necessary to treat depression, but optimal dosage data are lacking.

LITERATURE SUMMARY AND CRITIQUE

Almost all SAM-e clinical findings have used the parenteral formulation. Oral studies were typically open studies, and double-blind studies were of a small population. SAM-e's absorption from the gastrointestinal tract is questionable, so it is not valid to compare parenteral results with oral results. The parenteral formulation has generally been shown to be more effective. Oral studies of SAM-e for depression are controversial, small, and flawed. Further research is needed to determine if oral SAM-e is an effective treatment for depression.[8–13]

Caruso I, et al. Italian double blind multicenter study comparing S-adenosylmethionine, naproxen and placebo in the treatment of degenerative joint disease. Am J Med 1987;83:66–71.
A total of 734 patients were enrolled to receive 1,200 mg oral SAM-e, 750 mg/d of naproxen, or placebo. Results showed equal efficacy in the SAM-e and naproxen groups. Both drugs were more effective than placebo, although SAM-e was tolerated better than naproxen. There was no difference between SAM-e and placebo in the number of side effects.

Maccagno A. Double-blind controlled clinical trial of oral S-adenosylmethionine versus piroxicam in knee osteoarthritis. Am J Med 1987;83:72–7.
This double-blind study compared 1,200 mg/d of SAM-e to 20 mg of piroxicam. A total of 45 patients were followed for 84 days. The results showed similar efficacy and tolerability between the two treatments. The only significant difference was that the SAM-e patients maintained their improvement longer after treatment was stopped.

REFERENCES

1. Osteoarthritis: the clinical picture, pathogenesis, and management with studies on a new therapeutic agent, S-adenosylmethionine. Proceedings of a symposium. Am J Med 1987;83:1–110.
2. Baldessarini RJ. Neuropharmacology of S-adenosyl-L-methionine. Am J Med 1987;83:60–5.
3. Stramentinoli G. Pharmacologic aspects of S-adenosylmethionine. Pharmacokinetics and pharmacodynamics. Am J Med 1987;83:35–42.
4. Bell KM, et al. S-adenosylmethionine blood levels in major depression: changes with drug treatment. Acta Neurol Scand Suppl 1994;154:15–8.
5. Osman E, Owen JS, Burroughs AK. S-Adenosyl-L-methionine—a new therapeutic agent in liver disease? Aliment Pharmacol Ther 1993;7:21–8.
6. Friedel HA, Goa KL, Benfield P. S-adenosyl-L-methionine. A review of its pharmacological properties and therapeutic potential in liver dysfunction and affective disorders in relation to its physiological role in cell metabolism. Drugs 1989;38:389–416.

7. Iruela LM, et al. Toxic interaction of S-adenosylmethionine and clomipramine. Am J Psychiatry 1993;150:522.
8. di Padova C. S-Adenosylmethionine in the treatment of osteoarthritis. Review of the clinical studies. Am J Med 1987;83:95–103.
9. Reynolds EH, Carney MW, Toone BK. Methylation and mood. Lancet 1984;ii:196–8.
10. Bradley JD, et al. A randomized, double blind, placebo controlled trial of intravenous loading with S-adenosylmethionine (SAM) followed by oral SAM therapy in patients with knee osteoarthritis. J Rheumatol 1994;21:905–11.
11. Bottiglieri T, Hyland K, Reynolds EH. The clinical potential of ademetionine (S-adenosylmethionine) in neurological disorders. Drugs 1994;2:137–52.
12. Volkmann H, et al. Double-blind, placebo-controlled cross-over study of intravenous S-adenosyl-L-methionine in patients with fibromyalgia. Scand J Rheumatol 1997;26:206–11.
13. Cohen BM, Satlin A, Zubenko GS. S-Adenosyl-L-methionine in the treatment of Alzeheimer's disease. J Clin Psychopharmacol 1988;8:43–7.

Sassafras

COMMON NAMES
Ague tree, saxifrax, cinnamonwood, saloop, smelling-stick

SCIENTIFIC NAME
Sassafras albidum

CLINICAL SUMMARY
Derived primarily from the roots of the tree. No clinical data support the use of sassafras, which contains safrole, a volatile oil found to be carcinogenic in animal models. Diaphoresis, hot flashes, and sedation have been reported following administration of small doses. Excessive doses can cause hallucinations, hypertension, and tachycardia.

CONSTITUENTS
Volatile oils: safrole, myristicin, L-hydroxysafrole; alkaloids: boldine, cinnamolaurine; other constituents: sitosterol, tannins, lignans.[1]

WARNINGS
Sassafras, containing safrole, has caused liver cancer in animal models and is classified as a carcinogenic substance. Risk increases with length of exposure and amount consumed. It is unsafe and ineffective.[2]

MECHANISM OF ACTION

Unknown at this time. Safrole, a volatile oil, is a known carcinogen. L-Hydroxysafrole can cause neurotoxicity and is believed to be carcinogenic as well.[3]

USAGE

Detoxification, health maintenance, inflammation, mucositis, rheumatoid arthritis, sprains, syphilis, urinary tract disorders.

ADVERSE REACTIONS

Common: Hot flashes and diaphoresis.
Toxicity: Hallucinations, hypertension, tachycardia, liver cancer, and death.[4,5]

DRUG INTERACTIONS

Barbiturates: Sassafras may have an additive effect.[6]

DOSAGE

No recommended dosage.

LITERATURE SUMMARY AND CRITIQUE

No studies justify the use of this herb.

REFERENCES

1. Newall C, et al. Herbal medicines: a guide for health-care professionals. London: Pharmaceutical Press; 1996.
2. Safrole. Ninth report on carcinogens [online]. Available at: http://ehis.niehs.nih.gov/roc/ninth/rahc/safrole.pdf (accessed Jul 12, 2001).
3. Foster S, et al. Tyler's honest herbal: a sensible guide to the use of herbs and related remedies. New York: Haworth Herbal Press; 1999.
4. De Smet PA, et al. Adverse effects of herbal drugs. Vol. 3. New York: Springer; 1997.
5. Haines JD. Sassafras tea and diaphoresis. Postgrad Med 1991;90:75–6.
6. Brinker F. Herb contraindications and drug interactions. 2nd ed. Sandy (OR): Eclectic Medical Publications; 1998.

Saw Palmetto

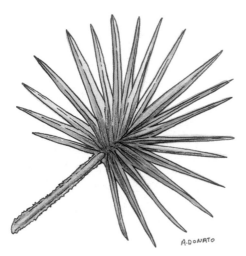

A. DONATO

COMMON NAMES
Saw, *Sabal serulata, Sabalis serulata*, palmetto berry, American dwarf palm tree, cabbage palm

SCIENTIFIC NAME
Serenoa repens

KEY WORD
Serenoa repens

CLINICAL SUMMARY

Derived from the berry of the plant. Saw palmetto is used primarily for symptoms related to prostatic conditions such as benign prostatic hypertrophy (BPH). Several actions are proposed, including antiandrogenic and anti-inflammatory activity. Numerous clinical studies have been conducted. Consistent efficacy of saw palmetto has been suggested for urinary symptoms, such as improvement in flow rate and reduced nocturia. Reported adverse effects are limited to gastrointestinal complaints such as nausea, vomiting, and diarrhea. No known drug interactions exist. Studies suggest that results may not be seen for up to 4 to 6 weeks after initiation. A recent laboratory analysis of six brands of commercially available saw palmetto revealed their actual fatty acid content to vary considerably from the labeled dosage, as has been found for many herbal products previously studied. Three brands contained less than 20% of the stated dosage.

CONSTITUENTS

Fatty acids: capric, caprylic, lauric, *cis*-linoleic, myristic, palmitic, stearic acid; steroids: β-sistosterol, campesterol, cycloartenol, lupeol, lupenone, stigmasterol; aliphatic alcohols; polyprenic compounds: arabinose, flavonoids, galactose, glucose, uronic acid; anthranilic acid; carotenes; lipase; tannins.[1]

WARNINGS

A recent laboratory evaluation of six commercially available brands of saw palmetto revealed actual fatty acid content to vary considerably from the labeled dosage, as has been found for many herbal products previously studied, from 3 to +240%. Three brands contained less than 20% of the stated amount. The authors recommend that patients who have not responded to over-the-counter saw palmetto try a second brand.[2]

MECHANISM OF ACTION

The mechanism of action is antiandrogenic. Studies have shown that a liposterolic extract of the berries reduced the uptake by tissue specimens of both testosterone and dihydrotestosterone (DHT) by more than 40%. This mechanism is confirmed by the observation that saw palmetto extract does not induce changes in the level of testosterone or other hormones in the plasma itself. Other studies have noted that it reduces the conversion of less active testosterone to the more active DHT by inhibiting the enzyme steroid 5-α-reductase. In addition to their antiandrogenic properties, anti-inflammatory and antiedematous activity have been demonstrated in the berries. This apparently results from inhibition of the cyclooxygenase and 5-lipoxygenase pathways, thereby preventing the biosynthesis of inflammation-producing prostaglandins and leukotrienes.[3,4]

USAGE

BPH, inflammation, promotion of urination, prostate cancer.

PHARMACOKINETICS

Analysis of saw palmetto components, including lauric acid, oleic acid, and β-sitosterol, in rats revealed wide distribution. Highest concentrations were found in abdominal fat, prostate, and skin, whereas lesser amounts were found in bladder and liver.[5]

ADVERSE REACTIONS

Infrequent: Intraoperative hemorrhage, gastrointestinal complaints, nausea, vomiting, and diarrhea.[6]

DRUG INTERACTIONS

No interactions have been reported.

LABORATORY INTERACTIONS

May prolong bleeding time. No significant change in mean serum prostate-specific antigen was noted.[6,7]

DOSAGE

Oral: BPH: 320 mg orally daily; may be administered in divided daily doses; duration is usually 3 months. A trial of 4 to 6 weeks may be necessary to see results.[8]

LITERATURE SUMMARY AND CRITIQUE

Over 100 open, controlled, and comparative trials have been conducted on saw palmetto.[9,10]

Marks LS, et al. Tissue effects of saw palmetto and finasteride: use of biopsy cores for in situ quantification of prostatic androgens. Urology 2001;57:999–1005.
Baseline androgen values were measured in surgically excised prostatic tissues. For control versus finasteride-treated men, tissue androgen values obtained with needle biopsy specimens were similar both for absolute values and percentage of change to those previously reported. Saw palmetto was found to induce suppression of prostatic DHT levels a modest but significant amount, supporting the hypothesis that inhibition of the enzyme 5-α-reductase is a mechanism of action of this substance.

Boyle P, et al. Meta-analysis of clinical trials of permixon (saw palmetto) in the treatment of symptomatic benign prostatic hyperplasia. Urology 2000;55:533–9.
All published clinical trial data on Permixon (saw palmetto) for the treatment of BPH consist of 11 randomized clinical trials and 2 open-label trials involving 2,859 patients. This meta-analysis of all available published trials revealed a significant improvement in peak flow rate and reduction in nocturia in Permixon patients compared with placebo.

Wilt TJ, et al. Saw palmetto extracts for treatment of benign prostatic hyperplasia: a systematic review. JAMA 1998;280:1604–9.
Studies were identified through MEDLINE (1966–1997). A total of 18 randomized, controlled trials involving 2,939 men met inclusion criteria and were analyzed. Treatment allocation concealment was adequate in 9 studies; 16 were double blind. The mean study duration was 9 weeks. Compared with men receiving placebo, men treated with saw palmetto had decreased urinary tract symptom scores and improvement in self-rating of urinary tract symptoms. Compared with men receiving finasteride, men treated with saw palmetto had similar improvements in urinary tract symptom scores. Adverse effects owing to saw palmetto were mild and infrequent; erectile dysfunction was more frequent with finasteride.

REFERENCES

1. Newall C. Herbal medicines: a guide for health-care professionals. London: Pharmaceutical Press; 1996.
2. Feifer AH, Fleshner NE, Klotz L. Analytical accuracy and reliability of commonly used nutritional supplements in prostate disease. J Urol 2002;168:150–4.
3. Tyler V. Herbs of choice, the therapeutical use of phytomedicinals. Binghamton (NY): Pharmaceutical Press; 1994.
4. Goldmann WH, et al. Saw palmetto berry extract inhibits cell growth and COX-2 expression in prostatic cancer cells. Cell Biol Int 2001;25:1117–24.

5. Chevalier G, et al. Distribution study of radioactivity in rats after oral administration of the lipido/sterolic extract of *Serenoa repens* supplemented with [1-14C]-lauric acid, [1-14C]-oleic acid or [4-14C]-β-sitosterol. Eur J Drug Metab Pharmacokinet 1997;22:73–83.
6. Cheema P, et al. Intraoperative haemorrhage associated with the use of extract of saw palmetto herb: a case report and review of literature. J Intern Med 2001;250:167–9.
7. Gerber G, et al. Saw palmetto (*Serenoa repens*) in men with lower urinary tract symptoms: effects on urodynamic parameters and voiding symptoms. Urology 1998;51:1003–7.
8. Blumenthal M, et al. Herbal medicine expanded Commission E monographs. 1st ed. Austin (TX): American Botanical Council; 2000.
9. Preuss HG, et al. Randomized trial of a combination of natural products (cernitin, saw palmetto, β-sitosterol, vitamin E) on symptoms of benign prostate hyperplasia (BPH). Int Urol Nephrol 2001;33:217–25.
10. Fagelman E, Lowe FC. Herbal medications in the treatment of benign prostatic hyperplasia (BPH). Urol Clin North Am 2002;29:23–9.

Schisandra

COMMON NAMES

Wu Wei Zi, schizandra, five flavor berry, fructus schisandra, gomishi, omicha, Ngu Mie Gee

SCIENTIFIC NAME

Schisandra chinensis

KEY WORD

Wu Wei Zi

CLINICAL SUMMARY

Derived from the fruit of the plant. This herb is used in traditional Chinese medicine for cough, wheezing, diarrhea, and spontaneous sweating. It is also used as an adaptogen. Various lignans are believed to be responsible for the activity of schisandra, but limited research evaluates its mechanism of action. In animal models, schisandra protects the liver against various toxins (eg, menadione), prolongs pentobarbital sleep time, and increases cardiac contractility without affecting blood pressure. No human trials have been performed with this supplement. Although no drug interactions are reported, schisandra may induce cytochrome P-450 and affect other metabolic pathways. No common adverse events are reported. Additional research is necessary to understand the efficacy and to uncover possible interactions associated with this supplement.

CONSTITUENTS

Lignans: schizandrin, γ-schizandrin, schizandrol, deoxyschizandrin; volatile oils; vitamins: A, C, E; others: hydrocarbon derivatives (eg, sesquicarene, β-2-bisabolene, β-chamigrene, α-ylangene), triterpenoid (nigranoic acid).[1-3]

MECHANISM OF ACTION

The mechanism of action is unknown. Schisandra has antioxidant activity. Animal studies suggest that water- and alcohol-based extracts promote myocardial contractility without effects on blood pressure, stimulate the respiratory center, induce uterine smooth muscle contractions, and increase hepatic glutathione levels and the activities of glucose-6-phosphate and glutathione reductase. Protection from hepatotoxicity and improvements in phase I metabolism are documented in rats administered 1 mL/kg carbon tetrachloride 24 hours after exposure to schisandra extract. Schisandra extract appears to increase DT-diaphorase activity within rat hepatocytes, resulting in protection from menadione-induced toxicity. In rats, repeated administration of schisandra extract at 10 mg and 25 mg doses reduces the extent of cycloheximide-induced amnesia. Nigranoic acid, a triterpenoid extract from schisandra plant stems, shows limited activity against human immunodeficiency virus (HIV)-1 reverse transcriptase in vitro at a median inhibition concentration IC50 of 200 µg/mL. Schisandrin B and schisandrol B have variable effects on pentobarbital-induced sleep in mice: 12.5 mg/kg prolongs sleep, whereas 100 mg/kg shortens the sleep interval. Schisandrin C increases pentobarbital sleep period at all doses.[1,3–9]

USAGE

Asthma, cough, diarrhea, indigestion, influenza, liver disease, premenstrual syndrome, strength and stamina, sweating.

PHARMACOKINETICS

No formal pharmacokinetic studies have been performed. Animal data suggest that schisandra increases metabolism via induction of cytochrome P-450 and/or the glutathione reductase pathway.[1]

ADVERSE REACTIONS

Heartburn, central nervous system depression.[2,10]

DRUG INTERACTIONS

No significant drug interactions have been reported, but schisandra may induce cytochrome P-450 and other hepatic metabolic pathways.[1]

LABORATORY INTERACTIONS

Lower aspartate transaminase, alanine transaminase, alkaline phosphate.

DOSAGE

Oral: Various doses and preparations have been used anecdotally. *Nonicteric hepatitis:* 3 g three times a day for 1 month.[1]

LITERATURE SUMMARY AND CRITIQUE

No noteworthy human studies have been conducted.

REFERENCES

1. Huang KC. The pharmacology of Chinese herbs. 2nd ed. New York: CRC Press; 1999.
2. Fetrow CW, et al. Professional's handbook of complementary and alternative medicines. Philadelphia: Springhouse; 1999.
3. Sun HD, et al. Nigranoic acid, a triterpenoid from *Schisandra sphaerandra* that inhibits HIV-1 reverse transcriptase. J Nat Prod 1996;59:525–7.
4. Ko KM, et al. Effect of a lignan-enriched fructus schisandrae extract on hepatic glutathione status in rats: protection against carbon tetrachloride toxicity. Planta Med 1995;61:134–7.
5. Zhu M, et al. Evaluation of the protective effects of *Schisandra chinensis* on phase I drug metabolism using a CCl4 intoxication model. J Ethnopharmacol 1999;67:61–8.
6. Hsieh MT, et al. The ameliorating effect of the water layer of fructus schisandrae on cyclo-heximide-induced amnesia in rats: interaction with drugs acting at neurotransmitter receptors. Pharmacol Res 2001;43:17–22.
7. Ip SP, Yiu HY, Ko KM. Schisandrin B protects against menadione-induced hepatotoxicity by enhancing DT-diaphorase activity. Mol Cell Biochem 2000;208:151–5.
8. Brinker F. Herb contraindications and drug interactions. 3rd ed. Sandy (OR): Eclectic Medical Publications; 2001.
9. Zhu M, et al. Improvement of phase I drug metabolism with *Schisandra chinensis* against CCl$_4$ hepatotoxicity in a rat model. Planta Med 2000;66:521–5.
10. Bensky D, Gamble A. Chinese herbal medicine: materia medica. Rev. ed. Seattle: Eastland Press; 1993.

Selenium

COMMON NAMES

Selenocysteine, selenomethionine, selenate, selenite

A. DONATO

CLINICAL SUMMARY

Selenium is an essential trace element required by the glutathione-peroxidase pathway. It acts as an antioxidant and regulates thyroid hormone action and the reduction of vitamin C. Selenium is used to treat and prevent cancer, to boost the immune system, and for cardiovascular and rheumatic disease. Bioavailability is dependent on organic versus inorganic supplements, ranging from 50 to nearly 100%. A recent analysis of five brands of commercially available selenium found that almost all contained up to 19% less than the labeled dosage. Methylation is the primary route of metabolism, with a majority eliminated via the kidneys. Clinical studies have evaluated the role of selenium in cancer prevention with intriguing results. SELECT (Selenium and Vitamin E Cancer Prevention Trial), conducted by the Southwest Oncology Group, is enrolling 32,400 men to study the effects of supplementation on the risk of prostate cancer; enrolment began in July 2001. Adverse events from selenium are usually gastric in nature, although chronic selenosis can occur with doses greater than 1,000 µg/d. This toxicity is characterized by muscle weakness, fatigue, peripheral neuropathy, skin rash, nail and hair changes, irritability, and possibly hepatic necrosis. Daily recommended intake is 55 µg, which is usually provided by seafood, meat, and fortified grain products. The tolerable limit is 400 µg, although all studies to date have been conducted with a maximum of 200 µg doses.

WARNINGS

A recent analysis of five commercially available brands revealed actual content variability to be between 81 and 123% of the stated dose. One brand varied by 54% between different lots of the same supplement.[1]

MECHANISM OF ACTION

Selenium is an essential structural element of the antioxidant enzyme glutathione peroxidase that takes part in a system to convert aggressive oxidation products and intracellular free radicals into less reactive or neutral components. Other biologic functions of selenium include regulation of thyroid hormone action and regulation of the reduction status of vitamin C.[2,3]

USAGE

Cancer prevention, cancer treatment, cardiovascular disease, immunostimulation, rheumatoid arthritis.

PHARMACOKINETICS

Absorption: Absorption of selenium is efficient and not regulated. More than 90% of selenomethionine, the major dietary form of the element, is absorbed by the same mechanism as methionine itself. Selenocysteine appears to be absorbed very well also. Of the inorganic forms, selenate is almost completely absorbed, but with a significant fraction lost in the urine before incorporation into tissue. Selenite has a more variable absorption probably related to interactions with substances in the gut lumen, but it is better retained, once absorbed, than selenate. Absorption of selenite is generally greater than 50%. Selenate and selenite are not major dietary constituents but are commonly used to fortify foods and as selenium supplements.

Distribution: Selenomethionine enters the methionine pool in the body and shares the fate of methionine until catabolized by the transsulfuration pathway, ultimately leading to the reduced form.

Metabolism/Excretion: Ingested selenocysteine, selenate, and selenite are all apparently metabolized by methylation to selenide. The selenide can be metabolized to selenophosphate, the precursor of selenocysteine in selenoproteins. The mechanism that regulates production of excretory metabolites has yet to be elucidated. The excretory metabolites appear in the urine primarily.[2]

ADVERSE REACTIONS

Chronic Selenosis (doses greater than 1,000 µg/d): Muscle weakness, fatigue, peripheral neuropathy, dermatitis, nail and hair changes/loss, garlic breath/body odor, irritability, growth retardation, hepatic necrosis.

Toxicity: Acute toxicity via selenium poisoning has occurred with either accidental or suicidal ingestion of gun bluing solution or sheep drench. Consumption of gram quantities of selenium can cause severe gastrointestinal disturbance, neurologic disturbance, acute respiratory distress syndrome, myocardial infarction, and renal failure.[2,4]

DRUG INTERACTIONS

Supplement Interactions: High doses of selenium may decrease vitamin C absorption.[4]

DOSAGE

Oral: Recommended Dietary Allowances
Men: 55 μg/d
Women: 55 μg/d
Pregnancy: 60 μg/d
Lactation: 70 μg/d
Tolerable upper intake level[2]: 400 μg/d

LITERATURE SUMMARY AND CRITIQUE

Clark LC, et al. Effects of selenium supplementation for cancer prevention in patients with carcinoma of the skin. A randomized controlled trial. JAMA 1996;276:1957–63.
A prospective, randomized evaluation of skin cancer prevention for patients with a history of either basal cell or squamous cell carcinoma. A total of 1,312 patients were randomized to receive either selenium 200 μg or a placebo daily and to return to the clinic every 6 months for follow-up evaluation. Enrolment began in 1983 and was completed in December 1993. The only adverse event involved gastrointestinal disturbances, which led to the withdrawal of consent in 21 selenium patients and 14 placebo patients. No chronic selenosis was noted. A total of 8,271 person-years of follow-up were accumulated and indicated no significant difference between treatment groups on the recurrence of squamous or basal cell carcinomas. The authors did note that there was a statistically significant reduced relative risk of carcinoma incidence (lung, colorectal, prostate) for patients receiving selenium; however, additional studies are needed to validate this.

REFERENCES

1. Feifer AH, Fleshner NE, Klotz L. Analytical accuracy and reliability of commonly used nutritional supplements in prostate disease. J Urol 2002;168:150–4.
2. Dietary Reference Intakes for vitamin C, vitamin E, selenium, and carotenoids. Washington (DC): National Academy Press; 2000.
3. Suadicani P, Hein HO, Gyntelberg F. Serum selenium concentration and risk of ischaemic heart disease in a prospective cohort study of 3000 males. Atherosclerosis 1992;96:33–42.
4. Pronsky ZM. Power's and Moore's food-medication interactions. 11th ed. Pottstown (PA): Food Medication Interactions; 2000.
5. Whitney EN, et al. Understanding normal and clinical nutrition. 4th ed. Belmont (CA): West Publishing; 1994.

6. Ip C. Lessons from basic research in selenium and cancer prevention [review]. J Nutr 1998;128:1845–54.
7. El-Bayoumy K. The protective role of selenium on genetic damage and on cancer [review]. Mutat Res 2001;475:123–39.
8. Klein EA, et al. SELECT: the selenium and vitamin E cancer prevention trial: rationale and design. Prostate Cancer Prostat Dis 2000;3:145–51.
9. Duffield-Lillico AJ, et al. Baseline characteristics and the effect of selenium supplementation on cancer incidence in a randomized clinical trial: a summary report of the Nutritional Prevention of Cancer Trial. Cancer Epidemiol Biomarkers Prev 2002;11:630–9.

Shark Cartilage

KEY WORDS
Neovastat, Cartilade, AE-941

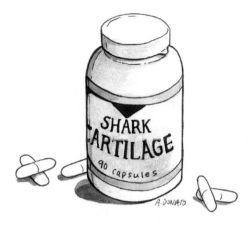

CLINICAL SUMMARY
Obtained from the spiny dogfish shark and hammerhead shark. This supplement is used to treat cancer, arthritis, osteoporosis, Kaposi's sarcoma, macular degeneration, psoriasis, and inflammatory disorders. It should not be confused with bovine cartilage, which has lower in vitro angiogenic activity. Many over-the-counter products contain mostly binding agents or fillers with little or no activity. The Federal Trade Commission has barred three manufacturers from making unsubstantiated claims of efficacy for their shark cartilage products. Shark cartilage extracts show strong antiangiogenic and antitumor activity in vitro and in animal models, but clinical use remains controversial owing to lack of bioavailability data and unsatisfactory patient outcomes in phase I/II trials. A case report of regression of Kaposi's sarcoma with long-term low-dose shark cartilage use is reported in the literature. The National Center for Complementary and Alternative Medicine is currently sponsoring trials of Neovastat (AE-941), a purified shark cartilage extract, in combination with conventional therapies for non–small cell lung cancer and BeneFin for advanced colorectal and breast cancers. A pilot study of shark cartilage in Kaposi's sarcoma, a phase III trial of Neovastat in metastatic renal cell carcinoma, and a registration phase II trial for refractory multiple myeloma are under way. Neovastat has proven to be effective against psoriasis. Most trials report low toxicity, but regular

consumption of a shark cartilage supplement was associated with reversible hepatic dysfunction in a 57-year-old man.

CONSTITUENTS

Glycoproteins: sphyrnastatins 1 and 2; glycosaminoglycans: chondroitin sulfate, keratan sulfate; calcium salts; protein: collagen.

WARNINGS

Commercially available supplements contain varying amounts of shark cartilage. Some are composed primarily of fillers and may not have any biologic activity.

Neovastat (AE-941) is a highly purified extract of shark cartilage. It is an investigational, new drug and is not available to the general public. Other shark cartilage products may not have similar properties.

MECHANISM OF ACTION

The glycoproteins sphyrnastatins 1 and 2 and other unidentified factors are thought to be responsible for the activity of shark cartilage, which shows strong antiangiogenic activity and inhibition of tumor neovascularization in numerous in vitro and animal studies. Both the crude extract and a heat-stable 10^3 to 10^4 molecular-weight fraction inhibit tumor neovascularization in rabbit corneas and embryonic angiogenesis in chorioallantoic membranes. Shark cartilage extract also interferes with bovine pulmonary artery endothelial cell adhesion via modification of focal adhesion protein organization. In vitro, a shark cartilage preparation protects *Escherichia coli* cells against hydrogen peroxide–induced lesions, suggesting a scavenger role for reactive oxygen species. U-995, which contains two shark cartilage peptides (10 and 14 kDa), inhibits human umbilical vein endothelial cell migration, disrupts tumor necrosis factor-α–induced angiogenesis, and prevents collagenase-induced collagenolysis in vitro. It also suppresses sarcoma-180 tumor growth in mice and B16-F10 melanoma cell metastasis in mice when administered intraperitoneally. Ingestion of shark cartilage powder dramatically reduces angiogenesis induced in mesenteric windows by mast cell stimulation in rats. Oral shark cartilage delays the development of streptozotocin-induced renal papillary and solid tumors in mice but does not reduce the number of lesions. A lower dose of oral commercially available shark cartilage failed to reduce tumor size or increase survival in mice implanted with SCCVII carcinoma.

AEterna Laboratories, Inc., the manufacturer of Neovastat (AE-941), a water-soluble shark cartilage extract, reports that, in vitro, this formulation inhibits embryonic vascularization, endothelial cell proliferation, tubulogenesis, vascular endothelial growth factor (VEGF) binding to endothelial cells, VEGF-dependent tyrosine phosphorylation of the VEGF receptor, and the VEGF-dependent increase in vascular permeability. It also inhibits serine elastase and matrix metalloproteinase activity (MMP-2, MMP-9, and MMP-12) via tissue inhibitor of metalloproteinase (TIMP)-like proteins. Oral administration of Neovastat results in a significant reduction in tumor volume in mice with subcutaneously grafted DA3 breast cancer or human glioblastoma cells, blocks medullary bone degradation and decreases tumor size in a mouse metastatic bone tumor model, and causes a decrease in the number of lung metastases in a Lewis lung carcinoma model. Neovastat can be used against psoriasis owing to its angiogenesis effect.[1-14]

USAGE

Arthritis, cancer prevention, cancer treatment, colitis, diabetic retinopathy, glaucoma, hemorrhoids, immunostimulation, inflammation, Kaposi's sarcoma, macular degeneration, osteoarthritis, osteoporosis, psoriasis, wound healing.

PHARMACOKINETICS

Large macromolecules such as those associated with the antiangiogenic properties of shark cartilage are not usually absorbed by the intestinal tract and may be digested by proteolytic enzymes in the gut, but studies show that certain large proteins can be absorbed. No bioavailability studies with shark cartilage preparations are published as it is unclear which active component to look for in the blood. One study in humans found a significant decrease in endothelial cell density within an inert subcutaneous implant following oral administration of a liquid shark cartilage extract, giving some support to the oral bioavailability of its antiangiogenic factors. The manufacturers of Neovastat (AE-941) claim that phase I/II trial results show that it is orally bioavailable and safe, but data from this study have not been published.[15,16]

ADVERSE REACTIONS

Infrequent: Nausea, vomiting, dyspepsia, constipation, diarrhea, anorexia, hypoglycemia in a known type 2 diabetic patient.
Case Report: A 57-year-old man experienced nausea, vomiting, diarrhea, anorexia, jaundice, low-grade fever, scleral icterus, and elevated liver function tests after consuming a shark cartilage supplement for 10 weeks. Normal liver function resumed after discontinuation of the supplement.[17]

DRUG INTERACTIONS

None known.

LABORATORY INTERACTIONS

Periodic liver function tests should be performed with long-term use.

CONTRAINDICATIONS

Patients with liver disease should use shark cartilage supplements with caution.

DOSAGE

Oral: *Tablets/capsules:* 2 to 6 daily. *Concentrates:* 1 to 2 tablespoons daily. *Ampules:* 1 ampule daily. *Neovastat:* 30 to 240 mL/d have been used in trials. *Cancer:* Typical doses are 500 to 4,500 mg/d, depending on the preparation; 80 to 100 g/d have been used in a clinical trial.

Rectal: 60 to 90 g of powder are mixed with water and administered as an enema.

A typical regimen costs about $700 per month.[18]

LITERATURE SUMMARY AND CRITIQUE

Unpublished Reports: A 16-week trial was conducted in Cuba in 29 patients with unspecified cancers; 15 were evaluable, of which 3 showed an unspecified response. In light of the "incomplete and unimpressive" data, the National Cancer Institute's (NCI) Division of Cancer Treatment decided not to pursue NCI-sponsored clinical trials of shark cartilage. Preliminary results of an ongoing clinical trial of high-dose oral or rectal shark cartilage showed that 10 of 20 cancer patients experienced improved quality of life, including less pain, after 8 weeks. Four patients showed partial or complete response, but the results and protocol of this study have not been published. Two additional unpublished phase II trials in cancer patients recorded no complete or partial responses.[15,19–22]

Miller DR, et al. Phase I/II trial of the safety and efficacy of shark cartilage in the treatment of advanced cancer. J Clin Oncol 1998;16:3649–55.

An open-label, nonrandomized phase I/II study of Cartilade shark cartilage supplementation in 60 patients (24 men, 36 women) with stage III and IV recurrent, previously treated, refractory, and/or metastatic cancer (14 lung, 18 breast, 16 colorectal, 8 prostate, 1 brain, 3 non-Hodgkin's lymphoma). Patients had Eastern Cooperative Oncology Group performance status of 0 to 2 and had not previously taken shark cartilage at doses 20% or greater of the protocol dose. Patients received 1 g/kg of shark cartilage powder daily in three divided doses and were evaluated at baseline and 6 and 12 weeks with a physical examination, laboratory and imaging studies, and Functional Assessment of Cancer Therapy-General (FACT-G). Dose was increased to 1.3 g/kg daily if no measurable response was seen at 6 weeks. Ten patients were either lost to follow-up or refused further therapy before 6 weeks. Five patients withdrew because of gastrointestinal toxicity. No complete or partial responses were observed, but 10 of 50 evaluable patients had stable disease for 12 weeks or more (range = 12 to 45.7 weeks, mean = 28.8 ± 9.9 weeks). Overall, no improvement in FACT-G quality of life scores was observed. Survival was not compared with a historical control, and the number of patients was too small to make meaningful statistical comparisons. This trial does not support the use of commercially available shark cartilage supplements in the treatment of end-stage cancers.

REFERENCES

1. Gingras D. Shark cartilage extracts as antiangiogenic agents: smart drinks or bitter pills? Cancer Metastatis Rev 2000;19:83–6.

2. Falardeau P, et al. Neovastat, a naturally occurring multifunctional antiangiogenic drug, in phase III clinical trials. Semin Oncol 2001;28:620–5.
3. Gomes EM, Souto PRF, Felzenszwalb I. Shark-cartilage containing preparation protects cells against hydrogen peroxide induced damage and mutagenesis. Mutat Res 1996;367:203–8.
4. Sheu JR, et al. Effect of U-995, a potent shark cartilage-derived angiogenesis inhibitor, on anti-angiogenesis and anti-tumor activities. Anticancer Res 1998;18:4435–42.
5. Barber R, et al. Oral shark cartilage does not abolish carcinogenesis but delays tumor progression in a murine model. Anticancer Res 2001;21:1065–70.
6. Horsman MR, Alsner J, Overgaard J. The effect of shark cartilage extracts on the growth and metastatic spread of the SCCVII carcinoma. Acta Oncol 1998;37:441–5.
7. Weber MH, Lee J, Orr FW. The effect of Neovastat (AE-941) on an experimental metastatic bone tumor model. Int J Oncol 2002;20:299–303.
8. Gingras D, et al. Matrix proteinase inhibition by AE-941, a multifunctional antiangiogenic compound. Anticancer Res 2001;21:145–56.
9. Dupont E, et al. Antiangiogenic and antimetastatic properties of Neovastat (AE-941), an orally active extract derived from cartilage tissue. Clin Exp Metastasis 2002;19:145–53.
10. Lee A, Langer R. Shark cartilage contains inhibitors of tumor angiogenesis. Science 1983;221:1185–7.
11. Davis PF, et al. Inhibition of angiogenesis by oral ingestion of powdered shark cartilage in a rat model. Microvasc Res 1997;54:178–82.
12. Chen JS, et al. Shark cartilage extract interferes with cell adhesion and induces reorganization of focal adhesions in cultured endothelial cells. J Cell Biochem 2000;78:417–28.
13. Oikawa T, et al. A novel angiogenic inhibitor derived from Japanese shark cartilage (I). Extraction and estimation of inhibitory activities toward tumor and embryonic angiogenesis. Cancer Lett 1990;51:181–6.
14. Sauder DN, et al. Neovastat (AE-941), an inhibitor of angiogenesis: randomized phase I/II clinical trial results in patients with plaque psoriasis. J Am Acad Dermatol 2002;47:535–41.
15. Ernst E, Cassileth BR. How useful are unconventional cancer treatments? Eur J Cancer 1999;35:1608–13.
16. Berbari P, et al. Antiangiogenic effects of the oral administration of liquid cartilage extract in humans. J Surg Res 1999;87:108–13.
17. Ashar B, Vargo E. Shark cartilage-induced hepatitis. Ann Intern Med 1996;125:780–1.
18. Fetrow CW, et al. Professional's handbook of complementary and alternative medicines. Philadelphia: Springhouse; 1999.
19. Mathews J. Media feeds frenzy over shark cartilage as cancer treatment. J Natl Cancer Inst 1993;85:1190–1.
20. Leitner SP, et al. Two phase II studies of oral dry shark cartilage powder (SCP) with either metastatic breast or prostate cancer refractory to standard treatment. Proc Am Soc Clin Oncol 1998;17:A240.
21. Rosenbluth RJ, et al. Oral shark cartilage in the treatment of patients with advanced primary brain tumors. A phase II pilot study. Proc Am Soc Clin Oncol 1999;18:A554.
22. Miller DR, et al. Phase I/II trial of the safety and efficacy of shark cartilage in the treatment of advanced cancer. J Clin Oncol 1998;16:3649–55.

Sheep Sorrel

A. DONATO

COMMON NAMES
Sorrel, dock

SCIENTIFIC NAME
Rumex acetosella

KEY WORD
Rumex acetosella

CLINICAL SUMMARY

Derived from the aerial parts of the plant. Sheep sorrel historically has been used to treat inflammation, scurvy, cancer, and diarrhea. The major constituents of sheep sorrel include anthraquinones, oxalates, and various vitamins. Consumption of large doses may result in diarrhea from the anthraquinones and renal and liver damage from the oxalate content. Sheep sorrel is one of the four ingredients in Essiac. There are no published trials evaluating the efficacy of sheep sorrel for any proposed claims.

CONSTITUENTS

Glycosides: hyperoside, quercitin-3d-galactoside; anthraquinones: emodin, aloe-emodin, chrysophanol, rhein, physcion; vitamins: A, B complex, C, D, E, K; others: oxalates, tannins.[1]

MECHANISM OF ACTION

The anthraquinones, including emodin, rhein, and physcion, stimulate peristalsis and increase the secretion of mucus and water into the intestine. They are also considered to be antioxidants and free radical scavengers.

USAGE
Cancer treatment, diarrhea, fever, inflammation, scurvy.

ADVERSE REACTIONS
Reported: Gastroenteritis, abdominal cramps, diarrhea leading to possible hypokalemia, renal and liver damage.[2]

DRUG INTERACTIONS
Diuretics: Potassium loss owing to stimulant laxative effect can increase the potential risk for hypokalemia.

LABORATORY INTERACTIONS
Anthraquinones can cause discoloration of the urine, interfering with urinalysis.[3]

CONTRAINDICATIONS
Patients with a history of kidney stones should not consume this herb.

DOSAGE
Oral: There is no recommended dosage at this time.

LITERATURE SUMMARY AND CRITIQUE
No clinical trials have been conducted to evaluate the efficacy of sheep sorrel for any proposed claims.

REFERENCES
1. Tamayo C, et al. The chemistry and biological activity of herbs used in Flor-essence herbal tonic and Essiac. Phytother Res 2000;14:1–14.
2. Fetrow CW, et al. Professional's handbook of complementary and alternative medicines. Philadelphia: Springhouse; 1999.
3. Newall CA, et al. Herbal medicines: a guide for health-care professionals. London: Pharmaceutical Press; 1996.

Shiitake Mushroom

A. DONATO

COMMON NAMES
Forest mushroom, lentinula, pasania fungus, lentinula, hua gu

SCIENTIFIC NAME
Lentinula edodes

KEY WORD
Lentinula edodes

CLINICAL SUMMARY

The entire mushroom may be consumed. It is a culinary staple in many Asian cultures. As a dietary supplement, shiitake mushroom is frequently used for cancer prevention and treatment. Lentinan, a polysaccharide, is believed to be the active component and has been studied extensively in Japan as an anticancer agent. Adverse events such as diarrhea, bloating, and eosinophilia have been reported with chronic use.

CONSTITUENTS

Polysaccharides: lentinan, 1-3-β-D-glucan; lipids: linoleic acid; ergosterol; amino acids: lysine, arginine, methionine, phenylalanine; minerals and electrolytes: potassium, calcium, magnesium, manganese, iron, copper, zinc; lignins.[1]

MECHANISM OF ACTION

The mechanism of action is attributed to the low concentrations of lentinan. Lentinan possesses immunoregulatory effects, antimicrobial properties, antiviral activity, and cholesterol-lowering effects.[1]

USAGE

Cancer prevention, cancer treatment, high cholesterol, immunostimulation, infections.

ADVERSE REACTIONS

None reported at normal doses.

Toxicity: Consumption of shiitake mushroom powder for a prolonged period of time has resulted in dermatitis, photosensitivity, eosinophilia, and gastrointestinal upset.[2,3]

DRUG INTERACTIONS

None known.

DOSAGE

No specific recommendation.

LITERATURE SUMMARY AND CRITIQUE

No significant clinical studies have been performed with the shiitake mushroom. However, lentinan, which is a polysaccharide component of the mushroom, has been studied extensively.

REFERENCES

1. Hobbs C. Medicinal mushrooms. 3rd ed. Loveland (CO): Interweave Press; 1996.
2. Hanada K, Hashimoto I. Flagellate mushroom (shiitake) dermatitis and photosensitivity. Dermatology 1998;197:255–7.
3. Levy AM, et al. Eosinophilia and gastrointestinal symptoms after ingestion of shiitake mushrooms. J Allergy Clin Immunol 1998;101:613–20.
4. Gordon M, et al. A placebo-controlled trial of the immune modulator, lentinan, in HIV-positive patients: a phase I/II trial. J Med 1998;29:305–30.

Sho-saiko-to

COMMON NAMES:
Xiao Chai Hu Tang, minor bupleurum decoction

CLINICAL SUMMARY
Sho-saiko-to (SST) or "Xiao Chai Hu Tang" is a classic Chinese botanical formulation widely known by its Japanese name. It is traditionally used to treat fever, malaria, gastrointestinal disorders, and chronic liver diseases. A prescription form has been used extensively in Japan, predominantly for hepatitis. SST and its isolated chemical components have demonstrated marked antiproliferative effects on hepatoma lines. Morphologic analysis of cells grown in the presence of SST showed evidence of apoptosis. SST has been shown to prevent liver injury and promote liver regeneration in animal models and has been demonstrated to enhance various aspects of immune function, including effects on killer cells, interleukins, interferon, and macrophages. There is also evidence that SST leads to enhancement of granulocyte colony-stimulating factor. Although SST has a good safety profile, its use has been associated with interstitial pneumonitis. SST should be used only under the supervision of a qualified practitioner. Clinical studies are currently under way to determine whether SST can increase survival in patients with liver cancer and to evaluate its therapeutic effect on hepatitis C.

CONSTITUENTS
SST is a mixture of seven botanicals: bupleurum root (Chai Hu), pinellia tuber (Ban Xia), scutellaria root (Huang qin), ginseng (Ren shen), Jujube (da zao), licorice (Gan cao), and ginger (Sheng jiang). A number of pharmacologically active components have been isolated, including the following: baicalin, baicalein, glycyrrhizin, saikosaponins, ginsenosides, wogonin, and gingerols. Given the complexity of SST, it is unlikely that all active components have been identified.[1]

WARNINGS
SST may cause interstitial pneumonitis, a potentially fatal condition. Concurrent use with interferon may increase this risk.[2]

MECHANISM OF ACTION

SST appears to have a multifactorial activity, inhibiting proliferation of hepatocellular carcinoma (HCC) cells, preventing liver injury, promoting liver regeneration, and enhancing immune function. Human studies have shown reduced incidence of HCC in users of ginseng, one of the botanicals in this formula. SST and its isolated chemical components have demonstrated marked antiproliferative effects on hepatoma lines in vitro. Of particular interest is that SST showed only minimal inhibitory effects on normal human peripheral lymphocytes even at high concentrations. Morphologic analysis of cells grown in the presence of SST showed evidence of apoptosis. SST has been shown to prevent liver injury and to promote liver regeneration in animal models. Rats treated with SST showed less fibrosis, as indicated by reduced liver hydroxyproline and a smaller increase in serum hyaluronic acid. Moreover, these rats developed fewer preneoplastic lesions. SST has also been demonstrated to prevent the development or metastasis of carcinomas other than HCC. SST can enhance various aspects of immune function, including effects on killer cells, interleukins, interferon, and macrophages. There is also evidence that SST leads to enhancement of granulocyte colony-stimulating factor.[3-12]

USAGE

Cancer prevention, cancer treatment, fever, gastrointestinal disorders, infections, liver disease, malaria.

PHARMACOKINETICS

Owing to the complexity of this formula, only limited data are available. One study indicated that the serum concentration of glycyrrhizin after a normal daily dose is 1.2 µg/mL.[13]

ADVERSE REACTIONS

SST-related pneumonitis was reported in 74 patients (approximately 1 in 20,000).[2]

DRUG INTERACTIONS

Anticoagulants/Antiplatelets: Theoretically, SST may cause additive effects when administered concurrently.
Interferon: Concurrent use may increase the risk of interstitial pneumonitis.
Monoamine Oxidase Inhibitors (MAOIs): Some ingredients, such as ginseng and licorice, may potentiate the activity of MAOIs.

LABORATORY INTERACTIONS

May affect asparatate transaminase and alanine transaminase.

CONTRAINDICATIONS

Women who are nursing or pregnant and people currently undergoing interferon treatment should not take SST.

DOSAGE

Varies between manufacturers. One company recommended 7.5 g/d orally, divided into three doses, before or between meals. The dosage may be adjusted according to age, body weight, and symptoms.[1]

LITERATURE SUMMARY AND CRITIQUE

Oka H, et al. Prospective study of chemoprevention of hepatocellular carcinoma with Sho-saiko-to (TJ-9). Cancer 1995;76:743–9.

Two hundred and sixty patients with cirrhosis were randomized using age, sex, hepatitis B antigen status, and liver function strata to treatment with SST or control. Patients were followed for 5 years with bimonthly α-fetoprotein measurement and quarterly ultrasonography. HCC diagnoses were confirmed by angiography, computed tomography, and, where indicated, biopsy. SST led to a one-third reduction in the incidence of HCC (23% versus 34%) and a 40% reduction in death (24% versus 40%). Analysis of this data suggests that SST has multifactorial action, both reducing the incidence of HCC and acting as a hepatoprotective agent.

REFERENCES

1. Honso professional catalog. Tempe (AZ): Honso USA, Inc; 2002.
2. Sato A, at al. Pneumonitis induced by the herbal medicine sho-saiko-to in Japan. Nihon Kyobu Shikkan Gakkai Zasshi 1997;35:391–5.
3. Oka H, et al. Prospective study of chemoprevention of hepatocellular carcinoma with Sho-saiko-to (TJ-9). Cancer 1995;76:743–9.
4. Yano H, et al. The herbal medicine sho-saiko-to inhibits proliferation of cancer cell lines by inducing apoptosis and arrest at the G_0/G_1 phase. Cancer Res 1994;54:448–54.
5. Sakaida I, et al. Herbal medicine Sho-saiko-to (TJ-9) prevents liver fibrosis and enzyme-altered lesions in rat liver cirrhosis induced by a choline-deficient L-amino acid-defined diet. J Hepatol 1998;28:298–306.
6. Ito H, et al. Effects of a blended Chinese medicine, xiao-chai-hu-tang, on Lewis lung carcinoma growth and inhibition of lung metastasis, with special reference to macrophage activation. Jpn J Pharmacol 1986;41:307–14.
7. Yamashiki M, et al. Effects of the Japanese herbal medicine "Sho-saiko-to" (TJ-9) on in vitro interleukin-10 production by peripheral blood mononuclear cells of patients with chronic hepatitis C. Hepatology 1997;25:1390–7.
8. Kakumu S, et al. Effects of TJ-9 Sho-saiko-to (kampo medicine) on interferon gamma and antibody production specific for hepatitis B virus antigen in patients with type B chronic hepatitis. Int J Immunopharmacol 1991;13:141–6.
9. Fujiwara K, et al. Regulation of hepatic macrophage function by oral administration of xiao-chai-hu-tang (sho-saiko-to, TJ-9) in rats. J Ethnopharmacol 1995;46:107–14.

10. Kaneko M, et al. Augmentation of NK activity after oral administration of a traditional Chinese medicine, xiao-chai-hu-tang (shosaiko-to). Immunopharmacol Immunotoxicol 1994;16:41–53.

11. Nagatsu Y, et al. Modification of macrophage functions by Shosaikoto (kampo medicine) leads to enhancement of immune response. Chem Pharm Bull (Tokyo) 1989;37:1540–2.

12. Yamashiki M, et al. Herbal medicine 'Sho-saiko-to' induces tumour necrosis factor-α and granulocyte colony-stimulating factor in vitro in peripheral blood mononuclear cells of patients with hepatocellular carcinoma. J Gastroenterol Hepatol 1996;11:137–42.

13. Mizoguchi Y, et al. The effects of sho-saiko-to on interleukin production by hepatic sinusoidal endothelial cells. J Med Pharm Soc 1989;6:172–6.

Skullcap

A.DONATO

COMMON NAMES
Huang Qin, baikal scullcap,
mad-dog herb, helmet flower,
hoodwort, quaker bonnet, Ou Gon

SCIENTIFIC NAMES
*Scutellaria baicalensis, Scutellaria
latifola*

KEY WORDS
Scutellaria, huang qin, baikal
skullcap

CLINICAL SUMMARY

Derived from the root of the plant. This herb is used in traditional Chinese medicine to treat a variety of conditions, including epilepsy, hepatitis, infections, and cancer. The flavonoid components of skullcap are thought to be responsible for its activity. Skullcap often is found in combination with other botanicals (eg, PC-SPES and Sho-saiko-to). In vitro and limited animal data suggest that its bioflavonoid components cause apoptosis in hepatoma cell lines, but additional research is necessary. Signs of skullcap toxicity include stupor, confusion, and seizures. In light of reports of hepatotoxicity that may be related to product contamination or skullcap itself, this supplement should be used with caution.

CONSTITUENTS

Flavonoids: baicalin, baicalein, scutellarein, wogonin, apigenin, hispidulin, luteolin, scutellarein; iridoids: catalpol; volatile oils: limonene, terpineol, β-humulene, caryophyllene; others: lignin, resin, tannin.[1–3]

WARNINGS

Products containing skullcap have been found to be contaminated with a similar-looking plant known as germander *(Teucrium chamaedrys)*, which can cause hepatitis.[2]

MECHANISM OF ACTION

In vitro studies suggest that flavonoid components of skullcap show anticancer activity. Induction of apoptosis in hepatoma G2, 3B, and SK-Hep1 cell lines occurs following 48 hours of exposure to baicalein, baicalin, and wogonin at a concentration of 25 to 100 µg/mL. Wogonin causes arrest at the G_1 phase, whereas baicalin and baicalein cause G_2/M accumulation. Additional in vitro studies show that baicalin at concentrations of 50 to 200 µg/mL activates caspase-3, resulting in apoptosis of Jurkat cells (leukemia-derived T cells). Baicalin also exhibits anti-inflammatory, antioxidant, and gram-positive antibacterial activity in vitro. Skullcap-derived flavonoids also prevent ethanol-induced hyperlipidemia, histamine release from mast cells, and catecholamine-induced lipolysis in animal models.[2-4]

USAGE

Atherosclerosis, cancer treatment, epilepsy, hepatitis, infections, inflammation, insomnia.

PHARMACOKINETICS

No pharmacokinetic evaluations of skullcap have been performed.

ADVERSE REACTIONS

Reported: Hepatotoxicity, pneumonitis.
Toxicity: Stupor, confusion, seizures.[2-5]

DRUG INTERACTIONS

Anticoagulants/Antiplatelets: Theoretically, skullcap may cause additive effects when administered concurrently.[6]

DOSAGE

No recommended dosage.

LITERATURE SUMMARY AND CRITIQUE

Skullcap has been studied in combination with other botanicals in formulations such as PC-SPES and Sho-saiko-to.

REFERENCES

1. Huang KC. The pharmacology of Chinese herbs. 2nd ed. New York: CRC Press; 1999.
2. Newall C, et al. Herbal medicines: a guide for health-care professionals. 1st ed. London: Pharmaceutical Press; 1996.

3. Chang WH, Chen CH, Lu FJ. Different effects of baicalein, baicalin, and wogonin on mitochondrial function, glutathione content and cell cycle progression in human hepatoma cell lines. Planta Med 2002;68:128–32.
4. Ueda S, et al. Baicalin induces apoptosis via mitochondrial pathway as prooxidant. Mol Immunol 2002;38:781–91.
5. Takeshita K, et al. Pneumonitis induced by Ou-gon (skullcap). Intern Med 2001;40:764–8.
6. Brinker F. Herb contraindications and drug interactions. 3rd ed. Sandy (OR): Eclectic Medical Publications; 2001.

Slippery Elm

COMMON NAMES
Indian elm, red elm, gray elm

SCIENTIFIC NAME
Ulmus rubra

KEY WORD
Ulmus rubra

A.DONATO

CLINICAL SUMMARY
Derived from the inner bark of the tree. Slippery elm has been used historically for gastrointestinal disorders, skin ulcers or abscesses, cancers, cough, fevers, and inflammation. The primary constituent is mucilage, which is thought to account for the demulcent effects. To date, no human or animal studies have been performed to evaluate the efficacy of any proposed claims. The toxicity of slippery elm is low based on chemical components. No adverse reactions or drug interactions are reported in the literature. Slippery elm appears to be safe for coughs and minor gastrointestinal complaints, but it should not be used to treat severe conditions such as cancer or bronchitis.

CONSTITUENTS
Carbohydrates: mucilage (hexose, pentose, methylpentose), galactose, glucose, galacturonic acid; phytosterols: β-sitosterol, citrostandienol, dolichol; fatty acids: oleic and palmitic acid; others: tannin, calcium oxalate, cholesterol.[1,2]

MECHANISM OF ACTION
Mucilage is responsible for the demulcent, emollient, and antitussive properties. Insoluble polysaccharides in mucilage (hexose, pentose, methylpentose) form a viscous

material following oral administration or when prepared for topical use. Fiber content is thought to reduce gastrointestinal transit time, act as a bulk-forming laxative, and adsorb toxins. The tannin component has been shown to exhibit astringent activity.[1,2]

USAGE
Bronchitis, cancer treatment, cough, diarrhea, fever, inflammation, peptic ulcers, skin abscesses, skin ulcers, sore throat.

ADVERSE REACTIONS
No adverse reactions have been reported.

DRUG INTERACTIONS
Theoretically, slippery elm may slow the absorption of concomitantly administered oral medications.[3]

DOSAGE
Oral: No standard dosage exists.

LITERATURE SUMMARY AND CRITIQUE
No human or animal studies have been performed to evaluate the efficacy of any proposed claims.

REFERENCES
1. Newall C, et al. Herbal medicines: a guide for health-care professionals. 1st ed. London: Pharmaceutical Press; 1996.
2. Tamayo C, et al. The chemistry and biological activity of herbs used in Flor-essence herbal tonic and Essiac. Phytother Res 2000;14:1–14.
3. Brinker F. Herb contraindications and drug interactions. 3rd ed. Sandy (OR): Eclectic Medical Publications; 2001.

Soy

COMMON NAMES
Soybean, soya, *Glycine soja*, tofu, miso, tempeh

SCIENTIFIC NAME
Glycine max

A.DONATO

CLINICAL SUMMARY
Derived from the legume of the plant. Patients take soy to treat and prevent cancer, heart disease, and menopausal symptoms. Soybeans contain various proteins, vitamins, and minerals, as well as significant amounts of isoflavones (eg, genistein, daidzein, and glycitein), and are a good source of fiber. Isoflavones are considered phytoestrogens and exhibit both selective estrogen receptor modulator activity and nonhormonal effects. Clinical data suggest that soy isoflavones are no more effective than placebo for treating menopausal symptoms in patients with breast cancer. Epidemiologic, laboratory animal, and in vitro data suggest that soy may be used as an alternative to conventional hormone replacement therapy to treat menopausal symptoms but with questionable efficacy. Other data suggest that soy may slow bone density loss and prevent breast cancer, but clinical results are inconsistent. Evidence suggesting that soy proteins have a protective effect against prostate cancer is primarily epidemiologic or in vitro. It is unknown whether isoflavones influence hormone-dependent cancers. Numerous studies indicate that soy lowers total cholesterol levels. Animal and human studies reveal that soy protein can decrease low-density lipoprotein (LDL) cholesterol, inhibit LDL oxidation, and possibly increase high-density lipoprotein (HDL) cholesterol. Genistein specifically appears to increase blood vessel flexibility.

CONSTITUENTS

Isoflavones: genistein, daidzein, glycitein; glucosides; phospholipids: phosphatidyl-choline, lecithin, linoleic acid, oleic acid; protein; carbohydrate.[1,2]

MECHANISM OF ACTION

Soy contains significant amounts of the isoflavones genistein (4'5,7-trihydroxy-isoflavone), daidzein (4',7-dihydroxyisoflavone), and glycitein (4',7-dihydroxy-6-methoxyisoflavone). In perimenopausal women, the estrogenic effects of soy isoflavones are weak because estrogen is abundant. At menopause, it is believed that this effect increases owing to the decrease in endogenous estrogen. Animal studies suggest that genistein and daidzein have an ability to prevent or reduce bone loss in a manner similar to that of synthetic estrogen owing to increased β versus α estrogen receptor binding. Soy may also contribute to maintaining bone density by causing less calcium to be excreted in the urine. Soy's capacity for osteoporosis prophylaxis is based largely on hypotheses rather than clinical data.

Several mechanisms for the chemopreventive effects of dietary soy are proposed. Soy-beans contain at least five anticarcinogenic phytochemicals: isoflavones, saponins, phy-tates, phytosterols, and protease inhibitors. Pilot results suggest that soy isoflavones have antioxidant activity. Genistein demonstrates antiproliferative effects in multiple cell lines, including breast cancer (estrogen receptor positive and negative), prostate cancer, neu-roblastoma, sarcoma, and retinoblastoma. Other soy isoflavones (eg, daidzein, etc) demonstrate growth inhibition of breast cancer cell lines, although the action is weaker than with genistein. Genistein may act as an antiestrogen by competing for receptor binding, possibly resulting in reduced estrogen-induced stimulation of breast cell prolif-eration and breast tumor formation. Alternatively, soy isoflavones may reduce breast cancer risk by decreasing endogenous ovarian steroid levels.

Genistein and other phytoestrogens inhibit the growth of androgen-dependent and -independent human prostate cancer cell lines. Rather than inhibit etiologic factors, soy protein extracts appear to influence the progression of established tumors. Other pro-posed mechanisms of prostate cancer prevention include genistein-induced prostate can-cer cell adhesion, direct growth inhibition, and induction of apoptosis. Growth inhibi-tion appears to be independent of genistein's estrogenic effects.

The exact mechanism for soy's cholesterol-lowering effect remains unknown. Pro-posed mechanisms include phytoestrogen-induced hyperthyroid state and increased excretion of bile acids, which may enhance removal of LDL. Isoflavones also may inhibit oxidation of LDL. So far, the soundest support is for altered hepatic metabolism with enhanced removal of LDL and very-low-density lipoprotein by hepatocytes.[1–7]

USAGE

Cancer prevention, cardiovascular disease, high cholesterol, menopausal symptoms, osteoporosis.

PHARMACOKINETICS

Absorption: Prior to absorption, isoflavones undergo extensive metabolism in the intestinal tract. Genistein is formed from biochanin A and daidzein from formonentin. Genistein, daidzein, and glycitein may be metabolized further to specific metabolites such as equol, *O*-desmethylangolensis, dihydrogenistein, and p-ethylphenol. Many variables can affect this metabolism. A 2001 analysis of 33 phytoestrogen supplements and extracts demonstrated notable differences in isoflavone content compared with the manufacturer's claims. Qualitative and quantitative differences in plasma concentrations of isoflavones were observed based on the type of supplement used. Such variations in pharmacokinetics and metabolism should be taken into consideration when conducting clinical studies.

Metabolism/Excretion: Following absorption, isoflavones undergo enterohepatic circulation, are secreted into bile, and are eliminated via the kidneys primarily as glucuronide conjugates. However, a portion of isoflavones in the portal blood can escape first-pass liver uptake, entering peripheral circulation. The plasma half-life of genistein and daidzein is approximately 8 hours. In adults, peak concentrations occur in 6 to 8 hours.[8]

ADVERSE REACTIONS

Reported: Flatulence, allergic reactions.

DRUG INTERACTIONS

Tamoxifen: Animal studies suggest that genistein, a soy isoflavone, may antagonize the effects of tamoxifen on estrogen-dependent breast cancer (MCF-7).[9]

CONTRAINDICATIONS

Soy is contraindicated in patients who are hypersensitive to soy products. There is an ongoing debate as to whether soy should be contraindicated in those with estrogen-dependent tumors.[10]

DOSAGE

Oral: Most soy foods contain about 30 to 40 mg of isoflavones per serving. Clinical trials have used the following dosages: *Menopausal symptoms:* 100 mg isoflavones once daily. *Cholesterol reduction:* To qualify for the US Food and Drug Administration's health claim, each serving has to contain at least one-quarter of the daily 25 g of soy protein daily (6.25 g of soy protein). Several recent trials have demonstrated that isoflavones in supplement form are ineffective in reducing serum cholesterol concentrations.

LITERATURE SUMMARY AND CRITIQUE

Van Patten CL, et al. Effect of soy phytoestrogens on hot flashes in postmenopausal women with breast cancer: a randomized, controlled clinical trial. J Clin Oncol 2002;20:1449–55.

A prospective, randomized, double-blind evaluation of soy milk containing 90 mg isoflavones on postmenopausal breast cancer patients 4 months status post-treatment experiencing hot flashes. Patients consumed 250 mL of soy milk ($n = 59$) or placebo rice milk ($n = 64$) twice daily for 12 weeks. The study allowed patients to take prescription medications and complementary therapies for hot flashes, provided that the dose was stable for greater than or equal to 4 months. Primary outcome was the number of hot flashes as recorded by patients in a daily menopause diary. Of 157 randomized patients, 9 were ineligible after randomization for reasons unknown, and 25 dropped out for various reasons, including 10 patients who were intolerant to the study drug (soy $n = 7$, placebo $n = 3$). Both the active and the placebo groups demonstrated a reduction in the number of hot flashes per day, 54% and 58%, respectively. Adverse events were primarily gastrointestinal in nature, including abdominal bloating and flatulence. The authors suggest that soy milk delivering 90 mg/d isoflavones is no more effective than placebo for the management of hot flashes experienced by postmenopausal breast cancer patients.

Han KK, et al. Benefits of soy isoflavone therapeutic regimen on menopausal symptoms. Obstet Gynecol 2002;99:389–94.

This double-blind, placebo-controlled study evaluated the change in menopausal symptoms, endogenous hormone levels, and cardiovascular risk factors in response to 4 months of daily 100 mg of soy isoflavone. Eighty postmenopausal women (aged 45–55) were randomized to receive either the isoflavone ($n = 40$) or placebo treatment ($n = 40$) daily. The isoflavone capsules were composed of soy protein 50.3 mg (60%) and isoflavone 33.3 mg (40%); each contained 23.3 mg of genistein, 6.2 mg of daidzein, and 3.8 mg of glycitein. Changes in menopausal symptoms were assessed at baseline and after 4 months of treatment by means of the menopausal Kupperman index, a numeric conversion index that evaluates 11 menopausal symptoms, including hot flashes (vasomotor), paresthesia, insomnia, and headache. Endogenous hormone levels (follicle-stimulating hormone, luteinizing hormone, and 17β-estradiol) were measured at the same visits. Menopausal symptoms of women using isoflavone were significantly lower during treatment than at baseline and compared with women taking a placebo. Similarly, although the isoflavone treatment did not appear to alter blood pressure, plasma glucose, or HDL or triglyceride levels, it did result in a significant decrease in total cholesterol and LDL compared with baseline and with the placebo group. Estrogen levels rose with isoflavone treatment, but transvaginal sonography studies identified no significant increase in endometrial thickness. The soy isoflavone regimen at the dosage used appears to be a safe and effective option for postmenopausal symptoms, with the added feature of providing potential cardiovascular system benefits at the same time.

Potter SM, Baum JA, Teng H, et al. Soy protein and isoflavones: their effects on blood lipids and bone density in postmenopausal women. Am J Clin Nutr 1998;68 Suppl:1375S–9S.

A double-blind, parallel-group study conducted over a 6-month period in 66 post-menopausal women to examine the effect on blood lipids and bone density of soy protein (40 g/d) containing varying concentrations of isoflavones. Participants were hyper-cholesterolemic and living freely in the community. A 14-day control period in which participants followed a National Cholesterol Education Program Step 1 low-fat, low-cholesterol diet was followed by a 6-month period in which subjects were randomly assigned to either (1) Step 1 diet with 40 g of protein daily from casein and nonfat dry milk (control), (2) Step 1 diet with 40 g of protein daily from isolated soy protein containing 1.39 mg isoflavones/g protein, or (3) Step 1 diet with 40 g of protein daily from isolated soy protein containing 2.25 mg isoflavones/g protein. Significant increases were observed in bone mineral content and density in the lumbar spine for the group taking the higher isoflavone-containing product compared with the control group. No significant decreases in total cholesterol or total triacylglycerols were observed in the subjects taking isoflavones, although HDL cholesterol rose significantly in both groups compared with the control group. In sum, both the moderate- and high-concentration isoflavone dosages decreased risk factors for cardiovascular disease, but only the higher concentration demonstrated an ability to protect against spinal bone loss.

Ingram D, et al. Case-control study of phyto-oestrogens and breast cancer. Lancet 1997;350:990–4.

In this case-control study, an inverse relationship between the risk of both pre-menopausal and postmenopausal breast cancer and a high intake of phytoestrogens (as measured by the urinary excretion of two classes of phytochemicals, lignans and isoflavonoids) was observed. Women with newly diagnosed breast cancer who completed questionnaires and provided 72-hour urine collection and blood samples were matched with breast cancer–free women. The analysis consisted of 144 pairs of individually matched subjects (by age and residential area, among other factors). A significant reduction in breast cancer risk was observed with high excretion of both equol and enterolactone. A reduction in risk—but not a significant one—was observed with the excretion of other phytoestrogens.[11–35]

REFERENCES

1. Huang KC. The pharmacology of Chinese herbs. 2nd ed. New York: CRC Press; 1999.
2. Schulz V, et al. Rational phytotherapy: a physician's guide to herbal medicine. 4th ed. New York: Springer; 2001.
3. Hasler CM, Finn SC. Soy: just a hill of beans? J Womens Health 1998;7:519–23.
4. Messina M, Barnes S. The role of soy products in reducing risk of cancer. J Natl Cancer Inst 1991;83:541–6.
5. Djuric Z, et al. Effect of soy isoflavone supplementation on markers of oxidative stress in men and women. Cancer Lett 2001;172:1–6

6. Lissin LW, Cooke JP. Phytoestrogens and cardiovascular health. J Am Coll Cardiol 2000;35: 1403–10.
7. Peterson TG, et al. The role of metabolism in mammary epithelial cell growth inhibition by the isoflavones genistein and biochanin A. Carcinogenesis 1996;17:1861–9.
8. Fair WR, Fleshner NE, Heston W. Cancer of the prostate: a nutritional disease? Urology 1997;50:840–8.
9. Ju YH, et al. Dietary genistein negates the inhibitory effects of tamoxifen on growth of estrogen-dependent human breast cancer (MCF-7) cells implanted in athymic mice. Cancer Res 2002;62:2474–7.
10. Lichtenstein AH. Soy protein, isoflavones and cardiovascular disease risk. J Nutr 1998;128: 1589–92.
11. Setchell KD, et al. Bioavailability of pure isoflavones in healthy humans and analysis of commercial soy isoflavone supplements. J Nutr 2001;131:1362S–75S.
12. Hsieh CY, et al. Estrogenic effects of genistein on the growth of estrogen receptor-positive human breast cancer (MCF-7) cells in vitro and in vivo. Cancer Res 1998;58:3833–8.
13. Albertazzi P, et al. Dietary soy supplementation and phytoestrogen levels. Obstet Gynecol 1999;94:229–31.
14. Anderson JW, Johnstone BM, Cook-Newall ME. Meta-analysis of the effects of soy protein intake on serum lipids. N Engl J Med 1995;333:276–82.
15. Barnes S. Molecular targets for dietary prevention of prostate cancer: soy products and genistein. National Cancer Institute Meeting; 2000 Jun 16.
16. Barnes S, Peterson TG, Coward L. Rationale for the use of genistein-containing soy matrices in chemoprevention trials for breast and prostate cancer. J Cell Biochem Suppl 1995;22:181–7.
17. Barnes S, et al. Soy isoflavonoids and cancer prevention. Underlying biochemical and pharmacological issues. Adv Exp Med Biol 1996;401:87–100.
18. British Menopause Society. Isoflavones in the management of the menopause. Proceedings supplement from an educational meeting, London, September 2000. J Br Menopause Soc 2001; 7(1).
19. Cassidy A, Bingham S, Setchell KD. Biological effects of a diet of soy protein rich in isoflavones on the menstrual cycle of premenopausal women. Am J Clin Nutr 1994;60:333–40.
20. Cline JM, Hugher CL Jr. Phytochemicals for the prevention of breast and endometrial cancer. Cancer Treat Res 1998;94:107–34.
21. Fournier DB, Erdman JW Jr, Gordon GB. Soy, its components, and cancer prevention: a review of the in vitro, animal, and human data. Cancer Epidemiol Biomarkers Prev 1998;7:1055–65.
22. Goodman MT, et al. Association of soy and fiber consumption with risk of endometrial cancer. Am J Epidemiol 1997;146:294–306.
23. Han KK, et al. Benefits of soy isoflavone therapeutic regimen on menopausal symptoms. Obstet Gynecol 2002;99:389–94.
24. Horn-Ross PL, Hoggatt KJ, Lee MM. Phytoestrogens and thyroid cancer risk: the San Francisco Bay Area Thyroid Cancer Study. Cancer Epidemiol Biomarkers Prev 2002;11:43–9.
25. Ingram D, et al. Case-control study of phyto-oestrogens and breast cancer. Lancet 1997;350:990–4.
26. Messina MJ, Loprinzi CL. Soy for breast cancer survivors: a critical review of the literature. J Nutr 2001;131:3095S–108S.
27. Messina MJ, Persky V, Setchell KD, Barnes S. Soy intake and cancer risk: a review of the in vitro and in vivo data. Nutr Cancer 1994;21:113–31.
28. Moyad MA. Soy, disease prevention, and prostate cancer. Semin Urol Oncol 1999;17:97–102.
29. Potter SM, Baum JA, Teng H, et al. Soy protein and isoflavones: their effects on blood lipids and bone density in postmenopausal women. Am J Clin Nutr 1998;68 Suppl:1375S–9S.
30. Scambia G, et al. Clinical effects of a standardized soy extract in postmenopausal women: a pilot study. J North Am Menopause Soc 2000;7:105–11.

31. Setchell KD. Phytoestrogens: the biochemistry, physiology, and implications for human health of soy isoflavones. Am J Clin Nutr 1998;6:1333S–46S.

32. Severson RK, et al. A prospective study of demographics, diet, and prostate cancer among men of Japanese ancestry in Hawaii. Cancer Res 1989;49:1857.

33. Upmalis DH, et al. Vasomotor symptom relief by soy isoflavone extract tablets in post-menopausal women: a multicenter, double-blind, randomized, placebo-controlled study. Menopause 2000;7:236–42.

34. Kumar NB, et al. The specific role of isoflavones on estrogen metabolism in premenopausal women. Cancer 2002;94:1166–74.

35. Van Patten CL, et al. Effect of soy phytoestrogens on hot flashes in postmenopausal women with breast cancer: a randomized, controlled clinical trial. J Clin Oncol 2002;20:1449–55.

St. John's Wort

A.DONATO

COMMON NAMES
Saint John's wort, *Hypericum*,
goatweed, God's wonder plant,
witches' herb

SCIENTIFIC NAME
Hypericum perforatum

KEY WORDS
Hypericum perforatum, Saint
John's Wort

CLINICAL SUMMARY

Derived from the aerial parts of the plant. St. John's wort is generally used for depression, seasonal affective disorder, and anxiety. Products currently are standardized based on hypericin content, although the hyperforin and bioflavonoid contents are believed to be responsible for activity. St. John's wort is metabolized primarily by the liver. Numerous studies comparing St. John's wort with placebo or standard antidepressants suggest that it may be as effective as imipramine or selective serotonin reuptake inhibitors (SSRIs) to treat mild to moderate depression. St. John's wort should not be used for patients with severe depression. Studies also show possible efficacy in the management of anxiety and premenstrual syndrome, although additional research is necessary. St. John's wort can interact with many medications owing to induction of cytochrome P-450 3A4 and other mechanisms. Significant interactions include decreased efficacy of antiretrovirals, cyclosporin, tacrolimus, antiepileptics, irinotecan, and other chemotherapeutic agents. Serotonin syndrome may occur when combined with sympathomimetics, antidepressants, or triptans (serotonin 5-hydroxytryptamine$_1$ agonists). Frequently reported adverse events include nausea, headache, constipation, dizziness, confusion, fatigue, and dry mouth. St. John's wort should not be taken with other medications and should be used under medical supervision.

CONSTITUENTS

Anthraquinones: napthodianthrones, including hypericin and pseudohypericin; phloroglucinols: hyperforin, adhyperforin; flavonoids: hyperin, hyperoside, quercetin, kaempferol, rutin, hyperoside; bioflavonoids: amenotoflavone, II8-biapigenin; phenols: caffeic, chlorogenic, paracoumaric, parahydroxybenzoic acid, hyperfolin; volatile oils: methyl-2-octane, trace amounts of monoterpenes (limonene) and sesquiterpenes; (caryophyllene, humulene); tannins: proanthocyanidins.[1,2]

WARNINGS

May cause photosensitivity. St John's wort should be discontinued 1 week before surgery or chemotherapy.

MECHANISM OF ACTION

The overall mechanism of action for St. John's wort is unknown. The hypericin component was thought to be responsible for antidepressant activity, but conflicting reports exist. It was initially shown to inhibit monoamine oxidase, although this effect has not been demonstrated with use of the whole botanical. Hypericin demonstrates modest receptor affinity for muscarinic cholinergic and sigma receptors. In vitro studies with whole-plant extract of St. John's wort report weak inhibition of catechol O-methyltransferase and limited reuptake of norepinephrine. Hyperforin, a phloroglucinol, has been shown to inhibit the reuptake of serotonin, dopamine, norepinephrine, γ-aminobutyric acid (GABA), and L-glutamine in vitro. Analgesic and central nervous system activity may be attributable to the bioflavonoid content.[1-3]

USAGE

Anxiety, depression, fatigue, insomnia, pain, pediatric nocturnal incontinence, premenstrual syndrome, seasonal affective disorder, wound healing.

PHARMACOKINETICS

Hypericin: Oral administration peak concentration at approximately 2 hours; elimination half-life at approximately 25 hours. Steady-state concentrations with three times daily dosing occurred by day 4. Terminal half-life is 42 hours.

Hyperforin: Oral administration peak concentration occurred at approximately 3.5 hours. Elimination half-life is approximately 9 hours. Steady-state concentration with 300 mg St. John's wort (standardized to 14.8 mg hyperforin) is equal to 100 ng/mL.

Pseudohypericin: Oral administration peak concentration at approximately 30 minutes. Terminal half-life is approximately 23 hours.[4]

ADVERSE REACTIONS

Common: Headache, nausea, abdominal discomfort, constipation, dizziness, confusion, fatigue, dry mouth, sleep disturbances, and sedation.

Infrequent: Photosensitivity or photodermatitis, elevated liver function tests, acute neuropathy, increased prothrombin time.

Case Reports:

- Mania in three patients with underlying bipolar disorder. Resolved promptly in two patients following discontinuation, whereas the third experienced persistent agitation for several months.
- Serotonin syndrome: hypertension, diaphoresis, agitation, dizziness, and weakness with acute onset following 10 days of St. John's wort. Syndrome resolved following supportive care and discontinuation of St. John's wort.
- Erythroderma affecting both light-exposed and non–light-exposed areas of skin. Developed 4 days after initiation of St. John's wort and resolved after 5 weeks with concomitant oral steroids.
- Sexual dysfunction: decreased sexual libido that returned following discontinuation of St. John's wort.[1,2,4–7]

DRUG INTERACTIONS

Cytochrome 3A4: St. John's wort has been shown to induce cytochrome isoenzyme 3A4, therefore affecting metabolism of certain medications and reducing serum concentrations. Drugs metabolized by 3A4 include the following:

- *Theophylline.* Blood levels of theophylline may be significantly reduced, resulting in decreased efficacy.
- *HIV protease inhibitors.* Blood levels of indinavir, nelfinavir, ritonavir, and saquinavir can be significantly reduced, resulting in increased human immunodeficiency virus (HIV) viral load and development of viral resistance.
- *HIV non-nucleoside reverse transcriptase inhibitors.* Blood levels of efavirenz and nevirapine can be significantly reduced, resulting in increased HIV viral load.
- *Cyclosporine/tacrolimus.* Blood levels of cyclosporine or tacrolimus can be significantly reduced, resulting in decreased efficacy.
- *Diltiazem/nifedipine.* Blood levels of diltiazem or nifedipine can be reduced, resulting in decreased efficacy.

Irinotecan: Owing to changes in hepatic metabolism caused by St. John's wort, levels of irinotecan metabolite SN-38 may be lowered by as much as 40% for up to 3 weeks following discontinuation of St. John's wort.

Warfarin: May increase or decrease activity when administered concomitantly. International normalized ratio should be monitored routinely. S-isomer may have increased metabolism owing to CYP 3A4 induction. S-isomer may have decreased metabolism owing to CYP 1A2 inhibition.

Digoxin: Prolonged concurrent administration may result in decreased absorption of digoxin with lowered plasma concentrations.

Triptans: Increased serotonergic effect and possible serotonin syndrome when combined with sumatriptan, naratriptan, rizatriptan, or zolmitriptan.

SSRIs: Increased serotonergic effect and possible serotonin syndrome when combined with citalopram, fluoxetine, fluvoxamine, paroxetine, or sertraline.

Tricyclic Antidepressants: Increased serotonergic effect and possible serotonin syndrome when combined with nefazodone, amitriptyline, or imipramine. Possible reduction in efficacy of antidepressants owing to changes in metabolism.

Oral Contraceptives: May reduce blood levels resulting in decreased efficacy (ie, breakthrough bleeding or pregnancy).

Alcohol: May result in increased sedation.

Anesthetics: Case report of cardiovascular collapse (hypotension without anaphylactic symptoms) shortly after induction of general anesthesia with fentanyl, propofol, d-tubocurarine, and succinylcholine followed by nitrous oxide, oxygen, and isoflurane.

Chemotherapy: Owing to changes in hepatic metabolism caused by St. John's wort, chemotherapy levels may be altered, resulting in increased toxicity or decreased efficacy. Caution should be exercised when administering concomitantly with chemotherapy (ie, cyclophosphamide, paclitaxel, etoposide, irinotecan).

Tamoxifen: Owing to changes in hepatic metabolism caused by St. John's wort, levels of tamoxifen may be lowered, resulting in reduced efficacy.

Sympathomimetics: Concomitant administration may produce increased serotonergic activity and possible serotonin syndrome.[4,8–11]

LABORATORY INTERACTIONS

Elevated liver function tests.

CONTRAINDICATIONS

Pregnant or nursing women should not consume.

DOSAGE

Oral: Adults: 300 mg (standardized extract 0.3% hypericin) administered three times a day. Maximum 1,200 mg/d.

LITERATURE SUMMARY AND CRITIQUE

Shelton RC, et al. Effectiveness of St. John's wort in major depression: a randomized controlled trial. JAMA 2001;285:1978–86.

A prospective, randomized, multicenter, placebo-controlled evaluation of 900 to 1,200 mg/d of St. John's wort or placebo for major depression. A total of 167 patients completed the 8-week trial, 87 receiving placebo and 80 receiving St. John's wort. Patients who had previously taken St. John's wort, were refractory to traditional antidepressant, or had a history of concomitant psychological disorder (ie, panic, schizophrenia, bipolar disorder) were excluded. No significant difference was found between St. John's wort and placebo for measured outcomes including scores on the Hamilton depression scale, Hamilton Anxiety Scale, Beck Depression Inventory, and global assessment of function. This study indicates that St. John's wort should not be used as monotherapy in patients with severe depression. However, the results of this study do not represent those for patients with minor to moderate depression.

Brenner R, et al. Comparison of an extract of hypericum (LI 160) and sertraline in the treatment of depression: a double-blind, randomized pilot study. Clin Ther 2000;22:411–9.

Prospective, randomized evaluation in which patients with mild to moderate depression were given either standardized St. John's wort (900 mg/d) or sertraline (75 mg/d) for 7 weeks. A total of 28 patients (13 St. John's wort and 15 sertraline) were enrolled and included in the intent-to-treat analysis. Both treatment arms had similar Hamilton depression scores greater than 17. A total of 8 patients (5 St. John's wort and 3 sertraline) withdrew from the study at week 7 owing to either adverse reactions (4 patients) or withdrawn consent (4 patients). Statistical analysis of all enrolled patients demonstrated no significant difference between treatment groups, indicating that St. John's wort is as effective as sertraline for mild depression. However, the small sample size is probably inadequate for definitive conclusions to be drawn.

Schrader E. Equivalence of St. John's wort extract (ze 117) and fluoxetine: a randomized, controlled study in mild-moderate depression. Int Clin Psychopharmacol 2000;15:61–8.

A prospective evaluation of 240 patients randomized to receive 20 mg/d of fluoxetine ($n = 114$) or 500 mg/d of St. John's wort ($n = 126$). Both treatment arms had Hamilton depression scores of approximately 19.5. One patient in the St. John's wort group withdrew from the study immediately following baseline assessment and one patient in the fluoxetine group withdrew owing to adverse effects. Following 6 weeks of therapy, St. John's wort and fluoxetine were equally efficacious with respect to change in Hamilton depression scale and clinical global impression. Adverse events associated with St. John's wort were gastrointestinal disturbance, dizziness, and fatigue. Fluoxetine and St. John's wort appear to be equally efficacious for the management of mild to moderate depression.

Stevinson C, Ernst E. A pilot study of *Hypericum perforatum* for the treatment of premenstrual syndrome. Br J Obstet Gynecol 2000;107:870–6.

Small, prospective evaluation of women experiencing premenstrual syndrome (PMS) for at least two cycles prior to treatment with hypericum. A total of 96 patients were screened preliminarily; 69 patients were asked to continue into baseline evaluation, and 25 patients passed baseline screening and were enrolled into the trial. Six patients withdrew consent (3 for personal reasons, 1 had hysterectomy, 1 pregnancy, and 1 adverse reaction of "jitteriness"). Treatment dose of hypericum was 300 mg three times a day (standardized to 0.3% hypericin). Adverse events seen at initiation were gastrointestinal in nature and subsided during treatment. Following two cycles of therapy, a 51%

improvement in self-reported Daily Symptoms Ratings score from baseline was documented. This pilot study indicates a possible role for St. John's wort in the treatment of PMS, but larger studies are needed.

REFERENCES

1. Newall CA, et al. Herbal medicines: a guide for health-care professionals. London: Pharmaceutical Press; 1996.
2. Fetrow CW, et al. Professional's handbook of complementary and alternative medicine. Springhouse (PA): Springhouse; 1999.
3. Foster S, et al. Tyler's honest herbal: a sensible guide to the use of herbs and related remedies. New York: Haworth Herbal Press; 1999.
4. Barnes J, Anderson LA, Phillipson JD. St. John's wort (*Hypericum perforatum* L.): a review of its chemistry, pharmacology and clinical properties. J Pharm Pharmacol 2001;53:583–600.
5. Parker V, et al. Adverse reactions to St. John's wort. Can J Psychiatry 2001;46:77–9.
6. Holme SA, Roberts DL. Erythroderma associated with St. John's wort. Br J Dermatol 2000;143:1127–8.
7. Bhopal JS. St. John's wort-induced sexual dysfunction. Can J Psychiatry 2001;46:456–7.
8. Brinker F. Herb contraindications and drug interactions. 3rd ed. Sandy (OR): Eclectic Medical Publications; 2001.
9. Irefin S, Sprung J. A possible cause of cardiovascular collapse during anesthesia: long-term use of St. John's wort. J Clin Anesth 2000;12:498–9.
10. Mathijssen RAHJ. Modulation of irinotecan (CPT-11) metabolism by St. John's wort in cancer patients [abstract]. American Association for Cancer Research Annual Meeting; 2000; San Francisco, CA.
11. Mathijssen RHJ, et al. Effects of St. John's wort on irinotecan metabolism. J Natl Cancer Inst 2002;94:1247–9.

Stillingia

COMMON NAMES
Stillingia treculeana, queen's root, queen's delight, yaw root

SCIENTIFIC NAME
Stillingia sylvatica

CLINICAL SUMMARY

Derived from the root of the plant. This supplement is used to treat syphilis, bronchitis, constipation, hemorrhoids, and skin conditions and as part of the Hoxsey herbal tonic for cancer. Stillingia contains diterpene esters that cause mucosal irritation and skin eruptions. Other reported toxicities include vertigo, diarrhea, nausea, vomiting, muscle ache, pruritus, cough, fatigue, and sweating. No clinical data support the use of this supplement for any proposed claim. Significant toxicity can occur following administration.

CONSTITUENTS

Terpenoids: stillingia factors S_1 to S_8; diterpene esters: phorbol, ingenane, daphnane; volatile oils; others: sylvacrol, resinic acid, stillingine, tannin, hydrocyanic acid (leaf and stem).[1]

WARNINGS

The diterpene esters in stillingia are irritants to the skin and mucous membranes.[1]

MECHANISM OF ACTION
No studies have evaluated stillingia for any proposed claim. Stillingia contains diterpene esters, toxic irritants that can cause swelling and inflammation of the skin. Anecdotal in vitro research suggests that diterpene esters may have antitumor activity, but this has not been confirmed with stillingia root.[1,2]

USAGE
Bronchitis, cancer treatment, chest congestion, constipation, hemorrhoids, laryngitis, skin abscesses, spasms, syphilis.

ADVERSE REACTIONS
Toxicity: Vertigo, burning sensation on mucous membranes, diarrhea, nausea, vomiting, muscle ache, pruritus, skin eruptions, cough, fatigue, sweating.[1]

DRUG INTERACTIONS
None known.

DOSAGE
No dosage is recommended for this product.

LITERATURE SUMMARY AND CRITIQUE
No studies have evaluated stillingia root for any proposed claim.

REFERENCES
1. Newall C, et al. Herbal medicines: a guide for health-care professionals. 1st ed. London. Pharmaceutical Press; 1996.
2. Szallasi Z, et al. Nonpromoting 12-deoxyphorbol 13-esters inhibit phorbol 12-myristate 13-acetate induced tumor promotion in CD-1 mouse skin. Cancer Res 1993;53:2507–12.

Sun Farms Vegetable Soup

COMMON NAMES
Sun Soup, selected vegetables, SV

KEY WORD
Sun Soup

CLINICAL SUMMARY
Proprietary product that contains water, soybean, shiitake mushroom, mung bean, red date, scallion, garlic, lentil bean, leek, hawthorn fruit, onion, American ginseng, angelica root, licorice, dandelion root, senegal root, ginger, olive, sesame seed, and parsley. Sun Soup was developed by biochemist Alexander Sun, PhD, who has held faculty and research positions at the Yale University School of Medicine, the Mount Sinai School of Medicine, Rockefeller University, and the University of California, Berkeley. Patients use this supplement in conjunction with conventional therapies to prevent and treat cancer and human immunodeficiency virus/acquired immune deficiency syndrome (HIV/AIDS), promote weight gain, and as an immunostimulant. Sun Soup selected vegetables (SV) is offered frozen (FSV) or freeze-dried (DSV). No side effects have been reported other than bloatedness and fullness after ingestion. DSV exhibits antitumor activity in mouse models. Data from small open-label phase I/II studies of SV administered concurrently with conventional therapies for stage III and IV non–small cell lung cancer (NSCLC) suggest improvements in survival, Karnofsky Performance Scale (KPS) score, and objective tumor regression. Larger randomized studies are under way to substantiate these data. A phase II trial evaluating the immune-enhancing effects of SV on AIDS patients is under way at the Mount Sinai School of Medicine.

CONSTITUENTS
Ingredients: water, soybean, shiitake mushroom, mung bean, red date, scallion, garlic, lentil bean, leek, hawthorn fruit, onion, American ginseng, angelica root, licorice, dandelion root, senegal root, ginger, olive, sesame seed, and parsley.[1]

MECHANISM OF ACTION

Unknown. No formal studies have analyzed the activity of Sun Soup. The inventor suggests that the "modest" individual antitumor activities of chemicals in certain ingredients act synergistically. Quantitative analysis of DSV reveals approximately 63 mg of inositol hexaphosphate (IP_6), 2.6 mg of genistein, 4.4 mg of daidzein, and 15.5 mg of coumestrol per serving. In vitro and animal studies performed with IP_6 suggest that it slows the initiation and/or promotion, inhibits proliferation by chelation of metalloproteins, causes G_0/G_1 arrest, and induces differentiation of various cancer cell lines. In vitro, genistein inhibits angiogenesis, induces DNA damage in cancer cell lines, and, with daidzein and coumestrol, inhibits the growth of human prostate cancer cell lines. Genistein and coumestrol have been shown to induce reduced nicotinamide adenine dinucleotide phosphate:quinone reductase, a detoxifying phase II enzyme, in colonic cells, leading to possible antitumor effects. Shiitake mushrooms contain lentinan, a polysaccharide, which may act as an immunomodulator and enhance production of interleukin-1, tumor necrosis factor, lymphokine activated killer (LAK) cell activity, cytotoxic T lymphocytes, and cytotoxic peritoneal exudate cells. A mouse tumor model showed that mice fed shiitake extract, mung bean extract, or both exhibited tumor inhibition of 60%, 53%, and 82%, respectively, compared with the control group after 22 days.[1-4]

USAGE

Cancer prevention, cancer treatment, HIV and AIDS, immunostimulation, weight maintenance.

PHARMACOKINETICS

No formal pharmacokinetic studies have been performed on Sun Soup.

ADVERSE REACTIONS

Common: Gastrointestinal fullness or bloatedness after ingestion.[1]

DRUG INTERACTIONS

Although no drug interactions have been reported, theoretical interactions exist for several ingredients present at unknown concentrations in Sun Soup (please see individual chapters): lentinan, garlic, hawthorn fruit, ginger, licorice, soy, and American ginseng.

DOSAGE

Oral: Freeze-dried powder: 30 g daily. *Thawed soup:* 283 g, about 10 ounces. Sun Soup should never be boiled or microwaved.[1,2,5]

LITERATURE SUMMARY AND CRITIQUE

Sun AS, et al. Phase I/II study of stage III and IV non-small cell lung cancer patients taking a specific dietary supplement. Nutr Cancer 1999;34:62–9.

A small, open-label phase I/II study conducted in the Czech Republic evaluating the effect of 30 g daily of Sun Farm soup DSV on the survival of patients also using conventional therapies. Stage III and IV NSCLC patients in the treatment group ($n = 6$) chose to receive daily DSV supplementation for 4 to 17 months and were compared with a control group of similar patients ($n = 13$). Although demographics (age, body mass index, KPS) are reported to be similar between treatment groups, the authors do not describe previous or current oncologic treatments used. The primary end point was death or survival measured up to 24 months from date of entry. KPS improved in those receiving DSV (75 ± 8 to 80 ± 13) and declined in control patients (79 ± 8 to 55 ± 11) 1 to 3 months after entry. Weight change in the control, treatment, and toxicity study patients was $-12 \pm 5\%$, $-2 \pm 2\%$, and $+4 \pm 4\%$, respectively. Median and mean survival were 4 and 4.8 months in control patients and 15.5 and 15 months in treatment patients ($p < .01$). Duration of DSV treatment varied between patients; most patients failed to ingest DSV for the intended period because of a lack of motivation, monotony of the diet, and taste preference. No toxicity resulted from chronic administration (17–24 months) in a subset of stage I NSCLC patients ($n = 5$). Although the author reported improved survival in patients taking Sun Farm soup, additional large, randomized, controlled studies are required.

Sun AS, et al. Pilot study of a specific dietary supplement in tumor-bearing mice and in stage IIIB and IV non-small cell lung cancer patients. Nutr Cancer 2001;39:85–95.

A small open-enrolment trial evaluating the survival of 18 volunteer stage IIIB and IV NSCLC patients consuming 283 g daily FSV alone or as an adjuvant to conventional therapy compared with historical controls. A murine lung tumor model was used to evaluate tumor inhibition activity. Mice receiving 5% DSV had 53 to 74% tumor inhibition by day 23 compared with controls. The mean and median survival times of eligible NSCLC patients using FSV were 23.7 and 33.5 months, respectively—significantly greater than the historical mean survival time of 7 months. One-year survival of FSV patients was 71%. Ten of the 13 patients receiving conventional treatment with FSV had no new sites of metastasis. Using FSV alone, two patients had objective regression of lung lesions and stability of other lesions for 39 and 29 months. The average KPS of all eligible patients increased from 55 ± 13 to 92 ± 9 ($p < .05$). Four patients were unable to ingest FSV at full dosage or for more than 2 months and exhibited normal mean survival time within the historical range (3–10 months). Types of previous and concurrent oncologic treatments were not specified. A possible source of bias is the self-selection of highly motivated patients who sought new treatments after failing to benefit from conventional therapies, but this alone would not likely result in a threefold increase in survival time. This study represents more of a case report series than a clinical trial but points to the need for a larger, randomized, double-blind, placebo-controlled trial, which is now in progress.

REFERENCES

1. Sun AS, et al. Phase I/II study of stage III and IV non-small cell lung cancer patients taking a specific dietary supplement. Nutr Cancer 1999;34:62–9.
2. Sun AS, et al. Pilot study of a specific dietary supplement in tumor-bearing mice and in stage IIIB and IV non-small cell lung cancer patients. Nutr Cancer 2001;39:85–95.
3. Mitchell JH, Duthie SJ, Collins AR. Effects of phytoestrogens on growth and DNA integrity in human prostate tumor cell lines: PC-3 and LNCaP. Nutr Cancer 2000;38:223–8.
4. Wang W, et al. Induction of NADPH: quinone reductase by dietary phytoestrogens in colonic Colo205 cells. Biochem Pharmacol 1998;56:189–95.
5. Sun Farms Corporation Web site. Available at: http://www.sunfarmcorp.com/index.htm (accessed Mar 13, 2002).

Superoxide Dismutase

COMMON NAMES
Dismuzyme, rh-SOD, orgotein superoxide, bovine superoxide dismutase

SCIENTIFIC NAME
SOD

KEY WORDS
SOD, dismuzyme

CLINICAL SUMMARY
Superoxide dismutase (SOD) is a ubiquitous enzyme throughout the body. SOD supplements are not absorbed following oral administration, and no data support claims of improved health or antiaging benefit. Sublingual SOD has no supporting literature at this time. The parenteral formulation, Orgotein, is classified by the US Food and Drug Administration (FDA) as an orphan drug, not as a dietary supplement, for the treatment of familial amyotrophic lateral sclerosis.

MECHANISM OF ACTION
The enzyme SOD catalyzes the breakdown of superoxide radicals, which are toxic to living cells, into harmless components consisting of oxygen and hydrogen peroxide.[1]

USAGE
Antiaging, cystitis (radiation induced), inflammation, osteoarthritis, scleroderma, urinary tract disorders.

PHARMACOKINETICS
Oral SOD is acid labile and has no oral bioavailability even when administered as enteric-coated capsules.[2]

ADVERSE REACTIONS

Common (Parenteral): Allergic reaction or pain at the injection site.

DRUG INTERACTIONS

None reported.

DOSAGE

Parenteral: The FDA classifies injectable Orgotein as an orphan drug. *Interstitial and radiation-induced cystitis:* 12 mg injected into the bladder a total of six times. *Osteoarthritis:* 16 mg intra-articularly twice a day. *Radiation-induced cystitis:* 8 mg intramuscularly daily. *Kidney transplantation to reduce rejection risk:* 200 mg intravenously during surgery.

Oral: No dosage recommended; possibly ineffective.

LITERATURE SUMMARY AND CRITIQUE

Sanchiz F, et al. Prevention of radioinduced cystitis by Orgotein: a randomized study. Anticancer Res 1996;16:2025–8.

A total of 448 patients were randomly allocated to receive either radiotherapy or radiotherapy and SOD 8 mg/d intramuscularly after each radiotherapeutic application. Apart from cutaneous side effects, a highly significant incidence of radioinduced acute cystitis and rectitis was detected in patients not treated by SOD. The data support the contention that SOD is effective in decreasing acute radioinduced damage and also in preventing the appearance of more delayed disorders.

Land W, et al. The beneficial effect of human recombinant superoxide dismutase on acute and chronic rejection events in recipients of cadaveric renal transplants. Transplantation 1994;57:211–7.

A prospective, randomized, double-blind, placebo-controlled trial assessing the effect of intravenous rh-SOD 200 mg during surgery in cyclosporine-treated recipients of cadaveric renal allografts on both acute and chronic rejection events as well as on patient and graft survival. Outcomes were measured by analyzing patients' charts retrospectively. The results show that rh-SOD exerts a beneficial effect on acute rejection events (18.5% rejection compared with 33.3% in controls) as well as on early irreversible acute rejection (3.7% rejections compared with 12.5% in controls). With regard to long-term results, there was a significant improvement of the actual 4-year graft survival rate in rh-SOD-treated patients to 74% compared with 52% in controls.

McIlwain H, et al. Intra-articular Orgotein in osteoarthritis of the knee: a placebo-controlled efficacy, safety, and dosage comparison. Am J Med 1989;87:295.

A total of 139 patients with osteoarthritis of the knee were randomly assigned to receive one intra-articular injection of either placebo or SOD (8–32 mg) each week for 3 weeks. Results showed that SOD was effective in reducing symptoms of osteoarthritis for up to

3 months after treatment; 16 mg given twice a day was the most effective and best tolerated regimen.

Nielsen OS, et al. Orgotein in radiation treatment of bladder cancer. A report on allergic reactions and lack of radioprotective effect. Acta Oncol 1987;26:101–4.
A double-blind study in 60 patients was planned, but, owing to unacceptable side effects, only 30 patients were included. SOD was injected at a dose of 4 or 8 mg 15 minutes after each daily radiation treatment. No effect of SOD on tumor radiation response or on acute radiation reactions in the bladder and rectum was detected. Redness and allergic reactions were seen at the site of injection in 5 patients.

Kadrnka F. Results of a multicenter Orgotein study in radiation induced and interstitial cystitis. Eur J Rheumatol Inflamm 1981;4:237–43.
Thirty-two patients suffering from radiation or interstitial cystitis were treated with intramural SOD injections into the bladder wall. The injections were administered during 4- to 6-week intervals and were given one to six times. The dose of injection was 12 mg six times a day. In all patients, an improvement in symptoms was observed. SOD treatment tolerability was found to be from good to very good in 90% of the cases.

REFERENCES
1. McCord JM, Fridovich I. Superoxide dismutase. An enzymic function for erythrocuprein (hemocuprein). J Biol Chem 1969;244:6049–55.
2. DerMarderosian A, editor. The review of natural products. St. Louis: Facts and Comparisons; 1999.

Tea Tree Oil

COMMON NAME
Melaleuca oil from Australia

SCIENTIFIC NAME
Melaleuca alternifolia

KEY WORD
Melaleuca alternifolia

A.DONATO

CLINICAL SUMMARY
Oil derived from the leaf of the tree. Tea tree oil should only be used topically. Oral consumption has resulted in serious adverse events, including coma. The active components are thought to be terpinen-4-ol, α-terpineol, and α-pinene. In vitro antimicrobial activity has been demonstrated against *Candida albicans, Escherichia coli, Staphylococcus aureus, Pseudomonas aeruginosa, Staphylococcus epidermidis,* and *Propionibacterium acnes.* Clinical studies suggest efficacy in treating acne, tinea pedis, and distal subungual onychomycosis compared with standard therapies. Skin irritation and hypersensitivity reactions have been reported following topical administration.

CONSTITUENTS
Volatile oils: terpinen-4-ol, 1-8-cineole, α-terpineol, sesquiterpenoid, terpinolene.[1]

WARNINGS
Tea tree oil should only be used topically. Internal administration may cause severe toxicity. Both coma and neutrophil leukocytosis have occurred following oral administration.

MECHANISM OF ACTION

Tea tree oil, especially terpinen-4-ol, seems to have antimicrobial activity against all test organisms including *C. albicans*, *E. coli*, *S. aureus*, and *P. aeruginosa*. In addition, the constituents terpin-4-ol, α-terpineol, and α-pinene were found to possess antimicrobial effects against *S. epidermidis* and *P. acnes.*[2]

USAGE

Acne, burns, fungal infections, insect bites and stings, mucositis, skin infections, wound healing.

ADVERSE REACTIONS

Reported (Topical): Local skin irritation and allergic contact dermatitis. *Reported (Oral):* Disorientation, systemic contact dermatitis, coma, body rash, and neutrophil leukocytosis.[3,4]

DRUG INTERACTIONS

None known.

DOSAGE

Topical: Acne: A 5% solution applied daily has been used successfully in studies. *Athlete's foot:* A 10% solution in studies twice a day has been used. *Toe nail fungus or onychomycosis:* A 100% solution twice a day has been used.[5–7]

LITERATURE SUMMARY AND CRITIQUE

Buck DS, et al. Comparison of two topical preparations for the treatment of onychomycosis: *Melaleuca alternifolia* (tea tree) oil and clotrimazole. J Fam Pract 1994;38:601–5.
A double-blind, multicenter, randomized, controlled trial on 117 patients with distal subungual onychomycosis proven by culture. Patients received twice-daily application of either 1% clotrimazole solution or 100% tea tree oil for 6 months. After 6 months of therapy, the two treatment groups were comparable based on culture cure and clinical assessment documenting partial or full resolution.

Bassett IB, et al. A comparative study of tea-tree oil versus benzoyl peroxide in the treatment of acne. Med J Aust 1990;153:455–8.
A single-blind, randomized clinical trial on 124 patients to evaluate the efficacy and skin tolerance of 5% tea tree oil gel in the treatment of mild to moderate acne when compared with 5% benzoyl peroxide lotion. The results show that both products had a significant effect in ameliorating acne by reducing the number of inflamed and noninflamed lesions, although the onset of action with tea tree oil was slower. Fewer side effects were experienced by patients receiving tea tree oil.

Tong MM, et al. Tea tree oil in the treatment of tinea pedis. Aust J Dermatol 1992;33: 145–9.

One hundred and four patients completed a randomized, double-blind trial to evaluate the efficacy of 10% tea tree oil cream compared with 1% tolnaftate and placebo creams in the treatment of tinea pedis. Significantly more tolnaftate-treated patients (85%) than tea tree oil (30%) and placebo-treated patients (21%) showed conversion to negative cultures at the end of therapy. There was no statistically significant difference between tea tree oil and placebo groups. The tea tree group and the tolnaftate group showed significant improvement in clinical condition when compared with the placebo group. Tea tree oil appears to reduce the symptomatology of tinea pedis as effectively as tolnaftate 1% but is no more effective than placebo in achieving a mycologic cure.

REFERENCES

1. Osborne F, et al. Australian tea tree oil. Herb Med 1998;March:42–6.
2. May J, et al. Time-kill studies of tea tree oils on clinical isolates. J Antimicrob Chemother 2000;45:639–43.
3. Rubel DM, Freeman S, Southwell IA. Tea tree oil allergy: what is the offending agent? Report of three cases of tea tree oil allergy and review of the literature. Aust J Dermatol 1998;39:244–7.
4. Carson C, Riley TV, Cookson BD. Efficacy and safety of tea tree oil as a topical antimicrobial agent. J Hosp Infect 1998;40:175–8.
5. Bassett IB, Pannowitz DL, Barnetson RS. A comparative study of tea tree oil versus benzoyl peroxide in the treatment of acne. Med J Aust 1990;153:455–8.
6. Tong MM, Altman PM, Barnetson RS. Tea tree oil in the treatment of tinea pedis. Aust J Dermatol 1992;33:145–9.
7. Buck DS, Nidorf DM, Addino JG. Comparison of two topical preparations for the treatment of onychomycosis: *Melaleuca alternifolia* (tea tree) oil and clotrimazole. J Fam Pract 1994; 38:601–5.

Turmeric

A.DONATO

COMMON NAMES
Indian saffron, curcumin, jiang huang

SCIENTIFIC NAMES
Curcuma longa, Curcuma domestica

KEY WORDS
Curcuma longa, curcumin, Indian saffron, jiang huang

CLINICAL SUMMARY

Derived from the rhizome and root. This supplement is routinely used as a spice and coloring agent. Oral administration is well tolerated, but bioavailability is relatively low, approximately 60%. Following absorption, turmeric is rapidly metabolized. Although in vitro and animal studies suggest antiproliferative and preventive effects against cancer, human data are lacking. No significant adverse events have been reported. Patients with gastrointestinal disorders should not take this supplement. Recent animal studies indicate that dietary turmeric may inhibit the antitumor action of chemotherapeutic agents such as cyclophosphamide in treating breast cancer. More research is necessary, but it may be advisable for breast cancer patients undergoing chemotherapy to limit intake of turmeric and turmeric-containing foods.

CONSTITUENTS

Volatile oils: mainly sesquiterpenes and zingiberene and curcuminoids (curcumin); electrolytes: potassium; vitamins: ascorbic acid, carotene; polysaccharides.[1]

WARNINGS

Recent laboratory findings indicate that dietary turmeric may inhibit the antitumor action of chemotherapeutic agents such as cyclophosphamide in treating breast cancer. More research is necessary, but it may be advisable for breast cancer patients undergoing chemotherapy to limit intake of turmeric and turmeric-containing foods.[2]

MECHANISM OF ACTION

The mechanism of action is not fully understood. Turmeric has anti-inflammatory and choleretic action. Anti-inflammatory action may be attributable to leukotriene inhibition. Its curcuminoids (curcumin) and volatile oil are both partly responsible for the anti-inflammatory activity. Curcuminoids induce glutathione S-transferase and are potent inhibitors of cytochrome P-450. Turmeric acts as a free radical scavenger and antioxidant, inhibiting lipid peroxidation and oxidative DNA damage. It also inhibits activation of nuclear factor-κB[4], c-jun/AP-1 function, and activation of the c-Jun NH_2-terminal kinase (JNK) pathway. In vitro and animal models of breast cancer show that turmeric may inhibit chemotherapy-induced apoptosis via inhibition of the JNK pathway and reactive oxygen species generation. The isolated constituent α r-turmerone has been shown to arrest the reproduction and slaughterer activity of human lymphocytes, which may contribute to its anti-inflammatory action. Curcumin is more effective by parenteral injection than by oral ingestion. Curcumin has displayed antitumor activity and may be protective against some cancers, such as colon cancer. In laboratory tests, curcumin's antitumor actions appear to be attribuable to interactions with arachidonate metabolism and its in vivo antiangiogenic properties.[2,3]

USAGE

Cancer prevention, infections, inflammation, kidney stones, stomach and intestinal gas.

PHARMACOKINETICS

Bioavailability of curcumin is approximately 60 to 65% following oral administration. Metabolism is primarily via glucuronidation to glucuronide and glucuronide/sulfate metabolites. In vitro studies indicate inhibition of cytochrome P-450 1A1. Excretion of parent compound is primarily in the feces with metabolites present in the urine.[4,5]

ADVERSE REACTIONS

None known.

DRUG INTERACTIONS

Reserpine: Turmeric may reduce efficacy.
Indomethacin: Turmeric may reduce efficacy.

Anticoagulants/Antiplatelets: Turmeric may increase risk of bleeding.

Camptothecin: Turmeric inhibits camptothecin-induced apoptosis of breast cancer cell lines in vitro.

Mechlorethamine: Turmeric inhibits mechlorethamine-induced apoptosis of breast cancer cell lines in vitro.

Doxorubicin: Turmeric inhibits doxorubicin-induced apoptosis of breast cancer cell lines in vitro.

Cyclophosphamide: Dietary turmeric inhibits cyclophosphamide-induced tumor regression in animal studies.[2,6]

CONTRAINDICATIONS

Patients with bile duct obstruction, gallstones, and gastrointestinal disorders (including stomach ulcers and hyperacidity disorders) should not take this supplement.[7]

DOSAGE

Parenteral: Not available in the United States.

Oral: 250 to 500 mg three times a day. *Fluid extract:* 10 to 30 drops three times a day.

LITERATURE SUMMARY AND CRITIQUE

Human Data

James J. Curcumin: clinical trial finds no antiviral effect. AIDS Treat News 1996;242:1.

A randomized study of 38 patients to either high-dose or low-dose turmeric powder. Following 8 weeks of treatment, there was no demonstrated effect of turmeric on human immunodeficiency virus (HIV) viral load. A small increase in CD4 cells in the high-dose group and a consistent fall of CD4 cells in the low-dose group were documented, but neither result was statistically significant. This report of an abstract presented at the Third Annual Conference on Retroviruses and Opportunistic Infections demonstrated no efficacy of turmeric in treating HIV.

Animal/In Vitro Data

Li JK, et al. Mechanisms of cancer chemoprevention by curcumin. Proc Natl Sci Counc Repub China B 2001;25:59–66.

Curcumin has shown anticarcinogenic activity in animals as indicated by its ability to block colon tumor initiation by azoxymethane and skin tumor promotion induced by phorbol ester tissue plasminogen activator (TPA). Recently, curcumin has been considered by oncologists as a potential third-generation cancer chemopreventive agent, and clinical trials using it have been carried out in several laboratories. Curcumin possesses anti-inflammatory activity and is a potent inhibitor of reactive oxygen-generating enzymes, such as lipoxygenase/cyclooxygenase, xanthine dehydrogenase/oxidase, and inducible nitric oxide synthase. Curcumin is also a potent inhibitor of protein kinase C and epidermal growth

factor receptor tyrosine kinase. It is proposed that curcumin may suppress tumor promotion by blocking signal transduction pathways in the target cells.

Venkatesan N. Curcumin prevents Adriamycin nephrotoxicity in rats. Br J Pharmacol 2000;129:231–4.
This study investigated the effect of curcumin on Adriamycin (ADR; doxorubicin) nephrosis in rats. The results indicate that ADR-induced kidney injury was remarkably well prevented by treatment with curcumin. Treatment with curcumin markedly protected against
ADR-induced proteinuria, albuminuria, hypoalbuminemia, and hyperlipidemia. Curcumin restored renal function in ADR rats, as judged by the increase in glomerular filtration rate. The data also demonstrate that curcumin protects against ADR-induced renal
injury by suppressing oxidative stress and increasing kidney glutathione content and glutathione peroxidase activity. This suggests that administration of curcumin is a promising
approach in the treatment of nephrosis caused by ADR.

Kawamori T, et al. Chemopreventive effect of curcumin, a naturally occurring anti-inflammatory agent, during the promotion/progression stages of colon cancer. Cancer Res 1999;59:597–601.
This study was designed to investigate the chemopreventive action of curcumin when
administered (late in the premalignant stage) during the promotion/progression stage of
colon carcinogenesis in male F344 rats. The study also monitored the modulating effect of
this agent on apoptosis in the tumors. The results showed that the administration of 0.2%
curcumin during both the initiation and postinitiation periods significantly inhibited colon
tumorigenesis. In addition, administration of 0.2% and of 0.6% synthetic curcumin in the
diet during the promotion/progression stage significantly suppressed the incidence and
multiplicity of noninvasive adenocarcinomas and also strongly inhibited the multiplicity of
invasive adenocarcinomas of the colon.

Mehta K, et al. Antiproliferative effect of curcumin (diferuloylmethane) against human breast tumor cell lines. Anticancer Drugs 1997;8:470–81.
The antiproliferative effects of curcumin against several breast tumor cell lines, including
hormone dependent, hormone-independent, and multidrug lines, were studied. Curcumin
preferentially arrested cells in the G_2/S phase of the cell cycle. Curcumin-induced cell death
was attributable neither to apoptosis nor to a significant change in the expression of
apoptosis-related genes, including *BCL2* and *P53*.

Rao CV, et al. Chemoprevention of colon carcinogenesis by dietary curcumin, a naturally occurring plant phenolic compound. Cancer Res 1995;55:259–66.
This study was designed to investigate the chemopreventive action of dietary curcumin on
azoxymethane-induced colon carcinogenesis and the modulating effect of curcumin on the
colonic mucosal and tumor phospholipase A_2, phospholipase C-γ-1, lipoxygenase, and
cyclooxygenase activities in male F344 rats. The results indicate that the administration of
curcumin significantly inhibited incidence of colon adenocarcinomas ($p < .004$) and the
multiplicity of invasive, noninvasive, and total adenocarcinomas. Curcumin also significantly suppressed the colon tumor volume by more than 57% compared with the control

diet. Although the precise mechanism by which curcumin inhibits colon tumorigenesis remains to be elucidated, it is likely that the chemopreventive action, at least in part, may be related to the modulation of arachidonic acid metabolism.

REFERENCES

1. Leung AY, et al. Encyclopedia of common natural ingredients used in food, drugs and cosmetics. 2nd ed. New York: Wiley; 1996.
2. Somasundaram S, et al. Dietary curcumin inhibits chemotherapy-induced apoptosis in models of human breast cancer. Cancer Res 2002;62:3868–75.
3. Blumenthal, et al. Herbal medicine, expanded Commission E monographs. Austin (TX): American Botanical Council; 2000.
4. Asai A, Miyazawa T. Occurrence of orally administered curcuminoid as glucuronide and glucuronide/sulfate conjugates in rat plasma. Life Sci 2000;67:2785–93.
5. Ravindranath V, Chandrasekhara N. Absorption and tissue distribution of curcumin in rats. Toxicology 1980;16:259–65.
6. Brinker F. Herbal contraindications and drug interactions. 2nd ed. Sandy (OR): Eclectic Medical Publications; 1998.

Ukrain

SCIENTIFIC NAME
Chelidonium majus alkaloid—
thiophosphoric acid derivative

A·DONATO

CLINICAL SUMMARY

A semisynthetic proprietary product containing alkaloids and thiotepa. Patients use this product to treat cancer, human immunodeficiency virus/acquired immune deficiency syndrome (HIV/AIDS), and hepatitis C. Ukrain is promoted as a selective cytotoxic agent against cancer cells, but research results are inconsistent. Most studies regarding efficacy in vitro and in animal models were conducted by the manufacturer and published in the journal *Drugs Under Experimental and Clinical Research*. Anecdotal reports suggest efficacy in humans, and one phase II trial reports that Ukrain may prolong survival in pancreatic cancer patients when administered with gemcitabine. Although claimed to be without toxicity, reported adverse effects include injection site reactions, slight fever, fatigue, dizziness, nausea, and possibly tumor bleeding. Ukrain is not approved by the US Food and Drug Administration but is available in parts of Europe and from Tijuana clinics. Product labeling makes claims of efficacy and safety, which have yet to be definitively proven.

CONSTITUENTS

Alkaloid extract from *C. majus*, thiophosphoric acid derivatives (triethylene-thiophosphoric acid triamide, thiotepa).[1]

MECHANISM OF ACTION

The mechanism of action is unknown. Proposed activity includes cytotoxicity from effects on cellular oxygen consumption; inhibition of deoxyribonucleic acid (DNA), ribonucleic acid, and protein synthesis; and induction of apoptosis. In vitro studies demonstrate weak inhibition of tubulin polymerization, causing arrest at the G_2/M phase of the cell cycle. Limited in vitro data support the claim that Ukrain has selective cytotoxicity against cancer cells. Ukrain also is promoted for its claimed ability to increase total T-cell count and T helper lymphocytes, while decreasing T suppressor cells. In vitro activation of splenic lymphocytes also was reported.[1-3]

USAGE

Cancer prevention, cancer treatment, hepatitis, HIV and AIDS, immunostimulation.

PHARMACOKINETICS

Following administration, Ukrain distributes rapidly throughout the body, including the brain and central nervous system. Most of the compound remains unmodified and is excreted through the kidneys. Ukrain administered to rats intraperitoneally at a dose of 28 mg/kg revealed rapid distribution into the plasma and a biologic half-life of approximately 60 minutes. Acute toxicity studies indicate that the LD50 dose for intraperitoneally administered Ukrain in mice and rats is approximately 280 mg/kg. Maximum tolerated intravenous dose was 3.5 mg/kg in rats and 0.35 mg/kg in rabbits. Chronic toxicity studies in mice and rats with intraperitoneal administration revealed no apparent toxic effects.[4]

ADVERSE REACTIONS

Reported (Parenteral): Soreness at injection site, nausea, diarrhea, dizziness, fatigue, drowsiness, polydipsia, polyuria, and slight fever. Hematologic side effects and tumor bleeding were reported in a recent phase II trial.[1,5,6]

DRUG INTERACTIONS

None known.

DOSAGE

Each ampule contains 5 mg of *C. majus* L. alkaloid-thiophosphoric acid derivative in 5 mL of bidistilled water for injection. Dose-ranging studies have not been performed. *Intramuscular/Intravenous: Per cycle:* 5 to 50 mg administered every other day for 20 days followed by a 10-day rest period.

LITERATURE SUMMARY AND CRITIQUE

Gansauge F, et al. NSC-631570 (Ukrain) in the palliative treatment of pancreatic cancer: results of a phase II trial. Langenbecks Arch Surg 2002;386:570–4.

A randomized trial of Ukrain monotherapy versus gemcitabine versus Ukrain plus gemcitabine in patients with unresectable advanced pancreatic cancer. In arm A, 30 patients received 1,000 mg gemcitabine/m^2 weekly (first cycle: 7 weeks of therapy, 1 week of rest; second to twelfth cycles: 3 weeks of therapy, 1 week of rest). In arm B, 30 patients received 20 mg of Ukrain weekly (following the same cycle). In arm C, 30 patients received both agents at the same doses above. In the first week of the first cycle, arms B and C received 20 mg/d of Ukrain. No complete responses were documented. Significantly more partial responses were noted in arms B and C. Median survival according to Kaplan-Meier analysis was 5.2 months in arm A, 7.9 months in arm B, and 10.4 months in arm C. More patients in arms B and C had received prior chemotherapy or radiotherapy. Side effects were comparable between groups, except that arms B and C had more cases of fever, and each had two cases of tumor bleeding. Because of this, the authors recommend that Ukrain should be used only under medical control.

REFERENCES

1. Uglyanitsa KN, et al. Ukrain: a novel antitumor drug. Drugs Exp Clin Res 2000;56:347–56.
2. Colombo ML, Bosisio E. Pharmacological activities of *Chelidonium majus* L. (papaveracea). Pharmacol Res 1996;33:127–34.
3. Panzer A, et al. Ukrain™, a semisynthetic *Chelidonium majus* alkaloid derivative, acts by inhibition of tubulin polymerization in normal and malignant cell lines. Cancer Lett 2000;160:149–57.
4. Jagiello-Wojtowicz E, et al. Preliminary pharmacokinetic studies of Ukrain in rats. Drugs Exp Clin Res 1998;24:309–11.
5. Danysz A, Kokoschinegg M, Hamler F. Clinical studies of Ukrain in health volunteers (phase I). Drugs Exp Clin Res 1992;18:39–43.
6. Gansauge F, et al. NSC-631570 (Ukrain) in the palliative treatment of pancreatic cancer: results of a phase II trial. Langenbecks Arch Surg 2002;386:570–4

Valerian

A. DONATO

COMMON NAMES
Garden valerian, Indian valerian, Pacific valerian, Mexican valerian, garden heliotrope

SCIENTIFIC NAMES
Valeriana officinalis, Valerianae radix

KEY WORD
Garden heliotrope

CLINICAL SUMMARY

Derived from the root of the plant. This supplement is frequently used as a sedative to improve sleep. Studies demonstrate that valerian extract is more effective than placebo, but optimal dosing and administration data are conflicting. Valerian may have an additive effect when combined with barbiturates (eg, pentobarbital) and benzodiazepines (eg, alprazolam or triazolam). Safety information regarding long-term use is not available, although cases of hepatotoxicity and withdrawal syndrome have been reported. Common adverse events include headache and possible "hangover" effect.

CONSTITUENTS

Alkaloids: pyridine type, actinidine, chatinine, skyanthine, valerianine, valerine; iridoids: valepotriates, valtrate, didrovaltrate; volatile oils: monoterpenes (borneol), sesquiterpenes (β-bisabolene); other constituents: caffeic and chlorogenic acids, β-sitosterol, tannins, choline.[1]

WARNINGS

Long-term use has been associated with hepatotoxicity. Patients should be warned not to drive or operate dangerous machinery. Valerian should be stopped about 1 week before surgery because it may interact with anesthesia.[2,3]

MECHANISM OF ACTION

The active ingredients are not known. However, researchers believe that a mixture of constituents (valepotriates and volatile oils) is responsible. Many researchers believe that the sedative effect is attributable to the valepotriates, and others believe it is attributable to the valepotriate decomposition products (baldrinal and homobaldrinal). In vitro, valerenic acid decreases degradation of γ-aminobutyric acid (GABA). Valerenic acid in animals appears to inhibit the enzyme system responsible for the central catabolism of GABA, increasing GABA concentration and decreasing central nervous system activity. More recent studies have shown that aqueous extracts of the roots contain appreciable amounts of GABA that could directly cause sedation, but there is some controversy surrounding the bioavailability of this compound.[4–6]

USAGE

Anxiety, colic, insomnia, menstrual cramps, migraine treatment, sedation, spasms, stomach and intestinal gas.

PHARMACOKINETICS

One study demonstrated the onset of a sleep-promoting effect within 30 minutes of oral administration.[7]

ADVERSE REACTIONS

Common: Headache, uneasiness, cardiac disturbances, morning drowsiness, impaired alertness.[8]

DRUG INTERACTIONS

Barbiturates: Valerian lengthens the sedation time induced by barbiturates.
Benzodiazepines: Valerian may have an additive sedative effect.[9]

DOSAGE

Oral: Sleep: 400 to 900 mg administered 30 minutes to 1 hour before bedtime. *Restlessness and tension:* 150 to 300 mg daily.

LITERATURE SUMMARY AND CRITIQUE

Several clinical trials have been performed in humans to assess its sedative effects and found it to be effective in the treatment of mild-to-moderate sleeping disorders and states of restlessness and tension.

REFERENCES

1. Newall C, et al. Herbal medicines: a guide for health-care professionals. 2nd ed. London: Pharmaceutical Press; 1997.
2. Upton R, et al. Valerian root: analytical, quality control, and therapeutic monograph. Soquel (CA): American Herbal Pharmacopoeia; 1999.
3. Ang-Lee M, et al. Herbal medicines and perioperative care. JAMA 2001;286:208–16.
4. Schulz V, et al. Rational phytotherapy: a physician's guide to the use of herbs and related remedies. 3rd ed. Berlin: Springer; 1998.
5. De Smet PA, et al. Adverse effects of herbal drugs. New York: Springer; 1997.
6. Houghton PJ. The scientific basis for the reputed activity of valerian. J Pharm Pharmacol 1999;51:505–12.
7. Fachinformation: Sedalint® Baldrian, valerian extract. Munich: Sanofi Winthrop GmbH; 1996.
8. Plushner SL. Valerian: *Valerian officinalis.* Am J Health Syst Pharm 2000;57:328–35.
9. Brinker F. Herb contraindications and drug interactions. Sandy (OR): Eclectic Medical Publications; 1998.

Vitamin A

COMMON NAMES

Retinol, retinal, retinoic acid,
retinoid, retinol palmitate

CLINICAL SUMMARY

Derived from dietary sources and vitamin A precursors such as beta-carotene, alpha-carotene, and cryptoxanthin. Patients take this supplement to treat and prevent cancer. Vitamin A is also used for eye conditions, kidney stones, and acne and to improve immune function and growth and development in children. Vitamin A is necessary for normal differentiation of corneal, conjunctival, and retinal membranes; growth and development; and immune activation. Current data are inconsistent regarding its anticancer activity. Vitamin A derivatives are in use and under study as prescription chemotherapeutic agents for cancer. Clinical data suggest that the prescription form of vitamin A may be effective against growth retardation and acne. Adverse effects from chronic vitamin A supplementation include nausea, vomiting, headache, stomatitis, blurred vision, muscular discoordination, and hepatotoxicity. Signs and symptoms of toxicity are nonspecific and may include diplopia, headache, insomnia, microcytic anemia, neutropenia, coagulation abnormalities, and bone and skin changes. Pregnant women should not consume vitamin A supplements because chronic consumption of 5,000 IU or greater may cause teratogenic effects. Supplementation with doses greater than the recommended daily allowance may result in toxicity, and patients should be monitored accordingly.

MECHANISM OF ACTION

Vitamin A is essential for a variety of physiologic processes. The retinal form of vitamin A is required for vision in the conversion of light to neuronal signals. Retinoic acid is necessary for maintaining normal differentiation of corneal, conjunctival, and retinal membranes, including the photoreceptor cone and rod cells of the retina. Other biologic functions of vitamin A include significant roles in embryonic development, maintenance of epithelial cell integrity in many body tissues, and proper immune activation through cell differentiation and proliferation.[1]

USAGE

Acne, cancer prevention, Crohn's disease, enhancing tissue integrity, eye disorders, gastrointestinal disorders, growth and development, immunostimulation, infections, kidney stones, menorrhagia.

PHARMACOKINETICS

Absorption: Absorption efficiency of preformed vitamin A is generally high, ranging from 70 to 90%. Intestinal absorption follows the breakdown of retinyl esters in the gut lumen. Solubilized retinyl esters and triglycerides are hydrolyzed to retinol by hydrolases. At the brush border, specific transport proteins facilitate retinol uptake. At normal physiologic concentrations, retinol absorption is saturable owing to carrier-mediated transport. However, at higher pharmacologic concentrations, absorption appears to be unsaturable.

Distribution: In the presence of adequate vitamin A intake, more than 90% of total body stores is located in the liver as retinyl esters. Vitamin A is fat-soluble and distributes widely to sites throughout the body, including adipose tissue.

Metabolism/Excretion: The majority of vitamin A metabolites are excreted in the urine. Retinol also is metabolized in the liver to various products, which can be conjugated prior to excretion in the bile. This additional excretion pathway is postulated to serve as a protective mechanism for decreasing the risk of excess hepatic vitamin A storage.[1]

ADVERSE REACTIONS

Reported: Nausea, vomiting, headache, stomatitis, blurred vision, muscular discoordination, elevated liver function tests.

Chronic Toxicity or Hypervitaminosis A: Usually associated with chronic intakes of more than 30,000 IU of vitamin A. The clinical picture is complex and nonspecific and may include diplopia, headache, insomnia, microcytic anemia, neutropenia, coagulation abnormalities, hepatotoxicity, bone and skin changes, and other nonspecific adverse effects.[1-3]

DRUG INTERACTIONS

Warfarin: Large doses of vitamin A may increase the anticoagulant effects of warfarin.

Alcohol: Ethanol can compete with retinol for alcohol dehydrogenase, leading to reduced levels of retinol oxidation to retinaldehyde and retinoic acid.[1,4]

CONTRAINDICATIONS

Owing to possible teratogenicity, women who are pregnant should not consume vitamin A supplements.

DOSAGE

Recommended Dietary Allowances:
  Men: 900 µg/d
  Women: 700 µg/d
  Pregnancy
  14 to 18 years: 750 µg/d
  31 to 50 years: 770 µg/d
  Lactation
  14 to 18 years: 1,200 µg/d
  19 to 50 years: 1,300 µg/d
Tolerable Upper Intake Level:
  Men: 3,000 µg/d
  Women
  14 to 18 years: 2,800 µg/d
  19 and older: 3,000 µg/d
  Pregnancy/lactation
  14 to 18 years: 2,800 µg/d
  19 to 50 years[1,2]: 3,000 µg/d[1,2]

LITERATURE SUMMARY AND CRITIQUE

Meyskens FL, et al. Randomized trial of vitamin A versus observation as adjuvant therapy in high-risk primary malignant melanoma: a Southwest Oncology Group study. J Clin Oncol 1994;12:2060–5.

A prospective, observational evaluation of 100,000 IU of oral vitamin A supplementation given for 18 months to patients with completely resected melanoma (Breslow thickness > 0.75 mm) on recurrence rates and survival. Patients were stratified based on the thickness of the primary lesion excised, randomized to vitamin A ($n = 119$) or observation only ($n = 121$), and followed for a mean duration of 8 years. Primary outcome was disease-free survival or death from time of registration. Vitamin A supplementation had no significant treatment effect. Disease-free survival and overall survival were similar between treatment groups. Numerous grade 3 ($n = 13$) and 4 ($n = 3$) toxicities were reported by patients receiving vitamin A, including headache, thrombocytopenia, nausea, elevated liver function test, and neurologic complaints (eg, dizziness, emotional or personality changes). High-dose oral vitamin A supplementation does not appear to influence recurrence or survival following complete resection of melanoma.

Van Zandwijk N, et al. EUROSCAN, a randomized trial of vitamin A and *N*-acetyl-cysteine in patients with head and neck cancer or lung cancer. J Natl Cancer Inst 2000;92:977–86.

A prospective, open-label, randomized evaluation of vitamin A (300,000 IU daily for 1 year followed by 150,000 IU daily for 1 year), *N*-acetylcysteine (NAC) (600 mg once daily for 2 years), both agents, or placebo in patients with non–small cell lung cancer (NSCLC), laryngeal cancer, or cancer of the oral cavity. The primary end points were event-free survival, overall survival, and occurrence of second primary tumor. A total of 2,573 patients were randomized to vitamin A ($n = 647$), NAC ($n = 642$), both agents ($n = 643$), or placebo ($n = 641$). Demographics appear to be similar between treatment arms, but no statistical tests were reported. Five-year survival, event-free survival, and development of secondary tumors were not significantly different between treatment arms. Adverse events were reported by approximately 25% of patients receiving vitamin A alone or in combination with NAC. Reactions included gastric events, skin rash, transient elevations in liver function tests, and bone pain. Nearly 18% of patients receiving NAC alone reported adverse events related to gastric events and skin rash. The authors concluded that vitamin A alone or in combination with NAC or NAC alone is no better than placebo in improving survival or decreasing second tumors for patients with primary NSCLC or head and neck cancers.

REFERENCES

1. Dietary Reference Intakes for vitamin A, vitamin K, arsenic, boron, chromium, copper, iodine, iron, manganese, molybdenum, nickel, silicon, vanadium, and zinc. Washington (DC): National Academy Press; 2001.
2. Pronsky ZM. Power's and Moore's food-medication interactions. 12th ed. Pottstown (PA): Food Medication Interactions; 2002.
3. Russell RM. The vitamin A spectrum: from deficiency to toxicity. Am J Clin Nutr 2000;71: 878–84.
4. Leo M, et al. Alcohol, vitamin A, and β-carotene: adverse interactions, including hepatotoxicity and carcinogenicity. Am J Clin Nutr 1999;69:1071–85.

Vitamin B_6

COMMON NAMES
Pyridoxine hydrochloride, pyridoxal, pyridoxamine, pyridoxic acid, and the phosphorylated forms pyridoxal phosphate, pyridoxamine phosphate, and pyridoxine phosphate

SCIENTIFIC NAME
Pyridoxine

KEY WORD
Pyroxidine

CLINICAL SUMMARY
Derived from various dietary sources. Patients use vitamin B_6 to treat heart disease, hypertension, peripheral neuropathies, palmar-plantar erythrodysesthesia (PPE), carpal tunnel syndrome, and diabetes. Vitamin B_6, or pyridoxine, is a water-soluble vitamin. Phosphorylated metabolites of pyridoxine are involved in amino acid metabolism, the transsulfuration pathway of homocysteine to cysteine, and glycogen phosphorylase, which mobilizes glucose from glycogen. Infrequent adverse events include headache, nausea, sedation, and mild paresthesias. Chronic consumption of large doses may cause severe neuropathies, ataxia, respiratory difficulties, and profound sedation, although reversal usually occurs following discontinuation. Preliminary data suggest that vitamin B_6 may be of benefit for PPE and carpal tunnel syndrome, but additional studies are necessary. Studies of its efficacy in diabetes, heart disease, premenstrual syndrome, and hypertension show inconsistent results.

MECHANISM OF ACTION
Vitamin B_6 is a water-soluble vitamin. It exists as an alcohol (pyridoxine), aldehyde (pyridoxal), or amine (pyridoxamine). Pyridoxal phosphate (PLP), phosphorylated pyridoxal, is the major coenzyme form and the most abundant in animal tissue. PLP is the cofactor

for over 100 enzymes used in amino acid metabolism, including aminotransferases, decarboxylases, racemases, and dehydrases. In particular, it acts as a coenzyme for cystathionine β-synthase and cystathioninase in the transsulfuration pathway from homocysteine to cysteine. It also facilitates mobilization of glucose units from glycogen via glycogen phosphorylase.[1,2]

USAGE

Alcoholism, asthma, cardiovascular disease, carpal tunnel syndrome, circulatory disorders, diabetes, homocystinuria, hypertension, immunostimulation, peripheral neuropathy, pregnancy-related nausea and vomiting, premenstrual syndrome.

PHARMACOKINETICS

Absorption: Vitamin B_6 is absorbed by nonsaturable passive diffusion. Absorption in the gut involves phosphatase-mediated hydrolysis followed by passive transport of the non-phosphorylated form into the mucosal cell.

Distribution/Metabolism: Most of absorbed vitamin B_6 is then phosphorylated to PLP. PLP is the major form of the vitamin in plasma, where it is bound primarily to albumin. Non-phosphorylated vitamin B_6 is distributed by erythrocytes. The bulk of vitamin B_6 stores is in muscle.

Excretion: Elimination half-life is estimated to be 15 to 25 days. Metabolites of vitamin B_6 are excreted primarily in the urine as 4-pyridoxic acid. Other forms of the vitamin are also found in urine to a lesser extent. Vitamin B_6 is also excreted in the feces, but microbial synthesis of vitamin B_6 in the lower gut makes it difficult to evaluate the extent of excretion.[1,2]

ADVERSE REACTIONS

Infrequent: Headache, drowsiness, mild flushing, and paresthesias.

Toxicity: Chronic dosing of vitamin B_6 (200 mg and greater) may result in severe peripheral sensory neuropathies, ataxia, respiratory difficulties, profound sedation, and vomiting. Toxicities appear to be reversible following discontinuation.[2,3]

DRUG INTERACTIONS

None known. However, isoniazid, levodopa, alcoholism, and possibly oral contraceptives may reduce the circulating plasma levels of vitamin B_6 and its metabolites.[2]

DOSAGE

Oral (from the literature): *Palmar-plantar erythrodysesthesia:* Approximately 200 mg daily. *Carpal tunnel syndrome:* 100 mg daily. *Diabetic neuropathy:* 150 mg daily. *Prevention of isoniazid neuropathy:* 10 to 25 mg daily.

Recommended Dietary Allowances:
  Men
  19 to 50 years: 1.3 mg/d
  51+ year: 1.7 mg/d
  Women
  19 to 50 years: 1.3 mg/d
  51+ years: 1.5 mg/d
  Pregnancy: 1.9 mg/d
  Lactation[2]: 2.0 mg/d[2]

LITERATURE SUMMARY AND CRITIQUE

Fabian CJ, et al. Pyridoxine therapy for palmar-plantar erythrodysesthesia associated with continuous 5-fluorouracil infusion. Invest New Drugs 1990;8:57–63.
A small, prospective, open-label evaluation of pyridoxine supplementation, 50 or 150 mg/d, on previously untreated patients developing PPE from protracted infusions of 5-fluorouracil (5-FU) 200 mg/m^2/d. Pyridoxine was initiated in five patients once grade 2 skin toxicity was noted. Four of five patients had a reduction to grade 1 skin toxicity and were able to continue 5-FU therapy. Patients supplemented with pyridoxine received an average of 8 months 5-FU compared with 4.5 months in six control patients. No adverse effects were attributed to pyridoxine therapy. Additional studies are necessary to establish the role of pyridoxine in treating PPE.

Levin ER, et al. The influence of pyridoxine in diabetic neuropathy. Diabetes Care 1981;4:606–9.
A small, prospective, double-blind, randomized evaluation of 4-month vitamin B$_6$ supplementation on diabetic peripheral neuropathy. Patients were administered 50 mg pyridoxine or identical placebo every 8 hours. Outcomes measured included patient self-assessment of neuropathic symptoms and motor nerve conduction velocity tests. Six of nine patients receiving pyridoxine and four of nine patients receiving placebo reported improvements in diabetic neuropathy. There was no difference in motor nerve conduction velocity of fasting plasma glucose between groups. Administration of 150 mg vitamin B$_6$ daily for 4 months did not significantly improve diabetic neuropathies.

REFERENCES

1. Zempleni J. Pharmacokinetics of vitamin B$_6$ supplements in humans. J Am Coll Nutr 1995;14:579–86
2. Dietary Reference Intakes for thiamin, riboflavin, niacin, vitamin B$_6$, folate, vitamin B$_{12}$, pantothenic acid, biotin, and choline. Washington (DC): National Academy Press; 2000.
3. Pronsky ZM. Power's and Moore's food-medication interactions. 11th ed. Pottstown (PA): Food Medication Interactions; 2000.

Vitamin C

COMMON NAMES
Ascorbate, sodium ascorbate

SCIENTIFIC NAME
Ascorbic acid

KEY WORD
Ascorbic acid

CLINICAL SUMMARY

A water-soluble vitamin necessary for a variety of physiologic functions in the human body. Patients use this supplement as an immune stimulant and antioxidant, to prevent and treat cancer and infections, to improve wound healing, and to promote heart health. The body cannot synthesize vitamin C. Physiologic processes that require vitamin C include formation of collagen, catecholamines, and carnitine in addition to tyrosine metabolism, peptide synthesis, and antioxidant activity. The pharmacokinetic profile is significant for nonlinear absorption and elimination, decreased and increased, respectively, which occurs with increasing oral doses. Potential adverse effects are gastrointestinal in nature, although hypoglycemia and hypotension are documented for doses greater than 1 g/d. Patients with a history of oxalate kidney stones, renal insufficiency, glucose-6-phosphate dehydrogenase (G6PD) deficiency, or hematochromatosis should not take supplements of vitamin C. Clinical studies suggest no survival advantage or antineoplastic activity with vitamin C. In addition, in vitro and animal studies suggest that cancer cells preferentially uptake vitamin C, suggesting that high-dose supplementation may be detrimental for cancer patients undergoing radiation or chemotherapy. Three clinical trials in end-stage cancer patients at the Mayo Clinic show no benefit and significant adverse effects from high-dose vitamin C. Some data suggest that vitamin C may reduce the severity and duration of respiratory infections in otherwise healthy patients, although no prophylactic benefit has been demonstrated. The daily recommended intake of vitamin C is 75 to 125 mg/d with a tolerable upper limit of 2,000 mg/d.[1]

MECHANISM OF ACTION

A water-soluble antioxidant, vitamin C reacts directly with superoxide, hydroxyl radicals, and singlet oxygen molecules. Ascorbic acid promotes wound healing by serving as a reductant in the pathway for the formation and polymerization of collagen. Vitamin C deficiency thus results in impaired wound healing and scurvy. Vitamin C is important for the synthesis of catecholamines and carnitine, in addition to the conversion of folic acid to folinic acid. It is also involved with tyrosine metabolism and peptide synthesis. During a state of infection, vitamin C may reduce inflammation caused by oxidizing chemicals released by phagocytic leukocytes following activation. Vitamin C also may inhibit free radical inactivation of nitric oxide, thereby improving endothelium-dependent vasodilation.[2–5]

USAGE

Asthma, bronchitis, cancer prevention, cancer treatment, cardiovascular disease, cataracts, common cold, glaucoma, hypertension, immunostimulation, infections, Parkinson's disease, strength and stamina, wound healing.

PHARMACOKINETICS

Absorption: Intestinal absorption occurs through a sodium-dependent active transport process that is saturable and dose dependent. Approximately 70 to 90% of the usual dietary intake of ascorbic acid (30–180 mg/d) is absorbed, although absorption falls to 50% or less with increasing doses above 1 g/d. The bioavailability of vitamin C from food or supplements is not significantly different.

Distribution: Dehydroascorbic acid is the form of the vitamin that primarily crosses the membranes of cells, after which it is reduced intracellularly to ascorbic acid. High levels of the vitamin are maintained in the pituitary and adrenal glands, leukocytes, eye tissue and humors, and the brain, whereas relatively low levels are found in plasma and saliva.

Metabolism/Excretion: Owing to homeostatic regulation, the biologic half-life varies widely from 8 to 40 days and is inversely related to body pools. Renal excretion increases proportionally with higher intakes. With large intakes of the vitamin, unabsorbed ascorbate is degraded in the intestine, a process that may account for the diarrhea and intestinal discomfort occasionally reported by people ingesting large doses.[6]

ADVERSE REACTIONS

Common: Nausea, diarrhea, stomach cramps, and possible hypoglycemia and hypotension with doses greater than 1 g.

Reported: In patients with a history of kidney stones, increased oxalate kidney stone formation occurs with possible nephrolithiasis, acute renal failure, or renal insufficiency. In patients with G6PD deficiency, hemolytic anemia may occur at high doses.

Toxicity: Excessive use of chewable tablets may break down tooth enamel, increasing the risk of dental caries.[2,7]

DRUG INTERACTIONS

Iron: Ascorbic acid increases iron absorption and modulates transport and storage in the body. Significant in patients with hematochromatosis.[6,7]

LABORATORY INTERACTIONS

High-dose ascorbic acid supplementation may alter results of urine glucose testing strips and may cause a false-negative guaiac (occult blood) test.[3]

CONTRAINDICATIONS

Patients who should avoid high-dose vitamin C include those with recurrent kidney stone formation, renal impairment or on chronic hemodialysis, hematochromatosis, and known G6PD deficiency. Large doses of vitamin C may induce copper deficiency.

DOSAGE

Oral: Recommended Dietary Allowances:
  Men: 90 mg/d
  Women: 75 mg/d
  Smokers: 35 additional mg/d
  Tolerable upper intake level[6]: 2,000 mg/d

LITERATURE SUMMARY AND CRITIQUE

Creagan ET. Failure of high dose vitamin C (ascorbic acid) therapy to benefit patients with advanced cancer. A controlled trial. N Engl J Med 1979;301:687–90.

A prospective, randomized evaluation of 123 patients with advanced solid tumor cancers refractory to prior treatment. Patients were randomized to receive either 10 g of ascorbic acid orally per day or placebo. No significant difference in demographics or diagnosis existed between treatment groups. No survival advantage with vitamin C supplementation was documented, nor was a significant difference in adverse events between treatment groups. Salvage therapy with 10 g/d of ascorbic acid showed no benefit in the treatment of solid tumors.

Engelhart MJ, et al. Dietary intake of antioxidants and risk of Alzheimer disease. JAMA 2002;287:3223–9.

A population-based, prospective cohort study evaluating antioxidant intake and risk of developing Alzheimer's disease. Subjects ($n = 5,393$) were at least 55 years old, free of dementia, and noninstitutionalized and had reliable dietary assessment at baseline. Dietary intake was assessed by self-reported checklist and interview with a dietitian using the semi-quantitative food-frequency questionnaire (SFFQ). After a mean follow-up of 6 years, 146 patients developed Alzheimer's disease. After adjustments for age, sex, baseline Mini-Mental State Examination score, alcohol intake, education, smoking habits, pack-years of smoking, body mass index, total energy intake, presence of carotid plaques, and use of supplements, high intakes of vitamin C and vitamin E were correlated with a lower risk of Alzheimer's disease. However, the apparent association may be caused by the influence of a preclinical illness on diet or diet recall/reporting because the SFFQ itself may indirectly assess cognitive functioning. Furthermore, the multiple comparisons made suggest that some associations may be owing to chance and that the critical p value should be set lower than .05.[8]

Moertel CG. High-dose vitamin C versus placebo in the treatment of patients with advanced cancer who have had no prior chemotherapy. A randomized double-blind comparison. N Engl J Med 1985;312:137–41.

A prospective evaluation of 100 patients with confirmed adenocarcinoma who had not received any prior chemotherapy, stratified by time since diagnosis, site of metastases, and measurable disease following enrolment. Patients were randomized to receive either vitamin C 10 g/d orally or identical placebo and continued treatment until marked progression of disease or inability to take oral medications. No significant difference between treatment groups was documented. Of 19 patients receiving vitamin C with clearly measurable disease, there was no evidence of tumor regression. One-year survival, evaluating 85 of 100 patients, showed no advantage for patients receiving vitamin C supplementation.

Karlowski TR, et al. Ascorbic acid for the common cold. A prophylactic and therapeutic trial. JAMA 1975;231:1038–42.

A prospective evaluation of 311 National Institutes of Health employees randomized to receive either 3 g of vitamin C per day orally or identical placebo for prophylaxis and an additional 3 g at the onset of presumed respiratory infection. Four treatment groups were established for prophylaxis and supplement during infections, respectively: placebo/placebo, placebo/ascorbic acid, ascorbic acid/placebo, and ascorbic acid/ascorbic acid. No significant adverse events were reported during the study. The study failed to show a reduction in the number of colds during respiratory season with ascorbic acid prophylaxis. A statistically significant reduction in illness symptoms and duration was demonstrated, but it is questionable whether this was clinically meaningful. The authors reported that a substantial number of patients were able to break the blinding of the trial by tasting the contents of the capsule, but additional analysis revealed no change in previous conclusions.

REFERENCES

1. Agus DB, Vera JC, Golde DW. Stromal cell oxidation: a mechanism by which tumors obtain vitamin C. Cancer Res 1999;59:4555–8.
2. Sauberlich HE. Pharmacology of vitamin C. Annu Rev Nutr 1994;14:371–91.

3. DerMarderosian A, editor. The review of natural products. St. Louis: Facts and Comparisons; 1999.
4. Hemila H. Vitamin C and the common cold. Br J Nutr 1992;67:3–16.
5. Taddei S, et al. Vitamin C improves endothelium-dependent vasodilation by restoring nitric oxide activity in essential hypertension. Circulation 1998;97:2222–9.
6. Dietary Reference Intakes for vitamin C, vitamin E, selenium, and carotenoids. Washington (DC): National Academy Press; 2000.
7. Foley DJ, White LR. Dietary intake of antioxidants and risk of Alzheimer disease. JAMA 2002;287:3261–3.

Vitamin E

COMMON NAMES
Tocopherol, α-tocopherol, *dl*-tocopherol, tocotrienol, RRR-α-tocopherol

SCIENTIFIC NAME
d-α-Tocopherol

KEY WORDS
d-α-Tocopherol, tocopherol

CLINICAL SUMMARY

Derived from plant oils and various foods. Patients use vitamin E to prevent and treat heart disease, cancer, diabetes, and Alzheimer's disease. Natural food sources include plant oils, wheat germ, eggs, green leafy vegetables, and whole grains. Vitamin E acts as an antioxidant, preventing the propagation of free radical reactions and protecting polyunsaturated fatty acids within membrane phospholipids. Although sold in a variety of formulations, only the *d*-isomer is considered active. A recent analysis of seven brands of commercially available vitamin E revealed actual content to vary considerably from the labeled dosage. Most research describes vitamin E in terms of milligrams, but most products are sold in international units (IU). The conversion is 1 IU natural vitamin E equals 0.67 mg *d*-α-tocopherol and 1 IU of synthetic vitamin E equals 0.45 mg *d*-α-tocopherol. Studies evaluating vitamin E supplementation suggest that it may reduce the risk of some cancers, help prevent and treat heart disease, improve immune response in the elderly, and slow the progression of Alzheimer's disease. However, 200 mg of vitamin E per day have no effect on reducing the incidence of acute respiratory tract infection. There are no significant adverse effects associated with vitamin E, although toxicity may occur with chronic supplementation of doses greater than 800 IU. Vitamin E theoretically may enhance the activity of warfarin, but data are inconsistent. Prothrombin time (PT) and international normalized ratio (INR) should be monitored when vitamin E supplementation is initiated or discontinued in patients receiving warfarin.

WARNINGS

A recent analysis of seven brands of commercially available vitamin E revealed actual content to vary considerably from the labeled dosage, from 59 to 157% of stated amount.[1]

MECHANISM OF ACTION

Vitamin E is a fat-soluble vitamin that acts as an antioxidant. The d-α-tocopherol isomer is believed to have the majority of activity. Natural vitamin E supplements contain d-α-tocopherol derived from plant oil sources, whereas synthetic supplements are composed of a racemic mixture of d- and l-α-tocopherol. The major function of d-α-tocopherol is to prevent the propagation of free radical reactions by acting as a peroxyl radical scavenger and protecting polyunsaturated fatty acids within membrane phospholipids and in plasma lipoproteins. α-Tocopherol reportedly causes inhibition of protein kinase C activity, which is involved in cell proliferation and differentiation in smooth muscle cells, human platelets, and monocytes. Vitamin E enrichment of endothelial cells down-regulates the expression of intercellular adhesion molecule 1 and vascular cell adhesion molecule 1, thereby decreasing the adhesion of blood cell components to the endothelium. Vitamin E also up-regulates the expression of cytosolic phospholipase A_2 and cyclooxygenase-1, which leads to the release of prostacyclin, a potent vasodilator and inhibitor of platelet aggregation in humans.[2]

USAGE

Alzheimer's disease, arthritis, cancer prevention, cardiovascular disease, cataracts, diabetes, immunostimulation, Parkinson's disease, wound healing.

PHARMACOKINETICS

Absorption: Vitamin E absorption is low in humans, although the precise bioavailability is unknown. Absorption from the intestinal lumen is dependent on biliary and pancreatic secretions, micelle formation, uptake into enterocytes, and chylomicron secretion, which has been suggested as the most important factor for efficient absorption. All forms of vitamin E (eg, solubilized, natural, and synthetic) have similar intestinal absorption of d-α-tocopherol.

Distribution: Vitamin E is fat soluble. It distributes throughout the body and is primarily stored in adipose tissue and various organs.

Metabolism/Excretion: α-Tocopherol can be oxidized to the tocopheroxyl radical one-electron oxidation product, which can be reduced back to the unoxidized form by reducing agents such as vitamin C. Further oxidation of the tocopheroxyl radical forms tocopheryl quinone, the two-electron product. The tocopheryl quinone is not converted back to tocopherol in any physiologically significant amounts. The major route of excretion of ingested vitamin E is fecal elimination owing to its relatively low intestinal absorption, although vitamin E metabolites appear to be primarily eliminated via the kidneys. Excess α-tocopherol, as well as forms of vitamin E not preferentially used, is probably excreted unchanged in bile.[2,3]

ADVERSE REACTIONS

Toxicity: Thrombophlebitis; long-term consumption of doses greater than or equal to 400 to 800 IU/d may cause fatigue, dizziness, weakness, headache, blurred vision, and rash.[2,4]

DRUG INTERACTIONS

Warfarin: It has been reported that vitamin E at doses greater than 400 IU/d may increase the effect of warfarin, although data are inconsistent. PT and INR should be monitored if vitamin E supplementation is initiated or discontinued.[5,6]

LABORATORY INTERACTIONS

PT and INR should be monitored if vitamin E supplementation is initiated or discontinued.[5]

DOSAGE

Oral: Conversion factor: Synthetic vitamin E – 1 IU (USP) = 0.45 mg *d*-α-tocopherol. Natural vitamin E – 1 IU (USP) = 0.67 mg *d*-α-tocopherol.
Recommended Dietary Allowance for d-α-tocopherol:
  Men: 15 mg/d
  Women: 15 mg/d
  Pregnancy: 15 mg/d
  Lactation: 19 mg/d
  Tolerable upper intake level[2]: 1,000 mg/d

LITERATURE SUMMARY AND CRITIQUE

Taylor HR, et al. Vitamin E supplementation and macular degeneration: randomised controlled trial. BMJ 2002;325:11–6.
A prospective, randomized, controlled trial of vitamin E 500 IU versus placebo for 4 years in 1,193 healthy volunteers aged 55 to 80. Patient characteristics were similar between groups, but the vitamin E arm had a slight excess in the number of patients with cortical lens opacities. Power to detect a 50% reduction in the incidence of early age-related macular degeneration (AMD) was 82%. Primary outcome was development of early AMD in annual retinal photographs, which was 8.6% in the treatment arm versus 8.1% in the placebo group. For late disease, incidence rates were also similar. These results indicate that daily supplementation with vitamin E does not prevent the development or progression of AMD. However, the relatively short follow-up and low proportion of cigarette smokers are weaknesses of this study.

Engelhart MJ, et al. Dietary intake of antioxidants and risk of Alzheimer disease. JAMA 2002;287:3223–9.

A population-based, prospective cohort study evaluating antioxidant intake and risk of developing Alzheimer's disease. Subjects ($n = 5,393$) were at least 55 years old, free of dementia, and noninstitutionalized and had reliable dietary assessment at baseline. Dietary intake was assessed by self-reported checklist and interview with a dietitian using the Semi-quantitative Food-Frequency Questionnaire (SFFQ). After a mean follow-up of 6 years, 146 patients developed Alzheimer's disease. After adjustments for age, sex, baseline Mini-Mental State Examination score, alcohol intake, education, smoking habits, pack-years of smoking, body mass index, total energy intake, presence of carotid plaques, and use of supplements, high intakes of vitamin C and vitamin E were correlated with a lower risk of Alzheimer's disease. However, as has been pointed out, the apparent association may be caused by the influence of a preclinical illness on diet or diet recall/reporting because the SFFQ itself may indirectly assess cognitive functioning. Furthermore, the multiple comparisons made suggest that some associations may be owing to chance and that the critical p value should be set lower than .05.[7]

Morris MC, et al. Dietary intake of antioxidant nutrients and the risk of incident Alzheimer disease in a biracial community study. JAMA 2002;287:3230–7.

A prospective study of antioxidant intake from diet and supplements and the risk of Alzheimer's disease in 815 subjects 65 years and older. Dietary intake was assessed by a self-administered food frequency questionnaire a mean of 1.7 years from baseline. After a mean of 3.9 years, 131 subjects developed incident Alzheimer's disease. Lower risk of developing Alzheimer's disease was associated with higher intake of vitamin E from diet (not supplements) after adjusting for age, education, sex, race, apolipoprotein E (APOE), and length of follow-up (p for trend =.05) and only for subjects who were apo E-IV negative. This study is criticized for its short follow-up and the fact that dietary assessment occurred 1.7 years into the study, for which it can be considered a cross-sectional study for some of the cohort. Cross-sectional studies are subject to exposure ascertainment bias. The multiple comparisons made suggest that some associations may be owing to chance and that the critical p value should be set lower than .05.[7]

Yusuf S, et al. Vitamin E supplementation and cardiovascular events in high-risk patients. N Engl J Med 2000;342:154–60.

A prospective, double-blind, randomized, 2×2 factorial design study to investigate the effects of vitamin E supplementation on cardiovascular events. Patients were randomized to receive ramipril or placebo with either 400 IU natural vitamin E or placebo. This study reported results from patients receiving placebo and either vitamin E or placebo. Primary outcomes were cardiovascular events and death. A total of 4,761 patients received vitamin E and 4,780 were given placebo. No statistical difference was found between treatment groups for myocardial infarctions, strokes, death from coronary heart disease, or death from any cause. No significant adverse events were reported. This study suggests that supplementation with 400 IU natural vitamin E does not reduce the risk of cardiovascular events in high-risk patients.

Sano M, et al. A controlled trial of selegiline, α-tocopherol, or both as treatment for Alzheimer's disease. N Engl J Med 1997;336:1216–22.
A prospective, randomized, double-blind evaluation of selegiline alone or with 2,000 IU of α-tocopherol, compared with placebo, for the progression of Alzheimer's disease. A total of 341 patients with a Clinical Dementia Rating of 2 were enrolled. Primary end points were inability to perform at least two of three basic activities of daily living, institutionalization, a Clinical Dementia Rating of 3, and death. Estimated median survival was 670 days in the α-tocopherol group, 655 in the selegiline group, 585 for combination treatment, and 440 for placebo. No significant adverse effects were attributed to α-tocopherol. The authors suggest that treatment with α-tocopherol improves the median survival and delays the progression of Alzheimer's disease compared with placebo.

Heinonen OP, et al. Prostate cancer and supplementation with α-tocopherol and B-carotene: incidence and mortality in a controlled trial. J Natl Cancer Inst 1998;90:440–6.
A prospective study of α-tocopherol and beta-carotene supplementation in male smokers ages 50 to 69 years. The trial was originally designed to test the effects of supplementation on lung cancer. A 2 × 2 factorial design was used, and patients were adequately randomized to receive 50 mg of α tocopherol, 10 mg of beta-carotene, both supplements, or placebo. A total of 29,133 patients were enrolled, with 7,286 receiving α-tocopherol, 7,278 receiving both supplements, 7,282 receiving beta-carotene, and 7,287 randomized to placebo. There were 246 incidences of prostate cancer: 46 patients receiving α-tocopherol, 56 patients receiving both supplements, 80 patients receiving beta-carotene, and 67 patients receiving placebo. Compared with the placebo group, the incidence of prostate cancer for patients receiving α-tocopherol alone was 36% less (CI = −56 to −6%). The results suggest that male smokers supplemented with 50 mg α-tocopherol may reduce the risk of prostate cancer.

α-Tocopherol, Beta Carotene Cancer Prevention Study Group. The effect of vitamin E and beta carotene on the incidence of lung cancer and other cancers in male smokers. N Engl J Med 1994;330:1029–35.
A prospective, randomized evaluation of male smokers, ages 50 to 69, from Finland. Subjects received supplementation with 20 mg of beta-carotene alone ($n = 7,282$), 50 mg of α-tocopherol alone ($n = 7,286$), combination ($n = 7,278$), or placebo ($n = 7,287$). Patients were followed for 5 to 8 years or until death. The primary end point was incidence of lung cancer. Data analysis revealed an increased number of deaths from lung cancer, ischemic heart disease, and hemorrhagic stroke for subjects receiving beta-carotene, with an 8% higher mortality rate over those not receiving beta-carotene. The authors suggest that although beta-carotene has previously been shown to reduce the incidence of certain cancer, male smokers may be at an increased risk of lung cancer when administered beta-carotene supplements.

Parkinson Study Group. Effects of tocopherol and deprenyl on the progression of disability in early Parkinson's disease. N Engl J Med 1993;328:176–83.
A prospective, randomized, double-blind study using a 2 × 2 factorial design that aimed to establish the effects of 2,000 IU of tocopherol with or without 10 mg of deprenyl on the

progression of Parkinson's disease. A total of 800 patients were enrolled, with 192 allocated to vitamin E plus placebo and 215 randomized to deprenyl and vitamin E. Progression of disease was defined as the addition of levodopa for management of Parkinson's disease. No significant adverse effects were associated with vitamin E. Final analysis of the data suggests that 2,000 IU of vitamin E has no effect on the progression of Parkinson's disease.[7–12]

REFERENCES

1. Feifer AH, Fleshner NE, Klotz L. Analytical accuracy and reliability of commonly used nutritional supplements in prostate disease. J Urol 2002;168:150–4.
2. Dietary Reference Intakes for vitamin C, vitamin E, selenium, and carotenoids. Washington (DC): National Academy Press; 2000.
3. Brody T. Nutritional biochemistry. San Diego(CA): Academic Press; 1999.
4. Pronsky ZM. Power's and Moore's food-medication interactions. 11th ed. Pottstown (PA): Food Medication Interactions; 2000.
5. Corrigan JJ, Marcus FI. Coagulopathy associated with vitamin E ingestion. JAMA 1974;230:1300–1.
6. Kim JM, White RH. Effect of vitamin E on the anticoagulant response to warfarin. Am J Cardiol 1996;77:545–6.
7. Foley DJ, White LR. Dietary intake of antioxidants and risk of Alzheimer disease: food for thought. JAMA 2002;287:3261–3.
8. Packer L, Weber SU, Rimbach G. Molecular aspects of α-tocopherol antioxidant action and cell signaling. J Nutr 2001;131:369S–73S.
9. Whitney EN, et al. Understanding normal and clinical nutrition. 4th ed. Belmont (CA): West Publishing; 1994.
10. Olmedilla B, et al. A European multicentre, placebo-controlled supplementation study with α-tocopherol, carotene-rich palm oil, lutein or lycopene; analysis of serum responses. Clin Sci (Lond) 2002;102:447–56.
11. Preuss HG, et al. Randomized trial of a combination of natural products (cernitin, saw palmetto, β-sitosterol, vitamin E) on symptoms of benign prostatic hyperplasis (BPH). Int Urol Nephrol 2001;33:217–25.
12. Graat J, et al. Effect of daily vitamin E and multivitamin-mineral supplementation on acute respiratory tract infections in elderly persons: a randomized controlled trial. JAMA 2002;288:715–21.

Vitamin O

COMMON NAME
Stabilized oxygen

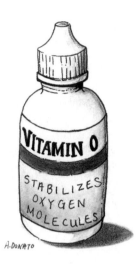

CLINICAL SUMMARY

Food supplement advertised on the Internet and elsewhere purported to contain 30,000 ppm stabilized oxygen molecules in a liquid solution of sodium chloride and distilled water. Vitamin O is promoted to prevent and treat cancer, human immunodeficiency virus/acquired immune deficiency syndrome (HIV/AIDS), cardiovascular disease, pulmonary disease, and other chronic illnesses by detoxifying the body and improving metabolism via high doses of molecular oxygen. Its supposed anticancer activity is based on the false theory that cancer cells grow in an oxygen-poor environment and cannot proliferate in oxygen-rich conditions. Vitamin O was advertised in national newspapers for mail-order purchase until the Federal Trade Commission (FTC) filed a complaint against its marketers, Rose Creek Health Products, Inc., and Staff of Life, Inc., in March 1999. The FTC found, contrary to advertisement claims, that Vitamin O does not allow oxygen molecules to be absorbed through the gastrointestinal system, does not prevent or treat any physical ailment or disease, does not have a beneficial effect on human health, has not been proven effective by medical or scientific research, and was not developed by NASA for the use of astronauts. The defendants were fined and are barred from marketing this or any other product with unsupported claims.

CONSTITUENTS

Vitamin O is purported to contain 30,000 ppm stabilized oxygen molecules in a liquid solution of sodium chloride, trace minerals, and distilled water.[1]

WARNINGS

The FTC charged the marketers of Vitamin O with making false health claims in March 1999, for which the marketers paid $375,000 in consumer compensation. No health claim made for Vitamin O has been substantiated.

MECHANISM OF ACTION

Vitamin O's supposed efficacy is based on the idea that most degenerative diseases (eg, cancer, arthritis, heart disease, Alzheimer's disease, chronic fatigue syndrome) result from decreasing levels of atmospheric oxygen caused by industry and deforestation. Stress, toxins, and the modern diet of processed foods, fats, sugar, alcohol, white flour, and caffeine are said to make the body oxygen deficient because more oxygen is required to metabolize them. Vitamin O's marketers misappropriate the discovery of higher atmospheric oxygen levels in past geologic eras to conclude that the human body evolved to function at higher concentrations of oxygen than are now available. They argue further that the dissolved oxygen content of most people's bodies is considerably lower than that needed to maintain energy and metabolism and that the lower the level of dissolved oxygen in a person's body, the greater susceptibility to disease. No advertisement claim is supported by laboratory or clinical evidence. Despite claims, gaseous oxygen is not absorbed through the gastrointestinal tract. Vitamin O does not contain 30,000 ppm oxygen as the maximum solubility of oxygen in water at room temperature is 7,500 ppm.[1]

USAGE

Arthritis, cancer prevention, cancer treatment, cardiovascular disease, central nervous system relaxation, chronic obstructive pulmonary disorders, cognitive improvement, common cold, headaches, HIV and AIDS, hypertension, infections, influenza, insomnia, recovery from illness, strength and stamina.

PHARMACOKINETICS

No formal pharmacokinetic studies have been performed.

ADVERSE REACTIONS

None known.

DRUG INTERACTIONS

None known.

DOSAGE
Oral: 15 to 20 drops two to three times a day.[2]

LITERATURE SUMMARY AND CRITIQUE
No clinical or laboratory study evaluates the efficacy of Vitamin O supplements.

REFERENCES
1. Mighty Vitamin O [Bio/Tech News Web site]. Available at: http://www.biotechnews.com (access date unknown).
2. Federal Trade Commission v. Rose Creek Health Products, Inc., The Staff of Life, Inc., and Donald L. Smyth. Complaint For Permanent Injunction and Other Equitable Relief. Mar 15, 1999. Available at: http://www.ftc.gov/os/1999/9903/rosecreekcmp.htm (accessed Apr 10, 2002).
3. Federal Trade Commission. Marketers of 'Vitamin O' Settles FTC Charges of Making False Health Claims; Will Pay $375,000 for Consumer Redress. News release; May 1, 2000. Available at: http://www.ftc.gov/opa/2000/05/rosecreek2.htm (accessed Apr 5, 2002).

Willow Bark

A.DONATO

COMMON NAMES
Bay willow, black willow, white willow

SCIENTIFIC NAME
Salix alba

KEY WORD
Salix alba

CLINICAL SUMMARY

Derived from the bark of the tree. Willow bark contains salicin, the phytotherapeutic precursor of aspirin (acetylsalicylic acid). Products should be standardized to the content of salicin, with daily doses ranging from 60 to 120 mg/d. Caution should be exercised in patients with known allergy or intolerance to aspirin or nonsteroidal anti-inflammatory drugs (NSAIDs). Willow bark should not be administered to children with a fever owing to the risk of Reye's syndrome. Adverse reactions are analogous to those seen with aspirin, including gastrointestinal bleeding, nausea, and vomiting. May have an additive effect with aspirin and NSAIDs and should therefore not be administered concurrently. Clinical studies demonstrate the efficacy of willow bark in the management of back pain and osteoarthritis.

CONSTITUENTS

Glycosides: salicin, salicortin, picein, fragilin, tremulacin, triandrin; esters of salicylic acid; tannins; catechins; flavonoids.[1]

MECHANISM OF ACTION

All of the phenolic glycosides of willow bark have similar physiologic and pharmacologic effects. In the intestinal tract and the liver, the phenolic glycosides convert to the active principle salicylic acid. Because of the time required for this conversion, the therapeutic properties of willow bark are expressed more slowly but continue to be effective for a longer time than if salicylate itself were administered. The tannins have astringent properties, and in vitro tests show that salicin and salicortin inhibit cyclooxygenase and an irreversible inhibition of thrombocytes is unlikely. Therefore, no increased interaction with anticoagulants should occur.[2,3]

USAGE

Fever, headaches, inflammation, influenza, muscle pain, pain, weight loss.

PHARMACOKINETICS

In a pharmacokinetic study in humans, three tablets containing willow bark (standardized to a total dose of 55 mg of salicin) were administered to 12 male volunteers in three doses over a period of 8 hours. The calculated half-life of salicin in the plasma was approximately 2.5 hours.[4]

ADVERSE REACTIONS

Infrequent: Nausea, vomiting, gastrointestinal bleeding, tinnitus, and renal damage.[5]

DRUG INTERACTIONS

No interactions have been reported. However, owing to the variable salicylate content found in willow back, there are theoretical interactions.

Anticoagulants/Antiplatelets: Theoretically, willow back may increase the risk of bleeding. *NSAIDs:* Theoretically, willow bark may cause increase the risk of bleeding and gastrointestinal mucosal damage.

LABORATORY INTERACTIONS

Owing to the unknown salicylate factor, use caution in interpreting test results that are sensitive to salicylates.

DOSAGE

Oral: Willow bark standardized to 60 to 120 mg of salicin administered daily.

LITERATURE SUMMARY AND CRITIQUE

Few controlled studies have been performed in humans; however, the pharmacologic actions of salicylates are well published and applicable to willow bark.

Chrubasik S, et al. Treatment of low back pain exacerbations with willow bark extract: a randomized double-blind study. Am J Med 2000;109:9–14.

Two hundred and ten patients were randomly assigned to receive an oral willow bark extract with either 120 mg or 240 mg of salicin or placebo, with tramadol as the sole rescue medication in a 4-week blinded trial. The principal outcome measured was the proportion of patients who were pain free without tramadol for at least 5 days during the final week of the study. One hundred and ninety-one patients completed the study; the number of pain-free patients in the last week of treatment was 27 (39%) of 65 in the group receiving 240 mg of salicin, 15 (21%) of 67 in the group receiving 120 mg of salicin, and 4 (6.8%) of 59 in the placebo group. Significantly, more patients in the placebo group required tramadol during each week of the study.

Schmid B, et al. Efficacy and tolerability of a standardized willow bark extract in patients with osteoarthritis: randomized, placebo-controlled, double blind clinical trial. Phytother Res 2001;15:344–50.

Seventy-eight patients were evaluated in this prospective study. Willow bark standardized to 60 mg of salicin or placebo was administered as two tablets twice daily for 14 days. A significant decrease in joint pain was reported in the willow bark treatment group compared with placebo. No significant change in stiffness or physical function was found. Adverse events were comparable between treatment groups. Willow bark was effective in reducing pain associated with osteoarthritis of the knee or hip.

REFERENCES

1. Newall CA, et al. Herbal medicines: a guide for health-care professionals. 1st ed. London: Pharmaceutical Press; 1998.
2. Tyler V. Herbs of choice: the therapeutic use of phytomedicinals. Binghamton (NY): Pharmaceutical Press; 1994.
3. Wichtl MW. Herbal drugs and phytopharmaceuticals. Boca Raton (FL): Medpharm Scientific Publications; 1994.
4. Blumenthal M, et al. Herbal medicine expanded Commission E monographs. 1st ed. Austin (TX): American Botanical Council; 2000.
5. Schulz V, et al. Rational phytotherapy: a physician's guide to herbal medicines. 3rd ed. Berlin: Springer; 1996.

Zinc

COMMON NAMES

Zinc gluconate, zinc sulfate, zinc acetate

A. DONATO

CLINICAL SUMMARY

Naturally occurring element necessary for several human physiologic functions. Patients use this supplement to shorten the duration of the common cold, as an immunostimulant, and to treat male infertility (sperm motility), diabetes, rheumatoid arthritis, and loss of taste resulting from head/neck radiation therapy. Zinc possesses antioxidant activity and is necessary for enzymatic reactions, formation of bone, and regulation of synaptic signaling. Topical administration of zinc (eg, lozenges or nasal spray) may affect the ability of rhinovirus to infect humans and replicate inside a host. Numerous studies show that zinc may reduce the duration of the common cold, but data are inconsistent, and adverse events are reported in approximately half of all subjects. Two small studies offer conflicting results regarding the efficacy of oral zinc for taste preservation following head/neck radiation therapy, and additional research is necessary. Commonly reported adverse events include nausea, diarrhea, and taste disturbances. Chronic toxicity consisting of copper deficiency, headache, nausea, and fatigue may occur with doses as low as 100 mg/d. Zinc may reduce the bioavailability of fluoroquinolones or tetracyclines when administered concomitantly; zinc should be given 2 hours before or 4 hours following these medications. If initiated within 24 hours of onset, short-term use of zinc lozenges may be effective for reducing the duration of symptoms associated with the common cold with low toxicity.

MECHANISM OF ACTION

Zinc performs a number of catalytic, structural, and regulatory functions. Many specific enzymes depend on zinc as a cofactor, including ribonucleic acid polymerases, alcohol dehydrogenase, carbonic anhydrase, and alkaline phosphatase. Zinc is essential for the structural formation of many biologically active molecules (eg, copper-zinc dismutase), particularly enzymes with domains capable of zinc coordination. Zinc has been shown to influence both apoptosis and protein kinase C activity. Zinc is necessary for immunocompetence and has a regulatory role in normal synaptic signaling. Supplemental zinc (lozenge or nasal administration) may reduce the ability of the rhinovirus to attach to the human respiratory tract. Zinc appears to complex with viral coat proteins and alter assembly of viral particles.[1,2]

USAGE

Cancer prevention, common cold, diabetes, immunostimulation, infertility, macular degeneration, rheumatoid arthritis.

PHARMACOKINETICS

Absorption: Most exogenous zinc is absorbed transcellularly in the small intestine, where the jejunum exhibits the greatest transport rate. Absorption kinetics are saturable, and the efficiency of intestinal zinc absorption increases with transit time and zinc deficiency. Substantial amounts of zinc also enter the intestines endogenously. Balanced absorption and secretion of endogenous zinc reserves maintain homeostasis.

Distribution: Over 85% of total-body zinc is incorporated into skeletal muscle and bone. Plasma zinc, bound primarily to albumin at a concentration of approximately 10 to 15 μmol/L, represents only 0.1% of total-body levels.

Metabolism/Excretion: Zinc is eliminated mainly in the feces, quantities ranging from less than 1 mg/d with a zinc-poor diet to greater than 5 mg/d with a zinc-rich diet. Intestinal secretions provide the major route of endogenous zinc excretion. Biliary secretion of zinc is limited. Urinary losses are less than 10% of normal fecal losses but increase concomitantly with increases in muscle protein catabolism owing to starvation or trauma. Zinc loss from the body also is attributable to epithelial cell desquamation, sweat, semen, hair, and the menstrual cycle.[1]

ADVERSE REACTIONS

Common (Oral): Taste disturbances, nausea, vomiting, dyspepsia, diarrhea.

Toxicity (Oral): Intake of 100 to 300 mg/d may result in chronic toxicity including copper deficiency, depressed immune function, headache, chills, fever, and fatigue.[3]

DRUG INTERACTIONS

Fluoroquinolones: Concomitant administration of zinc results in reduced bioavailability of fluoroquinolones (eg, ciprofloxacin, levofloxacin, gatifloxacin). Zinc should be administered either 2 hours before or 4 hours following fluoroquinolones.

Tetracyclines: Concomitant administration of zinc results in reduced bioavailability of tetracyclines (eg, doxycycline, minocycline). Zinc should be administered either 2 hours before or 4 hours following tetracyclines.

Minerals/Vitamins: Although human studies have been equivocal, patients should take zinc 2 hours before or after foods high in calcium, phosphorus, bran fiber, or phytate to avoid nonabsorbable complexes.[1,4]

DOSAGE

Intranasal (Common Cold): 1 puff of zinc nasal gel (Zicam) in each nostril every 4 hours. *Oral:* Dose of zinc varies (10–23 mg per lozenge) in clinical trials. *Male fertility:* 220 mg of zinc sulfate twice daily. *Common cold:* Children: 10 mg zinc gluconate lozenge dissolved in the mouth five times a day (ages 5–11) or six times a day (ages 12–17). Adults: 10–13.3 mg zinc gluconate lozenge dissolved in the mouth every 2 hours while awake. *Preservation of taste in patients receiving radiotherapy for head/neck cancer:* 18–45 mg elemental zinc capsules three times a day given during and 1 month following radiation therapy. *Prevention of opportunistic infections in patients with HIV/AIDS on zidovudine (AZT):* 200 mg/d of zinc sulfate. *Rheumatoid arthritis:* 220 mg of zinc sulfate three times daily.

Recommended Dietary Allowances:
   Men: 11 mg/d
   Women: 8 mg/d
   Pregnancy
   14–18 years: 13 mg/d
   19–50 years: 11 mg/d
   Lactation
   14–18 years: 14 mg/d
   19–50 years: 12 mg/d
Tolerable Upper Intake Level (UL):
   Adults: 40 mg/d
   Pregnancy/lactation
   14–18 years: 34 mg/d
   19–50 years[1,4–10]: 40 mg/d

LITERATURE SUMMARY AND CRITIQUE

Macknin ML, et al. Zinc gluconate lozenges for treating the common cold in children: a randomized controlled trial. JAMA 1998;279:1962–7.

A prospective, randomized, double-blind study that evaluated the efficacy of 10 mg of zinc gluconate (*n* = 124) or placebo (*n* = 125) lozenges (Cold-Eeze) administered to

schoolchildren (grades 1–12) within 24 hours after reporting two of nine symptoms associated with the common cold. Lozenges were to be taken five or six times a day. Primary
outcome was resolution of symptoms as reported by the subject. Demographics were similar between treatment groups except history of asthma: 7.5% in the zinc group and 14.2%
in the placebo group. Time to symptom resolution was 9 days for both arms, with a confi-
dence interval for the zinc and placebo groups, 7 to 10 days and 8 to 9 days, respectively. No
difference in resolution of individual symptoms or days absent from school was found. A
significantly greater number of patients receiving zinc reported taste disturbances, diarrhea,
and nausea. The results suggest that a 10 mg zinc lozenge administered five to six times daily
does not improve resolution of symptoms associated with the common cold.

**Mossad SB, et al. Zinc gluconate lozenges for treating the common cold. Ann Intern Med
1996;125:81–8.**
A prospective, randomized, double-blind study that evaluated the efficacy of 13.3 mg zinc
gluconate ($n = 49$) or placebo ($n = 50$) lozenges administered to health care professionals
every 2 hours within 24 hours of reporting symptoms associated with the common cold.
The primary outcome was resolution of symptoms as reported by the subject. Time to complete symptom resolution was significantly shorter for patients receiving zinc lozenges
compared with placebo, 4.4 and 7.6 days, respectively. Significantly more adverse events
were reported in the zinc group, including nausea and taste disturbances. The number of
adverse events reported per patient was significantly higher in the zinc group compared
with the placebo group. A total of 51% of zinc patients experienced two or more side effects
compared with 10% on placebo. The results suggest that 13.3 mg zinc lozenges administered every 2 hours may be effective in reducing the duration of symptoms associated with
the common cold.

**Eby G, et al. Reduction in duration of common colds by zinc gluconate lozenges in a
double-blind study. Antimicrob Agents Chemother 1984;25:20–4.**
A prospective, placebo-controlled, double-blind evaluation of 23 mg zinc gluconate or
placebo lozenges every 2 hours while awake in patients who reported symptoms associated
with the common cold. A total of 146 subjects were enrolled with 120 data surveys returned,
of which 80 were complete. The primary outcome was resolution of all self-reported symptoms within 7 days of initiating intervention. Baseline symptoms were stated to be similar
between treatment groups, but initial symptom severity appeared to be less in the zinc
group. Analysis of patient surveys in which lozenges were initiated within 3 days of symptoms ($n = 65$) revealed that 86% of the zinc group ($n = 37$) had no symptoms by day 7 compared with 46% of the placebo group ($n = 28$). Although the data suggest that zinc lozenges
are effective in reducing the length of the common cold, there are several concerns with
regard to design and data reporting. It is unclear how randomization was conducted and
whether blinding of placebo was effective. Also, the authors state that children were eligible
for enrolment but do not state if any children were included in the analysis. Patients were
discouraged against using cough/cold remedies, but the authors failed to report whether
any were taken.

Hirt M, Nobel S, Barron E. Zinc nasal gel for the treatment of common cold symptoms: a double-blind, placebo-controlled trial. Ear Nose Throat J 2000;79:778–80.
A prospective, randomized, double-blind, placebo-controlled evaluation of 33 mM zinc gluconate ($n = 108$) or placebo ($n = 105$) intranasal gel administered as one puff in each nostril every 4 hours on upper respiratory tract symptoms associated with the common cold. Patients were randomized to treatment within 24 hours of onset of symptoms. The primary outcome was resolution of symptoms associated with the common cold. Average time to resolution for the zinc and placebo group was 2.3 ± 0.9 and 9 ± 2.5 days. The rate of adverse events was not significantly different between groups. Baseline demographics were not provided. The authors suggest that Zicam is effective in reducing the length of the common cold when initiated within 24 hours of symptom development.

Turner RB. Ineffectiveness of intranasal zinc gluconate for prevention of experimental rhinovirus colds. Clin Infect Dis 2001;33:1865–70.
A prospective, randomized, double-blind, placebo-controlled evaluation of 33 mM zinc gluconate ($n = 41$) or placebo ($n = 50$) intranasal gel. Patients were pretreated with nasal spray for 3 days, inoculated with rhinovirus types 23 and 39 via nasal wash, and then continued on current treatment for an additional 6 days. The primary outcome was incidence of viral infection. Viral shedding, severity of symptoms, and serum zinc levels were also measured. The rate of infection was approximately 75% in both treatment arms, and no difference in severity of symptoms was found. The author suggests that pretreatment with zinc intranasal gel has no effect on reducing the incidence of the common cold.

REFERENCES

1. Dietary Reference Intakes for vitamin A, vitamin K, arsenic, boron, chromium, copper, iodine, iron, manganese, molybdenum, nickel, silicon, vanadium, and zinc. Washington (DC): National Academy Press; 2001.
2. Hirt M, Nobel S, Barron E. Zinc nasal gel for the treatment of common cold symptoms: a double-blind, placebo-controlled trial. Ear Nose Throat J 2000;79:778–80.
3. Chandra RK. Excessive intake of zinc impairs immune responses. JAMA 1984;252:1443–6.
4. Pronsky ZM. Power's and Moore's food-medication interactions. 12th ed. Birchrunville (PA): Food Medication Interactions; 2002.
5. Caldamone AA, Freytag MK, Cockett AT. Seminal zinc and male infertility. Urology 1979;13:280–1.
6. Macknin ML, et al. Zinc gluconate lozenges for treating the common cold in children: a randomized controlled trial. JAMA 1998;279:1962–7.
7. Ripamonti C, et al. A randomized, controlled clinical trial to evaluate the effects of zinc sulfate on cancer patients with taste alterations caused by head and neck irradiation. Cancer 1998;82:1938–45.
8. Silverman JE, et al. Zinc supplementation and taste in head and neck cancer patients undergoing radiation therapy. J Oral Med 1983;38:14–6.
9. Mocchegiani E, et al. Benefit of oral zinc supplementation as an adjunct to zidovudine (AZT) therapy against opportunistic infections in AIDS. Int J Immunopharmacol 1995;17:719–27.
10. Simkin PA. Oral zinc sulphate in rheumatoid arthritis. Lancet 1976;ii:539–42.

Index